D1050042

GUIDE to the COLORADO MOUNTAINS

GUIDE to the COLORADO MOUNTAINS

ROBERT ORMES

with the

COLORADO MOUNTAIN CLUB

SIXTH EDITION

SAGE BOOKS

THE SWALLOW PRESS INC.

CHICAGO

Printed in the United States of America

Sixth edition
Fourth Printing, 1973

Sage Books are published by
The Swallow Press Incorporated
1139 South Wabash Avenue
Chicago, Illinois 60605

ISBN 0-8040-0139-1
LIBRARY OF CONGRESS CATALOG CARD NUMBER 72-115033

TABLE OF CONTENTS

ERRATA SHEET

Page	*Line*	
28	18	NNW should real NNE
41	23	July *T&T* should read July 1970 *T&T*
46	35	13,110′ should read 13,310′
66	16	echo should read who
102	21	W to E
103	7	West Brush should read East Brush
113	32	Last sentence should read: Or from the Twin Lake Village Main Range Trail sign jeep 4 miles to 10,500′ and climb via marked 4-mile trail.
118	7	. . . Huron summit. Then should read Go straight up on tertiary intrusives (chiprock) or east and up on grassier slopes.
118	9	13,920 should read 13,957
119	20	13,250 should read 13,230
	32	after Granite. Drive 1½ miles and walk 1 mile, or jeep 2½ miles to sign; and walk 3 miles to Main Range Trail; at 10,000′.
120	13	13,200′ should read 13,230
122	2	zig zag jeep road should read dying old trail.
125	32	Delete building to end of paragraph. Should read location, from which climb to the saddle above and follow the ridge N to the top.
128	7	SSE should read SSW
141	15	Delete sentence.
141	26	Sentence beginning The other should read Or you can stay along the creek 3 miles and climb left to the maroons with moderate loose-rock hazard.
142	9	Snowmass Peak should read Snowmass
143	29	Snowmass Mountain should read Pierre Lakes Basin
166	21	NW should read W
168	31	west should read east
175	21	14,100 should read 14,165
187	28	NW should read NE
	29	Add Rough for novices.
187	30	Iron Nipple, 13,828′, is should read The 13,828′ N point is
188	33	and strikes left . . slopes should read then left and up S slopes
199	16	E of I-70 should read E of I-25
209	20	N of Colona and 2 miles S of should read S of Colona and 2 miles N of
216	17	NW should read NE
217	4	S2, 13,468 should read Mt. Ridgway, 13,468
218	12	but has a should read but has been climbed since.
221	29	Delete final sentence of paragraph
222	26	13,664 should read 13,864
274	31	Shoshone Dam should read Shoshone Power Plant

TABLE OF MAPS AND ILLUSTRATIONS

PREFACE TO THE SIXTH EDITION

This is in many respects a new book. Though it has borrowed some material from the earlier versions, each slightly updated since the first edition of 1952, many more areas and more climbs and trail trips in the same areas are included. Two aspects of the early emphasis on 14,000-foot peaks remain—the list of these, and the first edition maps drawn by Douglas Waterman. We have kept short sections on rock climbing, kayaking, and spelunking, but dropped the chapters on motoring, railroads and ski areas.

It would be impossible to list all the contributors to this book. We have to thank as a group some forty Forest Service officials and a few in the Park Service for their patient attention to questions sent out in a busy season. U.S. Geological Survey maps, which are invaluable for understanding terrain, have this year become available in either finished or preliminary form for all the mountain ranges of interest, and U.S.G.S. personnel have given aid of other sorts in addition. Besides the localized guide material in the Colorado Mountain Club's periodical *Trail and Timberline*, which we have acknowledged in the text as borrowed, we have drawn heavily on Trip Reports and other help from the *T & T* editor, the Publications Committee and various members of the club who have given of their special skills and services.

The book is and is not a publication of the Colorado Mountain Club. The club furnishes much of the information, owns the copyright, and shares in the proceeds. But the club cannot be held responsible for the editor's vagaries. One of these is to jump the gun with names where they seem needed and have some chance of official acceptance. A second is to interject occasional anecdotage or attempts at levity. The third is to include a sometimes too large element of guesswork as to routes. Each of these has a partial excuse. As to names, it is hoped their use will hasten and broaden their acceptance. The needless verbiage is merely an escape for the writer from the endless continuum of factual statements. And as for the guess-work, it is inevitable; all the information received is partial, much is confusing, and some is conflicting. There is no correct guidebook. However, most of the past improvements in the Guide have come from letters pointing out errors and omissions—letters which would not have been written if the errors had not appeared in the authoritative guise of print.

Please send your corrections and additions to the editor, at Colorado College, Colorado Springs, or to the Colorado Mountain Club, 1723 East 16th Avenue, Denver.

INTRODUCTION TO THE COLORADO MOUNTAINS

Colorado's mountains are the ganglionic center of the inland Rockies. Three-fourths of the nation's land above 10,000 feet lies within the state, whose average altitude is about 6800 feet. Generally speaking, it is mountainous everywhere west of a longitude line through Denver, with the ranges of greatest importance forming a thick, squarish J, with its horizontal fan running west from the foot of the vertical. Big mesas, some as high as 10,000 feet, take up much of the space within the J. The summit altitudes of the mountains tend to a remarkable sameness: more than 50 have tops over 14,000 feet and none reach 14,450 feet. Five times as many are in the 13,000-foot class.

The Continental Divide enters and leaves Colorado on almost the same line of longitude—a line that cuts the mountainous two-thirds of the state in half. But the Divide jogs far away from this line; in the northern part it bulges eastward into Rocky Mountain National Park and the Boulder district; in the southern part it bulges westward into the San Juan. Of the major peaks only a few are on the spine itself, but most of them cluster in its neighborhood.

The Colorado ranges are neither so young and precipitous as the Swiss Alps nor so old and rounded as the Appalachians. The basic sculpturing of them was done by stream erosion. Glaciers, mainly those of the Pleistocene Ice Age, ate their way among the peaks to form numberless cirques and to scoop out little lake beds in the U-shaped valleys. Post-glacial erosion has formed great talus slides on many of the upper slopes.

Most of the high peaks build up snowbanks that last all summer, and some have steep snow-and-ice gullies on their less sunny exposures. But of the great glaciers only a few tag ends are left.

GEOLOGY

The Colorado mountains are divided for simplicity into two portions: those mountains which are a part of the Rocky Mountain System extending from Canada through central New Mexico, and less regular offshoots to the west of the Rockies which do not share the typical architecture of the main Rocky Mountains.

The Colorado portion of the Rocky Mountains is characterized by a series of linear ranges trending north and north-northwest and consisting primarily of segments uplifted during Laramide deformation, some 60 to 70 million years ago. The easternmost Colorado Rockies are called the front ranges—the trend made up of the large Front Range to the north, and a topographically lower continuation, the Wet Mountains, to the south. These ranges have Precambrian crystalline rock cores which are flanked by layered sedimentary rocks, Paleozoic through Mesozoic in age. The upturned eroded edges of the sedimentary rocks are visible in the foothills belt of the mountains. Faulting of the border zone of the front ranges has occurred in places.

The western portion of the Rocky Mountain trend, called the back ranges of Colorado, is separated from the front ranges by a series of parks, or high intermontane structural basins (North, Middle, and South Parks, and the Wet Mountain Valley). From north to south the back ranges consist of the Park Range, the Gore Range, the Sawatch, Ten-Mile, and Mosquito Ranges, and the Sangre de Cristo Range. The back ranges are characterized by complex folds and thrust faults instead of the more simple anticlinal or arch-like structures shown by the front ranges. Some of the back ranges contain Precambrian crystalline rocks at their cores; others exhibit Paleozoic through Mesozoic sedimentary layers at their crests. The illustration, Cross Sections of Colorado Mountains, Section A shows the generalized structure across the northern Colorado Rockies: Gore Range to Front Range. Section B shows the structure across the southern Colorado Rockies:

Sangre de Cristo Range to Wet Mountains or Cuerna Verde Range.

West of the main trend Rockies lie some irregular ranges characterized by Laramide doming, post-Laramide intrusion and uparching, or post-Laramide extrusion of volcanic rocks. The large portion of the San Juan Mountains province consists of post-Laramide volcanic rocks as do the West Elk Mountains. As shown by Section C, the western edge of the San Juan Mountains is made up of a deeply eroded Laramide domal structure where the Precambrian rocks appear flanked by the Paleozoic-Mesozoic sedimentary rocks. In places, the volcanic rocks are intruded by post-Laramide igneous rocks. The Elk Mountains, Section D, consist of high-standing sedimentary rocks which have been uparched during invasion of post-Laramide igneous rocks. Portions of Grand Mesa and the White River Plateau country have volcanic rocks exposed at their summits.

(The above geological summary and some scattered notes in the text were contributed by John H. Lewis of Colorado College.)

WILD LIFE

A typical game estimate of the Forest Service included within their portion of the state's territory about 6000 black bear, 200,000 mule deer, 30,000 elk, and 4000 bighorn sheep. There are a few antelope within the mountain parks, and a handful of mountain goats have been obtained on an interstate exchange.

The fish in mountain waters are mainly trout. Those most frequently planted are rainbows and loch leven, with some German browns in the lower altitudes, brook trout in a few streams that seem to favor them, and for the high country native cut-throats.

Frequently seen small animals are the very numerous marmot, inhabitant of rock slides, tundra, and upper altitude forests; the little cony, which squeaks sepulchrally from under the talus blanket; the black and gray tree squirrels; the friendly, tameable ground squirrel; the oversized pack rat, named for his habit of carrying off sticks, napkin rings, and soap; the little striped chipmunk, fantastically quick of movement; the porcupine; and the snowshoe and cottontail rabbits.

There are foothill regions with some pheasants and turkeys. Game birds are few in the mountains. Sagehens also are found below 7000 or 8000 feet, and above these altitudes a blue grouse occasionally startles the mountaineer with his noisy take-off. The high altitude ptarmigan does his escaping with camouflage. He is snow white in winter and rock mottled in summer, and a hiker is likely to spot the shadow before he sees the bird.

Other favorites in the bird world are the saucy crested blue jay of the ponderosa pine belt, the juncos and chickadees, the thieving Canada jay or camp bird of high altitudes, the woodland musicians—Towsend's solitaire and Audubon's hermit thrush—and the fluffy little American pipit and browncapped rosy finch that one sees feeding on the snowbanks and shooting over the high ridges in the wind.

THE FORESTS

In eastern Colorado the plains run up to 5000 feet or above before they break into the frontal foothills. The plains grassland gives way to a broad belt of forests running up to a timberline of 11,000 or 12,000 feet.

It is possible to recognize four different vegetational zones based on increasing altitude. The first is the stands of stubby piñon pine and occasional junipers. This zone is not found everywhere, being more common on the western slope and in the southern part of the eastern slope. Ponderosa pine occurs in the next higher zone. It may be alone or may have a lower fringe of scrub oak communities or mingle with the piñon and juniper on its warmer, sunnier exposures. It is abundant, and holds the lowermost mountain slopes. At the third level comes Douglas fir. It often grows side by side with ponderosa but characteristically selects the north slopes of ridges, leaving the south slopes to the sun-loving pine. Above the ponderosa pine belt, Douglas fir often occurs in virtually pure stands. Above the Douglas tree and continuing up to the alpine meadows is a fourth belt composed of Engelmann spruce and subalpine fir. The former contributes most to the dwarf timber or elfin wood of timberline.

Where extensive logging or forest fires have occurred in either of the upper three belts, there lodgepole pine may be found. It is exceedingly common in the northern half of the mountainous area of the state. In the Douglas fir belt two other interesting but rather uncommon evergreens may be found in the more favorable situations such as along canyon bottoms. Besides Engelmann spruce, the dwarf trees of timberline may also be, in the southern half of the state, bristlecone (or foxtail) pine, and, in the northern half of the state, the limber (or flexilis) pine. All of the timberline trees may be found down as low as the Douglas fir belt, the specimens generally increasing in size with decrease in elevation.

The most common deciduous tree in the mountain regions is the whitebarked aspen, whose leaves rustle with the faintest breeze and in the fall turn the hillsides to gold. The tree is more common in the Douglas fir and the higher spruce and subalpine fir belts but may also be found with ponderosa pine. Forest fires greatly encourage the spread of aspen, whose underground parts are not usually destroyed by the conflagration. The aspen gains a head start in growth over its competitors. Later the slower growing evergreens will shade out the aspens. Alders are quite common along streams in the middle mountains, and lower down these give way to the cottonwoods or poplars.

THE TUNDRA

The type of vegetation most closely associated with the mountain heights is the meadow-like tundra, which begins usually at timberline and extends as far upward as the plants may find suitable soil.

The typical alpine meadows are found on gentler slopes, flat ridges, valleys, and basins, where the soil has become relatively stabilized and the water supply is more or less constant. In such areas, sedges and grasses form a rather dense sward, well known to stockmen for its summer grazing value. Better remembered, however, are the dozens of kinds of bright-flowered plants that are mixed in with the grasses, or occupy the fringe areas of boulder fields, steeper slopes, and exposed places where the soil is in early stages of formation. Fortunately, the blooming periods of these plants do not coincide, so that one may expect a showing of some sort throughout the short summer season. Outstanding are the yellows of mountain avens, little-old-man-of-the-mountain, cinquefoils, and buttercups; the reds of king's crown and paintbrush; the blues of forget-me-nots and polemoniums; the whites of bistorts, candytuft, sandwort, mountain dryad, and arctic gentian; and the pinks and purples of daisies, alpine primrose, cushion-pink, and pentstemons.

Many of the lively hues of the high places are due to the lowly lichens. These occur as green, orange, reddish, gray, or black crustlike growths over rocks, often resembling nothing less than splashes of bright-colored paint. As pioneer plants, they are very valuable agents in the process of producing soil from bare rock.

Scarcely anywhere are the rigors of climate and soil better reflected in vegetation than here in the alpine community. There are no trees, and the only shrubs are alpine willows, which are prostrate mat-formers. The bulk of the species are perennial herbs that are true dwarfs, not just lower altitude plants that are stunted by more severe conditions of higher locations. Some of these special conditions are frequent high winds, great extremes and sudden changes of temperature, strong actinic light, and a short growing season. Most of the plants are so well adapted to the alpine meadow environment that they do not thrive well where milder conditions prevail.

Of special interest in connection with the plants of the Colorado tundra is their geographic distribution. Several of the species may also be found in Alaska, on the seacoast of Greenland, and on the mountain summits of Europe and Asia—for example, the alpine lily and the cushion pink. Other species, such as the alpine primrose, are endemic to the southern Rockies. Still others including dwarf hawksbeards and alpine meadow rue are shared with the Sierras. It is believed that during the ice age the tundra of the far north was continuous with that of the Rocky Mountains. Today, however, our tundra exists only on the well-separated mountain peaks like vegetation-islands in a sea of sharply contrasting plant communities of lower levels.

ADMINISTRATION

A large percentage of the mountain areas lie within twelve national forests and the Rocky Mountain National Park. There are also in the high country some public domain lands, some state forest lands and some ranch lands, the largest of these last having come down through the old Spanish land grants.

The national forests have an area of more than 20,000 square miles. They are administered from a general office in Denver, from supervisory offices for the individual forests, and by the rangers of local districts. Forest Service policy seeks to preserve the balance which will best conserve water, timber, soil, forage, and recreation resources. The Forest Service maintains numerous campgrounds and picnic grounds and has given aid and cooperation toward the development of ski areas.

The Rocky Mountain National Park, dedicated to recreation, covers about 400 square miles of mountainous scenery, ranging in altitude from 7600 feet to 14,256 feet at the summit of Longs Peak. Adjacent to the western boundary of the Park is Shadow Mountain National Recreation Area, including two large reservoirs offering water sports. Scenic roads and trails, mountain shelters, camp grounds, and ranger programs of lectures and conducted tours make Rocky Mountain National Park especially attractive to uninitiated mountain recreationists. Lodging, food, and riding horses are available at the edge of the Park in Estes Park on the east and the village of Grand Lake on the west.

The Colorado State Fish, Game and Parks Department, operating with a central office in Denver and regional ones in Fort Collins, Colorado Springs, Grand Junction and Montrose, administers fish and game laws, works to improve fishing conditions and to maintain a balance between the game and the forage available for it, and operates camping facilities, most of them in the neighborhood of lakes. The State Forestry Service takes care of a state forest in the Rawah Range and also works in other areas where there are problems of tree disease.

COLORADO HERITAGE

THE INDIANS

Colorado has a varied heritage from the Indians. The most spectacular relics are the Balcony House, and the Cliff Palace—those dwellings of a race of cliff lovers and balance climbers. Elsewhere in the dry country there are pictographs like those in Pats Hole of the Dinosaur Monument, along the squaws' water trail into the Gunnison Gorge, on the Apishapa. The redskins sometimes left sign up high, too. Old Man Gun, an Arapaho, made an eagle trap on the top of Longs Peak so he would have feathers for his war bonnet. The Hayden Survey men who made the first recorded climb of Sierra Blanca reported that Indians had stolen their long uphill march: there were remains of a stone enclosure which some brave must have used when he made signal fires on the summit.

When the mountain men first came into Colorado around the turn of the century, they benefited by the Indian trails everywhere. The plains tribes had sallied into the highland from the east and fought battles in South Park, and the Navajos had come up into the southwest. The Utes were the true mountain people, the "dwellers of the turquoise sky," as they translate their tribal name. They were possessors of the mountains at the turn of the century when seven tribes of them were soaking their joints in every spring from Steamboat to Pagosa.

Arrowhead collections and Indian battlefields testify to the struggles between different tribes. There are legends of the struggle, too, like the story which made the Utes shun Grand Lake: the Arapahos came over the Divide to hunt; the Utes, to prepare for the coming fight, put their women and children on a raft and shoved them out on the water. In a squall all the passengers were dumped off and drowned. People who sail the lake know the suddenness of these squalls and are inclined to believe the story. To the Indians it is proved by the cloud spirits that rise from the water each morning.

Fremont, "the pathfinder," was guided over many of the Indian routes by the mountaineers. Some of the trails have disappeared; others have become automobile routes. The most famous is Ute Pass, west of Colorado Springs. It was a main artery both for the Utes and for the plains Indians who camped at Manitou Springs and traveled to South Park for meat, scalps, or salt. (The salt springs near Antero Junction gave the Park its Creole name *Bayou Salade.*) Trail Ridge Road from Estes Park to Grand Lake follows the old Indian trail, with occasional markers showing exactly where the trail originally ran. Cochetopa Pass likewise was an Indian trail. In 1858 when Major Bradford wanted to build a toll road to California Gulch (later Leadville) from Denver he asked the Indians where to lay it out. With a few variations, they pointed out the present Turkey Creek, South Platte, Kenosha Pass and South Park highway route. George Jackson followed the old Ute trail to Bergen Park, so says his diary, when he went into the hills to discover the first gold near Idaho Springs.

THE SPANISH

Naturalists say that the oldest evidence of Spanish penetration into Colorado is botanical—weeds that were brought to the edge of the state by Coronado's animals in 1540 and that have since climbed into the hills. Oñate founded Santa Fe in 1598—little old New England wasn't born yet—and afterward the Spanish came into Colorado's mountain barrier looking for gold. The earliest of these northward sallies cannot be dated, but Don Juan Maria Rivera carved a cross dated 1765 on a Gunnison River cottonwood tree, and in the easily remembered year of 1776, when Escalante traveled over the creeks emptying into the San Juan River, they already had Spanish names. The La Plata Mountains, too, were probably named in disappointment that their ores were silver (*plata*) instead of gold.

San Luis, Colorado's oldest town, was founded by Spanish settlers in the San Luis Valley, and like the New Mexico rootland it has retained its Spanish American character despite the shift to American sovereignty. Spanish names ran all the way across the southern Colorado mountainland from Trinidad and the Culebra Range to Rico and the Dolores River. Mexican land grants are responsible for the private ownership of large areas of mountain country in the Culebra, Sangre de Cristo, and Southeast San Juan Ranges.

THE FRENCH

In 1682 La Salle fought mosquitoes down the Mississippi and claimed all the land drained by its tributaries for France. French voyageurs canoed up these tributaries until the water became unnavigable, and then continued across land afoot or horseback. By 1740 the Mallet brothers had reached Santa Fe, where they were not welcome. Spain also claimed the land the French were infiltrating.

Spain was powerless to keep the cheerful French trappers out of the west, however, just as England could not keep them out of the northwest. St. Louis, founded by Choteau in 1765, fed Creoles into the western plains and mountains.

The French trappers came in greater number to Yellowstone and Missouri headwaters than to Colorado, and their rendezvous were generally to the north and northwest. Nevertheless, they left names on some of Colorado's waterways. In the north there are the Cache la Poudre River, the Bijou (a misspelling of Bijeau, a trapper Major Long hired as a scout), and the Platte; Colorado Springs' Fountain is still remembered as the Fontaine qui bouille (Fountain which bubbles); and the name Purgatoire has won out over its cowboy translation the Picketwire.

THE MOUNTAIN MEN

With the Louisiana Purchase the French trappers became American citizens. James Purcell, who wintered in South Park in 1802–3, was the first of the American "mountain men" to join them. The beaver boom, when fashionably dressed men in Paris, London, and New York were wearing beaver hats, was what brought these men west. They trapped the streams from the Canadian Rockies to Santa Fe.

One of the first organized companies was that of Ezekiel Williams. It came out in 1811 and worked the following year in and around South Park. Some of Williams' men went over the range and were never heard of again. Choteau and DeMunn of St. Louis sent other trappers into the country.

Spain slowed the trappers down for a time, expelling some of them by armed force, but after 1821, when Mexico took over in Santa Fe, the trade became better than ever. Jacob Fowler, for whom the town Fowler is named, began in 1821 using the Taos Trail which ran over Sangre de Cristo Pass, just north of La Veta Pass. Antoine Roubideau set up a fur trading post near Montrose; others opened one at Browns Hole which they called Fort Davy Crockett—doubtless the first invasion of Colorado by Texans. Larger trading posts were built on the plains—Bent's Fort on the Arkansas and a string of forts on the South Platte north of Denver.

In 1824 Ashley of St. Louis collected men to trap in the west and was the first to go boating on the stretch of the Green River now in the Dinosaur Monument. Among Ashley's men was Jim Bridger, who guided Sir St. George Gore into the mountains, who told tall tales of the Yellowstone geysers, and who died blind on a farm in Missouri. Jim Beckwourth was another; the mulatto son of a slave woman and an Irish overseer, he became a Crow chieftain. Others were Thomas Fitzpatrick of the Broken Hand, who knew the west as well as anyone; Louis Vasquez, one of the brothers who left their names on Vasquez Peak near Berthoud Pass; Jedediah Smith, who pioneered the cross country trails with a Bible in one hand and a rifle in the other; and Jim Baker, who spent the last years of his life on the Little Snake River in northwest Colorado surrounded by innumberable offspring. Most famous of them all was Kit Carson, the government's liaison officer to the Indians. In the '40's he was Fremont's scout three times in trips across Colorado.

Bill Williams was another of these mountain men. He had been a preacher, an adopted Osage and a trapper when he joined Fremont on the latter's disastrous trip into the La Garita Mountains in 1848. He returned to the scene for records the following summer, and was later found propped against a tree with an arrow through his heart.

In 1866 Marcy wrote that there still remained "a few of the semi-civilized white men called mountaineers."

THE EXPEDITIONERS

Lieutenant Zebulon M. Pike was sent west to report to Jefferson on the vast Louisiana Purchase. In November of 1806 he came up the Arkansas to the present site of Pueblo, and with a small group of his men headed for Pikes Peak. His try for the peak was the first recorded attempt on any Colorado mountain. He reached an intermediate summit, possibly the Miller Mountain named for one of his soldiers.

Major Long's 1820 expedition, concerned like Pike's with the Louisiana Purchase boundary, was a piedmont trek southward between the areas of Fort Collins and Pueblo. Three side trips were made into the mountains—one towards Longs Peak, one up the South Platte, and a third to Pikes Peak.

There were independent expeditioners who wrote books about their travels in the West, notably the Englishman Ruxton and the American Fremont. Fremont had explored for the army and knew mountains well, but when he set out in winter to find the best railroad route through the ranges he ran into disaster in the La Garita Mountains. At the start he had 33 men and 100 mules. At the end he staggered into Taos with 22 men and no mules.

S. F. Beale, the man who had carried a bag of gold from Sutter's Fort in California to Washington, crossed the Colorado mountains in 1853 in the hope of finding a central passage between the South Pass of Wyoming and the Spanish Trail south of the mountains. Beale's trip through Cochetopa Pass and across the Uncompahgre, the Gunnison and the Colorado, was written up by his companion Mr. Heap, who told of a 16-day side trip to Taos for supplies, of swinging packs across the Lake Fork, Peru fashion, and of crossing the rivers with canoes, rafts, and bull boats.

In the same year Captain Gunnison was assigned to explore the central of four possible railroad routes across the country. For the twenty wagons in his train he built a road—over Sangre de Cristo Pass, over Cochetopa Pass, down the Gunnison, and out to Utah, where he was killed by Indians.

Botanist Charles Christopher Parry spent several summers in the Rockies, climbing many of the Front Range peaks. He is responsible for the naming of Grays, Torreys, Englemann, Audubon, and other summits; Parry Peak was named for him. Other naturalists in the Parry tradition accompanied the survey parties.

INDIANS AND WHITES

Up to the 1830's, relations between redskins and whites were friendly. Some of the trappers lived with Indian women, and Indians sometimes supplied pelts. Then silk hats replaced beavers; skins dropped from six dollars to one; and trappers took to collecting buffalo hides. As the Indians were dependent on buffalo, trouble began.

A treaty in 1849 awarded $5000 to the Indians, but the whites kept coming and the buffalo kept going. By 1852 the Utes and their plainsmen cousins, the Comanches, Apaches, Cheyennes, and Kiowas, stirred up so much trouble that the Army built Fort Massachusetts on the Ute Creek that runs off Sierra Blanca. For six years it was a base for Indian chases. From it Col. St. Vrain, with Kit Carson as a guide, pursued the red-shirted chief Tierra Blanca through Cochetopa Pass. From it Col. Fauntleroy chased a band across Poncha Pass and killed forty of them above Salida.

In 1858 the Army abandoned Fort Massachusetts and established Fort Garland a few miles farther from the mountains.

The gold rush that began in 1859 and the creeping settlement that accompanied it did no good for Indian relations. The whites were pushing the Indians back, and no reminiscence of a pioneer excludes a tale of the Indians—how they burned the settlers' houses around Mancos, how Colorow set a fire in '79 which burned in North Park, Middle Park, and the country near Steamboat Springs, how they begged for biscuits from every woman's kitchen.

Parleys were held between the raiding Indians and the encroaching whites. Chief Ouray, then thirty, was the government-appointed spokesman for the redskins; Kit Carson and after him Otto Mears spoke for the whites. Mears conversed in both Ute and English with a thick Russian accent.

By 1868 Ouray and his followers were settled on Los Pinos Reservation west of Cochetopa Pass, and Chief Douglas, with a northern division of the tribe, was on the White River near Meeker. A third of the Western slope belonged by treaty to the Utes, but the inevitable trespassing process jumped forward with the development of gold mines in the San Juan in 1873.

The Southern Utes were moved west to the Uncompahgre River country south of Montrose in 1873, where they watched the miners advance farther and farther into their territory. The White River Utes went on the warpath about the time silver was found on the Roaring Fork. In 1881, after the Thornburgh Battle and Meeker Massacre of 1879, they were pushed into the Uintah Basin in Utah. This has been the main reservation ever since, with a few Utes living near Ignacio and the Sleeping Ute Mountain in southwest Colorado. Chief Ouray died disillusioned in 1880. Not even his last request was granted—that his bones lie undisturbed in an unknown grave. After his wife Chipeta died in 1924, his remains were brought down from the mountains and buried at the Ignacio Agency, half in the Protestant and half in the Catholic cemetery—an act symbolic of his life of tragic compromises. In 1950 the Utes were awarded judgments by the U.S. Court of Claims of over $31,000,000 for their illegally removed lands.

THE SURVEYS

Early formal explorations in Colorado were generally the work of the Army. Macomb in the San Juans in 1859, Dodge, and the above-mentioned Pike, Long, Fremont, and Gunnison, were all employed by the War Department. More exhaustive surveys were made by the Bureau of Indian Affairs, Department of the Interior. King, Powell, and Hayden were rivals for the directorship of the U.S. Geological Survey formed in 1879; each of them had conducted surveys more exhaustive than were the earlier reports of the Army. King, and after him Powell, won the appointment, though for Colorado the Hayden Survey was by far the most important. To keep in the competition the Army had produced its own survey, the Wheeler. Like the others it contained exhaustive reports by naturalists as well as topographic information.

The Hayden Survey made most of the recorded first ascents of Colorado high mountains, and their names and triangulated altitudes are generally very close to those which have since been determined by more thorough methods. Hayden's accomplishment was a tremendous one. He inspired deep loyalty though he pushed his men and himself unmercifully; his name with the Indians was He-who-picks-up-stones-while-running.

The Survey began in 1873 with three divisions working until 1876 in Colorado and 1878 in Wyoming. The first year Marvine went to Middle Park, Gannett to South Park, and Wilson to the San Luis Valley. Gradually they worked west with occasional changes of personnel. The Hayden *Atlas of Colorado*, published in 1878, now a collector's item, is remarkably accurate and made beautiful with soft colors and fine profile sketches. Hayden's men published 77 books of findings.

Also in 1873, the War Department sent Lt. Wheeler into the West. The Colorado Division of his survey went into South Park, the Gunnison, and the upper Arkansas, sometimes working the same range at the same time as the Hayden men. Lt. Marshall, who discovered Marshall Pass—lowest route from Arkansas to Gunnison drainage—was in charge. He reported having occupied 36 peaks over 13,000 feet, many of them on first ascents. The Wheeler Survey, which published very usable maps and 41 volumes of findings, was the nearest rival to that of Hayden.

Powell's official Survey, which began in 1871, covered country west of the mountains in southern Utah and northern Arizona. Powell had come out in '67 and '68 and climbed Longs Peak, Pikes Peak, and Mount Powell. In 1869 he boated down the Green and Colorado Rivers, stopping at Pats Hole long enough to climb Echo Rock. Having only one arm, he got stuck on the rock—couldn't get up, couldn't get down. In lieu of rope, his climbing comrade rescued the major with long underwear.

The King Survey, ordered in 1871 and starting east from California, was mainly concerned with exploring the land along the Union Pacific Railroad and the fortieth parallel. It is remembered for King's debunking of a fake diamond field north of Vernal, Utah. A company was selling shares in the venture in San Francisco. They had salted the field with diamonds, rubies and sapphires.

Prout, a civilian engineer, ran an exploring trip in 1873 for the Army's Lt. Ruffner of Leavenworth to determine the position of the 107th meridian Ute treaty boundary, and unofficially to look over the Indian country. He traveled up the Rio Grande, and along the Animas, visited Lake San Cristobal and the Gunnison, and returned to the San Luis Valley. A second trip took him north into Taylor Park, across to Twin Lakes, and through the Elks. He called the Elks "high, rugged and confused."

THE MINE BOOM

Free gold was panned in Denver in 1858. In 1859 the Gregory strike launched Central City and Blackhawk. From this center the panners pushed into South Park and shortly afterward north to the Blue and south to the Wet Mountain Valley. In the era, which lasted into the middle seventies, the only processes which supplemented panning were the arrastres and stamping mills. Gold was the only metal the miners sought during the period. In 1878 Leadville became a silver camp whose production soon advanced to a peak of $23,000,000 in 1892. It was in this year that gold first surpassed the $5,000,000 mark, largely because of cowboy Bob Womack's discovery of gold-bearing quartz veins at Cripple Creek. By the '90's there were smelters for the precious metals in Leadville, Colorado City, Denver, Pueblo, and Durango. The process of mining and milling had become largely a venture for big capital, not a little of which came into Colorado from England. In the last quarter of the nineteenth century strikes were made at Ouray, Silverton, Telluride, Rico, and Creede. Tom Walsh, owner of a Silverton smelter used for baser metals, discovered in 1895 that the tellurium ores contained gold. His Camp Bird Mine near Ouray brought him $25,000,000 in the next two decades.

The mining industry and the railroading and lumbering that went with it have left the most lasting and the most picturesque of all the signs that the mountain visitor finds in his wanderings—the ghost towns, the mills, the railroads, the roads and the trails, the mines and prospect holes.

ORGANIZATIONS

The latter day explorers of the mountains have joined together in a variety of clubs: Isaac Waltoners and others devoted to the conservation of game, lore clubs like the

Colorado Railroads

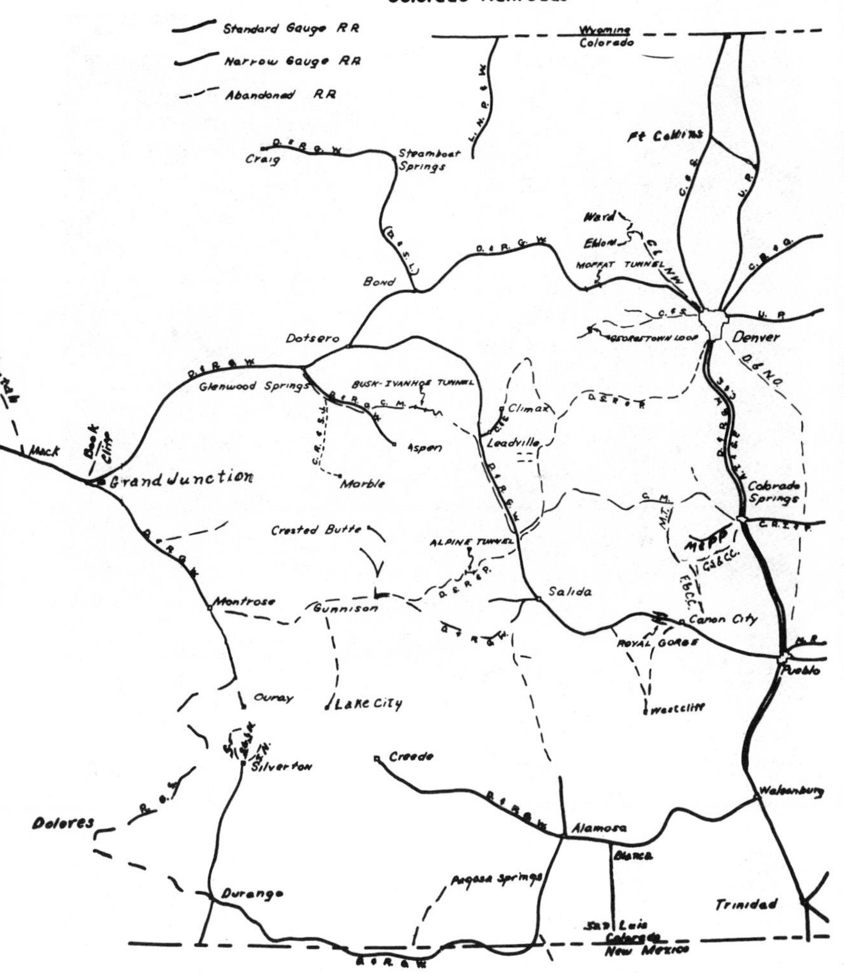
Standard Gauge RR
Narrow Gauge RR
Abandoned RR
Wyoming
Colorado
Ft Collins
Craig
D & R G W
Steamboat Springs
L. N. P. & W.
C. & S.
U. P.
Ward
Eldora
MOFFAT TUNNEL
C. B. & Q.
Bond
Dotsero
C. & S.
GEORGETOWN LOOP
U. P.
Denver
D & N.O.
Glenwood Springs
BUSK-IVANHOE TUNNEL
Climax
Leadville
Aspen
Mack
Book Cliff
Grand Junction
Marble
Colorado Springs
Crested Butte
C. M.
C. R. I. & P.
ALPINE TUNNEL
M & P P
Montrose
Gunnison
Salida
Canon City
ROYAL GORGE
Pueblo
Ouray
Lake City
Westcliff
Silverton
Creede
Walsenburg
Dolores
Alamosa
Blanca
Durango
Pagosa Springs
Trinidad
San Luis
Colorado
New Mexico
D & R G W

Old mine building at 14,000 feet on Mount Democrat. *H. L. Standley photo.*

Denver Posse of Westerners and the Pikes Peak Historical Society, and mountain picture makers like the William H. Jackson Camera Club. There are groups, both organized and informal, of bird watchers, of botanists, of crystal hunters and mineralogists, of riders of the bridle trails. There are several Ghost Town Clubs dedicated to hunting down the vanishing data and relics of the mining era. There is the AdAmAn Club, whose fireworks have greeted each New Year on top of Pikes Peak since 1922. There have been numerous outing groups, especially in the college towns—notably the university hiking and outing clubs, the Saturday Knights, who since 1903 have been settling the world's affairs and enjoying their weekly pot of coffee in some shelter spot of the Pikes Peak region. There is the Railroad Club; periodically its chuffachuff fans charter themselves rides. Ski clubs are innumerable and increasing.

The Colorado Mountain Club was founded in 1912. There is now a large membership in metropolitan Denver and there are several smaller chapters elsewhere. It has long conducted a program of one- and two-day trips in Colorado and extended outings both in the state and as far away as Japan, all under experienced leadership. Training classes are organized for rock climbing of different levels of intensity, and for ski touring and snow and ice climbing. The club rooms, presently at 1723 East 16th Avenue, Denver, serve as headquarters for a knowledgable secretary, a library and other sorts of information. Aspen, Boulder, Colorado Springs, Fort Collins, Los Alamos (New Mexico) and Pueblo have chapters, and the Denver Chapter has a Juniors organization. All welcome guests.

Members are kept informed about these and other activities by the monthly publication *Trail and Timberline*. Various maps, limited-area guide material, and matters of historical interest like the Kingery-Arps *High Country Names* are also available at the clubrooms.

The club is more and more concerned with the conservation of Colorado's vast mountain resources as the mountains provide recreation for more and more people, and as they are increasingly threatened with destructive forms of exploitation. Young people and newcomers will find that the club provides safe and sociable ways of learning how to enjoy the mountains and of joining the battle to protect them.

American Alpine Club members of Colorado and nearby states have organized as the Rocky Mountain Section. An office and a library are maintained in New York, and in Denver a branch library of the American Library Club is housed in the Conservation Section of the Denver Public Library. This nation-wide club sets high standards for membership eligibility. It sponsors mountain exploration on a world-wide scale.

INTRODUCTION TO CLIMBING

MOUNTAINEERING

The mountains are not hard to climb. The mining boom, which began in 1859 and lasted into the first decade of this century, has left a heritage of old roads and trails through the timber. It is these trails that link the automobile roads to the timberless upland where trails are not needed. They make the mountain tops accessible. All but a few summits can be reached by at least one route that is no more than steep mountainside hiking. Of those few exceptions nearly all can be reached by parties without special technical knowledge provided the leadership is experienced.

There are plenty of cliffs, however, for those who want to try out their ropes and hardware, and here and there an ice chute where crampon climbing or step cutting comes into play.

Though mountain weather tends to be unpredictable, the relatively dry climate makes for pleasant camping and climbing conditions.

The open season for high peaks is more or less from late June through early October, with wide variations in different years and with different climbs. Winter climbing is on the increase for slopes which do not avalanche, but special equipment and carefully graduated experience are necessary. Middle to late spring is usually the best time. Lower altitude mountain trails and trips are possible off and on through the winter as snow tends to melt off on sunny slopes up to 8000 feet.

SAFETY

Good mountaineering is safe mountaineering. It involves consideration of others, whether in dimming lights on the highway or in nailing in the belayer on a rock climb. Some of the ways to avoid trouble are these:

1. Reckon with conditions. High altitudes require warm clothing; even in midsummer there are freezing storms.

Sun glasses are necessary in snowy terrain. Rough mountain slopes demand sturdy shoes.

2. Start early. Mountain storms are more frequent in the afternoon than in the morning. Climbers should be prepared to turn back short of their goal to avoid after-dark travel.
3. Keep within sensible fatigue limits. Extreme weariness makes easy descents hazardous.
4. Avoid the rotten rock hazard in every way possible. A party should bunch in a loose-rock couloir, and on wider slopes they should angle away from the direct line of fall. Rocks should never be rolled for sport.
5. Snow slopes must be tested carefully. They may have hard spots that don't show or be soft at the edge. Any steep slope has avalanche possibilities.
6. The distress signal is three short, sharp whistles or calls repeated at intervals. Do not use anything that sounds like it unless you are in need.
7. In calculating how much time to allow, consider altitude and obstruction along with distance. People who walk 3 miles an hour on the level will normally go up hill at around 1. Given a small distance factor, 1000 feet of altitude per hour is close to normal. Minor rock problems, willow matting, bogs, windfall, ice, and other obstructions decrease speed incalculably. Darkness is an especially limiting factor.
8. When a swift stream must be crossed, No. 2 man belays from the shore while No. 1 crosses a full rope length downstream, tied in and leaning slightly against the rope. He then takes upstream position to belay No. 2.
9. Climbing alone in the mountains is not for the inexperienced. If you do it, leave word where you are going and stay with your plan. Keep a wide margin of safety in your movements.

10. If you get lost, it is better to attract attention with a small fire (green leaves make it smoky) than to wander about in panic. Dry matches and a candle butt are easy to carry.

MAPS

Although there are some maps in this book, a satisfactory coverage of so much terrain would have been out of the question. We have had to assume that the guide will be read and used in conjunction with U.S.G.S. quadrangles, many of them in preliminary stages, the latter available from the Topographic Division, Denver Federal Center. As $7\frac{1}{2}'$ quadrangles are unwieldy in large numbers we are investigating the production contoured field maps with a more favorable scale.

It is wise to make use of U.S.G.S. quadrangle maps. Learning to read their invaluable contour lines is a simple matter. If the lines are well separated, the slope is gentle; if close, steep; if dense, it is a cliff. A series of V-shaped contours indicates either a ridge or a trough or valley. If there is no line of a creek to tell you which, there are other clues. A ridge leads to a master ridge or a peak; a trough leads to a valley with water. Water is downhill. Concentric circles indicate a cone with the top at the center. Most have far from circular summits, but the concentric pattern still holds.

With a little experience one can tell at a glance where the cliffs are. For instance, the Rocky Mountain National Park McHenry's Peak Quadrangle shows you gentle walking slopes on the west side of most of the peaks, and near-vertical cirques, often ice-filled, on the east. The Gore is a range of steep canyons, sometimes all but impassable, and pinnacled ridges, where even for experienced rock climbers a mile a day would be a rapid pace. The north peaks of the Sneffels Range, the San Miguel Range, the Needle Mountains and Grenadiers, the Crestone and Blanca sections of the Sangre de Cristo Range, and the Elk Range are all places where parties not familiar with the terrain should expect difficulties. Useful as they are the topographic maps have their limitations. They do not show narrow cliff bands which may be impassable, or the deadfall which may make an old trail hopeless.

ROCKY MOUNTAIN TRAIL

The **Rocky Mountain Trail,** as presently planned by the U.S. Forest Service with the Colorado Mountain Club collaborating, will have over 600 miles within Colorado, generally along or near the Continental Divide. The route, with a map by John Sudar, is described by Gale C. Kehmeier in a CMC pamphlet. Parts are along trails already in use, parts are planned or in construction, and parts are not yet determined. It will follow the North Park, Rabbit Ears, Never Summer, Front and Sawatch Ranges and proceed around the La Garita Mountains, the Bend and the Southeast San Juan to Cumbres Pass.

Some of those interested expect that in time it will resemble the Appalachian Trail in having hostels at convenient places along the way.

TRAILS AND MOTOR VEHICLES

Trail use by motor vehicles is under the regulation of the U.S. Forest Service where the trails or old roads are within the forests. More trails will be closed as erosion problems and crowding require. People intending to use vehicles in the forests would do well to check in advance with the nearest ranger station. Do not assume that jeep routes or trails mentioned in this book will be open. Those who do ride bikes and trail bikes will help their cause by obeying all restrictions, by staying strictly on the trails they are permitted to use, and by guarding against erosive practices.

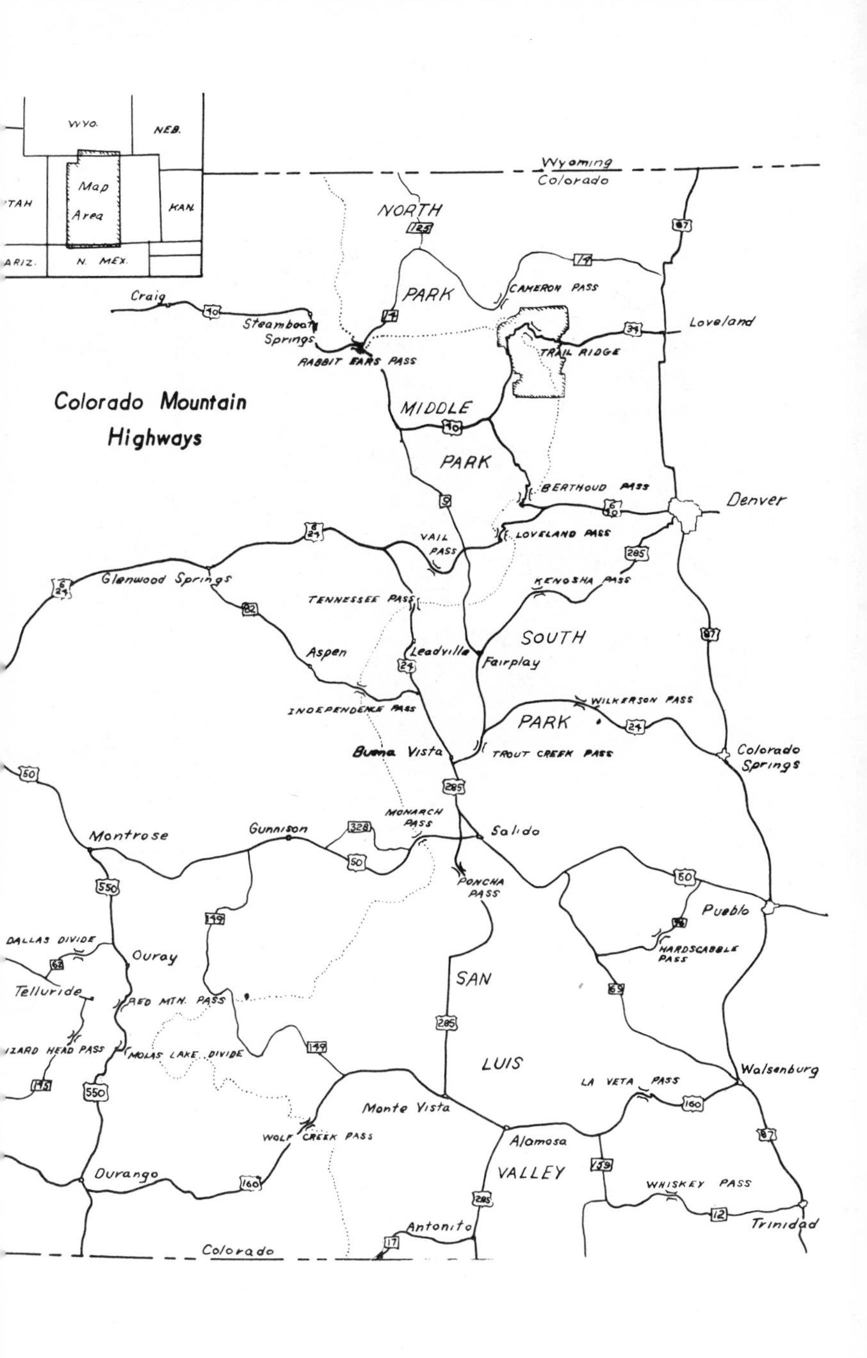

Colorado Mountain Highways
WYO.
NEB.
Map Area
TAH
KAN.
ARIZ.
N. MEX.
Wyoming
Colorado
NORTH
PARK
MIDDLE
PARK
SOUTH
PARK
SAN
LUIS
VALLEY
Craig
Steamboat Springs
RABBIT EARS PASS
CAMERON PASS
TRAIL RIDGE
Loveland
BERTHOUD PASS
Denver
LOVELAND PASS
VAIL PASS
KENOSHA PASS
Glenwood Springs
TENNESSEE PASS
Aspen
Leadville
Fairplay
INDEPENDENCE PASS
WILKERSON PASS
Buena Vista
TROUT CREEK PASS
Colorado Springs
MONARCH PASS
Montrose
Gunnison
Salida
PONCHA PASS
Pueblo
HARDSCABBLE PASS
DALLAS DIVIDE
Ouray
Telluride
RED MTN. PASS
IZARD HEAD PASS
MOLAS LAKE DIVIDE
Walsenburg
LA VETA PASS
Monte Vista
Alamosa
WOLF CREEK PASS
Durango
WHISKEY PASS
Antonito
Trinidad
Colorado
125
87
14
40
34
6 40
6 24
285
82
24
50
328
550
149
62
69
160
145
159
12
17

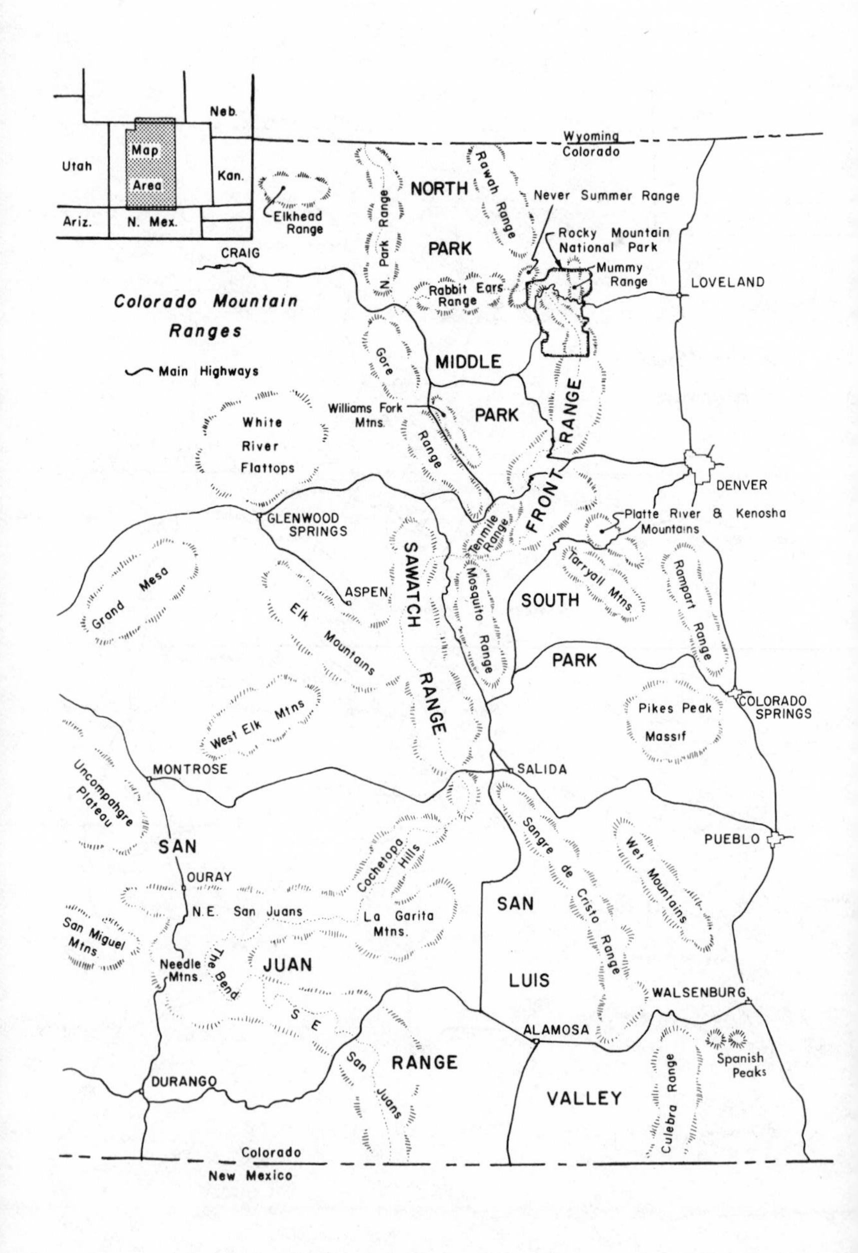
Neb.
Utah
Map
Area
Kan.
Ariz.
N. Mex.
Wyoming
Colorado
Elkhead
Range
NORTH
PARK
N. Park Range
Rawah Range
Never Summer Range
Rocky Mountain
National Park
Mummy
Range
LOVELAND
CRAIG
Rabbit Ears
Range
Colorado Mountain
Ranges
Main Highways
Gore
MIDDLE
PARK
Williams Fork
Mtns.
Range
FRONT
RANGE
White
River
Flattops
DENVER
GLENWOOD
SPRINGS
Platte River & Kenosha
Mountains
Tenmile
Range
SAWATCH
RANGE
Mosquito
Range
Tarryall Mtns.
Rampart
Range
Grand Mesa
ASPEN
Elk
Mountains
SOUTH
PARK
COLORADO
SPRINGS
Pikes Peak
Massif
West Elk Mtns
MONTROSE
SALIDA
Uncompahgre
Plateau
SAN
Sangre de Cristo Range
Wet Mountains
PUEBLO
Cochetopa
Hills
OURAY
N.E. San Juans
La Garita
Mtns.
SAN
San Miguel
Mtns
Needle
Mtns.
The Bend
JUAN
LUIS
WALSENBURG
S E
ALAMOSA
San
Juans
RANGE
Spanish
Peaks
DURANGO
VALLEY
Culebra Range
Colorado
New Mexico

THE MOUNTAINS

NORTH PARK RANGE

QUADS: Mount Zirkel, Mount Ethel, Boettcher Lake, Hahns Peak, Buffalo Pass, Rabbit Ears; Routt N F.

This range is traditionally known as the Park Range, but that name is duplicated in South Park. The mountains stretch from near Wyoming on the west side of North Park, 35 miles south to Rabbit Ears Pass. It is part of the Continental Divide, separating the Yampa from the North Platte. Summits, many of them planed off flat, are comparable in height to the Rawahs, 12,000′ plus a little. The range generally consists of metamorphic and igneous rock. The rough, hard Zirkel, Big Agnes and the Sawtooth Range are in a belt of hornblende schist and greenstone.

The main stretch of high country **(Mount Zirkel** to **Mount Ethel)** is contained in the Mount Zirkel Wilderness—20 miles long and 4-6 miles wide. There are many lakes in the cirques. The only road across is over **Buffalo Pass,** 10,325′, near the S end. It connects Hebron, 11 miles SW of Walden on State 14, with a road running N out of the center of Steamboat Springs. The W side is good, the E a little steep.

The road which runs closest to the Zirkel region leaves State 129 at Clark, 19 miles N of US 40 (starting 2 miles W of Steamboat Springs). It follows the Elk River NE 9 miles to Seedhouse Guard Station and 3 more to Slavonia.

The forest service maintains numerous camping places and a system of trails. The **Park Range Trail** begins at the end of a road running 2 miles N from **Rabbit Ears Pass** on US 40. It runs N, generally on the range crest, and in the main above timberline. At Gold Lake it dips W to meet the road from Slavonia. There is no trail along the Mount Zirkel wilderness, but it begins again at Diamond Park, 9 miles N of Seedhouse Ranger Station. It swings up by Lake Diana and then N down the Encampment River to Commissary Park on the state line. The S section is about 35 miles long, the N 25 miles.

Swamp Park Trail runs from 4 miles due N of Steamboat Springs northward through Elk Park, totaling 32 miles, to end at Seedhouse Ranger Station on Elk River. At Mad Creek it follows a canyon for 4 miles into Swamp Park. From this point on it is a machine-built trail. It passes through the burn at the head of Burn Creek, and then by a steep mountainside traverse reaches the South Fork of the Elk.

Fishcreek Falls Trail begins at Fishcreek Falls Camp Ground, 3 miles E of Steamboat Springs. Eight miles above the falls it reaches Long Lake, Round Lake, and Little Lost Lake on the North Park Range divide. Another stretch of 6 miles takes it to an E terminus near Cloverleaf Ranch in Willow Park, where a 10-mile county road runs out to State 14.

Seven Lakes Trail runs 6 miles W to the Divide from Big Creek Lakes Campground, which is reached by a 6-mile side road SW from Pearl in NW North Park. Branch trails fan out from both its termini to good fishing water. The Park Range has an E flank trunk trail parallel to the one on the crest. It runs from Big Creek Lakes to **Rabbit Ears Pass** through low altitude brush and light timber country.

North Gore Range Trail, a 30-mile route through lodgepole and spruce country, runs from **Lynx Pass** to **Rabbit Ears Pass.** The northern Gore Range has a crest trail system that connects with the **Park Range Trail** off the W side of Rabbit Ears Pass.

Mount Zirkel, 12,220′, can be approached from the E through Shaffer Ranch where horses would be useful. For the W side, drive 2 miles NW from Steamboat Springs on US 40, 19 N on State 129, and 12 NE on State 311 to Slavonia, 8350′. Take the trail up Gilpin Creek to the N side of Gilpin Lake 4 miles, then angle NNE (to right of timber) 1 mile to the ridge, and continue N 2 miles to summit. An alternate route with more trail and less scenery starts from Slavonia SE and uses 3 miles of trail along the N side of Gold Creek. When the trail turns S, a mine road continues N in Gold Creek to the S face of Mount Zirkel, which is easily climbed.

Big Agnes Mountain, 12,059′, has the same approach as for Mount Zirkel, and can be reached from Mica Basin. The trail to Mica Basin cuts left from 1½ miles NE of Slavonia and goes on above **Gilpin Trail.** Climb 2 miles to Mica Basin and E 2 miles to the summit ridge S of Big Agnes. A camp at Mica Basin would be close enough for an exploration of the rougher routes on Big Agnes and the Sawtooth Range immediately north of that lady. There is also a rough, sloppy, jeep road N from Seedhouse Guard Station along the Elk's North Fork to Diamond Park. From there you can get in close to the Sawtooth and Big Agnes on either of two 3-mile trails—one SE up Agnes Creek, the other E up the North Fork.

Hahns Peak, 10,839′, is a curiosity. Joseph Hahn found gold in the area in 1862, returned with friends to pan gold, and died in the spring of 1866 in an attempt to get back to civilization for food. The symmetrical cone named for him is far west of the range crest. It is a maze of roads of various ages including one which jeeps can ride to within ¼ mile of the top on the N side. The approach for cars is from Columbine, 30 miles N of US 40 on State 129. You drive 2 miles SE to the mine area, then climb 2 miles or so by a trail which starts at 9400′ on the W side and circles to the N for zigzags.

Mount Ethel, 11,924′, the southern high point, is virtually climbed on the **Park Range Trail.** It is about 9 miles N of **Buffalo Pass,** of which 5 can be done with a four-wheel vehicle. 11,705′ **Anvil Point,** a mile short of Mount Ethel but farther E off the trail, is also worth a visit.

Rabbit Ears Peak, 10,654′, is conspicuous beyond its altitude. You can get up to it on an old road which runs N from **Rabbit Ears Pass** on 40 and becomes the **Park Range Trail.**

RABBIT EARS RANGE

Quads: (W-E) Rabbit Ears, Spicer, Whiteley, Buffalo, and

Hyannis Peaks, Parkview and Radial Mountains, Rand; Routt and Arapaho N F's.

This range of only moderately high summits forms the south boundary of 30-mile-wide North Park. It carries the Continental Divide east from the North Park Range to the Rocky Mountain National Park stretch of the Front Range.

Whiteley Peak, 10,015′, conspicuously close from US 40, 7 miles SE of **Muddy Pass,** is best climbed from the SE ridge. It rises 2000′ in the mile or so.

Parkview Mountain, 12,296′, on the other end of the range off **Willow Creek Pass** (State 125—20 miles N from US 40) has a 4-wheel drive road to the Fire Lookout on top which turns left from State 125 just S of Willow Creek Pass at 9485′. Like all the lookouts it is selected for broadness of view. See Parkview and Radial Mountain Quads.

ELKHEAD MOUNTAINS

QUADS: Craig 1 SE and 4 NE, Elkhead 2 SW and SE, Bears Ears, Meaden Peak; 15′ Elkhead Creek; Routt N F.

This 18-mile long W-E range centers about 20 miles NNW of Craig, from which it is visible. It is crossed by a main N-S road between Slater and the Wyoming line, and State 13, which it meets 14 miles N of Craig. There are 2 trails running roughly parallel to the crest and 2-5 miles from it, one to the north through Lost Fork (where it crosses the road) and the other to the S. These join at the W end and connect with this same road on the E end—that through California Park. The latter is remote and reached only by dirt roads.

Bears Ears Peak, NW summit 10,577′, SE 10,494′, is the most tempting mountain, for an exploratory climb. It can best be reached from the S side trail. Head E down Sawmill Creek from 1½ miles S of the range crest on the N-S road. About 5 miles E of the road, you are directly under Bears Ears and can plan your mile or so of climbing to the N. Best bet: go right of SE summit. Spiral that and NW summits, both counterclockwise.

YAMPA WILLIAMS FORK MOUNTAINS

QUADS: 15′ Dayton Peak, Mt. Harris, Monument Butte; Routt N F.

The 8000 foot high points are SE of Craig between the Yampa River and its Williams Fork. As this area is privately held there are no developments for public use. (Without the word Yampa, the name duplicates that of the range W of the Blue River.)

FLATTOPS

QUADS: Steamboat Springs 30′; White River and Routt N F's.

The Flattops Wilderness is a land of lakes and forests at altitudes generally 9000-11,000′, between Steamboat Springs and Glenwood Springs. It is all andesite and basalt from late tertiary and perhaps quaternary flows which remain to us as plateaus with abrupt drop-offs at the edges. The first of the state's national forests was established on the White River Plateau in 1891, with the idea that its many resources might be saved from depletion. Ironically, its forests have suffered a tremendous devastation by beetles.

Access from the east is by State 131, running south from near Steamboat Springs up the Yampa River, and a road southwest from that along the Colorado River to Dotsero, on I-70. For a west approach one drives to Buford on either of two roads: one is State 132, running east 22 miles on the White River; the other is a 42 mile plateau road from I-70 at New Castle.

Trails and their branches run all over the Flattop Plateau, and beautiful tours past the lakes and cliffs can be put together with forest service maps and advice. The routes below are for those who want to try their ingenuity, or even their ropes, on those little mesas on the mesa—the peak tops—while their relatives whip the lakes.

A main crossroad, pretty well N in the area of prime interest, connects Phippsburg on State 131 with Buford.

Pyramid Peak, 11,611′, has a close trail approach from Oak Creek Guard Station, for which you drive 12 miles WSW from Phippsburg, taking a right at mile 2, a left at mile 6½ and a right at mile 7. From the guard station take the 3-mile jeep road left SSW to Sheriff Reservoir. Trail continues 2 miles toward Pyramid, then sidesteps it to the left. If our photo, taken and labeled in a rainstorm at dusk, indicates correctly, you will find the best approach from a mile farther, on the SSE side or ridge. We aren't sure.

Six miles from Sheriff Reservoir this trail meets with one coming south up the east fork of the Williams Fork from the Pyramid Guard Station. They continue S as one for 1½ miles to another junction, with a detour west for campgrounds and several small lakes. Another 1½ miles S and 3 miles SE takes you past the Devils Causeway to Stillwater Reservoir.

Stillwater Reservoir is reached by a 15-mile road SW from the S side of Yampa, on 131. It is the trailhead not only for the above route past Pyramid but for others.

A main cross trail, paralleling the main crossroad but 12 miles SSE of it and thus more in the heart of things, starts along the N side of Stillwater Reservoir and continues 30 miles or more to the South Fork Campground, the latter 10 miles SSE up the White River South Fork from Buford. From Stillwater, about 9500′, it climbs over a plateau pass at 11,300′, and at mile 7 reaches Trappers Lake. At miles 14–16 it passes between the Twin Lakes and connects with trails up the Marvine Creeks. (See below.)

A trail runs from the middle of Stillwater Reservoir 7 miles S to Stump Park and a jeep road that runs down the plateau W of Derby Creek to Burns.

Flattop Mountain, 12,493′, high point of the whole area, and **Dome Peak,** 12,176′, are on the front of the Flattops W of Toponas. They are reached from above trail. At mile 2 S of the reservoir, find the best way up E toward Flattop Mountain, and head ENE 2 miles to the top. Dome Peak is about 3 miles down the ridge, with a 400′ dip to be mastered before you climb to it. Return to the saddle, and descend W a mile then S a mile to a cross trail. The latter goes W 2½ miles to the **Derby Creek Trail** you started out on. It is then 6 miles back over the pass to Stillwater.

Derby Peak, 12,184′, is W of the trail down Derby Creek, and separated from it by the steep forewall of the mesa and its own 200′ step above that. From about mile 1½ S of Stillwater Reservoir, cut off right to get up on the mesa edge where it is passable, then head S 2½ miles on the crest, coming in to Derby far enough W to miss the abrupt N end.

The road E from Buford has a turn-off at mile 9 for Marvine Creek and another at mile 19 for Trappers Lake, 8 miles ESE by car. At mile 25 you reach **Ripple Creek Pass** and the ridge crest, at mile 36 the Pyramid Peak Guard Station and at mile 62 Phippsburg.

The Marvine road runs 4 miles upstream to a campground at 8200′, where the creek forks. Each branch has a trail to the main cross trail between Stillwater Reservoir and White River's South Fork. The right one takes you by a 12-mile route past Marvine Lakes. The left or E one climbs 6 miles to the plateau between the Marvine Peaks, Little on the left and Big on the right.

Little Marvine Peak, 11,948′, is 2 or 3 miles N up-ridge from where the trail finishes its climb to the plateau. **Big Marvine,** 11,875′, is 2½ miles WSW over high country from the same place. It is fairly well bulwarked with those big steps you see on the peaks, but nevertheless has a trail route through to the top.

Trappers Peak, 11,990′, is 5 miles SSW of the outlet of Trappers Lake. A trail from the W side of the outlet and lake, 8600′, runs SW 4½ miles, climbing to the plateau behind Temple Steps, the near peak across the lake from the approach road. At the trail T on the mesa, take the left one E and S 1½ miles to a stream crossing on the way to Wall Lake. Go W up stream until you have passed the N end of the peak, then head S to approach it on the W side.

Shingle Peak, 12,001′, can better be reached by taking the trail on the E side of Trappers Lake 5 miles SE past Parvin Lake to the plateau, and then 3½ SW to a trail junction. See if, by heading straight to it from the junction, you can climb on to the NNW ridge of Shingle Peak, a mile S. If you make that, the upper level of defenses a mile farther on should go.

Sheep Mountain, 12,246′, is an E point of the plateau Shingle Mountain is on. It is a 6-mile ridge crest walk from where you come to the plateau above Parvin Lake, 11 miles in all from Trappers Lake. The climb itself is easy: you go S 1½ miles on the plateau, then E, NE and SE on the dogleg ridge.

The plateau is also reached from the S by trails going NE up Lost Solar Creek and Park Creek. Take the Coffeepot Road N from US 6 about 15 miles to Budge's Lodge, at the junction of the South Fork of the White River and Nichols Creek (just SW of the Meadows). The trail goes W along the South Fork of the White 4 miles to junction with **Park Creek Trail.** Park Creek Trail goes NNE about 2½ miles to top of plateau, meets trail along Nichols Creek which returns 3 miles ESE to Meadows. From Budge's W along the **South Fork Trail** 7 miles is junction with **Lost Solar Creek Trail,** which also goes to top of plateau, 5 miles NE along Lost Solar Creek.

NORTHWEST CORNER

QUADS: Dinosaur National Monument (Special) and others.

Two features dominate the arid NW corner of Colorado. One is the Book Plateau with its vast mileage of Tawny Book Cliffs and also Roan Cliffs at the heads of the canyons. The other is the Dinosaur National Monument with its Lodore and Yampa Canyons, likewise carved from the tawny sandstone and with the saurian fossils for which it is named.

RAWAH RANGE

QUADS: Clark Peak and Rawah Lakes, Boston Peak, Chambers Lake, Gould, Johnnie Moore; Roosevelt N F.

This linear range, 15 miles long, running from NNW to SSE on the border of North Park, tops at around 12,000′ in pinkish Front Range granites deeply cut on the east side by glacial erosion. It is bounded on the north by the timbered saddle south of Johnnie Moore Mountain, and on the south by Cameron Pass, which separates it from the Never Summer Mountains. We use the name Rawah, Indian for wilderness, in preference to the traditional Medicine Bow, which is duplicated in a nearby range of southern Wyoming.

Except for North and South Rawah, Clark and the Diamond Peaks and Cameron Mountain, the summit names on this range are tentative conveniences. Those approved by the Colorado Mountain Club and federal agencies will be submitted to the U.S. Board of Geographic Names.

The Rawah has the cirques and lakes typical of glaciated ranges. The west side, much of it in forest below the 11,000′ timberline, is in Colorado's State Forest. The central lake district on the east side is in Rawah Wild Area.

On the west side there are some lumber roads, generally drivable, climbing west from Bockman Lumber Camp. From 2 miles N of Gould on State 14 (or about 10 miles W of Cameron Pass) a road starts N and runs W 4 miles to the camp, where you can inquire about approaches to the range immediately west. There is a road of sorts running from the camp 2 miles NW and 4 NE up the Canadian River to 10,400′, a mile and 600′ short of Jewel Lake. The lake is good camping and close under Sickle (head of the cirque, due north), with Clark to the right, and birdie ridge points running north.

At mile 15, 5 miles toward Walden on 14 from the above turnoff, a road goes in 3½ miles to the Smith Ranch. You go left (N) at ½ mile and right (E) at 1 mile, then straight east. A road SE from here also hooks up with the Jewel Lake road, but inquire here for the 5-mile jeep road in to Kelly Creek and the ponds there.

It may be possible to drive a car to the ponds, at 9400′; beyond them there is a jeep-width trail 2½ miles E and S to

Kelly Lake, 10,800′, beneath the roughest section of the range.

Mount Ashley, 12,376′, is a mile SE at the head of the Kelly Lake gulch, and not difficult to reach. **Island Lake Peak,** 12,175′, is closer, ENE, and sufficiently cliffy to require some exploring and perhaps experimenting with routes. For White-crown, Snowbank and South Rawah you should retreat ½ mile on the trail and then angle up the steep slope to the right to gain the ridge. For South Rawah alone, go N and a little left to the saddle W of Snowbank and then slantwise NNE to the ridge. South Rawah is a mile N of Snowbank along the ridge, and 550′ above the low point of the ridge.

Medicine Bow Trail starts 10 miles S of Mountain Home, Wyoming, on State 127. It runs down the range crest to Rawah Lakes, where it ties into the **Rawah Lakes Trail,** one of the better-built scenic trails. The latter passes the Rawah Peaks on the E, and the route continues via **West Branch** and **Fall Creek Trails** to Chambers Lake, 60 miles up the Cameron Pass Road from Fort Collins. This 40-mile trip is mainly above timberline except where it dips into the spruce timber of high valleys. Snow normally closes this trail by the end of September, and keeps it closed until mid July.

Since the peak climbs are beautiful and fairly short, and the trail approaches long, the Rawah climbs are particularly inviting as a backpack expedition along the above trail sequence, beginning at Chambers Lake.

Clark Peak, 12,951′, is the high point of the range. From Fort Collins drive 70 miles on US 285 and State 14 to Chambers Lake; from the south end of the lake, 9160′, take the trail 6 miles W and NW to the pass N of Blue Lake and climb 2 more miles SW on the ridge to summit.

Cameron Peak, 12,127′, is an easy mile E from the saddle above Blue Lake. It is well worth the climb for its view into the cirques farther north.

From the foot of the **Blue Lake Trail** a mile NW of the pass at 10,100′, you can turn up **West Branch Trail** and climb 1000′ (1½ miles) to Carey Lake and Island Lake. **Island Lake**

Peak goes best from Island Lake and a climb around S to the S saddle.

Whitecrown, 12,440′, is a mile farther N on the ridge, a pretty straight mile-long climb of 1400′ NNW from Carey Lake.

From the **West Fork Trail** it is 3½ miles down from Carey Lake, or 2 from the **Blue Lake Trail** terminus, to the **Rawah Trail,** which the **West Branch Trail** joins at North Fork and West Branch creek junction, 9600′. This point can also be reached from the Laramie River road at Tunnel Campground 8600′, 4½ miles north of Chambers Lake. The **West Branch Trail** starts here and climbs 4 miles and 1000′ to the junction. About 2 miles west of this junction, at 10,450′, the **North Fork Trail** branches to the right off the **Rawah Trail** and climbs 1½ miles to Twin Crater Lakes at 11,050′. **South Rawah Peak,** 12,644′, is a climb of 1½ miles across the basin to the northwest.

North Rawah Peak, 12,473′, is nearly 2 miles of ridge walk NNW from South Rawah, but there is only a moderate loss of altitude and a good cirque to look at on the way, and from the far summit there is a short descent NE to another side trail that assures good footing homeward from the east side of Lake Four. This trail drops to the **Rawah Trail,** which returns to the junction for **North Fork Trail,** about 3½ miles in all from North Rawah Peak.

Big South Trail from Big South Campground, 56 miles W of Fort Collins on State 14, runs S 13 miles on the Big South Cache la Poudre. The last 5 miles is way trail and is used to connect with **Hague Creek Trail** in the Rocky Mountain National Park. A sizable stream with interesting rock formations along the way makes this a pleasant trip.

Greyrock Mountain Trail climbs N 2 miles to the foot of **Greyrock Mountain** from 3 miles above Fort Collins waterworks on the Poudre River road. There is a 2-mile nature circle trail at the Fort Collins Mountain Recreation Area, 41 miles up the Poudre.

NEVER SUMMER RANGE

QUADS: Mount Richthofen, Bowen Mountain, Fall River Pass; or older small scale Rocky Mountain Park; Arapaho and Routt N F's.

This 10-mile range from Cameron Pass to Bowen Mountain is a southward continuation of the pink granite line of Rawah peaks. Its beautiful name is a translation of the Arapaho one. The cloud names were the idea of James Grafton Rogers, founder of the Colorado Mountain Club. Although Nokhu Crags give the range a rough north end, its other summits are generally of even slopes and are less deeply cirqued than either the Rawahs or the Front Range mountains to the south.

The Grand Ditch, which picks up water all along the east side of the range and takes it across the Divide at 10,175′ Poudre Pass, has a road—closed to traffic but available for horses and people—which limits the peak routes. Crossings include these: **Poudre Pass,** where you are some miles E of the N end of the range; **Thunder Pass Trail,** useful only for the rather long approaches from the W foot of the **Trail Ridge Road** to Mount Richthofen, Static Peak, or Lulu Mountain—a plank crossing not for horses; **Lake of the Clouds Trail** near Dutch Creek, well located for the central Lead, Cirrus, and Howard Mountains, and up Baker Gulch at the S end—useful mainly for reaching Parika Lake and the southwest chain—Bowen, Fairview and Parika. There are some coverings and culverts near the south end available to hikers who want to reach Nimbus, Stratus, or Baker Mountain. As the Park Service is presently negotiating with the ditch company for more crossings, it will be worth-while to send inquiries to the former at Estes Park.

Mount Richthofen, 12,940′, is high point of the range. One of the survey parties of the 1870's, probably Clarence King's, named this mountain after a scientific friend, Baron Frederick von Richthofen, who had worked with them on the California survey, and later first mapped the mountains in inner China. Mount Richthofen is reached from State 14. From 2 miles

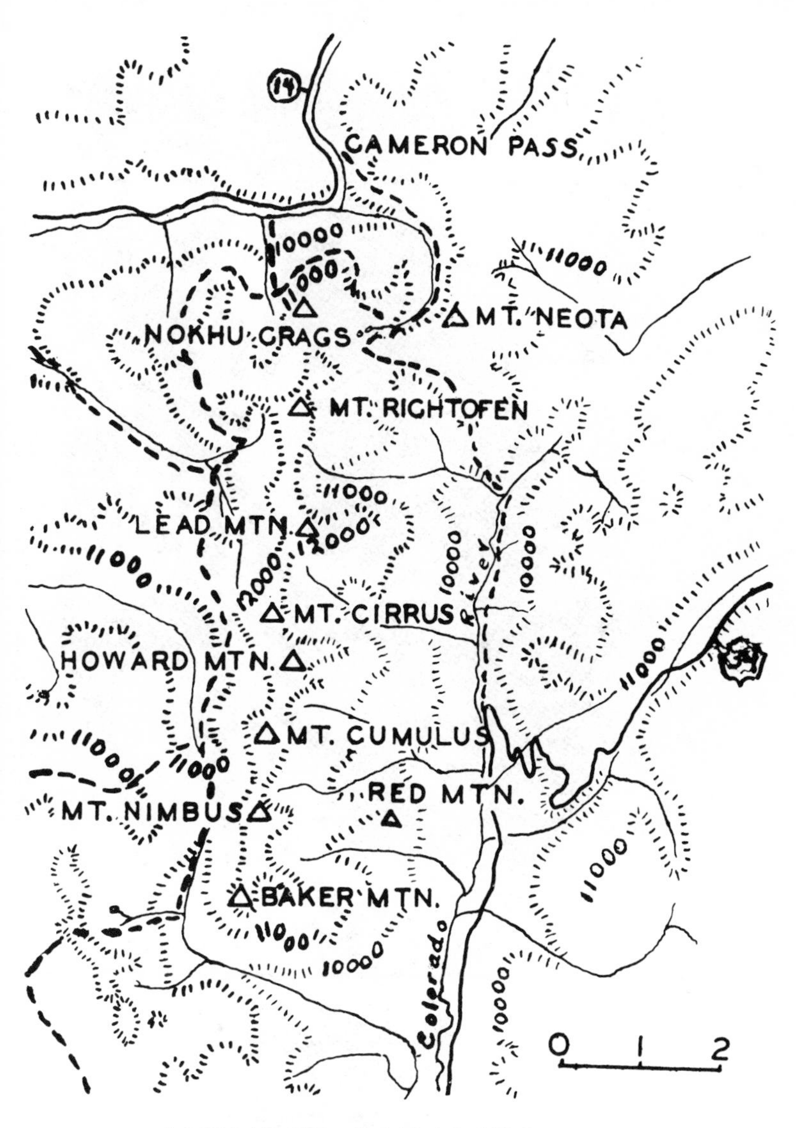

NEVER SUMMER
RANGE

Tepee Mountain under left flank of Mount Richtohofen. *Esther Holt photo.*

S and W of Cameron Pass a lumber road leads S and E a mile or so to the start of the trail to Lake Agnes (of Clark Peak Quad). Walk 3½ miles S, passing the lake on the west side; climb to the saddle and then E. Upper rock slopes are very unstable. From the lumber camp the climb is 3300′, 4 miles.

Nokhu Crags, 12,485′, E of Lake Agnes, can be visited en route by a strong party, or climbed more easily from the NNE ridge. For the latter, drive SSE 1.5 miles on the ditch road from Cameron Pass and then follow the ditch around to the ridge. There is good camping at or below Lake Agnes.

Richthofen is twice as long a climb from the west end of Trail Ridge Road. From Phantom Valley ranch parking area, 12 miles N of Grand Lake on US 34, at 9050′, take **Thunder Pass Trail** N 4 miles to ½ mile past the ditch crossing, and climb the 2-mile ridge to the W. **Lead Mountain,** 12,537′, can be combined with Richthofen, or climbed separately from the same trail. You cross the ditch and cut left (SW) for a half-mile, then go up Skeleton Gulch to the northwest ridge or the east saddle for the finish on the sharp ridge. **Cargo** and **Chisholm** recommend climbing W from the Phantom Valley, 9050′, to the ditch on **Red Mountain Trail,** and N on the ditch 1½ miles to Big Dutch Creek, where you can cross and go W on **Lake of the Clouds Trail** as far as the timberline. From there the climb is to the saddle E of the peak and up the ridge.

Howard Mountain, 12,810′, and **Mount Cirrus,** 12,797′, are approached from Lake of the Clouds at the head of Big Dutch Creek (see above for Lead Mountain). You can climb first up the Cirrus ridge ½ mile WNW from the lake, then dip to its 12,400′ south saddle and then climb up to Howard. For a shorter descent route, start E on the Howard ridge and cut ESE via Pinnacle Pool to Mosquito Creek. Follow the creek down to the trail, wading the ditch en route.

Mount Nimbus, 12,706′, is climbed from the Opposition Creek valley. Use the **Red Mountain Trail** from Phantom Valley, and a wooden aqueduct section of the ditch a little S of Opposition Creek to cross the ditch. Continue W along the creek drainage 2 miles to the north ridge of the peak at the head of the valley. It is .4 mile and 200′ altitude loss to continue S to 12,520′ **Mount Stratus,** and a considerable distance farther to Baker.

Baker Mountain, 12,397′, which is cliffed on the E, is best approached from 9 miles N of Grand Lake on US 34, where a turn-off leads to the Holzwarth Cabins and the ditch road. It is about 4 miles up hillside and W along the ditch to the Baker Gulch crossing, a good place to start the steep climb from 10,300′ to the top, a mile NNE. Total altitude is about 3400′.

Parika Peak, 12,394′, is about 2½ miles W via **Parika Lake Trail** from the same crossing of Baker Gulch, or in all 6½ miles.

Bowen Mountain, 12,524′, is also climbed from the ditch road S of where it crosses Baker Creek. Head WSW then W 1½ miles to the valley head, about 12,200′, and then SE along the ridge ½ mile to the top.

Cascade Mountain, 12,303′, is best climbed from the west side. From 2 miles W of Granby on US 40 drive 18 miles N on State 125, then drive E up Willow Creek 5 miles to a stream crossing (SW to NE side) at 9200′. Climb the timbered ridge NE 2½ miles to summit. It is a pretty mountain to approach and has a fine view of the Divide to the E.

The Outdoorsman's Guide to the Rocky Mountain National Park, to which I am indebted for some of the above route suggestions, gives a fuller treatment of routes and trails in the range.

MUMMY RANGE

QUADS: Trail Ridge, Estes Park, Comanche, Pingree Park; Older Rocky Mountain National Park is more condensed; Roosevelt N F; see also park folders and *Outdoorman's Guide.*

The Mummy Range gets its name from a resemblance it has to a reclining mummy. It is a 20-mile front range 10 miles east of the Divide between the Poudre and Fall Rivers. The west slopes tend to be smooth, the east cirqued. The higher southern part is in Rocky Mountain National Park.

Comanche Peak, 12,702′, and **Fall Mountain,** 12,258′, are end points of a 2-mile NW-SE ridge WSW of Pingree Park. They are best climbed from the Colorado State University Camp there. From US 287 NW of Fort Collins, drive 27.5 miles W on State 14 (2 miles beyond Fort Collins Mountain Park) turn left and go 14 miles SW and W to the camp. Continue 1 mile in Pingree Park to find a trail climbing out the north side to a road. Or try a short-cut road to this point from the campground 1 mile E of Pingree Park. If it drives, you save 400′ of climb from the 9050′ park to road level. Follow the road ½ mile W to where the trail starts. It climbs 4 miles to 11,300′ on the flat ridge crest, where there are ponds. Go NNW ½ mile to Fall Mountain and along the ridge to **Comanche.** From the latter descend E and ESE on the ridge to Fall Creek. It is 3 miles down to the end of the side road you started on and another 2½ down that to the camp.

The **Mummy Pass Trail** continues west 4½ miles from Mummy Pass to a trail on the upper Cache la Poudre River, and these in turn connect with long trails to Chambers Lake to the northwest and **Fall River** and **Trail Bridge Roads** to the southwest. There is a trail across the range north of the Comanche Peak-Fall Mountain ridge but none south of Mummy Pass.

Lost Lake, 10,714′, is reached by a trail from the Glen Haven road, for which you turn right off US 34 at mile 18 W of Loveland. At mile 6½ on this road keep right again for 3 miles up Dunraven Glade. At the 7900′ road end, the trail continues to a lake, where you are between the Stormy Peaks on the north and Mount Dunraven on the south.

Stormy Peaks, 12,418′, can be climbed from a camp at the lake on a 2-mile route ENE to NE. It takes you up through the highest available timber and across Stormy Pass. **Sugarloaf Mountain,** 12,130′, is 2½ miles W on the same ridge and, if you have an ice axe, makes a good combination climb, with a glissade from the head of the Big Thompson North Fork, a mile west of Sugarloaf on flat ground. It is 2 miles from Icefield

Pass, where the glissade is, past the two upper lakes to Lost Lake. **Hagues Peak** can also be climbed from a camp at Lost Lake. Go a mile W up the drainage and then climb SW up the steeper main stream to Dunraven Lake. It is about 5 miles to Hagues Peak and you can return by the above glissade route farther north.

Hagues Peak, 13,560′, is more often climbed by a long but beautiful route from Horseshoe Park, on the Fall River road. Starting just below the Power Plant at 8600′, the 5-mile **Lawn Lake Trail** climbs to the **Black Creek Trail** at 10,800′, and 3 miles NW to the 12,400′ saddle between Hagues Peak and Fairchild. Both peaks are within easy reach from a camp at Lawn Lake. Hagues Peak was named for Arnold and James Hague, King Survey geologists who climbed about Estes Park in the 1870's.

Mummy Mountain, 13,425′, is down an easy E and SE ridge 2 miles from Hagues Peak, with a 200′ climb to the summit at the end.

The **Ypsilon Lake Trail** leaves the **Lawn Lake Trail** 1½ miles above the start in Horseshoe Park. It is 3½ miles to the lake, at 10,600′. The route is used by rock climbers and those who want to give their ice axes a workout on the Ypsilon Y, high on **Mount Ypsilon.**

Fairchild Mountain, 13,502′, is a non-difficult climb from the lake. Heading N from the outlet, you climb 600′ in altitude, the last of it on a timbered ridge that runs NW. As the ridge steepens, turn right, N again, and contour NNW ½ mile to the upper Fay Lake. From here you can see your route. Fairchild is a long mile directly N and 2300′ higher. There are non-technical routes to **Ypsilon Mountain** from Ypsilon Lake—by detouring either N toward Fairchild or S over Chiquita.

The easiest approach to the southern summits is by way of the **Fall River Road.** It is one-way from Horseshoe Park up west.

Mount Chapin, 12,454′, **Mount Chiquita,** 13,069′, and **Mount Ypsilon,** 13,514′, are climbed in the order named from Chapin

Mount Toll (left) and Mount Audubon above Brainard Lake.

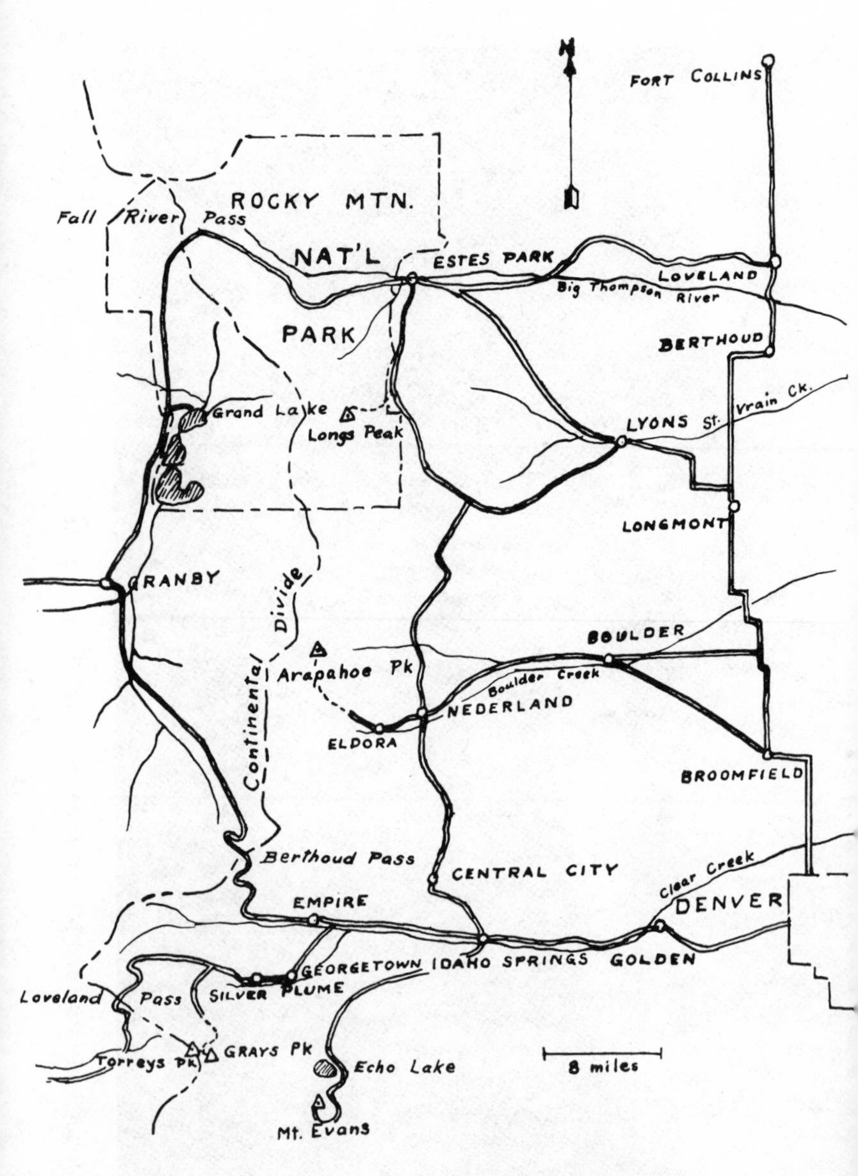

NORTH FRONT RANGE PEAKS

Pass. The trail starts N from $\frac{1}{4}$ mile above the second left road hairpin in the series of zigzags climbing out of Fall River, about mile $6\frac{1}{2}$ west of Horseshoe Park, or if you walk down Fall River Road, $1\frac{1}{2}$ miles from the **Trail Ridge Road.** The trail, starting at 11,000′ takes you .1 mile to the pass, where you leave it to go NE along the ridge. Mount Chapin is 200′ higher than the saddle to the N of it, and easily bypassed; Chiquita loses you only 100′, but is also easily by-passed. The trip to Ypsilon is about 5 miles.

FRONT RANGE

The Front Range, described below in geological terms, is used in an arbitrarily different sense in this book to include the section of the Continental Divide and certain offshoots, between Trail Ridge Road (Milner Pass) and Hoosier Pass. We separate it into the five sections treated below: National Park, Indian, James Peak, Loveland Pass and Southwest.

FRONT RANGE—NATIONAL PARK SECTION

QUADS: Longs Peak, McHenrys Peak, Allens Park, Isolation Peak, Estes Park (combined on older Rocky Mountain N Park Quad)—and see also Park Department folder map, Colorado Mountain Club's Front Range High Trail Map (U.S.G.S. based) and two guide books which go into more detail than this one: *The Rocky Mountain National Park—an Outdoorsman's Guide*, by Cargo and Chisholm, and *Longs Peak: Its Story and a Climbing Guide*, by Paul Nesbit. The July *T & T* has a full list of the Park's 85 summits and their altitudes, compiled by R. D. Martin.

Within the Park the Front Range angles SSE and S 20 miles from La Poudre Pass through the Wild Basin back ridge, where at the Park Boundary we change names to the Indian Section. The mountains are of typical Front Range granite and generally speaking rather flat-crested but with very deep cut glaciation on the east slopes. The glaciation has produced many Alpine lakes, often with cliffs at the back. Longs and Hallett

Peaks and some of the lower points have been areas of intensive rock climbing for many years. As is always true in the Rockies there is loose rock, ready to fall at a touch, even on the cleanest cliffs.

Because the Park is visited by many who have no experience in mountains and has many potential hazards of cliffs and ice, all climbers who depart from the marked trails or climb the high peaks must register their intentions and those who plan rock routes should obtain permission.

Camping is permitted only in designated places, but these are adequate for any excursions you may plan. Gate rangers will furnish the list on request.

EAST SIDE APPROACHES

For the string of peaks under consideration the main starting places are the Trail Ridge Road (US 34), Moraine Park, Bear Lake and nearby Glacier Gorge Junction, and Wild Basin, all of which have fine trail walks to various lakes, cirques and waterfalls.

Specimen Mountain, 12,489′, is an easy 2-mile trail climb from 10,750′ Milner Pass, 30 miles from Estes Park, 21 from Grand Lake on US 34. The trail goes N from near the upper end of Poudre Lake. From the top you look across W at the Never Summer Range, N along the Rawah, and across E at the smooth side of the Mummy Mountains. See the Fall River Pass Quad.

Mount Ida, 12,880′, is likewise reached from Milner Pass. Follow the trail S ½ mile, then NE a mile or so, when you cut off the right side, climbing to the ridge and Divide, which you follow SSE 3½ miles. Mount Ida looks down on the Gorge Lakes.

Gorge Lakes, the remote gems of Alpine scenery which lie between Mount Ida and Mount Julian, are one of the best trail-less trips in the park. You can go toward Mount Ida as above but turn off E from the Divide ½ mile and 400′ short of the summit. Near the end of the ridge you turn W to Arrowhead Lake. This is an altitude loss of 1200′, which you regain in segments as you go up past the lakes.

Mount Julian, 12,928′, is on the left or S side of the Gorge Lakes. You can climb from Highest Lake S to Cracktop, then along the narrow, rocky ridge to the E. The Gorge Lakes and Mount Julian or Ida can also be reached by dropping along Forest Canyon from ¼ mile E of the rock cut on the **Trail Ridge Road.** You drop 2000′ before you cross the canyon and start the climb to the lakes. With two cars this combines well with the ridge route above, since it is usually easier to climb up out of a steep spot than to descend into it.

Stones Peak, 12,922′, and **Sprague Mountain,** 12,713′, are climbed together if one of them is not enough. Drive to the west end of Moraine Park, 8150′, and take the **Fern Lake Trail** 2½ miles to the first switchback above the pool. Cross to the north side of Spruce Creek and bushwhack W up the rounded east ridge of Stones. It is 2 miles to timberline, where the ridge becomes sharp and turns NW to flank Hidden River. A mile and a half more along the ridge and a turn S does it. Sprague is a mile to the SW, with an 800′ drop between. Sprague is also at the end of a pleasant 4-mile walk NW along the Divide from Flattop, but you have to get to Flattop first.

Little Matterhorn, 11,586′, is a favorite of experienced climbers, being very handsome to look at and from, and offering the suggestion of a rock climb by the easiest route. A rope should be available whether it is used or not. Drive to Bear Lake, 9400′, and walk the trail 4½ miles W and N to the Odessa Lake outlet. Cross the creek and climb W and across a second creek, from Tourmaline Gorge. When you have bushwhacked to timberline continue WSW to S to reach the ridge W of the end point which constitutes Little Matterhorn. Another route approaches the summit ridge from the opposite side. From 3 miles up the Odessa Lake trail you turn off left for Lake Helene and switchback downhill NW from it till you can cross the west fork of Fern Creek and head up an obvious gully to the ridge.

Flattop Mountain, 12,324′, is a 4-mile trail climb from Bear Lake Parking area, 9400′. It is about 1½ miles W and N around Ptarmigan Point to Notchtop, another ½ mile to Knobtop, and ¾ mile more to Gabletop, all with very little loss of altitude. **Notchtop,** like Little Matterhorn, is down E off the gentle Divide ridge. It presents good climbing to those who approach from the valley below.

Hallett Peak, 12,713′, is ½ mile S and E around the Tyndall Glacier head from Flattop; **Otis Peak,** 12,486′, is another 1½ miles S around Chaos Canyon; and **Taylor Peak,** 13,133′, is 2 miles more S, past Andrews Glacier and the rough cliffs above Loch Vale. From Flattop to Taylor without the other peaks en route is a trip of 2½ miles with only 200′ altitude loss. Hallett and Otis are side trips of about 250′ each. **Mount Powell** is a bit far unless you go down off Thatchtop to Glacier Gorge with transportation arranged for, instead of returning via Flattop.

McHenrys Peak, 13,327′, is climbed from Black Lake, 5 miles from Glacier Gorge by marked trail. One skirts the lake to the left, climbs ½ mile farther S up the brook to Frozen Lake and then climbs ½ mile W to Stone Man Pass, and turning right, by the ridge to the top.

Mount Powell, 13,208′, can be climbed from Sky Pond, to which a 4½-mile trail, only cairn-marked the last part of the way, leads from Glacier Gorge Junction. It is a climb of ¾ mile from the pond up the north side of Powell, some of it probably on steep snow.

Thatchtop, 12,668′, juts NE a mile from Powell. Take the **Loch Vale Trail** from Glacier Gorge Junction 2¼ miles to the first sharp bend past the trail junction with Glacier Gorge. Just S across the creek you will get into the start of what *Outdoorsman's Guide* describes as a reverse south curve gully. It leads up to the easier tundra slope above. The climb is 2800′ from trail to summit in not much over a mile. You are in very handsome country here, with everything showing its teeth at you. Thatchtop is as often climbed from Solitude Lake.

Take the **Black Lake Trail** 4½ miles to a timberless patch just N of Shelf Creek, which comes in from the other (W) side of the canyon. Bushwhack up the right side of the creek to Shelf Lake, 1000′ higher. From Solitude Lake, a little farther up the shelf, cut S up a steep half-mile slope to summit.

Chiefs Head, 13,579′, is an easy ridge climb of 1 mile SE from Stone Man Pass. See the route for McHenrys Peak above, and McHenrys and Isolation Peak Quads.

Pagoda Mountain, 13,497′, is best ascended from the 13,100′ Longs-Pagoda saddle and the NNE ridge. You take the 5-mile **Black Lake Trail** from Glacier Gorge Junction and keeping SE from Black Lake climb 1½ miles to the saddle. It is a 7-mile trip one way, with a 4300′ climb. Black Lake is a good camping place.

The south peaks, Pagoda and Chiefs Head, are as often climbed from upper Wild Basin. Take the **Sandbeach Lake Trail,** 3½ miles W from its start at Copeland Lake, and angle right a little way up Hunters Creek for a camping place. **Chiefs Head** goes by the 3-mile southeast ridge including Mount Orton; for **Pagoda,** you climb Hunters Creek to the first lake above the camp, angle NE over a low ridge toward Meeker Peak and then climb the loose rock gully to the saddle W of Longs. **Longs Peak** can be climbed from here also, or with **Meeker Peak** by heading for the saddle between the two.

Longs Peak, 14,256′, is one of Colorado's great mountains, accessible to tourists under favorable conditions, yet well armored with steep to perpendicular faces. You need 4 quads to see it topographically: Longs, McHenrys and Isolation Peaks, and Allens Park. It was named for Major S. H. Long, who explored the plains in 1820. The first recorded climb was made by Major Powell and Denver editor William N. Byers in 1868, but Indians are said to have had an eagle trap on top earlier. Enos A. Mills gave it fame in his yarns. Since then ranger-patroled trails, high altitude shelters, and good rock have helped to keep its climbing tradition active. From Estes Park drive 10 miles S on State 7 and 1 mile W to a Ranger

Station and campground at 9400′. Climb or ride 7 miles W by bridle trail to Boulder Field, 12,600′. The Boulder Field is also reached by a 9-mile trail from Glacier Gorge Campground on the Bear Lake Road. From the Boulder Field a marked route climbs S over boulders and through a stretch hand-railed with cable to a sketchy trail higher up. A longer but more interesting route goes W through the Keyhole Ridge and turns S along marked rock ledges to approach the top from the SW. Unless it is icy neither route requires special skills or equipment, but the mountain is hard for the inexperienced or ill-conditioned. Camping is permitted at Jim's Grove, a halfway point near timberline on the N side of the trail and N of Alpine Brook. For the rock routes, which run all the way from easy to very difficult, see Nesbit.

Mount Meeker, 13,911′, is 500′ high on the Longs Peak side, so is sometimes climbed on the same excursion. The descent from Meeker to the **Longs Peak Trail** is a tedious piece of cross-country work. The pleasantest route to Meeker is one that takes you through the Wild Basin scenery on the way. Those who want to make it alone and in one day, bushwhack from the Horse-tooth–Lookout Mountain saddle, 10,200′, to and up the SE ridge. The saddle is 2½ miles WNW and S from Meeker Park. Total, 5½ miles, 5500′.

The **Longs Peak Trail,** running W from 10 miles S of Estes Park on State 7, has a branch running NW to Moraine Park and a spur in to Chasm Lake, where riders share the stone shelter hut with east face rock climbers and high country fishermen.

Eastward across the Tahosa Valley from Longs is the rigorous trail up to Twin Sisters Lookout. Look for the start 1 mile S of Wind River Pass on State 7.

The peaks W of Wild Basin are best enjoyed from the lakes designated by the Park Service as camping areas: Sandbeach, Thunder and Ouzel or Bluebird.

Mount Alice, 13,110′, and **Tanima Peak,** 12,420′, present formidable east fronts, but both can be climbed together from

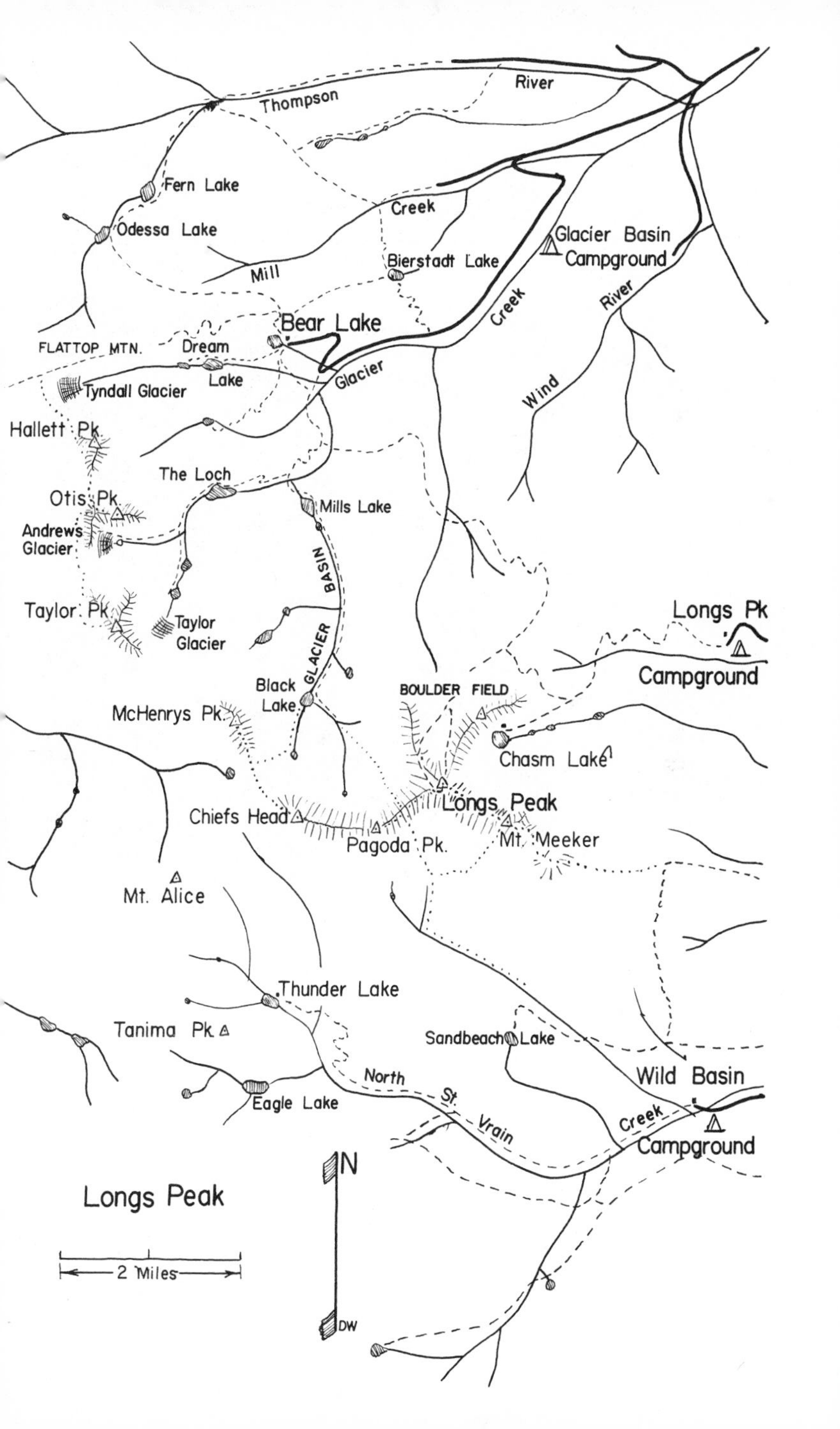

Thompson
River
Fern Lake
Odessa Lake
Creek
Mill
Bierstadt Lake
Glacier Basin
Campground
Creek
River
Bear Lake
FLATTOP MTN.
Dream
Lake
Tyndall Glacier
Glacier
Wind
Hallett Pk.
The Loch
Otis Pk.
Andrews
Glacier
Mills Lake
BASIN
Taylor Pk.
Taylor
Glacier
GLACIER
Longs Pk
Campground
Black
Lake
BOULDER FIELD
McHenrys Pk.
Chasm Lake
Longs Peak
Chiefs Head
Pagoda Pk.
Mt. Meeker
Mt. Alice
Thunder Lake
Tanima Pk.
Sandbeach Lake
North
St.
Vrain
Creek
Wild Basin
Campground
Eagle Lake
N
Longs Peak
2 Miles
DW

Longs Peak (left), Pagoda and Chiefs Head with Mount Meeker behind. *Kingery photo*

Thunder Lake. The pack in is on a 7½-mile trail W from 8400′ at Wild Basin to 10,600′. Start for the peaks along the N side of Thunder Lake, climbing W 1½ miles to the pass at the head of the drainage, 12,061′. Tanima is a climb of ½ mile ESE; Alice is a little over a mile N. It is possible to make a steep return from Alice by spiraling from SW at the top to S and E, and to follow the gulch 1½ miles SE along the headwater creek of the North St. Vrain, or to take a gentler route from Alice down the NNE ridge ½ mile, when you can follow a long ridge that cuts off at right angles to it.

Isolation Peak, 13,118′, is also accessible from Thunder Lake. A dimly marked trail goes S around the bench and up W to Box Lake, Eagle Lake and Frigid Lake, about 2½ miles in all. From Frigid there is a good route S around the ridge end and slantwise SW up the slopes of Isolation.

There is good camping also on the **Bluebird Lake Trail** at Ouzel Lake, 10,000′, or at Bluebird Lake 1000′ higher. They are 5½ and 7 miles respectively from the campground. Isolation Peak can be climbed quite directly from the latter. You continue W from the N side of Bluebird Lake all the way to the 12,200′ pass S of the summit, then work up the short steep ridge. Total, 2 miles from the lake.

Ouzel Peak, 12,716′, is a little longer and much gentler climb from the same pass. You head S around to E on the ridge crest. **Ogalalla** is another 1½ miles S along a gently rising ridge. The only practicable way down is to return to the saddle.

Copeland Mountain, 13,176′, juts far into the southwest corner of Wild Basin with a rough north face. The easiest route to it goes from the outlet of Ouzel Lake, 9800′, where you bushwhack S ½ mile up a timbered ridge and then SW to timberline another good ½ mile. From there it is a mile of rather steep trudging.

WEST SIDE APPROACHES

On the Grand Lake side of the park there are well maintained trails. **North Inlet Trail,** which takes off from the village of Grand Lake, connects via **Flattop Mountain Trail** with Bear Lake, 16½ miles. It also has a 3½ mile side trail south to Lake Nokoni and Lake Nanita, 10 miles from Grand Lake and 2400′ higher (10,800′).

Ptarmigan Mountain, 12,324′, is a short steep climb up ridge from the pass between the two lakes.

East Inlet Trail starts at West Portal, at the east end of Grand Lake, and climbs officially to camping at Lake Verna, 7 miles, and on up the valley in sloppier style to Fourth and Fifth Lakes, the latter above timberline and a cliff-blocked mile N of **Isolation Peak. Shadow Mountain,** S of Grand Lake, is a good conditioner. Drive S across the Grand Lake–Shadow Mountain channel and turn right. From the road end walk S along the east side of Shadow Mountain Lake. The trail starts a gentle climb after 1 mile. You ascend through 4 miles of timber to a fire lookout 1500′ above lake.

Mount Craig, 12,007′ is an imposing western extension from the Divide. To climb it, take the **East Inlet Trail** from 8367′ Grand Lake 5 miles W to Lone Pine Lake, 9900′. Head S from the southeast corner of the lake, following a minor ridge and bench for ¼ mile to the mouth of a steeply climbing U-shaped valley. After about 600′ of climbing in the valley it is feasible to work out of it to the right, where you continue on slopes of lessening steepness to the summit. It is wise to keep details of your route well in mind as any deviation on the descent may lead you into serious trouble. See Grand Lake and Isolation Peak Quads.

Ptarmigan Mountain, 12,324′, and **Andrews Peak,** 12,565′, can make a combined ridge climb from a camp at Lake Verna, 7 miles W of Grand Lake on the **East Inlet Trail.** To climb Andrews, which is 1½ miles N from the lake, you go diagonally upslope, angling well to left of the fall line. A 12,000′ bench makes it easy to avoid the high spots of the ridge on the 2-mile traverse to Andrews Peak. These peaks are on the spur of the Divide N of Mount Craig. See Shadow Mountain and McHenrys and Isolation Peaks Quads.

Mount Adams, 12,121′, is on another long spur E from the Divide, S of Mount Craig. Watanga and Hiamovi, up ridge from Adams, are remote, and best approached from the S, but Adams can be climbed by a mile-long NW ridge. Take the **East Inlet Trail** 4 miles to the junction for Paradise Creek and follow it S 1½ miles to a left turn. Instead of taking the turn of the main valley, continue S up a minor drainage line or up the small ridge to its left. The broad climbing ridge will be apparent when you have bushwhacked 1 mile on this line to timberline.

For some interesting Wild Basin to Grand Lake backpack trips, consult the *Outdoorsman's Guide.* The Grand Lake Ranger Station is also a good source for information.

A trail connects the S side of Grand Lake Village with the SE corner of Lake Granby. Starting as for Shadow Mountain above, the N part is along Shadow Mountain Lake; the S half is along Grand Lake and its Grand Bay. The trail is 13 miles long.

FRONT RANGE—INDIAN SECTION

QUADS: Monarch Lake, Isolation Peak, East Portal, Empire, Ward, Allens Park, Grand Lake, Nederland; Roosevelt and Arapaho N F map; Front Range High Trail Map (Colorado Mountain Club).

This section, likewise arbitrary, extends from the south border of the national park and Ogalalla Peak along the Divide through the Arapaho massif, where with a short jog west the James Peak Section carries on. The range crest is fairly straight, heavily glaciated, and drops off quite as steeply on the west side as on the east. A high flanking road along the east side, called the Peak to Peak Highway and numbered State 160, gives several fine prospects of the Indian Section. The prevalent rock of the summits is the Idaho Springs schist and gneiss.

Main approach valleys are the Middle St. Vrain (Peaceful Valley), the South St. Vrain (Brainard Lake), and the north fork of Middle Boulder Creek (Eldora) on the east side, and on the west three valleys east from Monarch Lake.

St. Vrain Glacier Trail starts 7½ miles W of State 160. From the exit for Peaceful Valley, drive W 1½ miles to the upper campground, and continue W on foot or with a rough country car for 6 more miles to a lake, where a trail starts on the S side of the lake and leads 3 miles W to timberline, ½ mile NE of the glacier series. From about 4 miles along the lumber road (5½ miles W from the Peaceful Valley exit), a trail crosses left and leads to the **Buchanan Pass Trail** (below).

Buchanan Pass Trail starts with the **Mount Audubon Trail** at Brainard Lake, 10,345′, and circles the mountain N and W to cross the Divide at 11,837′ and continue W for a total of 16 miles to Monarch Lake. Using the Peaceful Valley approach as a short cut, Buchanan Pass is about 3 miles from the lumber road.

Pawnee Pass Trail, formerly known as the Breadline Trail, runs over an 11-mile route parallel to the Buchanan, between Brainard and Monarch Lakes farther S. It can be used with the **Buchanan Pass Trail** to make a high country loop. Spur trails of the Pawnee run up under the spire of **Lone Eagle Peak** on the Cascade Creek side and to 13,000′ Isabelle Glacier on the Brainard Lake side. The route has high standard construction.

Arapaho Pass Trail climbs from the Fourth of July Campground above Eldora to the Divide W of the Arapaho Peaks and drops NW down Arapaho Creek to Monarch Lake, 12 miles in all. The W end is shortened with the use of the 4-mile **Caribou Trail** which meets the Arapaho on the pass and goes down W to a road up Meadow Creek. The latter road leaves US 40 3½ miles N of Fraser and runs 9 miles to Western Box Campground and on a rougher bed 2 miles more up Meadow Creek.

Ogalalla Peak, 13,138′, is climbed either from the **St. Vrain Glacier Trail** (see below) or from Wild Basin. One route started from a camp ½ mile above Ouzel Lake. The party turned off the trail to go left and S of Bluebird Lake, thence S to and up the creek coming from Junco Lake. From Junco Lake they climbed SW to Cony Pass, the saddle W of Copeland Peak. From the S side of Cony Pass, a short steep couloir led them to the Divide and an easy swing S to the summit. The **St. Vrain Glacier Trail** route goes this way. About 2 miles beyond the lakelet at the W end of the lumber road you can cut left off the trail and climb 1800′ to the Divide on a steepish ridge. By veering right you will come into the Divide a little E of the 12,000′ saddle above the easternmost glacier. The ridge is rough across the saddle and up the first pitch beyond, but after that settles down for a walk of 3 miles NW and around the bend to the Ogalalla summit.

St. Vrain Mountain, 12,162′, is a viewing point well E of the Divide. It goes by trail from Allenspark on State 7, where a dirt road with a many-name signboard takes you S 1 mile to the 8700′ start of a marked 4-mile trail to the mountain.

Lone Eagle Peak, 11,920′, named indirectly for Charles Lindbergh, first flier of the Atlantic, is a spire-shaped ridge end a mile W of the Divide. From Granby drive 5 miles N on US 34 and 10 miles SE on State 280 to Monarch Lake, 8340′. Starting E along the N side of the lake, take 9-mile **Cascade Creek Trail** E to Crater Lake and camp under the peak at 10,500′. The conventional route circles E under the peak and goes S about $\frac{5}{8}$ mile before turning to climb the E flank. The route starts up considerably S of the big chimney to the E, and then follows the knife edge N to the top. The peak has claimed fatalities; care should be taken to note landmarks for the return trip. Though topographically only a spur of Mount George, it is spectacular and so frequently visited. The rock, generally sound, has provided some fine technical climbs. As will be shown below, other Indian Section peaks are within the reach from Cascade Creek.

Mount Irving Hale, 11,754′, and **Hiamovi Mountain,** 12,395′, can best be reached from Roaring Fork Ranger station at the W end of Lake Granby. Drive 5 miles N on US 34 from 1 mile E of Granby and turn right for an 8-mile run E and around the lake end to Roaring Fork. The trail, starting at 8300′, climbs 3 miles up-creek to 9800′, then takes a side creek E 2 miles to Hiamovi-Irving Hale saddle and continues 2 miles E to 10,730′ Upper Lake, head of Hell Canyon. Irving Hale is an easy mile S from the saddle; Hiamovi is 2 miles ENE via the ridge.

Watanga Mountain, 12,375′, and **Mount Adams** can be climbed from mile 3. You turn N off the trail and climb on the main creek to Watanga Lake at 10,800′, 1½ miles. Adams is another 1½ miles N. Veer right to the saddle and then left to summit. For Watanga angle SE up the lakelets and to a ridge, then NE to the top, 2 miles.

From Upper Lake you can climb NW to the saddle, then E up-ridge and across gentle slopes to Ogalalla, total 2 miles.

Cooper Peak, 12,296′, and **Marten Peak,** 12,041′, are connected by a saddle ¾ mile S of Upper Lake. You can make a slantwise climb to the saddle, 11,600′, and get up the left ridge to Cooper Peak, and you can at least explore the summit of Marten Peak. They look down on Gourd, Island and other lakes.

Sawtooth Mountain, 12,304′, easternmost point of the Divide, is an easy climb of .4 mile SSE from 11,837′ Buchanan Pass. Its narrowness and the 600′ S side cliff make it one of the striking sights from the Peak to Peak Highway.

Mount Audubon, 13,223′, **Paiute Peak,** 13,088′, **Mount Toll,** 12,979′, **Pawnee,** 12,943′, **Shoshoni,** 12,967′, and others to the S are within climbing distance of the Brainard Lake Road, which runs 5 miles W from the N end of Ward on State 160. Brainard Lake, at 10,345′, has camping facilities. From the parking and camping area at the lake, 10,350′, a 4-mile marked trail leads to Audubon, largest and most conspicuous mountain in the area. With energy, one can drop 600′ on the ridge to the W and climb back to Paiute Peak, a mile away. It is another mile S to Mount Toll, for which you drop to 12,400′ and climb very steeply in a rotten rock couloir, to the sharp summit. From any of these points you can choose a route of descent to Blue Lake, 1 mile, and around its N shore to the

$2\frac{1}{2}$-mile trail E and home to Brainard Lake. To climb Toll alone or Toll with Pawnee take the **Blue Lake Trail** and a little short of the lake head W a mile (above its S side) to the Divide, 12,550′. The climb N to Toll is easier from this side, and Pawnee is likewise near and easy. A round trip is possible using the **Pawnee Pass Trail** a little S of Pawnee Peak for one way. Pawnee Pass, 12,541′, also gives an easy route to Shoshoni Peak, a mile S around the ridge line.

Apache Peak, 13,441′, **Navajo Peak,** 13,409′, and **Arikaree Peak,** 13,150′, are also within reach from Brainard Lake. Parties with these destinations take the **Pawnee Pass Trail** 3 miles to where it climbs away from Lake Isabelle. They continue along the South St. Vrain Creek N side another mile to a little lake S of Shoshoni Peak.

For Apache, the route goes SW and W for its S saddle, another mile with 1000′ of climbing at the end. The peak is 250′ higher, a short distance up-ridge NNW.

For the fine steep cone of Navajo, showpiece of the group, one goes from the lakelet SSW up Airplane Gulch, the left-hand choice of 2 ravines that present themselves. From Niwot Ridge, the summit can be taken either directly or on a clockwise spiral. Rope may be needed.

Arikaree Peak can be climbed by the route used for Navajo Peak as far as the climb up Airplane Gulch to Niwot Ridge. You then cross the basin to the S—a drop of 400′, and climb the peak by its N ridge. The round trip altitude climbed is 3600′, round trip distance 11 miles. Parties camped at 10,350′ under Lone Eagle Peak (see above) have climbed S in the valley and up Fair Glacier to the 12,750′ saddle S of it, 2 miles, where they made ascents of 13,441′ Apache Peak, $\frac{1}{3}$ mile ENE, and Navajo, $\frac{1}{2}$ mile SE along the ridge from it. Arikaree is $\frac{3}{4}$ mile farther SE on an obstacled ridge that dips to 12,560′ in the middle, climbs to 13,000′, and drops another 150′ before climbing the last 300′ to 13,150′ Arikaree.

The $3\frac{1}{2}$-mile stretch of watershed between Niwot Ridge and the E ridge of S Arapaho Peak has been closed by the city of

Boulder. Deschewa and other Divide points, and Albion and Kiowa peaks to the E, are needlessly difficult of access. Boulder officials should purify their water and their hearts.

Rainbow Lakes is a camping spot for the Arapaho climb. You turn W 7½ miles N of Nederland from State 160 and drive 5 miles to the 10,000′ camping area. The trail from the lakes is longer than that from the Fourth of July Mines; they meet on the saddle below S Arapaho.

North Arapaho Peak, 13,502′, and **South Arapaho Peak,** 13,397′, on Monarch Lake Quad, are rendered conspicuous by the lower smoother ridge to the S of them as well as by their own roughness. From the S side of Nederland drive 3½ miles W to Eldora and 6½ miles NW past Eldora to Fourth of July Campground at 10,200 feet. Continue on foot 2 miles W toward Arapaho Pass on trail to the location of Fourth of July Mines, 11,252′, then climb NE 1 mile to W-E saddle between Old Baldy and S Arapaho Peak at an elevation of 12,800′. From the saddle, climb ½ mile W up-ridge to the S summit and then ¾ mile N to the N summit via a paint-marked route. Arapaho Glacier lies E of both summits. Its crevasses, 1½ miles N of and 1000′ lower than the Baldy – South Arapaho saddle, are a 3-hour round trip from the saddle.

FRONT RANGE—JAMES PEAK GROUP

QUADS: East Portal, Empire, Berthoud Pass, Monarch Lake, Central City; Arapaho-Roosevelt N F; High Range Trail Map.

This group continues the Divide S and SW from Arapaho Pass to Berthoud Pass, 15 miles. We also include here a little material on the Boulder region to the east.

A road over Rollins Pass, 11,670′, route of the Moffat Railroad and now a scenic drive, crosses from Rollinsville, on State 119, to Winter Park, on US 40, about 35 miles. It is all passable for cars but some of the eastern portion is rough. The road runs west from Rollinsville to Tolland, east portal of the Moffat Tunnel now used by the railroad. Like the Indian section to the north, the section down to James Peak is best seen from the flanking Peak to Peak Highway, here State 160 N of Nederland, State 119 to the south. The Fall River Road, which leaves I-70 3 miles W of Idaho Springs, is the main line of approach to the James Peak section.

Arapaho Pass Trail, and the connecting **Arapaho Glacier Trail** E to Rainbow Lakes have been mentioned above.

Devils Thumb Pass Trail starts from 3 miles NW of Eldora on the Fourth of July Campground road, at 9600′, and climbs S ½ mile, then W 5 miles to 11,747′ Devils Thumb Pass on the Divide, and descends W 3 miles as the **Kings Lake Trail** to Devils Thumb Park. (The Kings Lake Trail is called the Corona on U.S.G.S. Quad.) **High Lonesome Trail** also runs to Devils Thumb Park but from Monarch Lake, 11 miles to the N, generally through timber country. Devils Thumb Park can be reached by a jeep road through ranch properties. The route starts at Fraser, goes 2 miles E, turns N and E a mile across Ranch Creek, then goes N 1½ miles and NE 2 miles to Cabin Creek, and up that to the park. These directions are very uncertain; field inquiry is necessary. There is a jeep approach to the **Devils Thumb Pass Trail.** A mile W of Eldora you take the left road through Hessie instead of the Fourth of July to the right. This climbs 1½ miles W to Jasper Creek and turns up the creek, WNW, for 2 more miles toward Devils Thumb Trail. The last mile or so may not go with a jeep.

There is a good round trip to and along the Divide, all by trail. Starting from Hessie or 1½ miles W where Jasper Creek meets the Middle Boulder, take the jeep trail and **Devils Thumb Trail** to the range crest. Turn S along **Kings Lake** or **Corona Trail** and go S 3 miles to the saddle S of Kings Lake and return down the south fork of Middle Boulder. It is 12-15 miles, depending on the starting point.

A shorter trip, from which you see even more lakes, takes off from East Portal, 9200′, 9 miles W of Rollinsville. From the S side of the tunnel you follow the road and pack trail WSW 4 miles to Rollins Pass, 11,860′, and walk N on the range crest

3½ miles to **Beacon Peak,** 12,072′. You could go farther but the SE ridge here is a good line of descent. Half a mile below timber, if you keep your aim with the upper part of the ridge, will bring you to the creek junction in Arapaho Creek. Follow the trail down the northeast side and when it turns right, shortcut to the tunnel.

Mount Neva, 12,814′, and **Mount Jasper,** 12,923′, can be climbed together from Fourth of July Campground. Climb by signed trail 3 miles to Jasper Lake; cut ½ mile to the right (NW) and go up the east ridge of Jasper, 1½ miles long. From Jasper follow the Divide W and N 2 miles to Neva. Drop off the N side (may be a good glissade) and past the E side of Lake Dorothy to **Arapaho Pass Trail** for the return. There is a west way, too. From Tabernash a 7-mile road leads to Western Box Campground, 11,850′ (See Strawberry Lake Quad.) Continue up Meadow Creek 4½ miles (first 2½ jeepable) to Columbia Lake, at timberline. Go right of the lake and to the saddle, ¼ mile SSW, and angle S up Neva's W face to the top.

Satanta Peak, 11,979′, is a short grass stroll N from Caribou Pass, W of Arapaho Pass, and thus likewise approachable from a camp on either side of the Divide.

James Peak, 13,294′, is on Empire Quad. Take Fall River road from 3 miles W of Idaho Springs, and drive 8 miles W and N to St. Marys Lake parking area, 10,000′. Walk to the right of the stream and lake to and up the glacier, and continue W on ridge, 4 miles in all. An even closer start can be made from Loch Lomond, for which you turn off left at Alice, a mile S of St. Marys Lake, and continue along the valley side on a chiprock road for 3½ miles to 11,200′. A short climb NE from the lake end puts you on the gentle ridge slopes; or take the rougher route with three big steps; up W past the lakes to the cirque head. From James Peak to 13,250′ **Mount Bancroft** is a longish mile with a dip to 12,600′, and you can go W another mile to **Parry Peak,** highest of the group at 13,391′. Best way down is back to the 13,000′ saddle E of Parry and then a contour a little S of Bancroft, where you go E to its ESE ridge and down that to your Lomond road.

Another James Peak route starts where the water syphon crosses US 40 at Jim Creek Valley. You climb Jim's Creek to road end and take directly E up slopes to Rogers Pass. It is then 2 miles S along the ridge to the peak. For a gentler grade, drive to Riflesight Notch at 11,000′ on the road W from Rollins Pass. An old road climbs from the Notch S along the hillside for 2 miles to Rogers Pass, and from there the **Ute Trail** takes you another mile along the crest to the ½ mile climb at the end—on the flat-faced north ridge.

Jeepers, you can almost drive to the top of James Peak. From Central City, drive up Main Street past town, and turning N at the cemeteries, continue 2 miles to the Apex road up North Clear Creek. (Apex road starts from State 119, 2 miles NW of Black Hawk). From Apex, which is 4 miles W and N from this junction, the road goes W crossing Elk Creek after 1½ miles and 2 miles later turns S and SW to get on the Kingston Peak saddle. It sidehills and climbs to 11,500′ between Kingston and James Peak, not much over a mile from the latter. The mayor of Central City tells us that jeeps are going wild in the hills there, and it may be that barriers will begin to appear. Central City was heavily mined, and so much of the mountain land is privately held. See Central City Quad.

James Peak bears the name of Dr. Edwin James, the first man on record to climb a 14,000-foot peak in the continental U.S.A. He, and two other men, climbed Pikes Peak in July, 1820. Major S. H. Long, the leader of their expedition, tried to change the name to James Peak, but Pike's name was too well established. In the 1860's, James name was given to the mountain west of Central City. It was long referred to as Jim Peak.

Mount Eva, 13,130′, and **Witter Peak,** 12,884′, are accessible from the Fall River road (see above for James Peak). Take the road for Alice and Loch Lomond, and when it turns N, 2½ miles W of Alice, leave the car and angle downhill W to Fall River. Cross to S and up to Chinns Lake. With jeep, you can get to Chinns Lake, on a road which crosses the creek where the main road takes a sharp right for Alice. Climb W 1½ miles past the lakes into the upper cirque, sidehill S to Witter Peak, walk around the ridge W and N 1½ miles to Neva and return via the cirque.

Breckinridge Peak, 12,889′, and **Mount Flora,** 13,132′, can be climbed from Empire. Take the main road up North Empire Creek, N from town, 2 miles to Conqueror Mine. Leave the car here at 9600′ and cross the creek to Lion Mines, where a trail takes off for Bill Moore Lake. About 2½ miles up you can cut left up the Breckinridge east ridge. You climb 1200′ on the ridge, then dip a little and climb 400′ more for Flora, a mile farther W.

From Berthoud Pass, hikers and sometimes skiers skirt N of Colorado Mines Peak and follow the Divide to Flora, Eva, and sometimes even Witter. When there is no snow cover the loose talus may drive you up over Colorado Mines Peak.

BOULDER AREA

Boulder (see Boulder and Eldorado Springs Quads) is naturally the center of much climbing activity. The tilted red sandstone Flatirons and other rocks within easy reach have been minutely routed by rock artists, and the less precipitous mountains of the area have a system of trails. In *High over Boulder*, Cleve McCarty and Pat Ament present both trails and climbs, the latter with fine diagrammatic drawings, in detail. Below are a few notes on major trails.

Green Mountain Trail makes a 7-10 mile round trip to Green Mountain from the end of Base Line Road (the 40th parallel of latitude). It runs into Gregory Canyon and climbs out to the S on any of several variations which lead summitward.

Flagstaff Mountain Trails lead both from the north side of Gregory Canyon and from a mile up Boulder Canyon on its south side to make a round trip of this Front Range viewpoint.

Royal Arch Trail runs up Fern Canyon from a mile south of Chautauqua grounds to the Royal Arch between two of the red sandstone Flatirons used as a climbing area by Boulder students. The round trip is 5 miles.

Thorodin Mountain, 10,555′, with **Odin,** which has a tower of 10,493′, gives a good off season hike to one of the best views of the Front Range. Drive up the Coal Creek road, State 72 N from Golden, S from Boulder, or through Arvada, to Camp Eden road, ½ mile E of Wondervu. Follow signs to Axton Ranch, past Highland Boys Camp and park outside the gate at 8750′, 3½ miles off 72. Walk W 1 mile on jeep road, keeping right. Trail continues to fork, ½ mile W, where you take left branch and zigzag 2 miles SSW through timber to summit. See Tungsten Quad.

FRONT RANGE—LOVELAND PASS SECTION

From Berthoud Pass to Argentine Peak, 12 miles S, the Continental Divide makes a great westward bend around the heads of the two Clear Creeks. On the Divide N of Loveland Pass are Vasquez Peak, Jones Pass and Pettingell, Citadel and Hagar Peaks. E of the Pettingell group, the two Clear Creeks are separated by a spur—Bard, Engelmann, and others. These are grouped below the *Clear Creek Group.*

From N of Jones Pass a Middle Park spur called the *Vasquez Mountains* goes off W and N to Byers Peak. When the Divide turns E south of Loveland Pass there are Grays and Torreys along it and the Evans massif on a big eastern spur. These are designated *Grays-Evans Group.* The approaches will be treated in this order.

CLEAR CREEK GROUP

Quads: Loveland and Berthoud Passes, Byers and Grays Peaks; Arapaho N F. This group includes the Divide peaks between Berthoud and Loveland Passes and the ridge between North and South Clear Creeks. The Williams Fork Mountains, though continuous with these on the NW, are treated elsewhere.

From Berthoud Pass, 11,300′, one looks N along the Continental Divide, or S at Engelmann Peak, and can climb along the Divide in either direction, E and N as above, to Breckinridge, or W and S.

Stanley Mountain, 12,521′, is a trip of about 3 miles. From the pass climb W up through the ski area and to the ridge, where you turn SW along the **Mount Nystrom Trail.** See Berthoud Pass Quad.

The road to Jones Pass, 12,541′, is steep but gravel surfaced and only rough enough to stop the more opulent cars. It leaves US 40 7 miles W of Empire, at the hairpin which starts the climb to Berthoud Pass, and keeping to right climbs 5½ miles. You see the Arapaho Peaks to the NNE and Gore Range and Holy Cross country to the W. The road drops on switchbacks to the valley bottom on the W side, but is only a jeep trail from there out. See Berthoud Pass and Byers Peak Quads.

Vasquez Peak, 12,947′, is approached from the above road. Drive only to where the road crosses the creek and makes a sharp bend to leave the creek, about 3½ miles from US 40. The peak is 2000′ above and 1½ miles NNE.

Mount Nystrom, 12,652′, is also available from here. Go on up the road as far as your car wants to. From Jones Pass or a shortcut below it, you have about 1½ miles N to where the ridge splits and you walk a mile NW from the Divide along the **Mount Nystrom Trail.**

Pettingell Peak, 13,553′, on Loveland Pass Quad, is reached from Silver Plume Campground, 10,300′, 7 miles W of Silver Plume. The route is 4½ miles long. Climb angling W from the campground to the steep part of Herman Creek and soon thereafter leave the gulch to work gradually to its N ridge. Thence W to the Divide and along that to the top.

Hagar Mountain, 13,195′, is climbed from Bethel Campground, a mile W of the above Silver Plume Campground, altitude 10,450′. A trail, good for ½ mile, starts up from the campground; the best route climbs to and along a bench on the N side of the creek and eventually climbs to the summit on its S ridge. 13,294′ **Citadel Peak,** which lies between the two, combines well with either.

Bard Peak, 12,641′, is 2 miles N of I-70 at Bakerville and almost 4000′ higher. Half a mile W of Bakerville an old road takes you on foot N and NE to the creek which debouches there. From a few yards higher on the creek, a trail angles off uphill at 30 degrees to the right of the brook. Go up this for $\frac{1}{4}$ mile, then angle back to the creek and head north for the summit, taking the split between the creek forks.

The ring of Clear Creek Peaks—Engelmann, which one sees straight across from Berthoud Pass, Robeson and Bard N of it, and to the W Parnassus and Woods—can all be reached from the Urad Mine provided permission is obtained on the ground. The Urad road turns left off the Jones Pass Road (see above) .2 miles W of US 40 and goes in S and W a mile. The route takes an ex-jeep trail (now closed to vehicles) from the mine area S a mile to near timberline on Ruby Creek, at which point 13,574′ **Parnassus** is $1\frac{1}{2}$ miles ahead, and 12,940′ **Woods,** easiest to gain, is $1\frac{1}{4}$ miles SW. **Bard,** the highest, is 2 miles SSW and the other two along the ridge N of it. If Bard is the objective climb to the Bard-Parnassus saddle. If you go N to **Engelmann** you can descend its NNW ridge to the mine.

VASQUEZ MOUNTAINS

QUADS: Byers Peak, Bottle Pass, Fraser, Berthoud Pass; Arapaho N F. The group consists of the horseshoe ridge around St. Louis Creek.

A fine system of trails connects the Middle Park ridges. **Nystrom Trail** climbs S from the top of the Winter Park Ski road to **Stanley Mountain,** in total about 10 miles, then 5 miles W over Vasquez Pass and Peak to **Mount Nystrom. St. Louis Trail** comes more directly to Mount Nystrom from a ridge knoll reached by road, 5 miles NNE. To reach the start of this one you drive W from Idlewild 12 miles on the Denver

Water Board road, or up St. Louis Creek from Fraser to the Fraser Experiment Station junction of roads and ½ mile E to the same point on Water Board road, then S from it 9½ miles (last 2 jeepish) to an 11,956′ knoll where the trail continues 4 miles S to **Nystrom.** It is 3 more miles SW to 12,246′ **St. Louis Peak,** and 7 more W and N to **Bills Peak,** near **Byers** on the Byers massif. There are lines of descent down both sides of the Byers massif. Since these follow the creeks, they suggest various backpack trips in combination with the ridges.

Byers Peak, 12,804′, has a 2½ mile trail from the north to the top, from Bottle Pass. From Fraser drive 12 miles W to Church Park, 2 miles SW to Keyser Creek, and 3 miles E. The trail continues E then S toward the peak.

GRAYS-EVANS GROUP

QUADS: Mount Evans, Grays Peak, Loveland Pass, Montezuma, Idaho Springs, Harris Park; Pike N F. Included here are peaks E and SE of Loveland Pass.

Grizzly Peak, 13,427′, is visible as one drives toward Loveland Pass from the W. It is a good high-country ridge tour of 2½ miles from the 11,990′ pass crest. You climb E along the crest most of a mile, then angle to the right to skirt the 12,915′ summit and continue along the ridge SE. Grizzly is sometimes climbed from the NE via Grizzly Gulch, tributary of Stevens Gulch below.

Grays Peak, 14,270′ and **Torreys Peak,** 14,267′, are named for the famous 19th Century botany professors of Harvard and Princeton. They are frequently climbed together. From Graymont (Bakerville) exit, 6 miles W of Georgetown on I-70, drive 4 miles or less S in Stevens Gulch to a camp around timberline. The 3000′ climb of Grays is on a trail 4 miles long which starts on the NW side of the creek. The route to Torreys is N from Grays along the ¾ mile ridge, with a 550′ drop. One does well to return to the saddle on the descent. For a S route to Grays, see Peru Creek below.

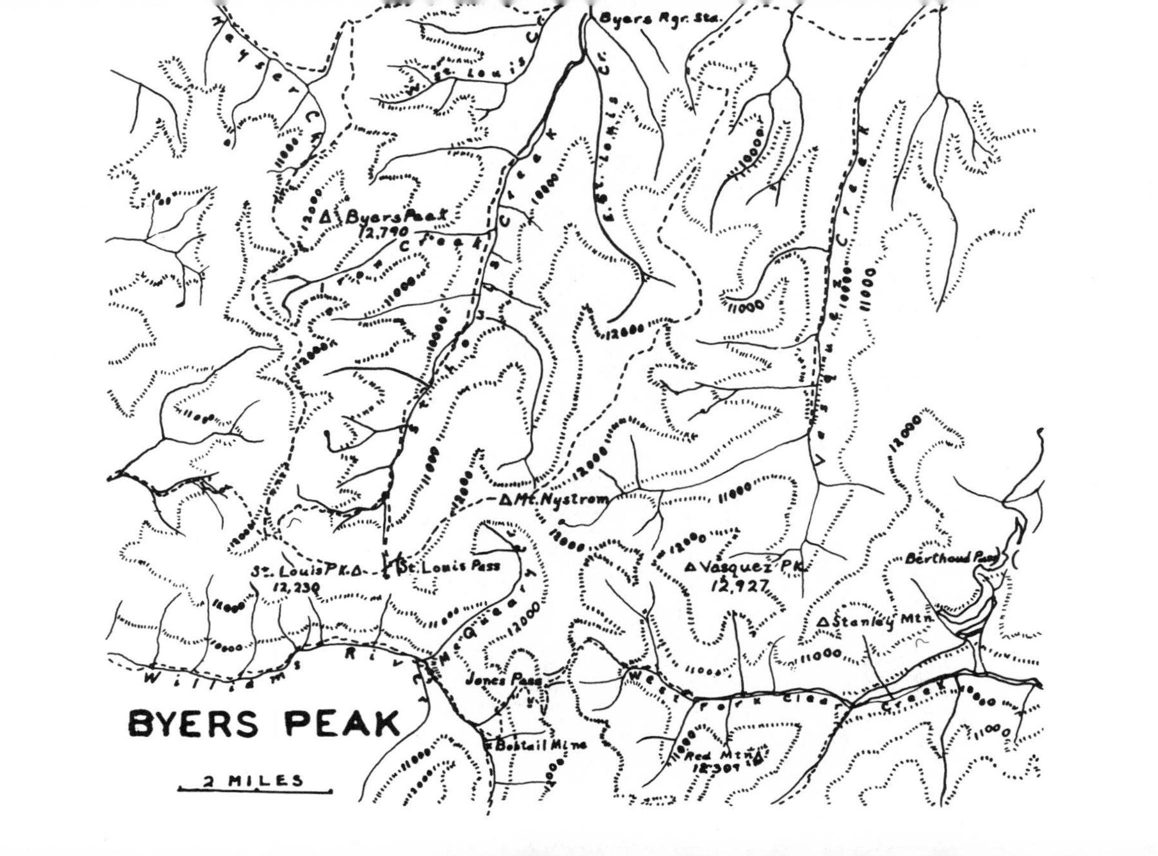
BYERS PEAK
2 MILES
Byers Rgr. Sta.
Keyser Ck.
W. St. Louis Cr.
E. St. Louis Cr.
Byers Peak
12,790
Iron Creek
St. Louis Creek
Vasquez Creek
Mt. Nystrom
St. Louis PK.
12,230
St. Louis Pass
Vasquez PK.
12,927
Berthoud Pass
Stanley Mtn.
Williams River
McQueary Cr.
Jones Pass
Bobtail Mine
West Fork Clear Creek
Red Mtn.
12,307
11000
12000
10000

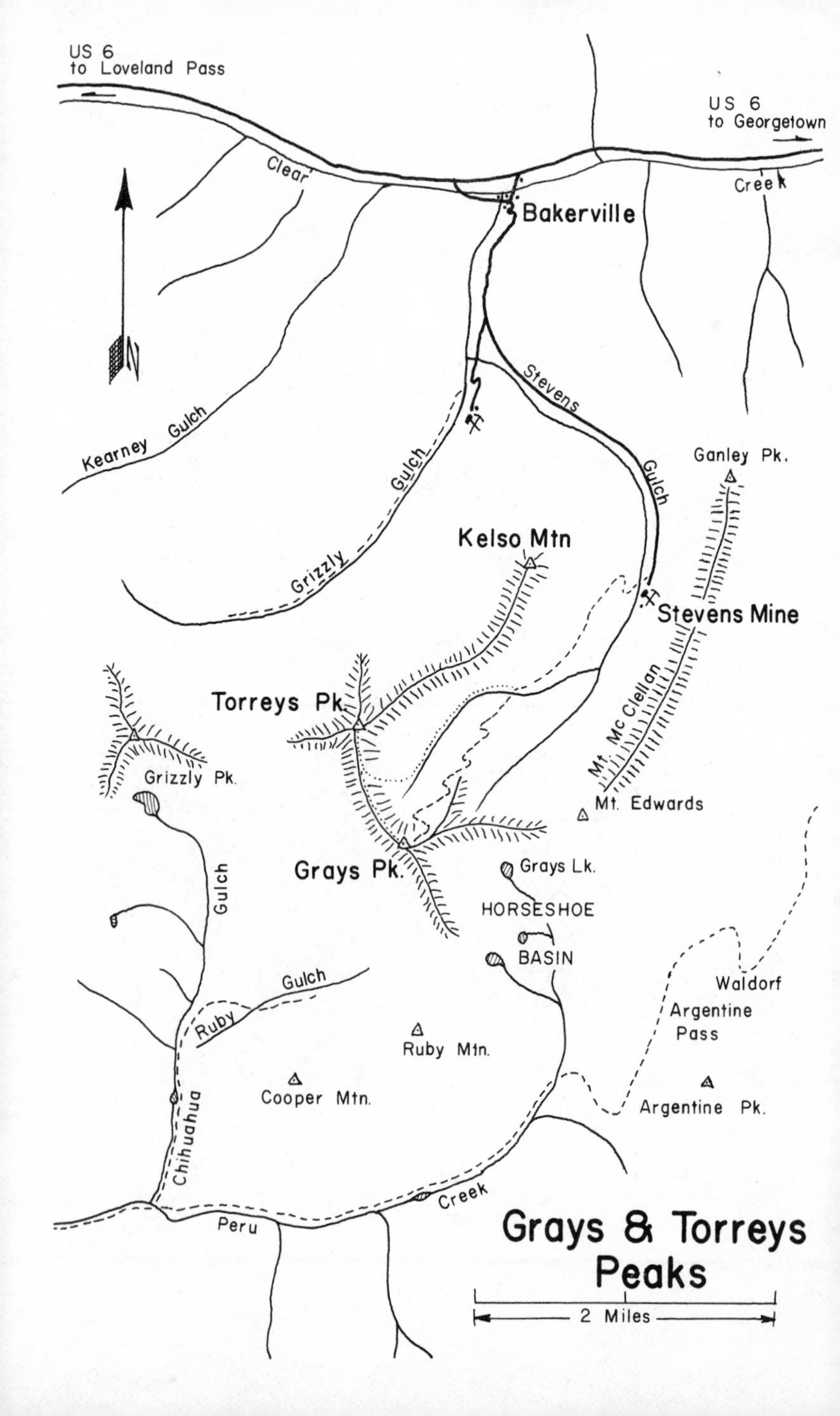

US 6
to Loveland Pass
US 6
to Georgetown
Clear
Creek
Bakerville
Kearney Gulch
Grizzly Gulch
Stevens Gulch
Ganley Pk.
Kelso Mtn
Stevens Mine
Torreys Pk.
Mt. Mc Clellan
Grizzly Pk.
Mt. Edwards
Grays Pk.
Grays Lk.
Gulch
HORSESHOE
BASIN
Gulch
Ruby
Waldorf
Argentine
Pass
Ruby Mtn.
Cooper Mtn.
Chihuahua
Argentine Pk.
Creek
Peru
Grays & Torreys
Peaks
2 Miles

Kelso Mountain, a mile W of the camping area in the gulch, is best climbed from the south. McClellan Mountain, though possible from the gulch, is much pleasanter from the east side. A jeep trail branches off from the Stevens Mine road 1½ miles S of I-70 and takes you 1 mile toward Grizzly Peak in Grizzly Gulch. From the main Stevens road the climb is 4½ miles and about 3100′. A mile above the jeep road, angle left (S) from the creek and find a route to the E ridge for a finish.

Guanella Pass, between Georgetown on I-70 and Grant on US 285, crosses the Clear Creek—South Platte divide 10 miles S of Georgetown. En route you pass the hydro-electric power plant which levels off peak load power demands by pumping water from lower pond to upper during light-load periods of the day. A branch road turns off right from 3 miles S of Georgetown and climbs W to the old railroad grade of the Argentine Central, then follows it 7 miles to Waldorf, where one of the many tunnels planned for the Divide was to go through to Peru Creek and the Snake River. From Waldorf, 11,600′, you can jeep SW to Argentine Pass or W up the railroad switchbacks to 13,000′ on **Mount McClellan.** The slopes on this side of the valley, including that of 13,850′ **Mount Edwards,** are well grassed steep walking country. Do not plan to jeep W off Argentine Pass. See Grays Peak Quad.

There is good camping a little below Waldorf, which is itself above timber.

Squaretop Mountain, 13,794′, is 4 miles W from the 11,670′ crest of Guanella Pass. Except for an abrupt section near the west end it is a gentle high country ridge climb.

Mount Bierstadt, 14,060′, is 3 miles ESE of the pass. From the crest walk far enough S to get past the marshes and then E up the ridge. A longer and wilder approach to both Bierstadt and Evans leaves the Guanella Pass road 5½ miles N of Grant, on US 285, and climbs by foot or jeep the first 3½ miles along Scott Gomer Creek and its Lake Fork to Abyss Lake. If the creek is too high for pedestrians, look for a footbridge about 2 miles up Scott Gomer Creek (¼ mile below deep ford). From creek junction of Lake Fork and Scott Gomer, one can follow the latter N to Abyss Shelter, then cut SE on a cairn line to and up the south ridge of Bierstadt.

Mount Evans, 14,260′, has a road to the top. From I-70 at either the exit for Bergen Park or Idaho Springs, take State 103 to Echo Lake, 21 or 14 miles respectively. (The Bergen Park route is higher and gives a fine sweep of the Divide.) From Echo Lake it is 14 miles to the top. At Summit Lake, mile 10 from Echo Lake, you are at 12,834′ and a steep half mile N of the summit. Climb anywhere E of the cliffs. To lengthen the walking distance, take the second of 2 right turns at about mile 10 from Idaho Springs on State 103 and drive 1½ miles S up Chicago Creek to Camp Shwayder, 10,200′. Jeep road and trail continue up-creek 3 miles to the lake. Climb the bench to the upper lake and head SE up the slopes to the right of Mount Warren to gain Summit Lake Basin. To shorten the climb drive to the cosmic ray laboratory just under the summit.

Mount Bierstadt is often packaged with Evans. Descend the west ridge of Evans 1½ miles and turn S along Sawtooth ridge ¾ mile to Bierstadt. The Sawtooth can be skirted on a high W side traverse, about 13,200′ at the low point. From Bierstadt return on traverse and climb ¾ mile NE to the saddle W of Summit Lake, 13,650′, and descend eastward down a steep couloir.

Rosalie Peak, 13,575′, is a down-ridge walk of 2 miles from the Mount Evans road. Leave the road where it crosses flats 2 miles SSE of Summit Lake and travel SE. You will drop to about 12,900′.

Mount Evans is named for the second governor of Colorado Territory, whose family still owns the land he acquired for his summer home on upper Bear Creek at the foot of Mount Evans. Mount Bierstadt is named for the 19th century artist whose romantic paintings of mountains are well represented by the oil depicting Longs Peak now hanging in the Western History Room of the Denver Public Library.

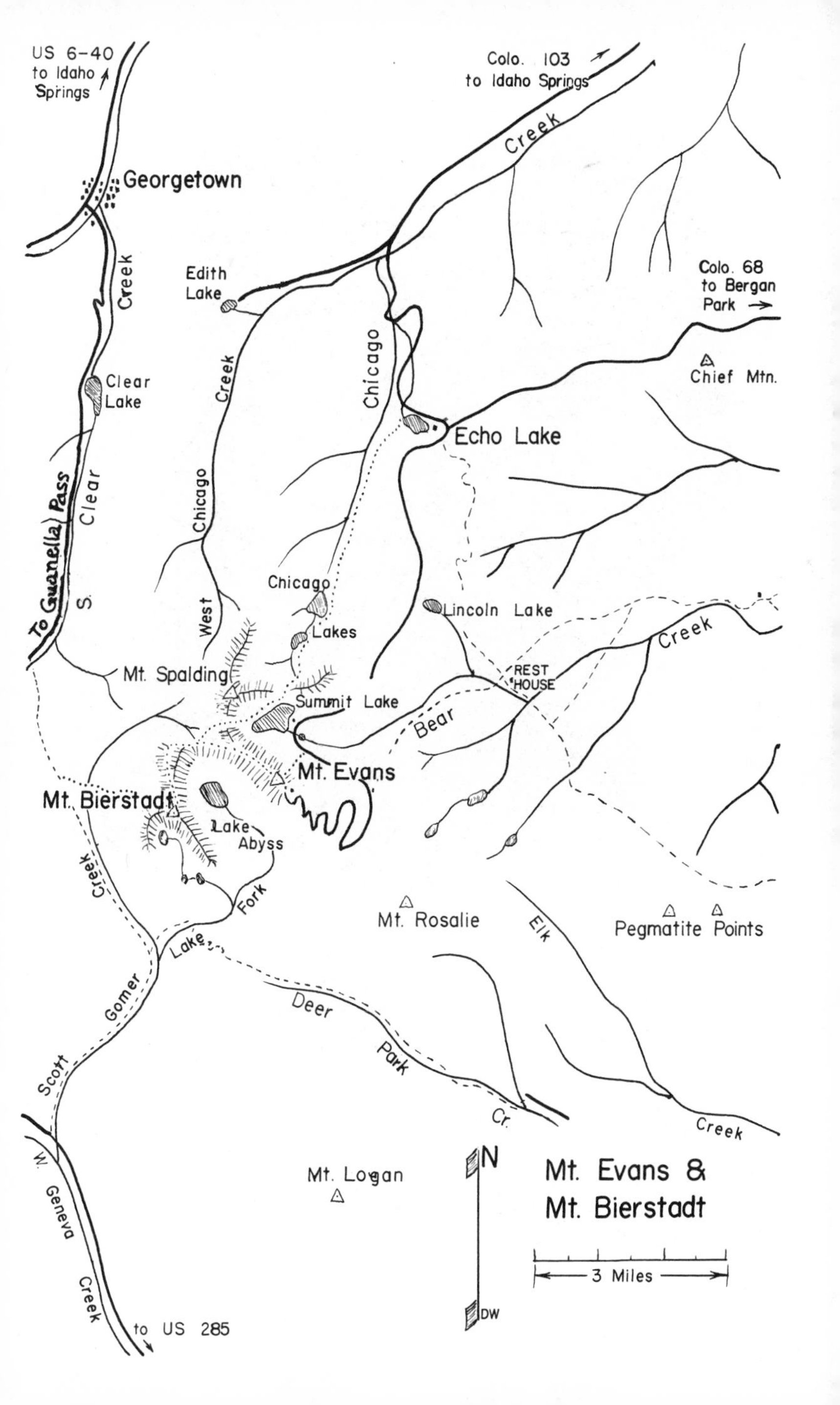

US 6-40
to Idaho
Springs
Colo. 103
to Idaho Springs
Creek
Georgetown
Creek
Edith
Lake
Colo. 68
to Bergan
Park
Chicago
Creek
Clear
Lake
Chief Mtn.
Echo Lake
To Guanella Pass
Clear
Chicago
S.
West
Chicago
Lakes
Lincoln Lake
Creek
REST
HOUSE
Mt. Spalding
Summit Lake
Bear
Mt. Evans
Mt. Bierstadt
Lake
Abyss
Creek
Fork
Mt. Rosalie
Elk
Pegmatite Points
Lake
Gomer
Deer
Park
Cr.
Scott
Creek
W.
Geneva
Creek
to US 285
Mt. Logan
N
DW
Mt. Evans &
Mt. Bierstadt
3 Miles

Mount Powell and the first tooth of Ripsaw Ridge. *Kingery photo.*

CLEAR CREEK TRAILS

The **Beaverbrook Trail** connects two scenic drives between US 6 in the valley and I-70 on topland west of Denver. From ½ mile W of the top of Mount Vernon Canyon turn right on Stapleton Drive and go to its north end. The signed trail descends N to Beaver Brook, then runs E and up to Windy Saddle, 4 miles toward Golden from the Cody Monument on Lookout Mountain road. The trail is on a proved right of way 10 feet wide and 8 miles long. The ends are about 7300′, low point 6600′. See Morrison and Evergreen Quads.

Squaw Mountain Trail starts at Squaw Pass Picnic Ground, 9 miles E of Echo Lake on State 103, and makes a 6-mile climb of 1100′ to the 11,483′ lookout and its view of the surrounding country.

Bear Creek Trail begins at Echo Lake on 103 and runs S to traverse the Vance Creek Basin, then turns E down to Bear Creek Guard Station. The trip is about 7 miles one way.

Other trails in the Echo Lake region include one to Lincoln Lake from 2 miles up-road from Echo Lake on Evans highway, and trips from the road-ends in all three Chicago Creeks, miles 7, 9, and 9½ from Idaho Springs on State 103.

From 5 miles WSW of Idaho Springs on 103 at 8400′ a steep old road climbs WNW to the ghost town of Lamartine, half buried among the aspens, 2000′ elevation in 4 miles. See Idaho Springs Quad.

Santa Fe Mountain, 10,537′, is a 3000′ climb accomplished most of the way on a 5-mile lumber road. Take the Soda Creek road S from Idaho Springs and turn left .1 mile S of the underpass. You cut left off Soda Creek road after .2 miles and go around the ridge end. The road climbs from 7600′ to 9800′. (See Idaho Springs and Squaw Pass Quads.)

Routes lead up **Flirtation Peak,** S of Idaho Springs and Virginia Canyon to the N. The latter continues via Russell Gulch to Central City, with numerous ramifications.

Georgetown Trails include the walk up the old railroad grade to Silver Plume, the powerline trail which climbs E to the

11,000′ summit of the ridge and gives a view of the Divide and the winding mine roads on 12,386′ Republican Mountain.

Trails climb high to old mines from Lawson and from Empire. The road S from Empire to Empire Pass turns W and runs 5 miles up Bard Creek. There are side branches from it to **Lincoln Mountain** on the N and to **Democrat** on the SW.

In lower country the **Mount Falcon Trail** starts from a ranch house 1 mile S of Morrison on Turkey Creek Road. With permission from the ranch owners, W of the road, it is possible to walk up an abandoned zigzag road to the ridge. At the saddle, the route turns right for ½ mile to Falcon's Wing formation, with views of peaks and prairies. A trip W from the saddle to the castle ruins (private property) makes a total trip of 5 miles with 1600 feet of elevation gained. The road and castle were built by John Brisben Walker, a Colorado promoter echo in 1910 dreamed of making a theater out of the Red Rocks. He also dreamed of building a Summer White House overlooking Bear Creek for the presidents of the U.S. The cement platform which was to be part of this house may be seen by walking north from the castle. The castle, which burned before it was occupied, was to be Walker's own home.

FRONT RANGE—SOUTHWEST SECTION

QUADS: Grays Peak, Montezuma, Boreas Pass, Jefferson, Keystone, Como, and Mount Lincoln 15′; (Old Como and Montezuma 15′ reduce bulk); Pike N F.

For this section—Argentine Peak to Hoosier Pass—there are several high climbing roads and jeep roads from which the many tops on and off the Divide are accessible.

The largest area for explorations is the Snake River, a valley with good camping places, mine roads and peaks in all of its several branches. The road turns off S from US 6 about 6 miles E of Dillon and runs E 4½ miles to a split in the valley. Peru Creek comes in from the E; the Snake takes you on a turn to the S.

For Peru Creek, continue E. You can follow it 4½ miles to where it curves northward and steepens, about 11,100′.

Argentine Peak, 13,738′, is 1¼ miles E. You can climb the slope or use the old Argentine Pass road which climbs to the saddle N of the peak in a steep zigzag.

From lower down in Peru Creek valley old mine roads lead up S to the Silver-Revenue-Decatur Mountain ridge from both Cinnamon Gulch and Warden Gulch, miles 9 and 7 from US 6. On the N side of Peru Creek a little W of Warden Gulch a walking road climbs steeply into the ponds and meadows of Chihuahua Gulch. About 2 miles up the gulch the road cuts back SE to climb into Ruby Gulch and runs up there to old diggings at 12,150′. Here you are on a south face route to **Grays Peak,** about a mile from the top. The ridge on your right connects 13,277′ **Ruby Mountain** and 12,792′ **Cooper Mountain,** likewise climbable. If instead of turning with the road into Ruby Gulch you continue N 1½ miles to the headwall of Chihuahua Gulch you will be on the 12,600′ saddle connecting **Torreys Peak** on the E with **Grizzly Peak** on the W—each about a mile away. The **Lenawee Mountain** ridge is the west wall of Chihuahua Gulch.

Returning to mile 4½ from US 6, if you keep on the main road S to Montezuma, 1 mile S of junction, you can probably get your car up most of the steep but good road to the Quail Mine, 3 miles E of the little town and 1200′ higher. A walk-road continues to 13,180′ **Santa Fe Peak,** a mile NE. By going from Montezuma to a junction 1½ miles S and keeping left up the Snake River you can drive a jeep or small car a good part or all the way to 12,096′ **Webster Pass,** 6 miles from Montezuma. Here you are between the easily accessible **Handcart Peak** (W) and **Red Cone** (E). From the base of the pass at 11,400′, an old walk-road climbs west a mile to a mine high on **Teller Mountain.**

Keystone Gulch, which comes into the Snake from the S about 2 miles E of the exit for Montezuma and the Snake River, has an 8-mile road S up the valley and the hillside east of it to the Erickson Mine. (You can reach this road by turning off US 6 for Montezuma and turning right at .2 mile.) The mine at the end, at 11,940′, gives a good look at the Gore and Tenmile Ranges. You can climb to the 12,408′ Keystone point and walk a gentle ridge E 2 miles to **Glacier Mountain,** 12,443′, or go N 1 mile to 12,585′ **Bear Mountain.**

From the northeast part of Breckenridge a road goes east up French Creek, driveable 5 miles or so. It is a pleasant 4-mile walk S up the valley to **French Pass,** 12,046′. From the pass a fairly sharp steep ridge leads a mile W to 13,679′ **Bald Mountain.** By climbing instead to the ridge ½ mile E, you can walk 1½ miles N along it to 13,370′ **Guyot.**

Bald Mountain yields its shortest route from 11,481′ **Boreas Pass,** reached by road from Como or Breckenridge (see below), where from the top you simply start E of the ditch and head N for 2 miles. Boreas Pass also gives access to **Red Peak** on the southeast end of Hoosier Ridge. You go W, keeping to the north side of the little and big humps on a gently climbing contour into a saddle 2 miles WSW from pass. Climb the steep ridge SSW another 1½ miles to the high point, 13,352′. The same summit can be reached from **Hoosier Pass,** 11,541′. It is about 5 miles of ups and downs, starting E up a slope with some deadfall and turning N along the ridge.

Between Guanella and Boreas Passes the South Park approaches to the Divide are longer than those from the Snake River roads. Hall Valley has a road system that leads to good camping and excursions. From Webster, 5 miles W of Santa Maria on US 285, the road runs off right to the Hall Valley Campground, 9750′, 5 miles NW. You can continue about 1½ miles before the road gets too rough for a car, or 4 miles in a jeep. At 11,600′ you are a mile S of **Teller Mountain** and ½ mile SW of **Handcart Peak,** both steep climbs.

From Hall Valley Campground a less conspicuous 4-wheel-drive road climbs right and NNW 3 miles up Handcart Gulch and continues a last mile up to **Webster Pass** on a more or less washed out trail. **Red Cone** is on your right, **Handcart Peak** on your left.

Whale Peak makes a good climb from Hall Valley. Turn off 1½ miles beyond the campground exit at a trail marked **"Gibson Lake."** From here, 10,316′, it is 2½ miles to the small lake at 11,850′, another bent mile to the top on either flanking ridge.

Glacier Peak, 12,853′, and **Whale Peak,** 13,078′, on Boreas Pass and Jefferson Quads, can be climbed from Jefferson Lake, for which a road turns N from US 285 at Jefferson. From Jefferson Creek Campground drive 1 mile N across a dam, go halfway up the lake, then slant N and NW through the timber ½ mile to the ridge. Glacier summit is at the northwest end. The 3-mile climb makes about 2100′. To visit Whale Peak, go N and E a mile along the Divide, with a loss of 200′ altitude. Return on the southeast ridge of Whale to a desirable dropping off point.

Georgia Pass, 11,585′, is approached by going from Jefferson on US 285 NW 1¼ miles, W 2 miles, then NW to a total of 7 miles on good road, to 10,375′. By jeep it is 3 more steeper miles to the pass. One can drive the topland nearly all the 5 miles E to **Glacier Peak** from pass crest. Or walk. Do not jeep down the north side of the pass without inquiry. **Mount Guyot,** 13,370′, is a mile W of the pass—a steep but simple ridge climb.

The Boreas Pass road leaves US 285 at the exit for Como. Most of it is on the Denver South Park and Pacific Railroad grade, a very pleasant drive. **Boreas Mountain,** 13,082′, like Bald Mountain mentioned above, is easily reached from the pass crest. You head up the slope ESE and climb 1500′ in little over a mile. The pass road gives good views of the Tenmile Range as you descend the west side to Breckenridge.

Mount Silverheels, 13,817′, is climbed by driving 6 miles NNW from Fairplay on Beaver Creek. Take the trail 2 miles N up Beaver Creek and climb 1½ miles E to the top. The mountain was named for a dance hall girl in Buckskin Joe, a town above Fairplay. The girl nursed the miners through a smallpox epidemic after all the proper women, if any, had left camp. See Mount Lincoln Quad.

WILLIAMS FORK MOUNTAINS

QUADS: Montezuma, Dillon, Ute Peak and Mount Powell, all 15′; in 7½′ quads the completed Loveland Pass will be joined by those temporarily designated Mount Powell NE and Ute Peak NW, SW and SE; Arapaho N F.

This minor range runs west 6 miles from a mile south of **Hagar Mountain** on the Divide to **Ptarmigan Peak,** 12,480′, and then another 25 miles NNW parallel with the Blue River. It is not to be confused with another range of the same name, which we label the Yampa Williams Fork Mountains. For climbers its main interest is the view it gives of the Gore Range across the valley.

A road climbs E to the crest in 6 rather steep miles from the Grand-Summit County line, 12½ miles S of Kremmling, 29 miles N of Dillon Dam, and circling the high points goes SSE about 6 miles at altitudes around 10,500′. You look into the northern Gore valleys from the N end; farther S you can see some of the middle valleys better. You also look off at **Pettingell, Byers Peak, Grays** and **Torreys** and others on the left side. Go early enough, for the Gores look best in the morning.

Coon Hill, 12,757′, the highest point, can be reached from the west portal of Straight Creek Tunnel on I-70. Walk up Straight Creek ½ mile and pick a route to the left.

You can walk 12 miles of the crest on the **Ptarmigan-Ute Peak Trail.** The **Ptarmigan Trail** itself starts up from the bottom of Straight Creek, but a good higher approach can be made from the west ridge of Hamilton Gulch, second right hand gulch as you descend from the tunnel and about 2½ miles E of it. A mile or so up, you can skirt the first summit on the left and go into **Ptarmigan Pass.** Skirt the next point high upon the right and continue over **Ptarmigan Peak** to the trail. At

Lone Eagle Peak and the higher ridge behind. *H. L. Standley photo.*

about mile 9 from Ptarmigan Peak it will take you almost to the top of 12,298′ **Ute Peak,** the best viewing point for the middle and south Gore valleys. 1½ miles farther is the best line of descent—a trail down N to camping on the Williams Fork and its auto road. Nearby Sugarloaf Campground is 25 miles from Parshall on US 40.

It is also possible to continue 2 miles farther NW on the ridge on a sketchier trail, where you drop into **Ute Pass** and can go down off the range on either side by a well-maintained trail. On the W you come down Pass Creek to ranch country about 5 miles down the Blue from Boulder Creek Campground.

GORE RANGE

QUADS: Minturn, Dillon, Mount Powell, Ute Peak, all 15′; White River and Arapaho N F's. The 15′ quads are in process of replacement with 7½'s. These are not as yet named but when available can be ordered as Minturn SE, Dillon NW, etc.

The Gore Range shortcuts 70 miles south across the big east bend of the Continental Divide, connecting **Rabbit Ears Pass** and **Fremont Pass** (Climax). Thus its line is a slightly S-curved southern extension of the North Park Range. It is cut through about ⅓ of the way down by the Gore Canyon of the Colorado River and near the south end by **Vail Pass.** The range was named after an Irish nobleman with an enormous bank account who hunted in the West for two years around 1855. To Jim Bridger, who served him as guide, he read Shakespeare. He had a wagon fitted up like a modern camper, a well-stocked wine cellar on wheels, and a full-sized bath tub, filled daily with warm water by his valet. Sir St. George Gore's retinue drummed up game for him to shoot every day from 10 o'clock on. It took the Gore Range years to recover from this wholesale slaughter of its wildlife.

The north part of the Gore crest peaks are metamorphic schist and gneiss produced from originally sedimentary rock. The central section is divided between the schist and gneiss prevalent on the east ridges, and granite up to the crest on the west side. The Willow Lakes section is granitic. A set of topographic eminences links the Gore and Tenmile ranges with the westward edge of the Front Range to the east. These mountains are called the Vasquez and the Williams River Mountains. They represent northwestward trending structural prongs of the central Front Range.

The range is more one of ridges than of separated peaks, but the ridges are generally strings of pinnacles and small peaks. There is a world of rock climbing, but the rock climbs are a mixture of easy scrambling and short problems. Rope should be taken for most high point climbs unless they have been previously scouted, because of possible cul de sac and descent problems. But the major hazard is often rotten rock, for which great care rather than rope is the answer.

There was almost none of the mining which in many mountain areas has provided roads up through the steep timbered valleys. The region is, in fact as well as by decree, a primitive area. It may be increased in acreage to Wilderness status.

In discussing the range we have covered mainly the trails and other approach routes, leaving the short and sometimes very hard details of the innumerable climbs to successive climbers, with the hope that even when they are repeating the climbs of others they won't know it.

On the east side the Gore is paralleled by the Blue River, tributary to the Colorado near Kremmling. The section of main interest, about 15 miles long, lies between Green Mountain and Dillon Dams. The range crest is 6-9 miles west of the paralleling main road along the Blue River, State 9, and visible from it only in fragments because of the nearby timbered slopes and the ridges that jut eastward.

A 19-mile road to **Meridian Mountain,** the last half closed to all but 4-wheel vehicles by a rough section, provides a high approach to the N end of the range, taking you close W of **Eagles Nest Mountain.** From 30 miles N of Dillon Dam, 11.7 miles S of Kremmling, turn W off State 9. Keep right at mile 3.5, and again at mile 8, where you leave the better road.

Avoid lesser unmarked lumber roads, usually lefts, here and above. At mile 11 take a left for Mahan Lake; at 12.5 keep to left (not to Mather Spring). At 13.8 keep right for Elliot Ridge, not Mahan Lake. The car can be left at the trail sign, mile 19, or perhaps a little closer to the top of 12,390′ **Meridian Mountain,** a mile beyond. See Mount Powell Quad.

For Cataract Crags only, you could take water along and camp on the Meridian ridge. For an attractive camp, climb over the Meridian summit and continue NE ½ mile to low point of saddle, where you can descend SE to timber and flatter ground. A suggestion of trail flanks the N crag (on your right) and takes you around it to Climbers Lake, 11,000′, 2 miles from Meridian.

Eagles Nest Mountain, 13,397′, is the NNW high point of a rough curving ridge directly E of Meridian Mountain. From the lake, go up-valley ¼-½ mile to cross the stream and pick a route angling ENE up slopes of broken rock and grass to the low point of the S ridge, which can then be followed N to the summit. To climb **Powell** from Eagles Nest, return to S saddle and either stay on the ridge or drop W and contour S for ½ mile, until the grassy climbing leads upward. One group found it best to drop 200′ below the low point of the saddle for the traverse between the peaks. The opposite direction—Powell to Eagles Nest—is harder.

Mahan Lake, reached from the above road on a 4-mile jeep side road, can be used as a campsite, and may go with a car in dry weather, but we recommend taking a 4-wheeler to the end of the higher road, especially for climbing S of Eagles Nest.

Mount Powell, 13,534′, is the high point of the range. It was first climbed by John Wesley Powell in 1868, a few days after his ascent of Longs Peak, and a year before he boated the Colorado River. To climb it from the lake, go upstream, cross and climb on grass and sheep trails to a flattish place left of saddle, and 100′ or so higher, at the head of the valley. Traverse SE of the ridge a few yards, then climb on its right side, traversing right only as forced. About 600′ higher, a little pass to the left puts you on a grass and small-scree slope to the left of the same ridgelet and avoids a very rotten gully continuation. Watch your bearings for the return. Another route, slower but perhaps better for large groups, climbs from the lake to the low point of the same valley-head saddle and then contours a mile SE and E to and across Powell's south saddle for a climb on the easy SSE side.

The unfolding views from **Mount Meridian,** then the saddle and then Powell itself, show you the range to the south for what it is—a spire-filled wilderness.

The **Cataract Crags** can be climbed by scrambling routes. The one nearest to Powell goes best from the side away from the valley-head saddle, to which you can pick a left side (S) traverse after climbing to the saddle.

The **Gore Range Trail,** over 50 miles long, travels generally along the E flank of the range. The part so labeled, of high standard, starts S from Cataract Lake (U.S.G.S. Lower Cataract). But by reason of a N end branch it actually starts from the road 1 mile N of **Mount Meridian.** It winds 12½ miles eastward past Mirror Lake, Upper Cataract Lake and Surprise Lake, at miles 5½, 7 and 10 respectively, to Black Creek. The rest of the distance, most of it at 9000′-10,500′ altitude is at this writing open to scooters and snow vehicles. (The old GR Trail NW from Eaglesmere Lake is discontinued—unmaintained and swampy.)

Generally the trails are suitable for and open to horse travel, but people intending to use horses should consult the rangers at Kremmling for the east side, Minturn for the west, since shortage of feed or trail conditions may require restrictions.

Although the trail is usually about 2½ miles W of State 9, there are few lines of access to it. After the Meridian road, the next on the E side is a 4-mile road from the SW side of Green Mountain Reservoir to 8600′ Cataract Lake. It starts 1½ miles E of Heeney or 5½ miles SW from the upper end of the reservoir.

From near the end of the Cataract Lake road a marked trail runs S 3 miles to the **Gore Range Trail,** meeting it near water-lily-covered Surprise Lake. Where the Cataract road ends a second trail runs off NW, W and S to the Gore Range Trail by a 6-mile route, meeting it ½ mile W of Surprise Lake. The combination with the connecting link of Gore Range Trail suggests a 10-mile circle with an 1800′ climb.

To climb **Eagles Nest Mountain,** use the south trail above, turn W on **Gore Range Trail,** and keep left after ¾ mile on the latter. This takes you to Upper Cataract Lake. Cross the creek and take the ridge from the W side of the outlet. There are some slow humps as you progress S to the summit.

A 1933 climb of this ridge was reported by Kenneth Segerstrom, who decided he and his partner were not first on the peak when they found a gun shell in a crevice near the top. It occurs to us that the evidence is not conclusive, crows and ravens being what they are.

Dora Mountain, 12,119′, is a flat-topped ridge-end overlooking Black Lake. The best route is from the **Gore Range Trail** just east of Surprise Lake, where you can climb SE and S to cross Otter Creek (1 mile along) before it gets canyoned. You are then 1 mile off Dora on the N ridge and can climb directly up though partly in timber and without benefit of trail.

The upper reaches of Black Creek, a good climbing point for the northern Gore Peaks, can be reached only with difficulty. A trail of sorts starts as a jeep road—very rough, we hear—from just S of the upper end of Green Mountain Reservoir and across from the cemetery. It climbs 3 miles SW to the **Gore Range Trail,** at 9350′. Go W (right) ½ mile, then leave the G R Trail and follow an unmaintained trail which sidehills up Black Creek canyon 8 miles to camp at the lake at 10,900′, at the foot of **Mount Powell,** on the central fork of Black Creek. From this lake camp a whole circle of summits can be climbed: **Dora, Eagles Nest, Powell,** and the climbers' lettered summits from C to N. There is precedent for calling this fork Torrent Creek, and the name may be one of those recommended by the Mountain Club to the U.S. Board of Geographic Names.

The route to **Powell** is a fairly direct one to and up its SE (easiest) side. For **Eagles Nest** you start the same way but traverse right to cross the saddle E of Powell. Continue along the flank of Powell and into the basin of Cliff Lake, where you can choose your route to the top. It is about 3½ miles, with a little altitude loss.

Of the lesser peaks some have problems and some don't. They are short enough climbs so that picking routes and experimenting with them is a major part of the fun.

The above jeep route used for Black Creek leads to a pleasant short trip off left from a mile above the **Gore Range Trail;** you turn off left for Lost Lake, up on a bench under the ridge. From the lake there is a 4-mile return trip by way of variation. Go E from the lake instead of retracing, and NW along the G R Trail.

Boulder Creek, 9 miles NW of **Silverthorne,** has over a mile of road and a Gore Range Trail access 2 miles more up-canyon from the road end. The **Boulder Creek Trail** continues up to shallow Boulder Lake at mile ½. Now obscure, the trail skirts swamps and talus to an upper lake, at 11,000′, 2 miles up canyon from the trail end. Here you are between the walls of the **Keller Mountain** ridge and the South Slate Creek ridge, both 13,000′ high. The headwall is a rough section of the range crest. The section of trail above the G R Trail is open to snow and trail vehicles.

Ralph Johnson, the District Ranger at Kremmling, tells us that Boulder Lake was raised 5 feet and increased from 1 acre to 30 by a dam in 1882. J. H. Gould had a water-powered mill there for 3 years. It became naturally stocked with trout about 1888 and attracted visitors. At the turn of the century some leading citizens appropriated it for recreation purposes. They raised the dam 3 feet and did some clearing of the ground. It was washed out in 1906 and not rebuilt.

The Boss Mine road up North Rock Creek, across from Blue River Campground, 6½ miles NW of Silverthorne, is the only one which takes you in past the Gore Range trail by car. It is 4½ miles to the mine on a rather sketchy but driveable road. Camping is possible along this road but better at maintained Blue River sites. From the mine area at 10,000′ you can climb out E to the ridge and up it, most of the way by trail, to **Keller Mountain,** 12,866′, which is a ridge end rather than a mountain. The outlook is fair and gets far better if you go along up-ridge to the valley head. It is a rough 2 miles. The valley head goes up to 13,000′, but the SE ridge, opposite the Keller, is low enough so you look across it to 13,356′ **Silverthorne** and **East Thorn,** which will start you making more plans. (Silverthorne and East Thorn are tentative names which have CMC approval only.)

The town of Silverthorne, named for an eminent judge of the region, has a 1½-mile access trail to the range trail, which it meets at South Willow Creek. You can go NW 3 miles on the range trail and a mile off left by trail to Salmon Lake at about 10,000′ on main Willow Creek. This side trail continues, unmaintained, to and up the string of Willow Lakes, 1½ miles farther. A camp at 11,250′ by the next to last lake on either creek branch is recommended. The valley head serves the most compact climbing area of the southern Gore. On the left is **Red Peak** and its bumpy east ridge, on the right, 13,330′ **East Thorn,** and on the range crest ridge between, the string of Zodiac Spires. (The Zodiac name first appeared in the Addison article mentioned below.)

The first rock climbers in the area seem to have been two parties with Mark P. Addison, who wrote of their climbs and enthusiastic impressions for the January 1957 *T & T*. They climbed Red Mountain by the north ridge, where they were roped but found little difficulty, and took in stride a couple of ridge spires on the way. Four or five of the eight Zodiacs gave them some interesting problems, and they came away with the impression there were plenty more. It would seem that most of the climbs are, or verge on, the technical. A 1968 climber describes an easy pull up rocks and steep talus to the east ridge of **East Thorn.**

Sections of the Gore Range Trail have been used for backpacks. One of the most attractive one-day or two-day trips would be to go in from **Silverthorne** and follow South Willow Creek up between **Red Peak** and **Buffalo Mountain** to its head under the range crest, where there are two lakelets at 11,500′, and then to climb out S over 11,900′ **Eccles Pass** to a trail down Meadow Creek and into Frisco. It is a 13-mile trip with 3200′ climb. **Red Peak,** 13,183′, has its recommended route on the S side, where the gradients are most favorable. Take the main trail 5 miles up South Willow Creek to about 11,000′, where you can select slopes to the peak itself, or to the range crest S of it.

Buffalo Mountain, 12,764′, is a good off-the-crest summit to climb to, and can be climbed from pretty well down the trail if you don't mind a long steep pull. A gentler route would take you perhaps 6 miles up the trail and then in a slow spiral counterclockwise to the SW saddle, from which you have a short climb E to the summit.

A road runs up North Tenmile Creek from US 6 at the W end of Frisco to the G R Trail, the first 2 miles good with a car, the third perhaps requiring a jeep. Scooters and snow vehicles may use this route where it continues above the G R Trail for 2 more miles W and N to timberline.

Vail Pass Peak, 12,513′, is N along the crest ridge 2 miles from 10,550′ **Vail Pass.** Climb the short slope to the E from the Pass top and head N; you will get a good though foreshortened view into the complexities of the Gore Range.

The W side of the Gore Range is normally approached on roads and trails from US 6 (I-70), but it may first be remarked that the Meridian Mountain road from the N links into the W side trail system. A mile N of the road terminus a jeep trail zigzags W off Elliot Ridge a mile to the **Piney Lake Trail.** To the right the Piney Lake trail goes NNW 3 miles on trail and

3 more on jeep road to the Sheephorn Creek road, the latter connecting with State 11, the Kremmling-to-State-Bridge road. To the left the Piney Lake Trail parallels the ridge in the opposite direction for 2 miles or so and then cuts around the side ridges southward into the Piney and drops to Piney Lake, about 6½ miles from the Meridian road. The trail would perhaps find its chief use in a range-circling backpack trip.

The Piney Lake road is the only car access route for middle and north climbs into the range. It turns off US 6 from the lower end of the Vail settlement and follows Red Sandstone Creek. It turns left after 2½ miles, and about 3½ miles farther keeps right for Piney Lake, about 11 miles from the highway. The lake is privately owned and the area around it closed. Plan to leave your car 2 miles short of the lake and carry camp to somewhere up E of it along the creek. (Jeeps go in to ¼ mile from the lake.)

The **Piney River Trail** goes from the lake 2½ miles NE to the bend, then SE 4 miles to the Piney-Booth Creek saddle at 11,750′, and continuing as the Booth Creek Trail, runs down to US 6.

Piney River has twice been used as base camp for Mountain Club expeditions. It is convenient for peak and pinnacle climbs from **Mount Powell** SE to **West Partner Peak,** 13,021′ headwall point of South Slate Creek. The route to Mount Powell goes up-trail to the bend at 10,000′, and then E and N 2 miles up steep slopes with moderate rock scrambling. The best finish is on the E side of the S ridge. The stretch of Ripsaw Ridge points (C to J) are in reach, but of course closer from camps farther up the valley. One party camped at the forks of the Piney, about 5 miles up-trail from the lake. **The Spider,** 12,655′, loomed above them and became the first object of interest. They found their way up it, first using the trail most of the way to the Booth Creek saddle, then cutting left to the Spider SSE saddle.

On the Piney Lake road, by keeping right at the first fork, mile 2½, you can take a road N for 3 miles and find a trail to

Lost Lake, on a branch of Red Sandstone Creek. The last mile of this road is for pick-up or jeep only. You can reach the Piney River from here by an old trail down to the lake or by bushwhack into the valley farther up.

A jeep road climbs 4 miles steeply up Spraddle Creek from the Vail Interchange to a shelf at 11,250′, just S of 12,096′ **Bald Mountain,** S end point of the ridge mentioned just above.

Booth Creek, 2½ miles E of Vail, has a trail which forks 2½ miles N of the highway. The right fork spirals left to a good-sized lake 1000′ higher at 11,500′. The trail-less right fork of this right fork climbs to a lakelet at 11,800′ right under the steep slope of 13,021′ **West Partner.** It is also under the pinnacle ridge that runs off SE from Spider Peak, 1½ miles NW. From I-70 to Booth Lake is maintained trail and closed to all vehicles. The left fork of the **Booth Creek Trail** climbs NW and N 3 miles after the forking to a pass, 11,750′, where as noted above it becomes the **Piney River Trail.** This is not maintained. The pass gives access to the W side of Spider and its pinnacled S ridge.

The **Pitkin Creek Trail** leaves the highway 3½ miles E of Vail, and climbs NW and N 7 miles to Pitkin Lake at 11,250′. **East Partner** is a mile E and **West Partner** a mile N, 1700′ higher up heavily tilted terrain. Pitkin and Bighorn are closed to vehicles at the primitive area boundary. The **Bighorn Creek Trail,** from 4 miles E of Vail and 1½ miles NW of Gore Creek curve, climbs 4½ miles to a mine property about 10,500′. The mile between the valley and the range crest to the E is abrupt. By climbing up the creek it appears one could flank it and come out near the upper (SW) end point of Keller Ridge.

Two trails climb toward the range from Gore Creek campground, 8750′. The right one keeps E 9 miles up the main creek to **Red Buffalo Pass,** about 11,750′, and down a little way to the Gore Range Trail. It is 8 more miles to the E terminus. This trail has a branch N from the Recen brothers' graves, about mile 6, to Main Gore Lake 1½ miles WSW of **Silverthorne Peak.** This should make the best approach for climbs on Silverthorne and the 1½ mile ridge to the west of it. It would work also for the Zodiac Spires west of Willow Lakes. Both this trail and the one below are closed to vehicles.

The left trail from the Gore Creek Campground climbs 4 miles NE into a lake in upper Deluge Creek. Here you have access by steep short climbs to the 13,000′ ridge points at the head of Rock Creek drainage. For those who like their climbing from the road, we suggest scaling the first half mile of Deluge Creek.

NAMES IN THE GORE RANGE

Doig Lake is named for a homesteader who hunted and explored the range. One of his trips took him down the cliffs to the little lake from flat Mount Dora. Elliot Ridge is named for a local man whom the Indians killed in revenge for Tabernash. Mahan Lake takes its name from early ranger, Stanley A. Mahan, who was killed in a hunting accident. The Forest Service finds precedent for a Bledsoe Creek, coming from the south into Slate Creek, 1 mile east of Slate Lake. The ridge end immediately east of this creek is called Bloodshaw Mountain; our policy is to seek acceptance for this name for the full ridge between Boulder Creek and the South Fork of Slate Creek. Likewise we would extend the name for Keller Mountain to Keller Ridge, applying it to the length of the ridge SE of Boulder Creek. For the branches of Black Creek we shall seek acceptance for the names Cliff Lake Creek, northernmost, rising between Eagles Nest and Powell; Torrent Creek for the two-forked central creek into which the above flows; and Black Creek for the longest fork, the southeast, now labeled Brush Creek on the 15′ Minturn Quadrangle.

Spider Peak, Vail Pass Peak, and East and West Partner Peaks, like others noted above are tentative names which have C.M.C. approval and will in most cases be submitted to the U.S. Board of Geographic Names. Some are suggested as replacements for a series of alphabetical designations which have been employed by Mountain Club climbers.

SOUTH GORE GROUP

QUADS: 15′ Minturn, Holy Cross, Mount Lincoln and Dillon; Arapaho and White River N F's.

This area, normally included with the Gore Range, stretches from Vail south to Leadville on the east side of Eagle River and Tennessee Creek. Black Gore and West Tenmile Creeks separate it from the Gore Range proper and Tenmile Creek from the Tenmile Range. The main appeal for mountaineers is for ski touring and for viewing other mountains.

The Shrine Pass road, starting just S of the top of **Vail Pass** at 10,600′, runs NW 2½ miles to a crest at 11,060′, and turns WSW down Turkey Creek to 8600′ Red Cliff and US 24. A turn in the canyon lets you see **Mount Jackson** and **Mount of the Holy Cross.**

Ptarmigan Hill is likewise a good lookout point for little effort. Turn in at the dismantled Camp Hale, 6 miles NNW of **Tennessee Pass** on US 24 (about 7 from Redcliff the other way), and from the S end of the camp, 9300′, drive the steepish but good road up Resolution Creek 6 miles to 11,750′. Climb ½ mile and 400′ W to the top.

The Eagle River East Fork, which cuts up E from the S side of the camp to Climax you will probably find closed for molybdenum mining operations.

Jacque Peak, 13,201′, is high enough to have some appeal as a climb and is a good ski ascent. We would recommend getting permission from the Amax security office at Climax to enter from where Kokomo was, in the valley 5 miles N of Climax on State 91. It is a 2-mile, 2600′ climb up the S ridge. You may be able to drive or jeep the first 2 miles, 600′, on an old mine road N from the Kokomo exit.

TENMILE RANGE

QUADS: Mount Lincoln and Dillon 15′; White River and Arapaho N F's. (7½′ quads will replace the 15′ with temporary designations Dillon SE, etc.)

This well-defined ridge climbs S from Frisco on I-70 12 miles to meet the Continental Divide W of Hoosier Pass, where it continues as the Mosquito Range. Most of the peaks are intimately visible from the Blue River Valley and from the Boreas Pass road SE out of Breckenridge. The latter is a mining town converted to the resort and skiing business, and taken up with private holdings. Climbs to the peaks are usually done from the east side; the higher northern ones are scaled with the help of old mine roads and new reservoir roads, which climb from State 9 up Spruce Creek, McCullough Gulch and Monte Cristo Creek.

Quandary Peak, 14,264′, is the high point. From Fairplay drive 14 miles N, or from Breckenridge 8 miles S, to Monte Cristo Creek, 10,800′. From ½ mile W of the highway bend you can climb N on stock drive up to the E ridge and follow it 2 miles to the top. The crest is broad enough to be skied most of the way in spring.

The Colorado Springs water road climbs in the Monte Cristo canyon to the dam incorporating Blue Lakes at 11,700′. Quandary Peak is a direct but extremely rough scramble on this side. **Fletcher Mountain,** 13,955′, is a 2-mile climb NW up the ridge from the reservoir. **Wheeler Peak,** 13,650′, is separated from Fletcher by a very slow serrated ridge with climbing problems along the way. We have not heard of a climb combining the two. The route to Wheeler goes from the reservoir straight W 2 miles to the ridge crest, 12,350′ and S for the final pitch. **North Star Mountain,** 13,350′, is very steep on this side. Save it for a road walk W from **Hoosier Pass,** 11,540′. The route shelfroads the S side to high mine buildings not far E of the summit point on the ridge.

McCullough Gulch has a walking road that starts 7 miles S of Breckenridge at 10,300′ on State 9 and climbs 2½ miles to 11,250′. Another mile of old trail climbs 500′ higher. The easy route in, however, is the N or right hand branch of the Colorado Springs water road which starts in up Monte Cristo Creek. You come N around the Quandary ridge end and up to the

11,700′ tunnel intake, where you are 2½ miles E of the range crest.

Pacific Peak, 13,975′, is a steep short summit pull from either the S or the E ridge. Climb to the NW corner of the widening valley and take your choice. **Fletcher Peak** can also be climbed from this side, with a finish on its E ridge. The 5-point Rock Fountain, sharply visible up the creek from State 9 at Quandary Lodge, makes an enjoyable obstacle route to Fletcher Mountain from its north saddle. **Quandary's** roughish west ridge is also available from the SW corner of the valley.

Spruce Creek has a road which cars can take for the first mile or so to where it branches left off the water intake (good) road. Jeeps go 2 more miles. It leaves State 9 from Goose Pasture Tarn, 3½ miles S of Breckenridge and climbs to 11,000′. A 2-mile trail goes on up to a bench and some lakes above 12,000′. Camping is good below timberline on Spruce Creek, near the road end. **Belle and Helen Peak,** 13,150′, juts out E of the range crest between Spruce Creek and its N tributary Crystal Creek. It is named (tentatively) for two gals who left the city and settled in their favorite place in old Breckenridge to write about the Tenmile Range and gold dredging and the mountain people. Their peak is best climbed from the E ridge, about 2½ miles up the Spruce Creek road. You rise 2000′ in the mile.

Crystal Peak, 13,015′, is at the head of the valley on the right side. From the jeep road end, climb up the bench past Mohawk and the other lakes to where you can choose a route for the saddle ¼ mile E of the summit, and continue up the ridge. It is something under 4 miles from the road end. **Pacific Peak** used to be climbed this way but is a shorter trip from McCullough Gulch. It goes from the S end of the Crystal-Pacific ridge.

A trail takes off up the right side of Crystal Creek from about mile 2 of the road and climbs (on the S side of the creek after you reach timberline) to a 12,000′ lake under **Peak Ten.** This and the climb up the next basin—either the one to the

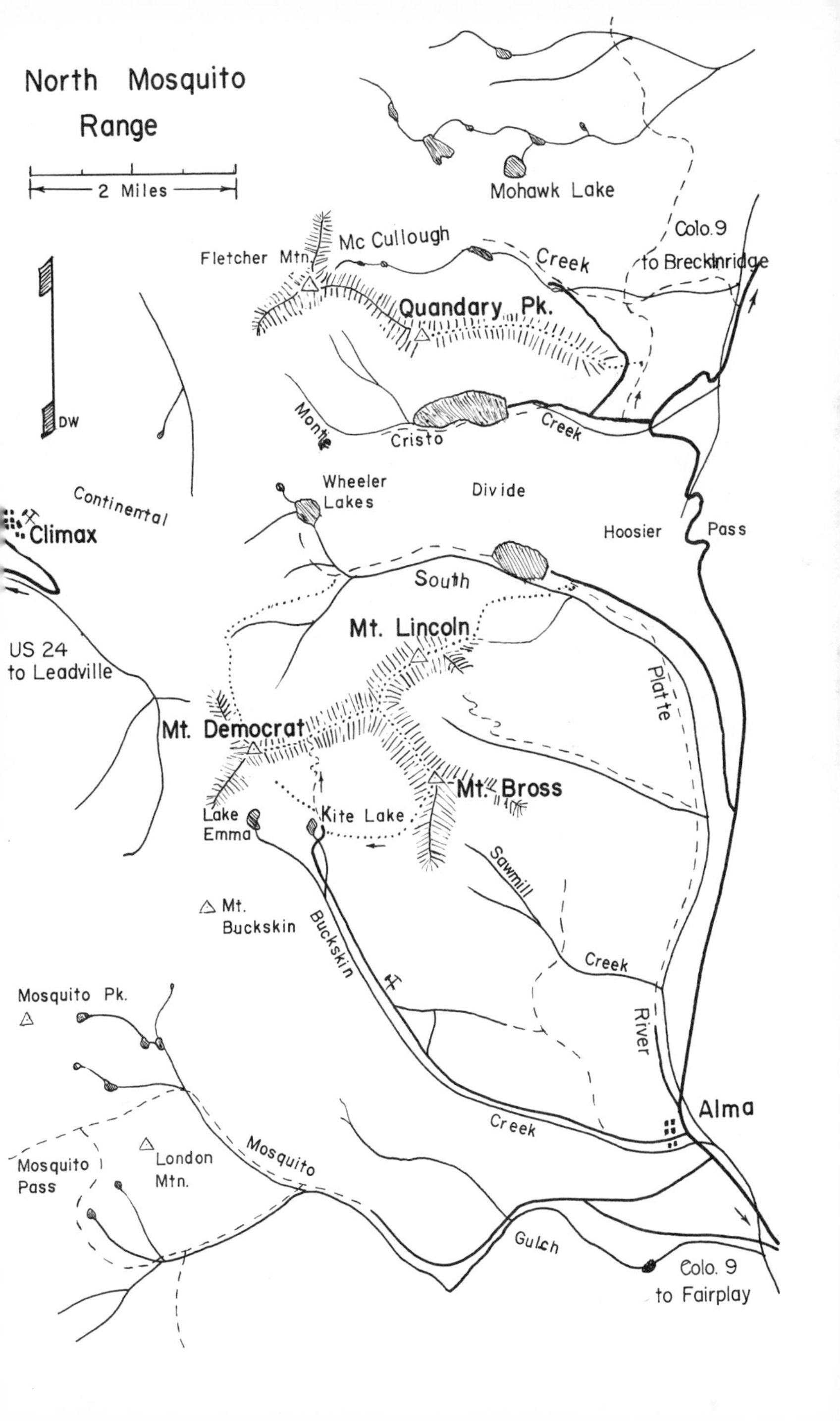
North Mosquito Range
2 Miles
DW
Mohawk Lake
Mc Cullough
Creek
Fletcher Mtn.
Colo. 9
to Breckinridge
Quandary Pk.
Montie
Cristo
Creek
Wheeler Lakes
Divide
Continental
Climax
Hoosier
Pass
South
Mt. Lincoln
US 24
to Leadville
Platte
Mt. Democrat
Mt. Bross
Lake Emma
Kite Lake
Sawmill
Mt. Buckskin
Buckskin
Creek
Mosquito Pk.
River
Alma
Creek
Mosquito Pass
London Mtn.
Mosquito
Gulch
Colo. 9
to Fairplay

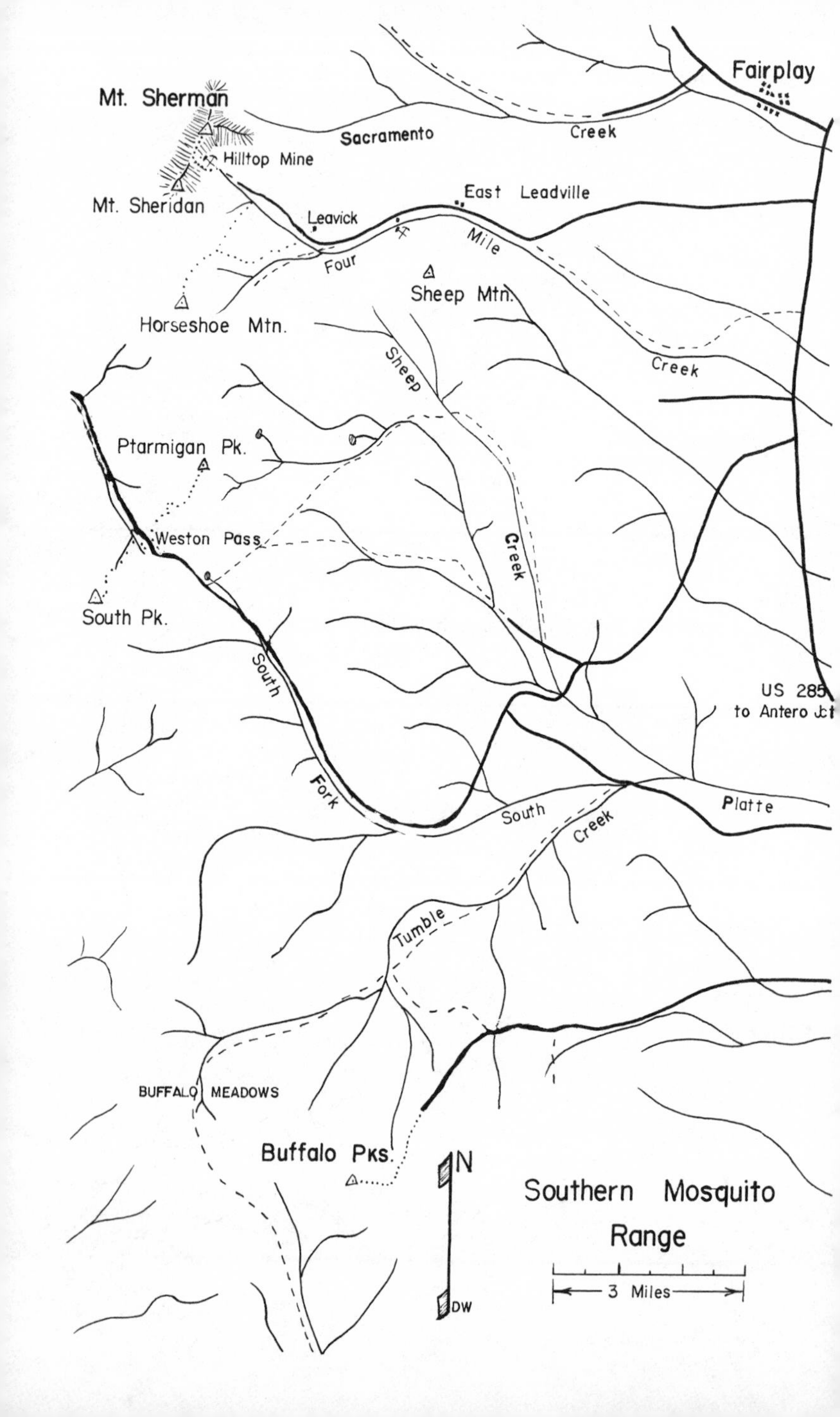
Mt. Sherman
Hilltop Mine
Mt. Sheridan
Fairplay
Sacramento
Creek
East Leadville
Leavick
Four
Mile
Creek
Sheep Mtn.
Horseshoe Mtn.
Sheep
Creek
Ptarmigan Pk.
Weston Pass
South Pk.
South
Fork
US 285
to Antero Jct
South
Platte
Creek
Tumble
BUFFALO MEADOWS
Buffalo Pks.
N
DW
Southern Mosquito
Range
3 Miles

W or the one to the S—is likely to keep you away from crowds.

Like the Gore and the Sawatch, the Tenmile Range has its east side flank trail. Running northward, this begins with the stock drive from near the mouth of Monte Cristo Creek and goes in and out until it contours to the range crest at 12,350′ between **Peaks Nine** and **Eight.** From a mile or so short of this point on the E side, a 6-mile continuation branches off N, and keeping generally below timberline, runs N down Miners Creek to the road end there. To find it from the N end, drive E from Frisco 1½ miles on State 9 and turn off N for 1½ miles on a road to Rainbow Lake. This trail provides access to the lower northern summits of the range, some of which present rough and interesting short climbs. From the range crest S of Peak Nine, the trail drops 2 miles down the W side as the **Wheeler Trail.** It ends at 9900′, 2 miles N of US 6 on State 91.

While not under maintenance, the Tenmile trails are generally in fair condition and easy to follow.

The W side of the range is evenly steep and its streams do not generally invite camping. Mayflower Gulch, however, has a road which turns E off State 91 about 6 miles S of US 6 and 6 miles N of Climax, and climbs 2½ miles to Boston, a ghost town remnant at 11,500′. Here you are about 1½ miles below **Fletcher Mountain** and the **Rock Fountain** to the N of it. This valley gives a route to **Pacific Peak.** Pacific Gulch comes into Mayflower Gulch about halfway up the latter, at 11,250′, and can be followed 1½ miles E into an upper cirque. The summit is then reached by climbing N to the W ridge and up it a short distance.

MOSQUITO RANGE

QUADS: Mount Sherman, South Mountain, Fairplay West and Jones Hill; 15′ Mount Lincoln and Buena Vista; Pike N F.

This range runs S from W of **Hoosier Pass** 35 miles to **Trout Creek Pass,** on US 24. Along with the Tenmile Range to the N, the main ridge does not dip below timberline from Frisco to S of **Weston Pass,** a total of 33 miles. High altitude mining has made for many old roads that make good walking and skiing routes. A road crosses the range centrally at **Mosquito Pass,** 7 miles straight W of Alma. A good deal of the cap is of early tertiary intrusive rock.

Mosquito Range names are of Civil War political vintage, with a rebellious Democrat thrown in afterward. Legend says that a mosquito lighted on the blank space left for the yet-to-be-decided name on a legal document, and thus gave the mine, the mountain, and the range its name. The Mosquitos were part of the previously named Park Range. Fairplay, the long-standing center for Colorado's placering operations, was named by protesting miners who were forced out of the earlier Tarryall camp.

Mount Lincoln, 14,286′, **Mount Democrat,** 14,148′, and **Mount Bross,** 14,172′, on Mount Lincoln Quad, can be climbed in one day by a moderately strong party. From Fairplay drive 6 miles NW to Alma on State 9. Turn W on Alma street and drive NW in Buckskin Gulch part or all of the 7 miles to Kite Lake, 12,000′. Climb 1 mile NW to the summit of Democrat, then go ENE 2 miles along the ridge and over Cameron to the summit of Lincoln; return to Cameron and go 1 mile SE to Bross; descend to where you left the car. The Democrat-Cameron ridge drops to 13,400′; Cameron-Lincoln ridge remains above 14,000′; Bross ridge drops to 13,850′. Camping is available in Buckskin Gulch before the last steep section of the road leading to Kite Lake.

Mount Buckskin, 13,858′, is a quick climb up the W ridge from Buckskin Gulch. It starts well from Kite Lake or from farther down the valley. The whole Buckskin SE ridge, including the broad lower part known as **Loveland Mountain,** is an interesting route, with mine roads and mines along the way.

In Buckskin Gulch one sees one or two arrastres, doughnut shaped pools formed in the rock of the streambed, where a stone dragged around a pole by a donkey provided a crude ore-crushing process. It attests to the Spanish influence on early mining methods in Colorado.

An alternate route for the Democrat-Lincoln massif takes you driving N through Alma to where State 9 starts the side hill climb to **Hoosier Pass.** Take the left hand road to the Montgomery Dam in the valley, 5½ miles from Alma, at 10,850′. Skirt the dam and follow the gulch W and SW 3½ miles where an old mine road doubles back right (N at first) and lets you climb to the NNW ridge of Democrat, 13,250′, on easy grades. Turn S on the ridge and circle left around an obstacle there to find a mine shaft at 13,350′, and continue on the ridge to the top. From Lincoln the descent is good a little to the right of N, on the ESE ridge. Work to the right if you encounter cliffs.

Traver Peak, 13,846′, **McNamee Peak,** 13,750′, and **Clinton Peak,** 13,853′, are clustered together along a mile of ridge at the west end of this valley, which is the headwater of the South Platte River. Start as for Mount Democrat, but take the first right hand road, which climbs W from 2 miles above the dam to Wheeler Lake, 12,183′, where you can choose a route to the range crest. The three peaks named are W to SW. **Wheeler Peak** is a mile NNW, up past a higher lakelet, as easy a climb from this side as from any other.

The Mosquito Pass road starts W off State 9 from a mile S of Alma, climbs in 9 miles from 10,250′ to 13,188′ on the range crest and then descends 8 miles to Leadville.

Mount Evans, 13,557′, is 2 miles S along the ridge from **Mosquito Pass,** and **Mosquito Peak,** with a more satisfying steep-cone top, is about as far north. Old roads, some of them revived for recent mining, climb about the hills of both Mosquito Creeks. The pass road is in North Mosquito; South Mosquito, which branches off left at mile 5, drives for a mile and, when ploughed for mining, opens on a broad ski-tour area. **London Mountain,** 13,194′, splits the Mosquito Creek drainage. It is a short climb up ridge from the W end, where Mosquito Pass road and an old alternative road to the pass from the S creek meet. Mosquito Pass has lately featured an annual burro race.

The gulches E of Leadville offer close approaches for those who like to prowl the old mines or climb to the summits. Mount Evans is at the head of Evans Gulch, reached by driving due W from upper Leadville. Iowa Gulch has a 5-mile road up to 11,000′ and a walking or jeep road 4 miles farther into the amphitheater circled by **Dyer, Gemini, Sherman,** and **Sheridan.** You can reach the Iowa Gulch road from the California Gulch, W from the S part of town. From about mile 4 in Iowa Gulch a road S takes you over toward Empire Gulch. Continue S to the Gulch on poorer road and walk E, 8 miles altogether, to a trail pass a mile N of **Horseshoe Mountain** on the range crest at 13,200′. Good country to see, but far longer than the E side approach. Check in Leadville for road conditions.

Mount Sherman, 14,036′, is an easy climb to start climbing 14'ers with. From Fairplay drive S on US 285 to 1.1 miles S of the State 9 exit, and W 11 miles to Leavick, where camp can be made at 11,000′. Leavick once had its railroad, and there is evidence of the end of the roadbed there. From Leavick a steep but good road leads WNW to an active mine at 12,200′. Climb WNW on the old road system which leads to higher mines, and veer right for the saddle and SW ridge of Sherman, which is 1½ miles N of the car-road mine.

Mount Sheridan, 13,748′, is straight W of the mine, a half-mile climb of 550′ from the same ridge saddle. Sheridan shows its skunk stripe of snow to all of South Park. **Horseshoe Mountain,** 13,898′, is seen from the Fairplay area for its horseshoe cirque on that side. To climb it you leave the Sherman road ¼ mile short of its end and go to the left up the benches to the ridge N of the Horseshoe cirque.

Weston Pass road crosses the range on a generally diagonal NW route from US 285 10½ miles NW of Antero Junction, or 10½ miles S of Fairplay. The road ends at Mount Massive Fishing Club not far S of Leadville on US 24. Keep left at the intersection at mile 7. The road has camping places along the way. The 14-mile E side is good though at the end steepish where it climbs to 11,900′. The descent W is of jeep rating.

Ptarmigan Peak, 13,739′, is a 2½ mile climb up the steep hillside N from **Weston Pass** by the W side and crest of the ridge. **Weston Peak,** 13,572′, is an easy half-mile E from the ridge end S of Ptarmigan. **South Peak,** a 12,892′ point 2 miles WSW of the pass, is a gentle walk with some mine relics to be seen en route. Start down the pass ¼ mile before turning off left on a road. If the pass is open for mining this makes a good short ski tour.

Buffalo Peaks, W summit 13,326′, on Buena Vista and Jones Hill Quads, have been a good place to see elk and bighorn. Drive 8 miles N from Antero Junction on US 285 (13 miles S of Fairplay) and 9 miles W on a lumber road to a right turn point at 10,200′, where you are 2 miles N of the NE peak. A trail climbs E from the E fork of Rough and Tumbling Creek part way up the broad N ridge of the E end of the massif. You can finish and go on to the other summits and make a high traverse back E toward the starting ridge, most of the way above timberline.

TARRYALL RANGE

QUADS: McCurdy Mountain, Topaz Mountain, Tarryall, Farnum Peak; Pike N F; see also U.S.F.S. Lost Park Trail sheet (Lake George Ranger Station).

This 25-mile NW-SE range parallels Tarryall Creek from SE of Jefferson to N of Lake George. It was named by miners in 1859 who panned gold "as big as watermelon seeds" out of the creek. Late comers, angry that they could find no good placers for themselves, said the place should have been called Grab All; they headed across South Park and founded Fairplay.

The N and S ends are a timbered ridge; the middle is higher, wider and rougher, and characterized by a wealth of warts, spikes, knobs, etc., of very red granite. It had once the largest concentration of bighorn sheep to be found anywhere. They are scarcer now. The Tarryall road, State 77, about 43 miles long, connects Jefferson on US 285 with US 24 a mile NW of Lake George. A second road goes N to the Tarryall from US 24 6 miles NW of Lake George, and a third goes in to the Tarryall Reservoir from US 24 at a point 4 miles W of Wilkerson Pass, and misses the central part of the range. Most of the river land is privately held but there are some forest service campgrounds and trails into the range.

The **Indian Trail** starts near a footbridge 4 miles SE of Tarryall Reservoir dam, 8½ miles NW of Tarryall. It crosses the creek and climbs NNE 3½ miles along Ute Creek from 8700′ to 11,300′, were it meets the **McCurdy Trail.** You can go N down Indian Creek to the Lost Park Road or turn E on the McCurdy. The latter climbs you 1½ miles to the flank of **Bison Peak,** turns to flank **McCurdy Mountain,** 1½ miles SE, and then continues by a swing SE over (tentatively named) **Jumble Mountain** and then S and W to return to the Tarryall River at Twin Eagles Campground, at the mouth of Hay Creek, 9 miles from McCurdy Mountain.

Bison Peak, 12,431′, and **McCurdy Mountain,** 12,168′, are side trips from this trail of less than a mile each and 500′ altitude gain. There are rock obstructions and some down timber from an old burn, and the top country is confusing enough so you might get lost for a time.

North Tarryall Peak, 11,902′, is a bushwhack climb of 1½ miles from the 10,670′ pass 13½ miles SE of Jefferson on Lost Creek road. You can start from the lumber camp, 2½ miles farther S, where you cross the marshy area and climb 3 miles up ridge. You will have help through the timber on lumber roads.

Anyone interested in walking trails in the rocky back country E of the Tarryalls should get the sheet of the Lost Creek Scenic Area from the Lake George Ranger Station. This shows the 17-mile trail from W of Goose Creek Campground N to Lost Park road. There are connecting trails NE to Wigwam Park and S to **McCurdy Trail.**

The Tarryall is now connected to Goose Creek by a road called the Matukat for a Lithuanian who lives in the region. From 8 miles N of Lake George on the Tarryall road you go E about 14 miles to connect with a road S from Goose Creek Campground.

PLATTE RIVER MOUNTAINS and KENOSHA MOUNTAINS

QUADS: Mount Logan, Shawnee, Topaz Mountain, Jefferson; Pike NF.

These oddly warted smoothtops are on a 14-mile split ridge running SE from just E of **Kenosha Pass.** The Platte Rivers are on the NE side of Craig Creek; the Kenoshas, running a little higher to 12,000′ summits, are on the southwest. One can walk or drive on a dirt road E from the pass 1½ miles to Kenosha Creek, 10,050′, and follow the drainage 4 miles to the **Twin Cones.** Don't be alarmed if you can count three; **Mount Blaine** is between and E of the twins. For a long high walk go down one ridge 6 or 8 miles, cross Craig Park's marshes and come up the other ridge.

Knobby Crest, 12,429′ is a high point of the Kenosha. To climb it turn E off US 285 from 3 miles W of **Kenosha Pass** (1 mile NE of Jefferson), and follow State 134, Lost Park road, 11 miles S to **Hooper Pack Trail,** 10,016′. Follow faint trail (not Hooper) E along N side of the creek past high beaver dams for ½ mile, then go generally NNE to summit, keeping to left of the large rock tower. Views include a sweep from Evans through Sawatch and Sangre de Cristo Ranges to the plains, and close-ups of the Front Range towers.

Windy Peak, 11,970′, names its quad. From the foot of the hill at Bailey on US 285 drive SE 5 miles. Keep right at the fork and continue 2½ miles to Sonderstrom Ranch, start of **Hooper Trail** leading W. Continue 2.5 miles on this trail to just short of the fork. Walking starts at 9300′ on a lumber road which cuts

SE. Take a timbering route S and continue 2 miles to summit over rocks or timbered slopes. This peak also goes from the trail up Rolling Creek. Drive 2 miles beyond Soderstrom Ranch and take the trail up Rolling Creek and its S fork. As the slope gentles about 2½ miles from the start, cut to right for 2½ miles to the right of and along the SE ridge.

Freeman Peak, 11,589′, the south end of the Kenoshas, is well fortified by bushwhacking terrain on steep slopes. From the Flying G Ranch W of Cheesman Lake and S of Wellington Lake, take the road N a mile to the cross trail to the left into Wigwam Creek. Follow the trail from 8200′ on the creek for 2 miles, then cut off right and work your way N up the slope, then NE. It is about 2 miles of hard work.

The Castle, 9691′, which rises from the west side of Wellington Lake, is reportedly a semi-technical climb, not for the inexperienced. There is about a mile of steep bushwhacking if you climb directly S from the Bancroft Ranch, ¾ mile N of the peak, or you can take the climb more gradually by climbing 1½ miles on the trail up Rolling Creek and its south fork and then cutting up the W slope, toward and then N of a lesser summit ½ mile SW of the Castle. The jumble of rock points can then be explored or climbed according to the party's makeup. See Windy Peak and Green Mountain Quads; for the roads, Pike N F.

PUMA HILLS

QUADS: Glentivar, Farnum Peak, Spinney Mountain, Tarryall; Pike N F.

This name applies to a clump of timbered hills running to 11,000′ summits on both sides of **Wilkerson Pass.** The high point, 11,570′, is 1½ miles SW of **Farnum Peak** and a mile SE of the end of the Packer Gulch road, a logging road that is normally good for car travel. You can get there by driving 2 miles W from the Tarryall Reservoir spillway and turning left rather than right on the main road to South Park. Keep left at mile 2½. The road climbs 8 miles total to 11,000′. The higher summit is the second one, ½ mile SE of road end.

The **Badger Mountain Lookout,** 11,294′, is close N of **Wilkerson Pass** and can be reached by car for a fine view of this part of the state. From Wilkerson Pass on US 24 drive 4½ miles W to crossroad, N for .4 mile, NE and E 2 miles, keeping right; then left (NE) 2 miles to **La Salle Pass,** where you take a right and continue 3½ miles SE to the summit. La Salle Pass, can also be reached from the E side off the second Tarryall road N from 24. If you like to pay more for such a view, scramble up from Wilkerson Pass. It's 1800′ in under 2 miles, steep and somewhat scratchy.

RAMPART RANGE REGION

Pike N F

The Rampart Range itself runs S from Devils Head to the Garden of the Gods at elevations around 9000′. There are many roads, campgrounds, lakes, ranches and resorts through the wide swath of timbered, middle-height, mountain country to the west, all in Platte River drainage southwest of Denver and northwest of Colorado Springs. It is well sprinkled with spectacular hunks of granite, and here and there a fair-sized mountain to climb. It is a good place for early and late season climbing, when the high mountains are closed.

The Rampart Range road runs N from .1 mile E of Balanced Rock in the W part of the Garden of the Gods at Colorado Springs. There are fine overlooks from the 9000′ crest if you go up this way, but it is a little rough and sometimes dusty. The easier approach by car is from Woodland Park, 20 miles NW of town on US 24. Go straight E from the Woodland Park main street and turn N with the main road there. It will take you 1½ miles N and a mile W to a junction. If you want to go S, turn right and keep right. You will find a road to the water and recreational development. If you want to go N toward Denver, keep left.

Ormes Peak, 9727′, high point of the range, was named for this editor's father, who made a widely used trail map of the region and presided over the Saturday Knights hiking club's coffee pot, only symbol of the group's organization since its inception in 1903. The "peak" rises about 300′ from the plateau and can be reached from a lumber road that turns E off the Rampart Range 3½ miles N of Ridge Crest Picnic Grounds. The main road goes NE to the new lake; keep right at mile 1 and go 1½ miles E. The summit is ½ mile N on the ridge.

There are pleasant walking and horsebacking byroads off both sides of the main road from the south end of the plateau N to Carrol Lakes road. These were used for early day lumbering.

Palmer Lake has a number of very interesting trail walks—one to an ice cave, others to granite formations and viewing points along the range W of town. If you are lucky you may be able to find a mimeographed sheet describing these routes. Otherwise inquire.

Academy Peak, or as Air Force people prefer to call it, **Mount Harmon,** 9385′, is the 3-top just back of the Academy. Inquire and get a road plot at either Academy entrance off I-25. Head for the Hospital, where you use the visitors' parking lot, about 7000′. Walk W 1 mile (first ¾ on dirt road) to a trail which takes you into and up Stanley Canyon. At mile 3 from start you cut right (NE) ½ mile up back slopes to the summits. Best view is from the cliff top or N summit, 9366′. See Cascade and Pikeview Quads. **Blodgett Peak,** the next peak S of the Academy, gives a similar fine view of the prairie.

Devils Head, 9748′, is the summit of greatest interest on the Rampart because of the rough points of rock that rise from it like the horns of a mythical monster. A short trail climbs to the fire lookout on top from 8800′ Devils Head Campground. The campground road turns E off the Rampart road 50 miles N of Colorado Springs, or you can go 20 miles WSW from Sedalia, starting on the road to Deckers. Turn S (left) at mile 10 from Sedalia.

Between the Rampart Range and the Tarryall and Platte River and Kenosha Mountains there is a wide valley largely forested with ponderosa pine trees and here and there punctuated by odd-shaped outcrops of the granite that underlies the area. State 67, which is parallel to the Rampart Range Road but more polished, runs north from Woodland Park to Deckers and then down the Platte to Sedalia. This, and the roads that run W from it and N to US 285, are the access routes to this middle basin and its west rim, the Kenoshas.

Thunder Butte, 7936′, on Westcreek Quad, is a hard scramble of 3 or 4 miles from the road a mile S and a mile W of **Westcreek,** 7600′. Use the old road and whatever trail you can find in Shrewsberry Gulch for 2 miles NW and then work N, bushwhacking up the steep slope to the summit. You can cross a dip NE and go SE for a mile if you want to visit the cliff top. The only report we have says it's all rough, and even the deer don't make trails.

Sheeps Nose is SW of Thunder Butte, just off the road from Westcreek to Florissant. You can get up through steep timber to the space among the summits.

To get to **Long Scraggy,** drive 2 miles S from Buffalo toward Deckers and follow the signs for Long Scraggy Ranch. The trail takes off above the embankment at the outskirts of the ranch. This high, rocky hill is on Deckers Quad, the higher N end, 8812′, 2 miles SE of the ranch.

Little Scraggy, 9192′, is another of those rock, bush and tree deals you can look into in the off-season. From 7 miles N of Deckers, you can leave your car at the bend where the road starts E, at 8100′, and clamber N a mile to the high point. From 4 miles S of Buffalo Creek you can drive W 2 miles and a little way toward the N end of the little monster on a side road.

Green Mountain, 10,421′, is 2 miles W from the starting point for the S end of Little Scraggy above.

PIKES PEAK REGION

QUADS: Manitou Springs, Pikes Peak, Cascade, Woodland

Park, Divide, Cheyenne Mountain, Mount Big Chief, Big Bull Mountain, Cripple Creek North, Cripple Creek South, Pike View, Mount Deception; Pikes Peak and vicinity has much of the above condensed; Pike N F *The Pikes Peak Atlas*, a thorough trail map and trail history, covers the area between the Air Force Academy and Little Fountain Creek, and between Colorado Springs and Cripple Creek. It suggests numerous trail trips including the various routes to Pikes Peak. There are some geological notes for the amateur.

The main large-capacity camping area in the region is at Manitou Park, 7 miles N of Woodland Park and US 24 on State 67.

Pikes Peak is farthest east of the big peaks; hence its early fame. It is accessible by road and rail as well as by trails from both sides. The maintained trail is **Barr's Trail** for which you drive W up Manitou Springs' main street to where it angles 70 degrees right to start up **Ute Pass.** You keep straight instead and drive to the parking lot for the cog railway and Manitou Incline Railway or a little farther. Continue up the valley on foot until road becomes trail and cuts to the right out of the canyon. The 12-mile climb starts at 6600′ and involves more base-to-summit altitude than any other in the state. It is very punishing unless you are in condition, and even if you are it will be more comfortable to camp en route. The usual place is at Barr's Camp, 9800′. The Chamber of Commerce will let you know whether this is maintained. The climb can be shortened at the bottom by using the Mount Manitou Incline Railway. From the top of the ride, take the higher of two trails running west. In about ½ mile the **Barr Trail** will come up to it from the left. The incline railway does not start early in the morning. See Manitou Springs and Pikes Peak Quads.

The Pikes Peak Highway, on the route of an earlier carriage road, leaves US 24 5 miles NW of Manitou Springs. It was built by Spencer Penrose and operated for an allotted period as a toll road. It is now managed and maintained by the city of Colorado Springs.

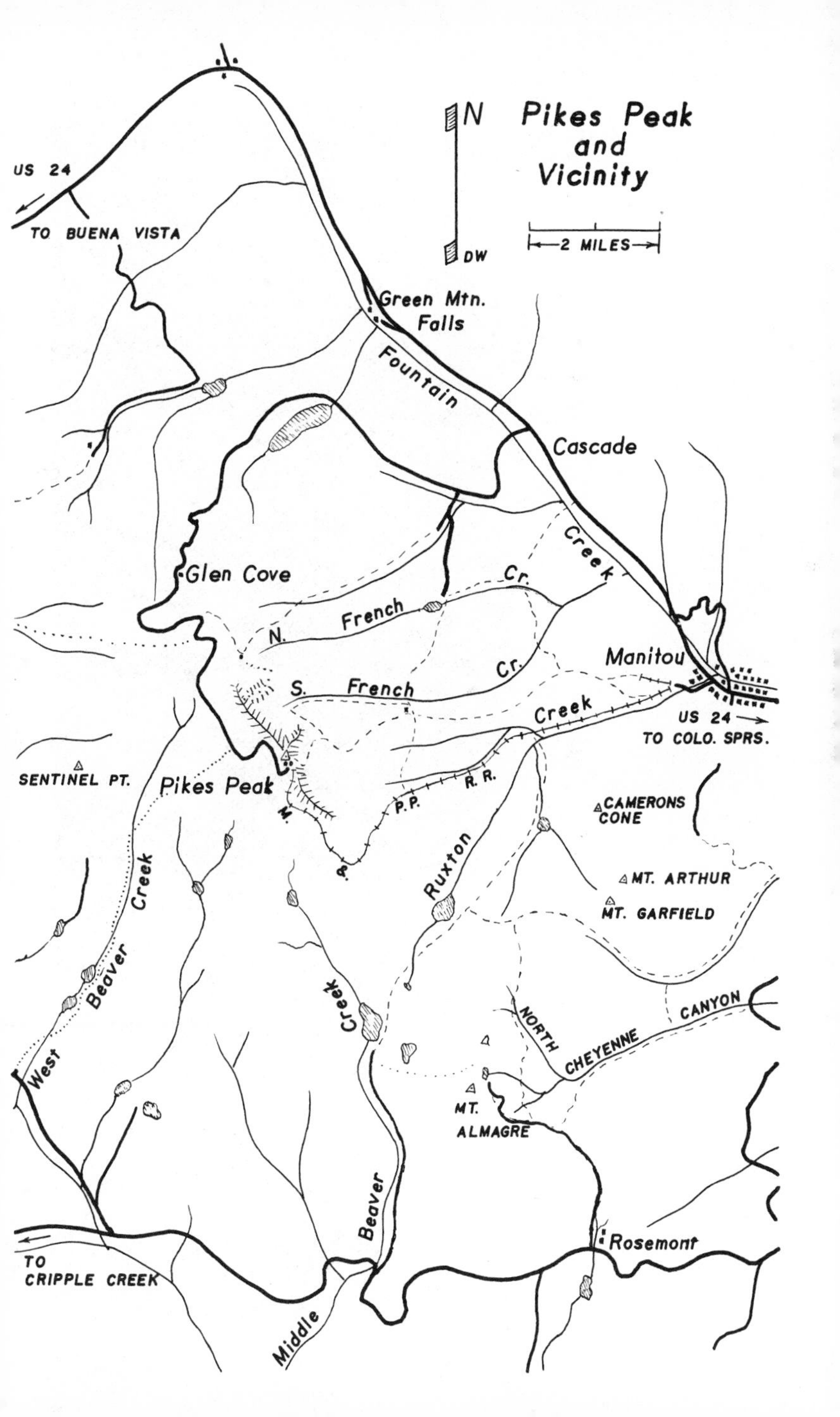
Pikes Peak
and
Vicinity
N
DW
2 MILES
US 24
TO BUENA VISTA
Green Mtn.
Falls
Fountain
Cascade
Creek
Glen Cove
N.
French
Cr.
S.
French
Cr.
Manitou
Creek
US 24
TO COLO. SPRS.
SENTINEL PT.
Pikes Peak
M.
P.P.
R.R.
Ruxton
CAMERONS
CONE
MT. ARTHUR
MT. GARFIELD
West
Beaver
Creek
Creek
NORTH
CHEYENNE
CANYON
MT.
ALMAGRE
Beaver
Rosemont
TO
CRIPPLE CREEK
Middle

The shadow of Pikes Peak on the prairie, from summit at sunset. *H. L. Standley photo.*

A pleasant climb of **Pikes Peak** makes use of the toll road to timberline, 1 mile beyond the Glen Cove building. A road turns off left, very unobtrusively but identifiable by a chain post. This takes you down to Elk Park Knoll where you leave your car, ¼ mile off the highway. From the little saddle on the way to the knoll an old walking road takes you S and downhill around into Ghost Town Hollow. Go up to where there is an old boiler and a creek flowing out of a mine mouth. Pick up some delicious water for the dry run ahead. You climb from 11,000′ diagonally eastward out of the valley to the ridge at 11,600′, going E just far enough to evade the cliffs. Cross the ridge flats till you can look into Bottomless Pit, to the S, and then climb up the ridge on the left side of the crest. When you come into the highway you can leave it again to go up the final cone on big broken rocks. It is 2¼ miles more with 1200′ climb. Since hitch-hiking is illegal, bum a ride back with the patrol.

The Mennonite road gives access to **Pikes Peak** from the northwest. You drive US 24 to the Divide, 27 miles NW of Colorado Springs, and turn S on 67 for 4½ miles to the road left to Mennonite Camp, which you take for 3 miles or so to a campground, picnic, and parking place at 10,000′. If you keep to the right (S) side of the stream, as you walk E up the creek, an old lumber road will take you most of the way to timberline. Then all you have to do is climb. You'll end up on a little spur road off the Pikes Peak Highway at "mile 16," the point from which people like to watch the Pikes Peak auto races, 12,300′. Shortcutting the road, it is about 3 miles more to the summit, 7 miles total.

Denver's mountain historian Louisa Arps has supplied many items of interest for this book, including the following information on Pikes Peak.

The mountain was the first 14,000-foot mountain in the United States to be climbed. This was on July 13, 14, and 15, 1820, in beautiful mid-summer weather with a sky so blue that Dr. Edwin James, botanist, wondered if the blue of the tundra flowers was not partially acquired from the blue of the sky.

Dr. James' companions were a soldier and a civilian employee of the Long Expedition. The climb was successful in spite of the fact that the climbers broke most modern mountaineering rules: the soldier, instead of "going light," carried a gun (in case of hostile Indians); they carried no emergency rations; they left their warm clothes in camp; the party did not stay together—the civilian got tired and took a nap below timberline, causing Dr. James to lose time and patience hollering for him. But the worse thing they did was to fail to put out their fire the morning after they bivouacked on the ascent. When they came off the mountain they found their cached supplies burned and a good part of the forest with them. Colorado's first careless campers!

Fourteen years before, in 1806, the man for whom Pikes Peak was named, Zebulon Montgomery Pike, left his main party in a breastwork built of 14 logs on the present site of Pueblo, and, with three companions, set out "to ascend the north fork [Fountain Creek] to the high point of the blue mountain, which we conceived would be one days march, in order to lay down the various branches and positions of the country." Legends have grown up about this attempt—one, that Pike actually climbed Cheyenne Mountain; another that he said Pikes Peak would never be climbed. Mountaineering scholars now think he came up South Turkey Creek and climbed Blue Mountain or another of the summits southwest of Cheyenne Mountain. Starting with an entry of November 24, 1806, his account reads thus:

> We marched at one o'clock with an idea of arriving at the foot of the mountain; but found ourselves obliged to take up our nights lodging under a single cedar, which we found in the prairie, without water and extremely cold . . . Distance, 12 miles.
>
> 25th November, Tuesday. Marched early, with an expectation of ascending the mountain, but was only able to encamp at its base . . . Killed two buffalo. Distance, 22 miles.

26th November, Wednesday. Expecting to return to our camp that evening, we left our blankets and provisions at the foot of the mountain . . . We commenced ascending, found it very difficult, being obliged to climb up rocks, sometimes almost perpendicular; and after marching all day, we encamped in a cave, without blankets, victuals, or water . . .

27th November, Thursday. Arose hungry, dry, and extremely sore from the inequality of the rocks on which we had lain all night, but were amply compensated for toil by the sublimity of the prospect below . . . Commenced our march up the mountain, and in about an hour arrived at the summit of this chain; here we found snow middle deep; no sign of beast or bird inhabiting the region. The thermometer . . . here fell to 4° below 0 [Réaumur reckoning; + 23° Fahrenheit]. The summit of the Grand Peak which was entirely bare of vegetation and covered with snow, now appeared at the distance of 15 or 16 miles from us; and as high again as what we had ascended and would have taken a whole day's march to have arrived at its base, when I believe no human being could have ascended to its pinical [*sic*]. This with the condition of my soldiers who had only light overalls on, and no stockings . . . the bad prospect of killing anything to subsist on . . . determined us to return . . . We descended by way of a long ravine with much less difficulty than contemplated. Found all our baggage safe but the provisions all destroyed. It began to snow, and we sought shelter under the side of a projecting rock, where we, all four, made a meal on one partridge, and a piece of deer's ribs, the ravens had left us, being the first we had eaten in 48 hours.

28th November, Friday. Marched at nine o'clock. Kept straight down the creek to avoid the hills. At half past one o'clock shot two buffalo . . . Encamped in a valley under a shelving rock . . .

29th November, Saturday. Marched after a short repast, and arrived at our camp before night.

Camerons Cone, 10,709′, is very steep on the E side and so best taken from behind. Use either the **Mount Manitou Incline** and the **Pipeline Trail** W from it, or the **Barr Trail** to its intersection with the Pipeline Trail, and follow the latter around S and W to the cog road on Ruxton Creek. Cross the creek and go S up the canyon on the other (E) side ½ mile. Start uphill to your left, off the stream line in a little side draw. Climb S from it a little way to the gravel-covered W ridge of the Cone. It is a 1-mile, 1500′ climb from the canyon floor. See Manitou Springs Quad.

The Gold Camp Road, on the bed of the Colorado Springs and Cripple Creek District Railroad, opens many trail trips and minor climbs. It turns S off Colorado Avenue on 26th Street and winds 24 miles in and out of the Cheyenne Canyons on 4% grade to Rosemont 9800′, before leveling off. There is a short cut to it up Cheyenne Canyon (continuation of Cheyenne Road and Cheyenne Boulevard), and a much higher one from just north of the arch introducing the **Cheyenne Mountain** and zoo and Ski Area road behind the Broadmoor Hotel.

Almagre Mountain, 12,367′, has a road to the top from Rosemont. To get the picture use Manitou, Big Chief, Pikes Peak and Big Bull Quads. Rosemont, once a settlement, is now identifiable only as a brook crossing at the bend of road N of the Penrose Reservoir. It is a smooth mountain, climbable from any direction with a map. Trails go up from North Cheyenne Canyon and from the water road above Clyde on the W side.

Mount Rosa, 11,499′, is a short but rewarding climb from Rosemont. Start directly E up a ½ mile draw. At the saddle turn left and up the 1¼-mile ridge which climbs 1500′ to the summit. See Mount Big Chief and Manitou Springs Quads.

SAWATCH RANGE

The Sawatch is long and complex, stretching from the Eagle River to Poncha Pass, 90 miles or so. Its limits are somewhat arbitrary in the north half but from Mount Massive south to

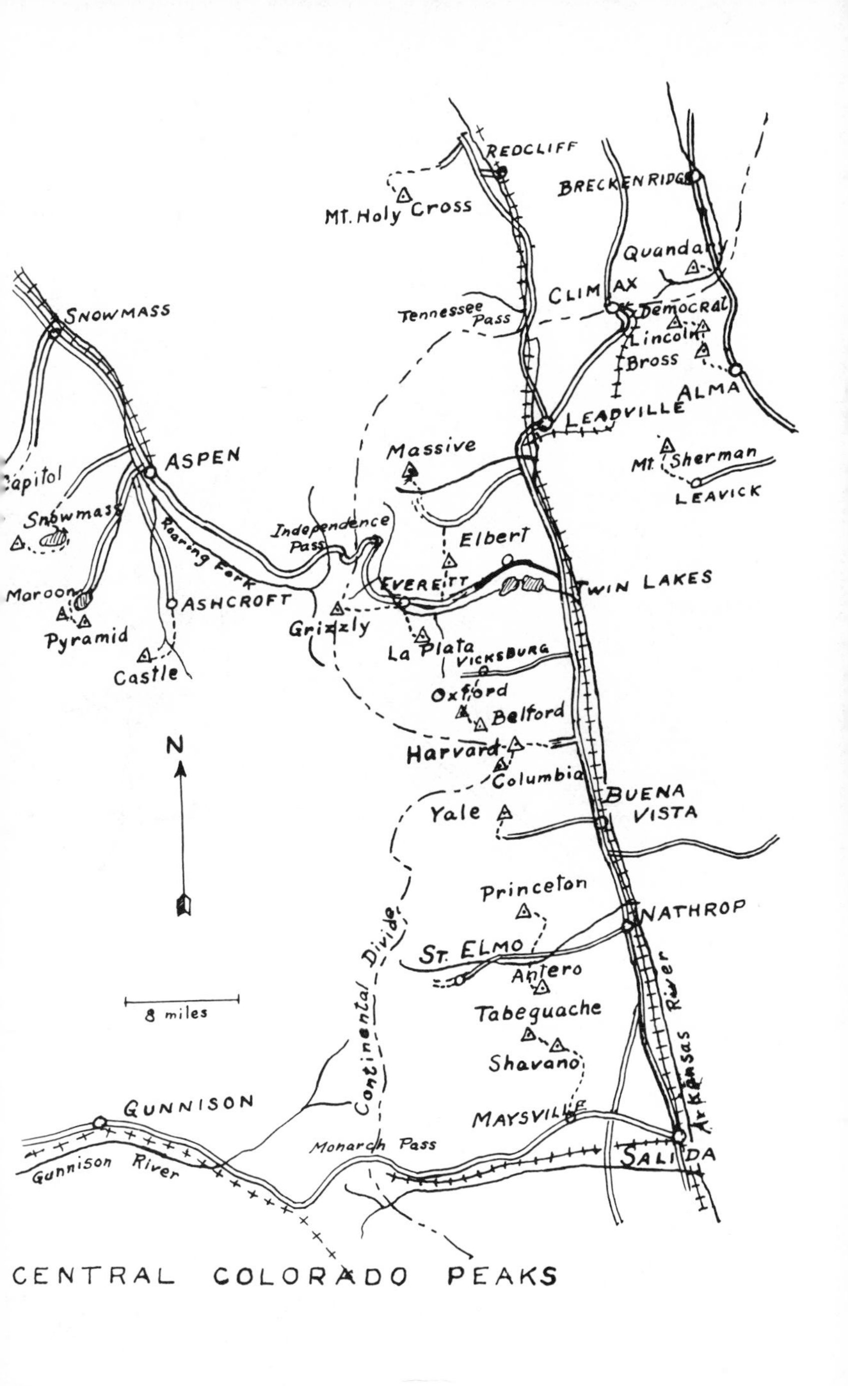

CENTRAL COLORADO PEAKS

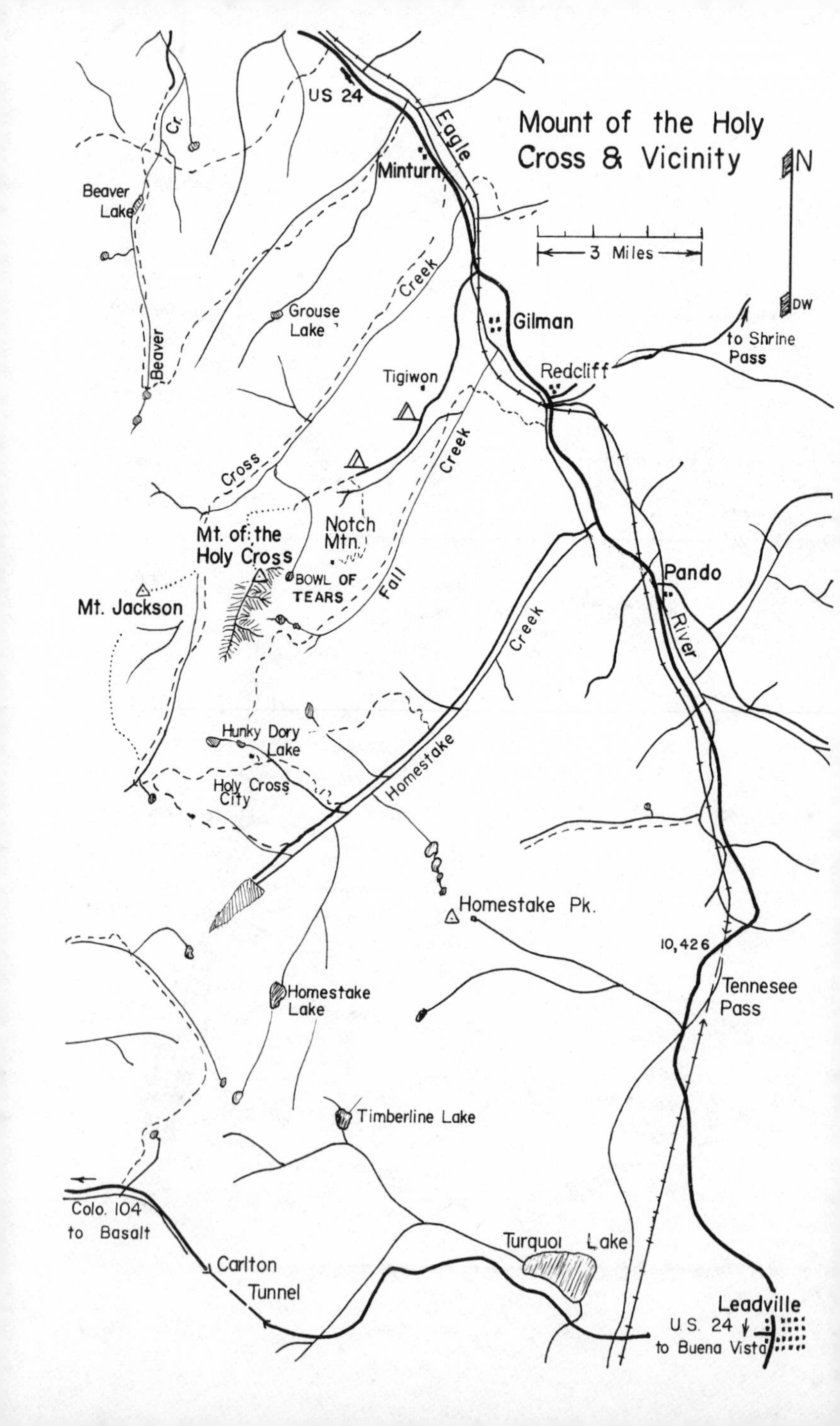
Mount of the Holy Cross & Vicinity
N
DW
3 Miles
US 24
Eagle
Minturn
Cr.
Beaver Lake
Beaver
Grouse Lake
Creek
Gilman
to Shrine Pass
Redcliff
Tigiwon
Cross
Creek
Notch Mtn.
Mt. of the Holy Cross
Mt. Jackson
BOWL OF TEARS
Fall
Pando
River
Creek
Homestake
Hunky Dory Lake
Holy Cross City
Homestake Pk.
10,426
Tennesee Pass
Homestake Lake
Timberline Lake
Colo. 104 to Basalt
Carlton Tunnel
Turquoi Lake
Leadville
U.S. 24 to Buena Vista

Antora Peak it forms a definite chain. It is separated into these sections in our treatment: *Holy Cross*, *Leadville*, *Collegiate*, and *Shavano*.

The word Sawatch—Indian for Water of the Blue Earth—is supposed to have been used for the lake which once covered San Luis Valley. Hayden called the range one of the grandest of eruptive masses on the continent.

SAWATCH RANGE—HOLY CROSS SECTION

QUADS: Mount Jackson, Ivanhoe Creek, Grouse Mountain; Holy Cross and Minturn 15′; For approaches only: Fulford, Mount Thomas, Meredith, Eagle, Edwards, Wolcott; Mount Jackson 30′, covering most of the area, is economical of space but only grossly informative; White River N F.

This part of the range extends S from the New York Mountains and Mount Jackson and the Holy Cross to Hagerman Pass. It lies between West Brush Creek and the Eagle River, but extends E of the Eagle River to the ridge SW of Gore and Black Gore Creeks. Vail Pass separates it from the Gore Range and Fremont Pass from the Tenmile and Mosquito Ranges.

WEST SIDE

Crooked Creek Pass separates the west group of the Holy Cross Section from **Red Table Mountain,** which we group with the Elk Range. The road climbs SW up West Brush Creek from the south side of Eagle, 6600′, on I-70, about 22 miles to the pass, 10,000′, flanking the long Red Table Mountain. Then it descends past Woods Lake to Ruedi Reservoir on the Frying Pan, another 10 miles. From the pass top a jeep road of increasing roughness and sometimes very steep grade climbs to **Mount Thomas,** E end of the Red Table ridge, where there is a superb view of the elusive ridges W of the Holy Cross. (Even with a jeep you may do better to come in to Red Table Mountain from the W as indicated with the Elk Mountains.) From Crooked Creek Pass and some of the open country S of Woods

Lake there are good views of the Fools Peak–Avalanche Peak ridges.

The Fulford Cave Campground connects by a 5-mile trail with the little fishing resort lake at the foot of **Crooked Creek Pass** (E side). The S end starts from the end of a road E of the N side of the resort lake and climbs to an 11,200′ pass. Both termini are at 9400′. At the pass it is crossed by a long ridge crest trail whose upper (E) end is a part of our recommended route (below) for **Fools Peak** from Woods Lake.

You get a fine look across at the Gold Dust ridge at the end of the first mile of this path (3½ miles total from the S terminus at the Crooked Creek lake). Come up from the lake to the saddle and turn E and SE on the ridge crest trail and follow it to the 12,041′ high ridge point. These trails N of Woods Lake are not maintained, but should not be hard to follow.

Woods Lake, a private resort run for fishermen, is on a 2-mile side road off the foot of **Crooked Creek Pass.** This resort, or Lime Creek to the W, where you can camp on forest land, is a good starting place for explorations of the **Avalanche Peak** ridge. (See Mount Jackson 7½′ quad.) From Woods Lake, drive or walk 2 miles W to Eagle Lake, and continue up Lime Creek SE 2 miles by trail to Fairview Lake, and then ½ mile farther, where a creek comes in from the west. Climb past the falls on this creek to a higher lake at 11,650′. Try for some trout and see what you can do about getting up to Avalanche Peak, .3 mile S of the lake and 1200′ higher. Fairview Lake would seem to be an exploration center for the whole muleshoe of peaks around the valley head lake. The latter is 2 miles beyond Fairview Lake at 11,200′ and the summits around it push 13,000′. Fairview Lake is directly under (¾ miles SW of) the rough, steep side of a mountain we shall call **Many Ribs Peak,** 13,116′ high.

Fools Peak, 12,960′, is a smooth cone as seen from the west. The route to it starts at Woods Lake, 9400′. Climb ½ mile W from the buildings to the 200′ ridge N of the lake, and on the ridge go 1 mile ENE to the steep mountain side of Fools Peak ridge. You climb N 1800′ to this ridge. At this point climb right instead of following the trail left, and keeping a little to the right around a 12,323′ ridge point, you go a mile E via the W saddle and cone slope to the top. See Mount Thomas and Mount Jackson Quads.

The Brush Creek road divides 10 miles SE of Eagle, the left fork following West Brush Creek to Yeoman Park Campground, 6 miles. It can be jeeped another mile upstream to Fulford Cave Campground. From here it is 5 miles by trail, still in West Brush Creek, to Mystic Island Lake. Within a mile around the valley head there are several peaks close over and under 13,000′. Lake Charles, a mile downstream from Mystic Island Lake, is between **Gold Dust Peak,** 1½ miles NNE, and **Fools Peak,** a mile S. It would seem a good center, at about 11,070′, for these and several other summits. The route to Fools Peak from this side would go directly up the slope S of the lake to the big bench there, and then veer right to the peak's W saddle, 12,100′, for the same smoothcone finish as above.

Gold Dust Peak, 13,360′, is climbed by way of the streambed ½ mile below Lake Charles. If you come up from below, climb along this stream to timberline, leaving the trail where the side stream enters West Brush Creek at a little round lake; if you come from Lake Charles, climb N from the lake about 300′ in altitude and then contour to creek. Above timberline you scramble up a couloir toward the base of the peak and then working to the left side achieve the W ridge, which gains the summit. It appears from the 30′ Mount Jackson Quad that the miner-designated Gold Dust Peak was the more accessible ridge point, ¾ mile E of what we call Gold Dust and 500′ lower.

New York Mountain, 12,550′, is 2 miles E of the ghost town of Fulford. From Yeoman Park a road cuts sharply to the left and climbs 3½ miles to Fulford, 9600′, and another 2 miles to the N, past Triangle Creek. About .7 mile past the Fulford street (which is a side road) a trail turns off right and climbs 2½ miles up the mountain's W ridge to timberline. It is jeepable most of the way. Above timberline on the trail's right fork, you turn S and are taken still higher to an easy finish on the W slope. It is worthwhile to go NE ¼ mile to the lower summit for a good look at New York Lake and the long N ridge of Gold Dust.

From Lake Creek School, ¾ mile W of Edwards on I-70, a road goes S 9 miles to Baryeta cabins on West Lake Creek. The last 6 miles of it is classified jeep. You keep right at mile 1½ and mile 4. Here you are about 4 miles N of New York Lake, but there is no mentionable trail.

East Lake Creek takes you 5 miles by car and another mile by jeep. You keep left at mile 1½. A trail continues 10 miles farther up the canyon, passing the Discovery Tunnel at mile 5. A backpack of 8½ miles on this 10-mile trail to a cabin site at 10,150′ would put you in the heart of this little-known valley. See Grouse Mountain and Mount Jackson Quads.

Mount Jackson, 13,657′, is 2 miles to the E of the above camping spot and reached by a route which bows slightly N from the direct line. Two rough, steep valleys suggest problem routes leading to **Gold Dust Peak:** one, directly W, takes you to a basin of lakelets which culminates in the NE headwall of the peak; for the other you would go S up the trail for a mile or so and then climb W to some larger lakes and an approach to the narrow S ridge of the peak. At the head of the valley 4 miles (2 of the 4 on trail) is **Many Ribs Peak,** with the usual parabolic slope line, and both sides of the valley are lined with rough sharp ridge points.

From the N side of Minturn a 9-mile trail runs SW up West Grouse Creek and crosses to the Turquoise Lakes, on Beaver Creek. A trail up Beaver Creek to the same lakes from Avon is a mile shorter and saves the 700′ climb over Grouse Mountain shoulder, but may be closed to the public by private owners who straddle it. From a camp at the lower lake, 11,050′, you are about a 2½-mile climb from **Mount Jackson.** Scramble W to the long N ridge and continue on it to the top.

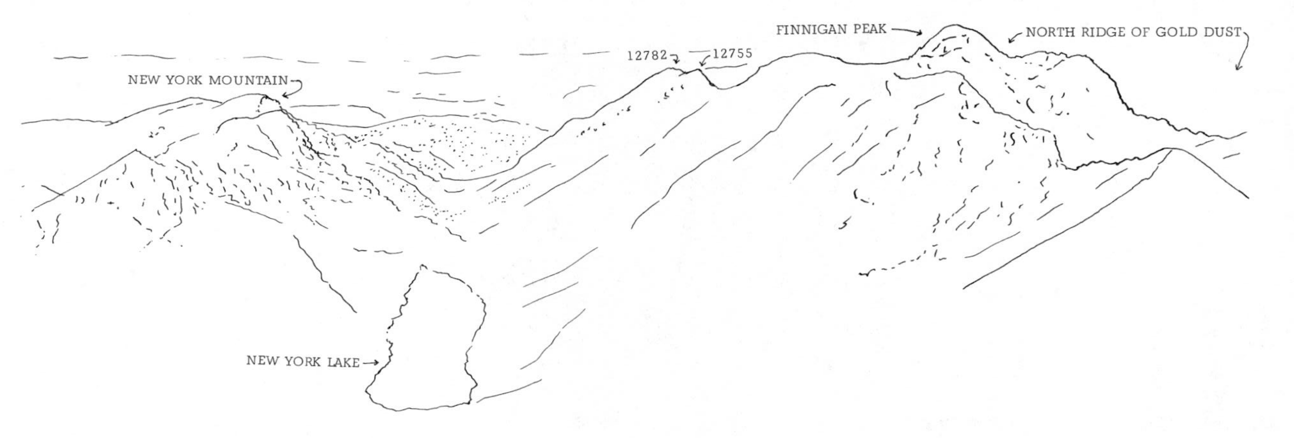

Looking north from Gold Dust Peak.

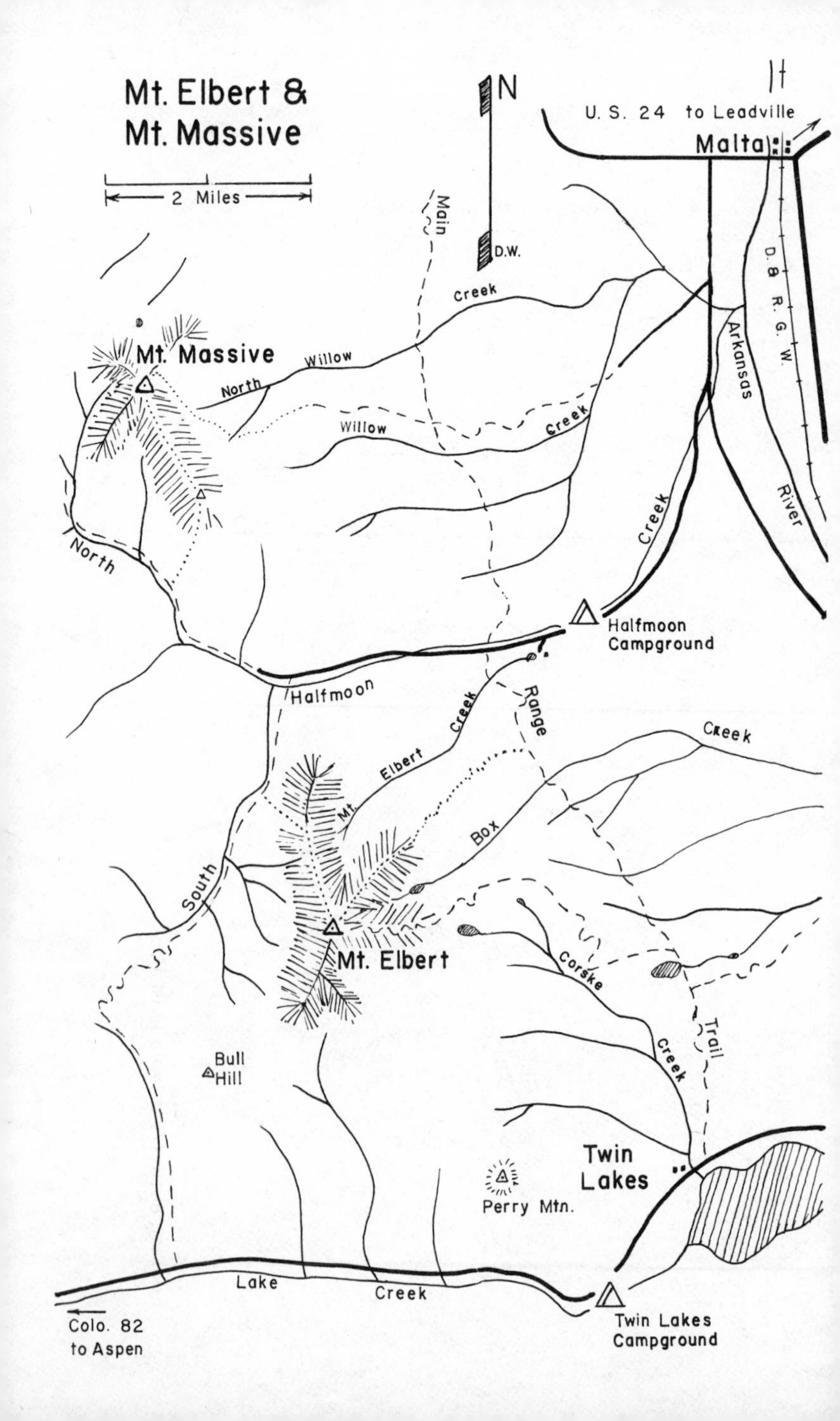
Mt. Elbert &
Mt. Massive
2 Miles
N
D.W.
U. S. 24 to Leadville
Malta
D. & R. G. W.
Main
Creek
Mt. Massive
North
Willow
Willow
Creek
Arkansas
River
Creek
North
Halfmoon
Campground
Halfmoon
Creek
Range
Creek
Mt. Elbert
Box
Mt.
Elbert
South
Mt. Elbert
Corske
Creek
Trail
Bull
Hill
Twin
Lakes
Perry Mtn.
Lake
Creek
Colo. 82
to Aspen
Twin Lakes
Campground

Cross Creek has a trail which runs its full length, 15 miles. It starts a mile or so S of Minturn on US 24, at 8000′, or you can reach it at 8300′ from the second left bend on the Tigiwon Road. It rises with the canyon to 11,000′, and then climbs out E over a 12,400′ pass at the N end of Holy Cross ridge. It connects there with trails to Holy Cross City and Homestake Creek, discussed below. This trail is too far E for the New York Mountain climbs, but it leads into little-visited country W of the Holy Cross, which it flanks.

South of Woods Lake there is a trail system mainly geared to reach some lakes but also useful for exploration of the ridges behind them. Just off the Crooked Pass—Frying Pan road on Woods Lake side road, the powerline road turns off S and goes 5 or 6 miles SSE to the Frying Pan North Fork, which it meets 2½ miles E of the Frying Pan River. A parallel trail runs SSE from Woods Lake to the North Fork, 9 miles. The first leg runs 2½ miles SE and then climbs E a mile to Tellurium Lake, 10,500′. The second runs S 2 miles to Last Chance Creek, where it meets a trail coming up the creek 2 miles E from the powerline road. Here the third lap climbs E out of Last Chance Creek to a bench 400′ higher and continues E to Henderson Park, 2 miles. The last lap runs S from a little E of Henderson Park on a jeep road SSW 2 miles to the North Fork, where it meets the trail up that stream to Savage Lakes.

From Henderson Park, 10,500′, on the above trail, a side trail of lower standard zigzags N 2 miles to little Josephine Lake, 11,400′. Here you are just under and W of the 12,180′ S ridge end of the long mountain chain S from **Gold Dust Peak,** and you can climb to it without problems.

The **Savage Lakes Trail** is a continuation of the North Fork Road. The car road runs from the Frying Pan 3 miles E to the campground. It is next a jeep road for 3 miles, and then a 3 mile maintained trail. Savage Lakes are at 11,000′, just over the Divide from the Sopris Creek Lakes. 13,083′ **Savage Peak,** which might be called the very end of the long Holy Cross S ridge, is an easy climb from the N Savage Lake by way of the pass and ridge. See Mount Jackson and Ivanhoe Creek Quads.

Carter Lake, about midway between Josephine Lake and the Savage Lakes, has 2 trail connections with the Savage Lake Trail, each 1½ miles long.

A trail of lower standard goes N from Carter Lake, 10,350′ and climbs by way of the main creek NNE 2½ miles to Blodgett Lake. On the way it passes several high lakelets, crosses the Divide at 11,850′. This links it with the **Eagle River Trails** up Cross Creek, Fall Creek and Homestake Creek.

A S fork of the **Savage Lake Trail** climbs from a mile W of Savage Lakes by way of Mormon Creek to Mormon Lake, 11,400′, just over the Divide from Upper Homestake and Bench Lakes. It then continues S, crossing a pass at 11,600′, and runs down Lyle Creek past Lyle Lake to the Carlton Tunnel-Ivanhoe Creek road. This is a 7-mile trail, with the pass in the middle.

EAST SIDE

East of the Mount of the Holy Cross the roads and trails follow the general up-valley path of NNE to SSW. See Minturn and Holy Cross 15′ quads (7½′ quads will be Minturn SW and Holy Cross NW).

The road to Half Moon Campground leaves US 24 2 miles S of Minturn, at 8,000′, and climbs 4 miles to Tigiwon Campground, 10,000′, and 500′ and 2 miles more to Half Moon. This campground, on a bench creek tributary to Fall Creek and called Notch Mountain Creek, is the trail head for the Holy Cross climb, for Notch Mountain, and for Hunky Dory Lake and Holy Cross City.

Mount of the Holy Cross, 14,005′, is a long massif with 3 successively lower summits along the south ridge which along with the rugged tilted block top help to make it recognizable from long distances. Its fame began with a photograph by William H. Jackson of the Hayden Survey. The best road view of the cross is from part way down the Shrine Pass road. **Shrine**

Pass is a summertime dirt surfaced shortcut from the summit of **Vail Pass** down Turkey Creek to **Red Cliff.**

To climb the mountain, take the trail from Half Moon Campground (see above) 2 miles to **Half Moon Pass,** 11,600′, and descend 2 miles on it 900′ to East Cross Creek. The trail crosses and continues to timberline on the simple north ridge route to the summit, 3 miles and 3300′.

A small party of climbers suffered their way up the cross itself in 1966. We understand their ascent was a success.

Notch Mountain, 13,734′, was placed there for people to look at the cross from. The viewing place, 650′ lower than the summit, is a climb of 2500′ and 4½ miles, all by gently graded and well-marked trail from the campground.

The **Notch Mountain Trail** takes off right from the longer trail, 9 miles, connecting Half Moon Campground with Hunky Dory Lake. About mile 4 the trail comes into Fall Creek and Lake Constantine; then it climbs 2½ miles to 12,600′ **Fall Creek Pass** and drops past some more lakes to Hunky Dory. From here a jeep road runs SE 3 miles down French Creek to the Homestake road. Another jeep road turns off this one a little below Hunky Dory and comes around a mile S to Holy Cross City. A branch of it goes NW ½ mile to Cleveland Lake; the main branch goes S and W a mile and continues W as a 3-mile trail W to Blodgett Lake, up against the Divide, where it connects with the trail NNE down Cross Creek (see above), and in the opposite direction with a trail in Frying Pan drainage that goes down to Savage Lakes—this by a low Divide pass, 11,850′, above Blodgett Lake.

Whitney Peak can be climbed from **Fall Creek Pass** on the above trail. By jeeping to Hunky Dory you would have 2½ miles of trail and a mile S on the ridge, and little over 2000′ of climb.

A mile E of Blodgett Lake on the **Hunky Dory Trail** is Treasurevault Lake. A trail turns S by way of the Missouri Lakes and E on Missouri Creek, total 4 miles, to meet the road up Missouri Creek.

Homestake Creek comes into the Eagle River 2 miles S of Redcliff exit and 20 miles N of Leadville. Homestake Reservoir, completed in 1969, supplies water for Colorado Springs and Aurora. The dam has more than doubled the length of Homestake Lake. Water is tunneled E under Homestake Peak ridge to the Arkansas Lake Fork, where it meets Frying Pan water from a similar tunnel through the Divide. Farther down the Arkansas the water is pumped up to a gravity pipeline into South Park.

A 9-mile road runs from US 24 up Homestake Creek to the dam. At the halfway point a 2½-mile trail cuts off to the W, climbing from 9000′ up the side hill to Whitney Lake at 11,000′. **Whitney Peak,** 13,272′, is a 1½-mile climb from Whitney Lake. Climb S out of the lake hollow and then up the E ridge and S slope.

At mile 6½ on the Homestake Creek road, a 2½-mile side road runs E up Missouri Creek to meet the road down Fancy Creek and the trail down Missouri Creek. From just short of the Homestake dam a 2½-mile trail climbs S up the East Fork of Homestake Creek to Lonesome Lake, rising from 10,000′ to 11,650′ in the 6 miles. The lower half is U.S.F.S. maintained. From 11,250′, near timberline on this trail, it is a 2-mile climb E to the summit of **Galena Mountain.** The first objective is the saddle on the Divide, 11,750′, to which you angle in the down-canyon direction. This puts you on the SW slope of Galena. **Homestake Peak,** 3 miles up the Lost Lakes creek, is probably easier from the other side.

The view NW from Leadville takes in the Galena to Homestake ridge, a 12-13,000′ section of the Divide, 10 miles away. Behind it is the long Homestake Creek; on this side several roads and trails climb to the lakes between **Mount Massive** and **Tennessee Pass.**

From 1½ miles SW of the pass a road cuts W 2 miles to the saddle where Wertz Ditch crosses the Divide at 10,000′. A jeep road turns up-ridge and continues NW 2½ miles to Slide Lake, 11,750′.

Homestake Peak, 13,211′, is a mile W of Slide Lake. To climb it, work W from a little S of the lake and climb to the saddle and up the peak's NE ridge.

West Tennessee Creek has a good but bumpy road, rated 4-wheel, starting from .7 mile SW of **Tennessee Pass.** It is 5½ miles to the Homestake Mine, 11,727′, where you are ½ mile N of the West Tennessee Lakes and ½ mile S of a 13,050′ ridge point jutting E from the Divide. The road starts at gravel pits off the highway.

The **Main Range Trail** starts off from the above road a mile W of US 24. This trail follows the full length of the Sawatch Range on its E side, at altitudes usually around 9000′, somewhere near midway up the timbered belt. A few of the sections have connecting links of road instead of trail. One of the trail's purposes is fire protection. Sections of it make excellent horseback trips, and for the mountaineer it is often a useful lateral or connecting trail between parallel ridges and valleys. It is presently logged at around 100 miles from **Tennessee Pass** to Indian Creek, 25 miles N of Saguache.

There is a route up Longs Gulch from 4 miles S of Tennessee Pass, 6 miles N of Leadville, for which you must get passage permission from the Homestake Trout Club. The trout club takes you a mile in; the next 2 miles is jeep road. By this time you are on **Main Range Trail,** which climbs S out of Longs Gulch 3½ miles W of the jeep road end and passes various lakes on its 6-mile winding route to Lake Creek. There are two routes of access to the trail S of Longs Gulch. The main one is the Lake Creek road. It runs W from central Leadville to a fork a mile out of town and angles NW (right fork) to the N side of Turquoise Lake and W to the E portal of Homestake Tunnel, at 10,000′, 7 miles.

A trail continues up Lake Creek 2½ miles to Timberline Lake, a good-sized body of water at 10,900′. 12,000′ summits of the Divide rise on 3 sides.

The **Main Range Trail** climbs N from a mile E of the end of the Lake Creek road, 2 miles N and E to Galena Lake, 11,000′.

Galena Mountain, 12,850′, is a 2-mile climb N from the top of the trail's zigzags at timberline, ½ mile W of Galena Lake on the Main Range Trail, a total of 3½ miles and 2850′ from the road.

A good jeep road climbs to the **Main Range Trail** higher up (at 11,250′) a mile NE of Galena Lake. For this, turn right off the Lake Creek road 1 mile N of the crossing of the river and railroad. Turn N (right) after 2 more miles and go on another 2 miles generally NW. Here you can climb WNW into the bowl of St. Kevin Lake, 11,800′, or climb to and up the E ridge of Galena or drop a little to Galena Lake and climb the mountain from the S.

SAWATCH RANGE—LEADVILLE SECTION

QUADS: Mount Champion, Thimble Rock, Independence Pass, 15′ Mount Elbert and Taylor Park; San Isabel and White River N F's. Preliminary Taylor Park SE etc. available.

This grouping covers the range south from Hagerman Pass through Twin Lakes and the Lake Fork. Some of the cap is granite, Mount Massive for instance; a good deal including Mount Elbert is in schist and gneiss of the Idaho Springs formation, and the south part is intrusive volcanic rock, including rough Grizzly Peak.

The **Main Range Trail,** described briefly with the Holy Cross Section above, is in good shape and continuous from West Tennessee Creek to Twin Lakes Village. Between Twin Lakes and Clear Creek some relocation is in order because of private holdings.

NORTH AND WEST APPROACHES

The Frying Pan Arkansas project has re-opened **Hagerman Pass,** traversed for some years by railroad tunnel. You drive W from central Leadville out past Turquoise Lake and up the Midland grade.

Just short of the Busk Ivanhoe Tunnel, 10,750′, which is 12 miles W of Leadville, a good trail winds S up the mountainside 3 miles to Native Lake, 1000′ higher. Other lakes in the Rock Creek drainage N of **Mount Massive** can be reached on sketchier trails from here.

After the tunnel, the road continues a little farther on grade and then separates from it to take a steep short route over **Hagerman Pass.** Railroad buffs like to prowl the remains of the Midland between the Busk Ivanhoe or Carlton Tunnel and the higher Hagerman tunnel which went through at 11,550′. They can view the remains of a magnificent curved trestle which made altitude through a burn in the forest.

The road over 11,950′ **Hagerman Pass** is steep but on good bed—about 3 miles to the pass from the tunnel.

For the area W of the Divide see Ivanhoe Creek, Meredith, Thimble Rock, and Independence Pass Quads. There is access to the long S branches of the upper Frying Pan River and the ridges that separate them in even parallels—the **Williams Mountains** and others.

From the elbow 13 miles down the road from Ivanhoe Lake and 3 miles up the road from Chapman Campground, a 5-mile road cuts SE up the Frying Pan River as far as Marten Creek. A trail parallels the road on the opposite (SW) side of the river. Where Granite Creek comes in from the S, about 3 miles above the start at Chapman Lake resort, a trail runs up Granite Creek and climbs the right side to Granite Lakes. These are near the head of the valley, at 11,400′ and 11,600′. Either would be a good approach place for an exploration of the ridge. Climb from the lakes W to the ridge, and head N to the 13,003′ high point.

Marten Creek has a longer trail S. Starting at 10,000′, it runs 7 miles up canyon to the Divide, which it crosses at 12,700′. This is not a constructed trail—little more than a route in places. On the far side of the pass it joins a better trail from the main **Frying Pan Trail** and they go down as one to the Independence Pass road. Their terminus is at the elbow where State 82 leaves the North Fork of Lake Creek to start its climb.

The **Frying Pan River Trail** is constructed and maintained all the way to Frying Pan Lakes, 10 miles in all. From the road end at Marten Creek to the lakes is 5 miles and 1000′; from there to the Divide at 12,500′, it is 3 more miles and a 1500′ climb on a lower standard trail. The junction with the **Marten Creek Trail** is between the two passes on the S side of the Divide. The ridge separating these trails is 5 miles long and moderately rough. It is topped with 7 or 8 evenly spaced 13,000′ summit points.

At Norrie Guard Station, 1 mile SE of the Frying Pan North Fork exit, a road runs off from the highway and then turns SSE for Chapman Lake, where it divides. One leg goes S 3 miles up Chapman Gulch and continues as a trail to the head of the gulch. The first 3 miles of trail is good, the next 3 not maintained. At the valley end the trail climbs out E over a 12,200′ ridge and makes a 2½-mile descent to the **South Fork Trail** at 10,550′.

The left fork of this road goes E around Chapman Lake before turning S to parallel the above **Chapman Gulch Trail.** From Norrie it is about 10 miles long. It continues as trail 2 miles more to meet the above climb-out trail from Chapman Gulch. From here on it is higher standard trail. The next 3½ miles takes it up to **South Fork Pass,** 11,800′, and a 4-mile downhill run to Lost Man Campground at the W foot of **Independence Pass,** 10,500′.

The **Williams Mountain** ridge, 13,382′ at the high point, is best climbed from Lost Man Campground. Take the 5-mile trail up Lost Man Creek to **South Fork Pass** and pick a 2-mile route NW to the rough summit.

Hunter Creek and Midway Creek have trails that come up to the Williams ridge from the other (W) side. These involve long approaches and doubtless do well for people who like to be alone.

Geissler Mountain, 13,360′, is a short climb from the end of the shelf road off the W side of **Independence Pass.** Go up the creek from the bend, 11,500′, to the pass at 12,800′, 2 miles N, and then a half mile to the right.

EAST APPROACHES

Mount Massive, 14,421′, was named by the Hayden Survey as Henry Gannett reports, but although several attempts have been made to substitute such men's names as those of Gannett and Winston Churchill, for the superior descriptive designation, none has succeeded. It was long rated first in altitude in the state. To climb it, drive W from US 24 at Malta, 4 miles W of Leadville. At mile 1 junction, drive 1.2 miles S. Keep right at this junction and drive 1½ miles SW. The 6-mile **Mount Massive Trail,** E route of ascent, starts from the end of a spur road that leads .7 mile W from this point to South Willow Creek, 9700′. There are some camping places before you reach timberline. Cars can go higher as follows: continue SW along Half Moon Creek to Half Moon Campground, 10,064′, about 6 miles from Malta. Camp, or continue 3½ miles W up the Creek and camp at 10,300′. Leaving the car at 10,300′, continue 2 miles NW on the N fork of the creek and choose an ascent route N 2 miles to summit.

Mount Elbert, 14,431′, is the state's highest peak, but smooth enough to have been climbed all the way on skis. From Half Moon Campground (see Mount Massive above) drive ½ mile W on the road to **Main Range Trail,** 10,060′. Walk 2 miles S on it, crossing one ridge and climbing to a second, the NE ridge, which has a marked trail leading up. Follow the ridge 2½ miles to summit. A route that is shorter but has poorer footing starts 2 miles farther W, from ¼ mile W of S Half Moon Creek, at 10,285′. The road grows rough before you get there. On foot you cross Half Moon and climb S 1 mile on an old road to a crossing of South Half Moon. From here or farther up the creek pick a route up the slope on your left to Elbert's N ridge and summit, 2½ miles distant. The longer **Mount Elbert Trail** from Twin Lakes village, 8200′, climbs N to W up the E ridge.

French Peak, 13,922′, **Casco Peak,** 13,884′, and **Bull Hill,** 13,773′, can be reached from farther up the **South Half Moon Trail,** which climbs to a mine property at 12,500′. It is also possible to jeep up the main Half Moon Creek 3½ miles beyond the mouth of South Half Moon to the Champion Mill, 11,600′. It is 1¾ miles up by the old road (sometimes jeepable) S and W to the mine, 12,900′, and another 750′ climb N to the Champion summit. **Deer Mountain** is also accessible, either N along a roughish 2½ miles of ridge or directly NW from the mill and over a 13,445′ S ridge point.

The ridge between the Lake Fork and Clear Creek has a number of good peaks E of the 14'er La Plata. From the W end of Twin Lakes village, 9200′, a road goes S 1½ miles. Where it turns E, a trail continues S 1½ miles to a forking in Willis Gulch. The S fork climbs to the 12,500′ saddle between **Quail Mountain** and **Mount Hope** and drops on S to the Clear Creek road W of Vicksburg. 13,461′ **Quail Mountain** is a short ridge climb to the E from this saddle. 13,943′ **Mount Hope,** the handsomest peak seen from Twin Lakes, is a mile W. To climb it, contour SW from the saddle to the couloir just S of the E ridge. Each of these is a 5-mile climb from Twin Lakes.

The SW fork of the above trail climbs 4½ miles to 12,100′ in the main Willis Gulch. From Twin Peaks on the right side around to Hope on the left, there are several 13,000′ summits. The one at 13,780′ a mile up-ridge from the Twins has fine cross canyon views of La Plata to the W and Hope to the SE.

La Plata Peak, 14,340′, is one of the most satisfying peaks in the whole range. A major problem for climbers has been getting across the Lake Fork, swollen through most of the summer from Western Slope water. Drive up State 82 5.8 miles from the center of Twin Lakes village. A bridge, privately owned, but not closed, takes you across the creek at 9850′. Keep S to the flume, which you walk E .1-.2 mile to Crystal Lake Creek. Find the old trail which climbs S along the W side of the creek to Crystal Lake, 1 mile. Continue S 2 more miles in a rocky valley until the basin permits you to spiral clockwise

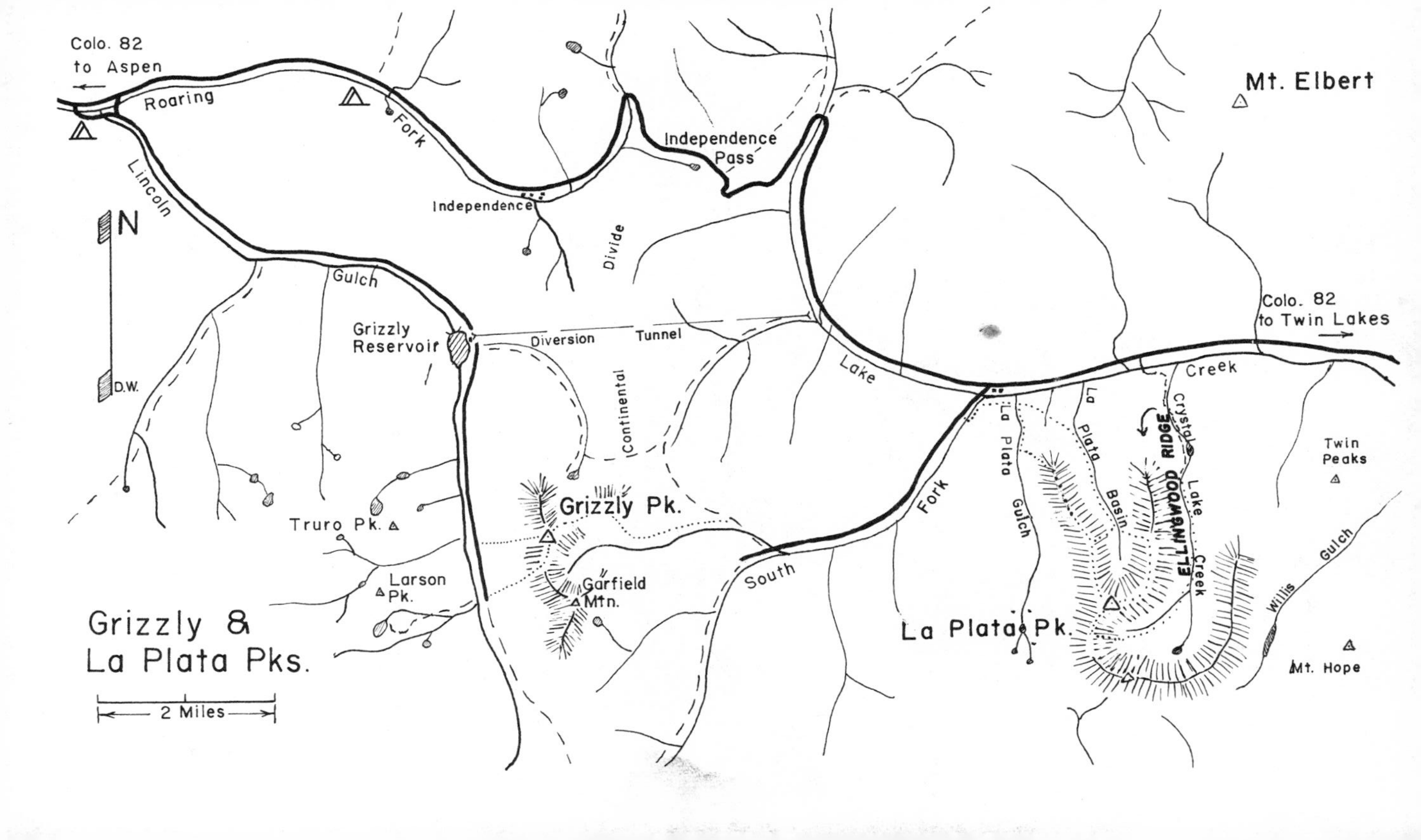
Colo. 82
to Aspen
Roaring
Fork
Lincoln
Gulch
N
D.W.
Independence
Independence
Pass
Divide
Mt. Elbert
Colo. 82
to Twin Lakes
Grizzly
Reservoir
Diversion
Tunnel
Continental
Lake
Creek
Grizzly Pk.
Truro Pk.
Larson
Pk.
Garfield
Mtn.
South
Fork
La Plata
Gulch
La
Plata
Basin
Crystal
Lake
Creek
ELLINGWOOD RIDGE
Twin
Peaks
Willis
Gulch
Mt. Hope
La Plata Pk.
Grizzly &
La Plata Pks.
2 Miles

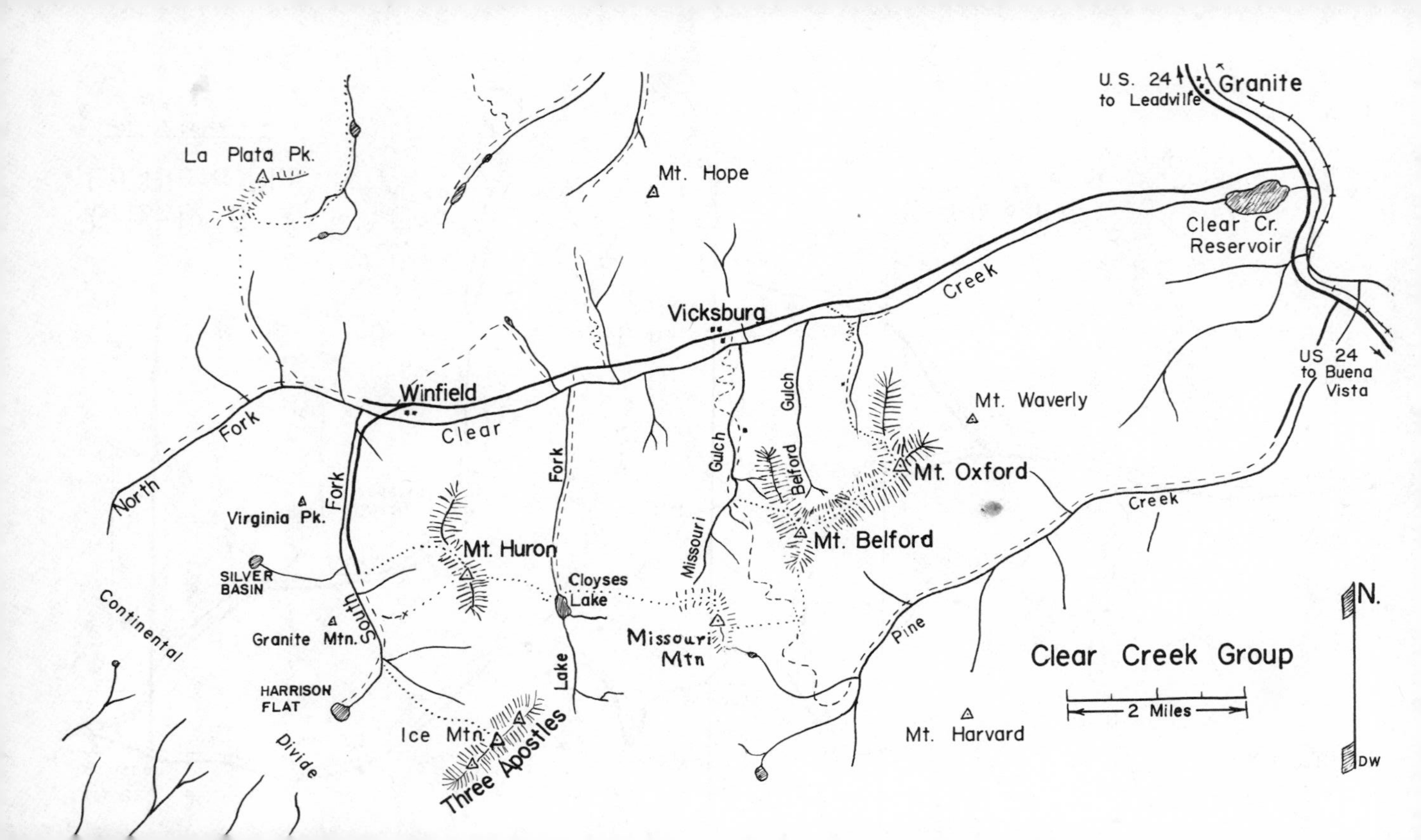

U.S. 24 to Leadville
Granite
La Plata Pk.
Mt. Hope
Clear Cr. Reservoir
Creek
Vicksburg
US 24 to Buena Vista
Winfield
Mt. Waverly
North Fork
Clear
Fork
Gulch
Gulch
Belford
Mt. Oxford
Virginia Pk.
Fork
Creek
Mt. Huron
Missouri
Mt. Belford
SILVER BASIN
Cloyses Lake
Continental
Granite Mtn.
South
Missouri Mtn
Pine
Clear Creek Group
N.
HARRISON FLAT
Lake
2 Miles
Ice Mtn.
Three Apostles
Mt. Harvard
Divide
DW

to the finish on the flat S ridge of La Plata. Be prepared for steep snow.

The traditional route up La Plata is by the next basin to the W. You can walk to it 1½ miles up the S side of the river from this crossing. Best route on the low part is on a little rib of a ridge just W of La Plata Creek. Continue up the basin, 2 miles in all, and from the flat part climb up to the right hand ridge. Or if you want a touch of the Ellingwood Ridge, cut up left to it and come down one of the other ways. I was one of three with Ellingingwood the first time it was climbed. He left us and crossed the basin. We didn't see him again till he came in to our camp at Everett at 9 that evening. He said he had dangled from a finger ledge for a full two minutes. I believe him—he liked to get into a nasty position and then play cat and mouse with the problem. Phil Carr describes the ridge climb in *T & T*, January, 1960. It takes a lot of time, and you should have a rope along. You can reach the ridge by angling directly up slope from the stream crossing.

The South Fork road is quite passable and has some good camping spots and, late in the summer, a profusion of fringed gentians—if you go up Peakaboo Gulch (right at mile 5) you get a splash of the unbelievable color of **Ruby Red Mountain. Grizzly Peak,** earlier rated as a 14'er, was climbed the first years from this side. You walked up the South Fork and the **McNasser Gulch Trail** 5 miles to make the final climb to and along a N and E ridge. South Fork turns left from 82 15 miles W of US 24.

Star Mountain, 12,941′, the centerpiece of the up-canyon view from down E on the Independence Pass road, is a rewarding 2500′ climb from 2 miles up the South Fork. There are other peaks, all quite approachable: 13,100′ **Middle Mountain,** which splits the valley, and 13,760′ **Garfield,** a mile S of Grizzly on the Divide.

The South Fork road beyond the Peekaboo Gulch exit can be jeeped for 3 miles S. It continues as a trail to the **Lake Pass,** which has lakelets on top at 12,230′, and then descends to Taylor River country.

Casco Peak is climbed from this side almost all the way by a trail N up Echo Creek Canyon, 13 miles W of US 24. Total altitude a little under 4000′, one-way mileage 4½.

Mount Champion, 13,646′, and **Deer Mountain,** 13,445′, are best climbed from the first bend in the Independence Pass road, 20 miles W of US 24, altitude 10,800′. For Champion you walk N ½ mile in the valley and then take to the ridge climbing NE on your right. For Deer you keep to the trail in the valley. When it climbs and divides on the hillside between the forks, keep right for the saddle and from that head ESE up the final ridge, another 1½ miles. A good long ridge trip could start with Deer Mountain and come S along the ridge over the 13,445′ point S of Deer and the 13,736′ point N of Champion, to Champion. Altitude gained, 4000′.

There is good range crest walking both N and S from **Independence Pass.** Going S, it is 3½ miles to a 13,198′ peak. Going N 2½ miles (left around the first hump) you climb to 13,711′, a very good lookout point for all the ridge country of the wide upper Frying Pan: Geissler and the rougher Williams Mountains beyond it to the NW, and two more long ridges E of them.

From 2 miles W of **Independence Pass,** where the hillside road becomes a valley road, and again at mile 6 where Lost Man Creek comes in, you are on the start of trails N into the Frying Pan ridge country which we have considered above with **Hagerman Pass.**

The turn-off to Lincoln Gulch is at mile 10 from Aspen, mile 11 from **Independence Pass.** A good road leads to the reservoir, 7 miles S, and some cars can continue S on a poor road 4 miles to Ruby, under the W side of **Ruby Red Mountain.**

From a mile short of Ruby, a trail climbs W 2 miles from 11,200′ to 12,300′ Petroleum Lake. **Larson Peak,** 12,908′, is close N, and the NW end of the Taylor River section of the Divide is to the W, with a string of 13,000′ ridge humps.

Midway between Grizzly Lake and Ruby a trail climbs W under the cliffs of **Truro Peak** to Truro Lake, 12,200′, and suggests a counterclockwise trip on to the summit of the peak, 13,282′.

There are ways to get up **Grizzly** from Grizzly Gulch, which has a trail starting E from midway along the reservoir, but we recommend driving 3 miles S from the dam. A climb ESE from 11,200′ takes you to the 13,500′ saddle immediately S of the peak.

SAWATCH RANGE—COLLEGIATE SECTION

QUADS: Mount Harvard, Buena Vista, Taylor Park, Mount Elbert, Garfield, all 15′; Ivanhoe Creek, Taylor Park NE, SE, etc. (in process); San Isabel and Gunnison N F's.

The group named for the Collegiate peaks in its midst includes the mountains between Clear and South Cottonwood Creeks, and west along the Roaring Fork–Taylor River Divide to Taylor Pass, where the Elks take over.

Most of the high parts of the mountains from north of Harvard to south of Yale are pre-cambrian gneiss and schist—wavy-textured precambrian rocks of the Idaho Springs formation. From Mount Princeton through Shavano the rock is intrusive volcanic of tertiary times. Although there are some rough places, the Sawatch Range does not generally have the grand cliffs one sees in the Front Range glaciated granite, and in the Elk Range, and San Juan areas.

CLEAR CREEK

The **Main Range Trail** is continuous between Clear Creek and Middle Cottonwood. The Clear Creek road leaves US 24 4 miles SE of the exit for State 82, 15 miles NW of Buena Vista, and runs W through Vicksburg at mile 8. It continues to Winfield, 4 miles farther, on a road somewhat rough but still passable by stock cars. There are attractive camping places at the small ghost town of Vicksburg, near the old mill 2 miles farther W, and beyond Winfield both S and W.

Huron Peak, 14,005′, on Harvard Quad, is 2½ miles S up a ridge from Winfield, the ridge includes **Cross Mountain,** 13,060′ **Middle Mountain,** and 13,523′ **Browns Peak.** You can usually drive a car 2 miles SSW from Winfield up the South Fork, where you are at 10,500′. About 4 miles from Winfield a trail climbs E from the road to a mine property a mile WNW of the Huron summit, to which you can climb on early tertiary intrusive matter now reduced to tiresome chiprock.

The Three Apostles, 13,920′ **Ice Mountain** and two flanking peaks of 13,863′ on the NE and 13,570′ on the W, are good scenery as you make this climb. They are at the head of the SSE branch of the South Fork, 2 miles S of the turnoff for Huron. For the climb of Ice Mountain, as I remember it, one continues S to and up the WNW ridge lifting Harry Standley's box of glass plates and a tripod consisting of three joined oak trees from shelf to shelf of a slippery grass slope. Eventually, however, one stands up for the summit push.

For people camping in the area there are other good climbs: **Winfield, Virginia** and **Granite** and several nameless 13'ers at the valley heads of both the North and the South Fork that overlook the milder Taylor River country. Trails climb up above 11,000′ on both sides of Granite Mountain, the wedge piece in the South Fork, and also along the North Fork.

La Plata Peak has an approach from this Clear Creek side. Bucolic-type cars can go 1 to 2 miles W from Winfield before settling quietly into wet earth. Continue on the N fork of the road to 3 miles W of Winfield. (Don't take a right at the cairn-marked road, which would take you up Black Bear Creek.) Continue to a point a little W of the W end of the road off **Mount Winfield,** visible across the valley. Your trail goes N up the E side of the stream for ½ mile, then crosses to the next valley W for the climb of 2½ miles up through timberline to the valley head and S ridge of La Plata, where you are 1½ miles from summit on easy grade.

Huron and Missouri have routes starting at mile 10 W of US 24, where there is a mill at 10,000′. A jeep road climbs along

Clear Creek's Lake Fork 4 miles to Cloheseys Lake, 10,900′. Here you are 1½ miles E of **Huron Peak,** and can climb to and up its E ridge, starting on a zigzag trail from the outlet of the lake. If you have time for some extra work take a saw. The trail is in bad need of clearing. For **Missouri Peak** you head NNE 2 miles up the ridge from the upper end of the lake and come to the crest ridge about ¾ mile NW of the summit for a pleasant level walk the rest of the way.

Mount Belford, 14,197′, and **Mount Oxford,** 14,153′, 1½ miles and a 650′ dip apart, are usually climbed together. From **Vicksburg,** 9650′, where you may camp, take a trail S across Clear Creek and 2 miles S up Missouri Gulch. Choose a route up Belford, 1½ miles SE, and return or continue ENE to Oxford. From Oxford descend to the Belford saddle and angle across its steep slope to Belford's S ridge for a return to Missouri Gulch. If the water is low you can go down Belford Gulch and ford Clear Creek to reach a road 1½ miles E of Vicksburg.

Missouri Mountain, 14,067′, is also climbed from Missouri Gulch. Stay on the trail from Vicksburg for 5½ miles to 13,250′ **Elkhead Pass** and climb W 1 mile keeping to the right side of the ridge. The pass is very steep at the end and may call for rope or ice axe. **Belford** is an easy climb along the ridge from Elkhead Pass.

A trail from ½ mile E of the Lake Fork mill, 9840′, climbs N along Sheep Creek to the 12,500′ saddle between Quail and Hope, 2 miles N of the Clear Creek road, and then drops to Twin Lakes. The two peaks, **Hope** to the left and **Quail** to the right, are short climbs from this saddle.

PINE CREEK TO COTTONWOOD CREEK

Pine Creek has fine possibilities as a mountain-climbing camp center. The road turns SW off US 24, 13 miles NW of **Buena Vista,** 4½ miles SE of **Granite,** and after 1½ miles continues another 2½ as a jeep trail to **Main Range Trail,** at 10,000′. 3 miles farther W and 800′ higher you meet the **South**

Pine Creek Trail, which climbs to the **Harvard** E ridge, 2½ miles SSE, crossing South Pine Creek en route. (See first route to Harvard below.) You have also a very direct route to Oxford and Belford. Leave the valley and climb along the creek coming in from the WNW off **Oxford,** keeping on its left side. Oxford is 1½ miles up the ridge, **Belford** is then 1½ miles W along it, with a drop of 350′, and if you spiral S and SW another mile to **Elkhead Pass,** you have a trail route back S to the valley and down it. **Missouri Mountain,** 13,881′ **Iowa Peak** and 13,904′ **Emerald Peak** provide a somewhat rougher ridge journey from the same pass. From the above **South Pine Creek Trail** junction continue SW on the **Pine Creek Trail** 3 miles, climb N 3 miles to **Elkhead Pass,** 13,200′, and climb SW to Missouri, 1 mile. Iowa and Emerald Peaks involve climbs of 250′ and 800′.

Mount Harvard, 14,420′, and **Mount Columbia,** 14,073′, are connected by a ridge and are often climbed together from any of several directions.

The first route: **The Harvard Trail,** marked on US 24 and starting about 7½ miles NW of Buena Vista, can be jeeped to a campground on Frenchman Creek. Stock car parties drive 5.6 miles from Buena Vista on 24, turn W, SW and S, and at .4 mile go straight W on **Jeep Trail No. 2236,** which will give 2 miles more driving to an old cabin at 8850′ where camping is good. Continue on foot or by jeep 2 miles W to **Main Range Trail,** 11,200′. Follow it to right around ridge and W to **Harvard Trail,** 1 mile. Harvard Creek (Frenchman on Harvard 15′ Quad), also good for camp at or above 10,600′, is on your right. The Harvard Trail and the **South Pine Creek Trail** take you to the Harvard E ridge, 2½ miles, which you follow 1½ miles W to the summit. For Columbia alone, continue up Harvard Creek on Harvard Trail 1 mile and then strike S another mile to summit. For Columbia after Harvard, retreat from Harvard 1 mile and cross the basin about 400′ under the rough ridge on the E side before climbing to Columbia from 12,800′.

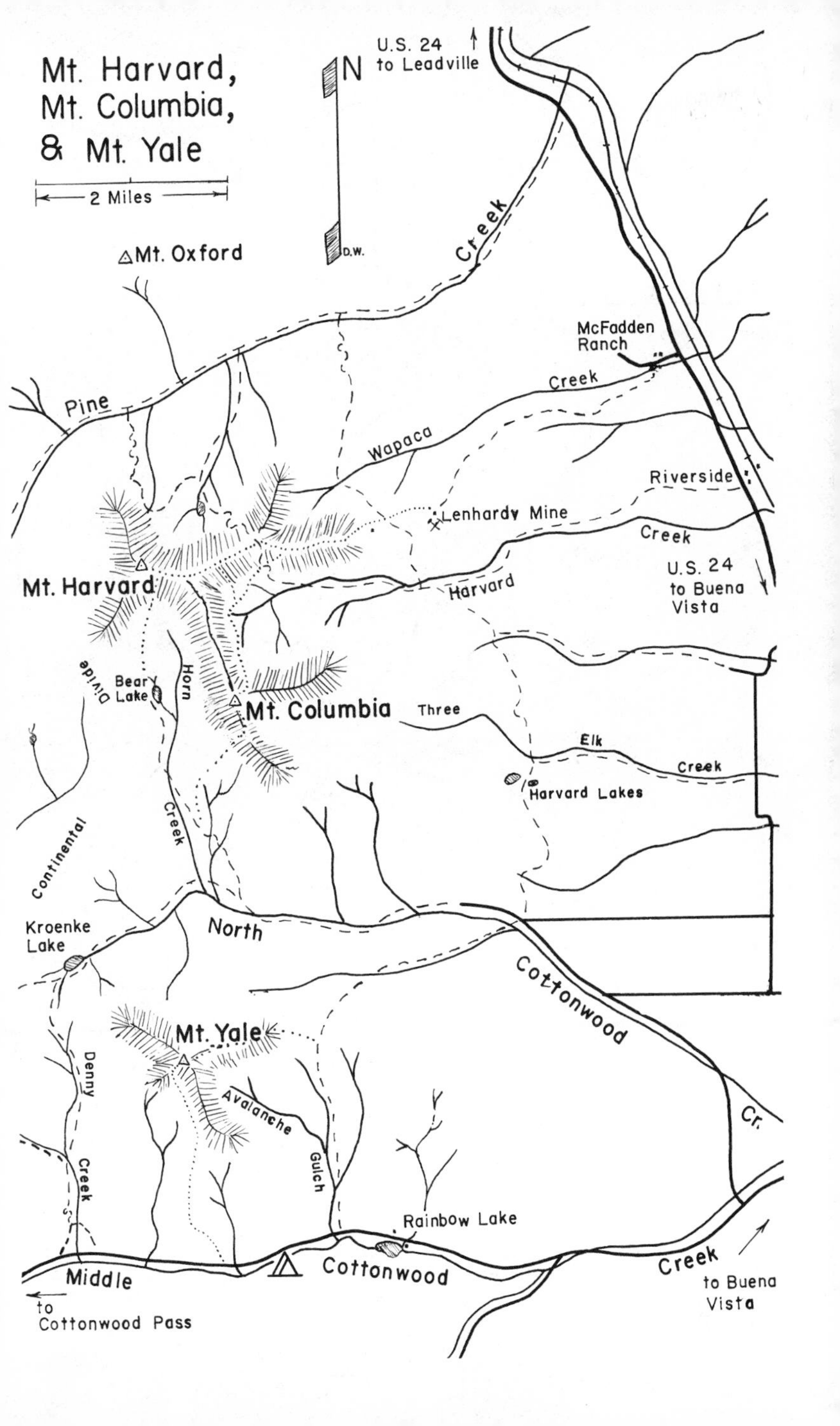
Mt. Harvard,
Mt. Columbia,
& Mt. Yale
2 Miles
N
D.W.
U.S. 24
to Leadville
Mt. Oxford
Creek
Pine
McFadden
Ranch
Creek
Wapaca
Riverside
Lenhardy Mine
Creek
Harvard
U.S. 24
to Buena
Vista
Mt. Harvard
Divide
Bear
Lake
Horn
Mt. Columbia
Three
Elk
Creek
Harvard Lakes
Creek
Continental
Kroenke
Lake
North
Cottonwood
Mt. Yale
Denny
Creek
Avalanche
Gulch
Cr.
Rainbow Lake
Middle
Cottonwood
Creek
to Buena
Vista
to
Cottonwood Pass

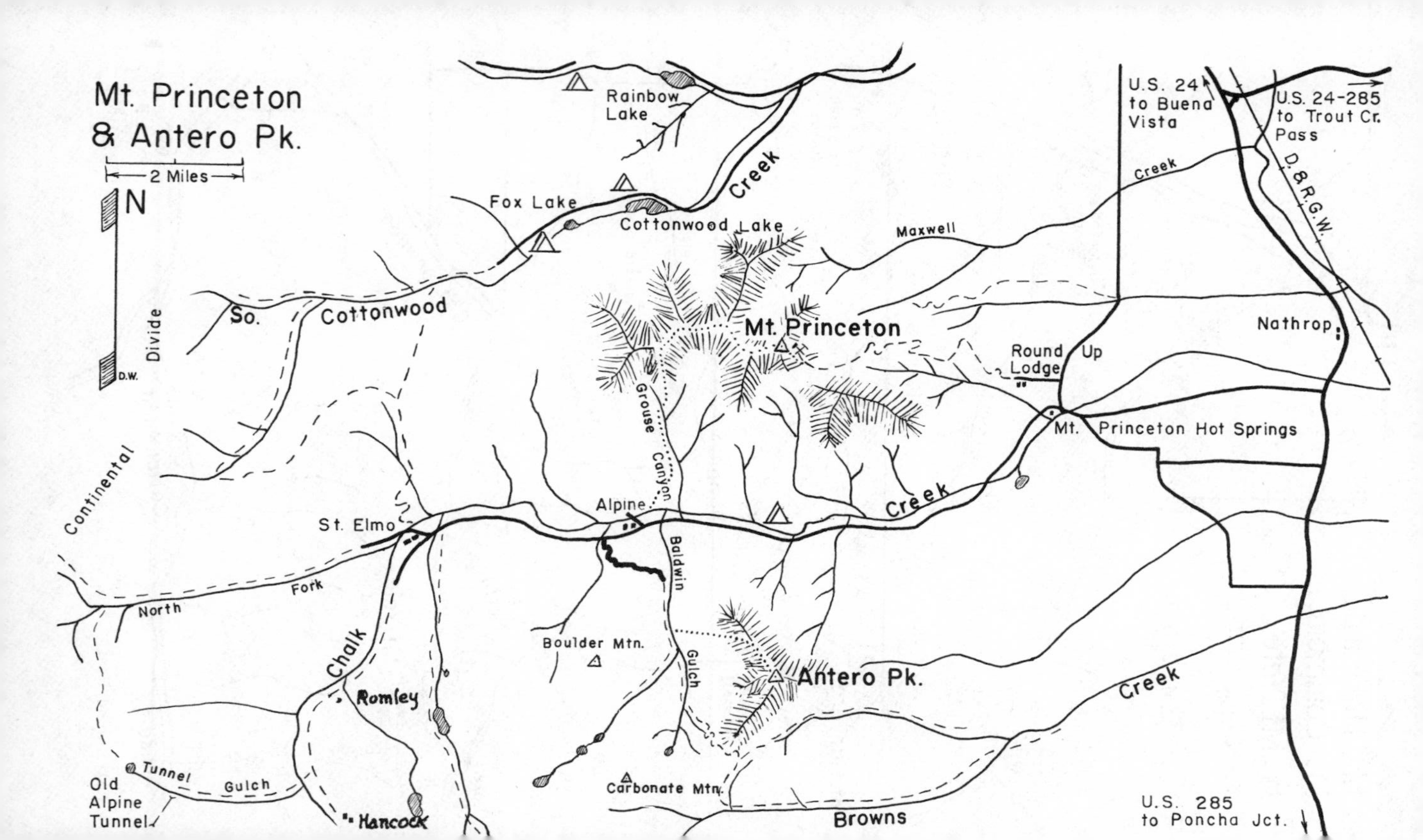
Mt. Princeton
& Antero Pk.
2 Miles
N
D.W.
Divide
Continental
Rainbow Lake
Creek
Fox Lake
Cottonwood Lake
So. Cottonwood
Maxwell
Creek
U.S. 24 to Buena Vista
U.S. 24-285 to Trout Cr. Pass
D. & R.G.W.
Nathrop
Mt. Princeton
Round Up Lodge
Mt. Princeton Hot Springs
Grouse Canyon
Alpine
St. Elmo
Creek
Baldwin
North Fork
Chalk
Boulder Mtn.
Gulch
Antero Pk.
Romley
Creek
Old Alpine Tunnel
Tunnel Gulch
Hancock
Carbonate Mtn.
Browns
U.S. 285 to Poncha Jct.

The traditional McFadden Ranch route to Mount Harvard is presently closed, but a road connects with it through the next ranch S of the McFadden, about 8 miles N of Buena Vista and 10 S of Granite. Drive W there past a trailer home where you ask permission, and pick up the ridge route for 4-wheel vehicles to the Lenhardi Mine, 4 miles from US 24, a traditional camp at 10,200′. Find a trail near the S side of the mine clearing leading up to a ridge and to **Main Range Trail,** ¼ mile. Continue W along the ridge 4 miles to the peak, skirting false summits. For Columbia alone, climb from the mine area to the trail as for Harvard but go left on it a mile. When it begins to lose altitude, contour SW into Harvard Creek. For the rest, see the first route above.

A satisfactory Harvard–Columbia route has been found from the S. Drive N .4 mile from Buena Vista traffic light, W 2 miles, N and NW 1 mile, S .2 mile and W 5 miles, to road end, where camp can be made at 9900′. Continue by foot on the opposite side of the creek 1½ miles and keep right at the junction; go 4 miles up Horn Fork to the Harvard summit. You can go to Columbia on the route described under First Route for both peaks, and then come S to N Cottonwood Creek 2 miles W of your car.

Mount Yale and 12,749′ **Birthday Peak** are also easily reached from this valley, especially if you camp farther up.

Harvard and Yale were named by J. D. Whitney, surveyor of California, when he brought Harvard's first Mining School graduates to Colorado in 1869. Gannett, one of his students who became a noted geologist, later named Princeton. Roger Toll named Columbia in 1916 when he was putting Colorado Mountain Club registers on the Sawatch peaks. Jerry Hart of Denver, Colorado Mountain Club member and a Rhodes scholar, named Oxford. Belford was named for an early Colorado politician, James B. Belford, whose nickname was "The Red Headed Rooster of the Rockies."

Mount Yale, 14,196′, has its most direct routes on the S side. The shortest one climbs directly from .2 mile W of 9600′

Collegiate Peaks Campground, 11 miles W of Buena Vista on State 11. Climb 1½ miles on a zigzag jeep road in Denny Gulch (not Denny Creek). Continue up the gulch ½ mile and scramble a steep slope to left (W) ridge and timber line, where you can go N a mile to a NW saddle at 13,500′ and SE ½ mile to summit. From the population centers on the plains, Yale makes the best 1 day or 1½ day peak climb in the Sawatch.

For an alternate route, climbers can drive 1½ miles W from the Collegiate Peaks Campground or 11 miles from Buena Vista, and jeep or walk the Hartenstein Lake road N for a mile or so and into the W fork of Denny Creek a little way before bushwhacking uphill NW back to Delaney Gulch and climbing the SW slope of Yale. The whole distance is 3½ miles.

The **Main Range Trail** crosses the E ridge of Yale 2 miles from the summit, at 11,900′. You can climb to it from Cottonwood Creek, 8½ miles W of Buena Vista, or from 7½ miles W of Buena Vista on the North Cottonwood road. See S approach to Harvard above. Both starting points are at about 9,350′ and 4 or 5 miles walking distance from the ridge. The ridge climb to the top is 2 miles, with a halfway level section for resting.

The Cottonwood Creek road has three branches. The access to North Cottonwood is given above with the S approach to **Mount Harvard,** above. The South Cottonwood road leaves the main or Middle Cottonwood road 7 miles from Buena Vista and goes 4 miles SW to Cottonwood Lake. One can continue W up the gulch 7 miles to Mineral Basin. On the right are **Gladstone Mountain,** 13,209′, and **Jones Mountain,** 13,221′, and on the Divide at the head of the valley 13,120′ **Mount Kreutzer.** On the S side is Ridge Twelve, the 12-mile ridge or range of 12,000′ and 13,000′ summits which connects **Princeton** with the Continental Divide. This ridge is crossed at altitude 12,310′ by a 6-mile trail from the South Cottonwood over to **St. Elmo,** on Chalk Creek. The trail starts at the mouth of Green Timber Creek, 4 miles W of Cottonwood Lake. It is not maintained but there is no problem finding it. You can also get up the ridge farther E on a trail that zigzags S from Fox

Lake, a mile W of Cottonwood Lake. The route is not maintained, and rated as poor.

The Middle Cottonwood car road climbs to **Cottonwood Pass** 17 miles W from Buena Vista and descends to the Taylor River, 9 miles. The summits near the pass are mild ones, but there is a good northward prospect of the **Apostles** ridge.

From the N end of Taylor Reservoir you drive E by jeep or pick-up 7 miles along Texas Creek, where you are at 10,000′. A 7-mile jeep trail continuing E puts you by a timberline lake, 11,600′, a mile N of **Birthday Peak.** From a mile N up the basin you can climb 1 mile NE to the S ridge of **Harvard.** By skirting right of the 13,562′ S point you can go 1½ miles to the summit with little loss of altitude.

Other Divide points can be reached from Texas Creek, notably the **Apostles,** for which you climb N from ½ mile beyond the Texas Creek road end. A trail climbs N 4 miles up Waterloo Creek to a lakelet under **Ice Mountain's** E cliffs.

The Pieplant road leaves the Taylor River road 3½ miles N of the Cottonwood Pass road end, and climbs to 10,800′ on the S slopes of 13,428′ **Jenkins Mountain,** perhaps the most conspicuous of the Taylor River row of summits. The climb, 2 miles in all, goes up the valley a little way and then left and up the steep S ridge to finish on the gentle W ridge.

The **Timberline Trail** skirts the Taylor River chain from 7 miles up Texas Creek NW 16 miles to the Pieplant road, climbing to 11,500′ between 10,000′ termini.

Mount Kreutzer, 13,120′, is an interest point near the spot where Ridge Twelve, running W from **Mount Princeton,** meets the Continental Divide. Kreutzer was the first national forest ranger. The best route to his peak is from Tincup, a little town on the Taylor River side of the Divide. Drive there from Taylor Reservoir or over **Cumberland Pass** from Pitkin. Drive W from Tincup 3 miles, a little short of Mirror Lake, and climb the 2000′ slope NE 1½ miles.

SAWATCH RANGE—CHALK CREEK SHAVANO SECTION

QUADS: Mount Harvard, Buena Vista, Poncha Springs, Garfield, Bonanza, all 15′; Pahlone Peak; San Isabel and Gunnison N F's. This group covers the range from Chalk Creek S to the Cochetopa Hills.

Chalk Creek, between Mounts Princeton and Antero, has a long road and a considerable history. A detailed guide by Helen Stiles was published by the Colorado Mountain Club in its August, 1969 *T & T* and is also available separately, under the title *Sawatch Range—Chalk Creek Area.*

The Chalk Creek road, State 162, goes W from US 285 at Nathrop, 8 miles S of Buena Vista, 16 miles N of US 50. It climbs 16 miles to St. Elmo, most of the way on the grade of the Denver South Park and Pacific Railroad. From there it continues right on a steepening road to **Tincup Pass,** 12,121′ on the Divide, and drops on rough jeep road to Mirror Lake and on better road to Tincup, about 7 miles off the top. This road, continuing via **Taylor Pass,** was the stage route to Aspen.

The pass has fine views and suggests a climb 1½ miles SW over to 13,124′ **Fitzpatrick Peak.**

Emma Burr Mountain, 13,544′, can be climbed from here. The route, E to the 13,190′ ridge point and then N, is about 3 miles, with 400′ altitude loss to be regained. See Garfield Quad.

A left fork from just E of St. Elmo turns S and follows the railroad grade to Hancock, 5½ miles. En route is Romley, station for the Mary Murphy Mine. At Hancock, the railroad grade turns NW and W for a 3½-mile walk—flowers between the ties—to the Alpine Tunnel through the Divide, built in 1882 as the first tunnel through the Divide, and abandoned in 1910. A climb of 350′ to the pass on the ridge shows you the railroad meadow on the other side. Jeeps climb to **Williams Pass,** starting W from Hancock, and turning left up valley after ¼ mile, at the pond on the railroad grade.

Mount Chapman, 12,184′, and the S summit of **Van Wirt,** 13,081′, are short climbs NW and SE from 12,100′ **Hancock Pass.** Start S from Hancock and take the first right turn. This road, possible for jeeps, goes W around the ridge end and S to the pass, 2½ miles. It drops into Brittle Silver Basin in Quartz Creek drainage. The old road S from Hancock climbs over 12,070′ **Chalk Creek Pass** and drops down the Middle Fork to Garfield, 9 miles total. Jeeps make the first 2 miles to Hancock Lake. The road, continuing to Maysville, was Col. Altman's toll route.

Sewanee Peak, 13,259′, the imposing cliffed one up valley from Hancock, is a climb from Chalk Creek Pass of 1¼ miles, E from the pass and then NW up-ridge. On the opposite side of the pass is a 13,257′ point midway between 13,056′ **Van Wirt,** to the right, and 13,375′ **Monumental,** to the left. The climbs all involve short distances.

Mount Princeton, 14,197′ is climbed from Alpine, 9250′, 11 miles W of 285. Cross Chalk Creek and walk ¼ mile N up Weldon Gulch. An inconspicuous road goes off right through aspen and climbs to Grouse Creek, 1½ miles E. Continue 1 mile up Grouse Creek and take the right branch 1½ miles NE to the saddle. Follow the ridge SE and E 1 mile over false top to summit.

Princeton is also climbed from the E. Park the car near Young Life's Frontier Camp, which is on a terrace at 8800′. Inquire about access to the road at wrangler's cabin—it may be open to four-wheel-drive vehicles as far as the chalet at timberline. Pick up the road and walk or drive it to just above the last trees on the left at timberline. Switch to trail which leaves the road on the right side. Follow the trail over an intervening ridge and traverse across the bowl in a northerly direction to trail's end at an old mine building. Climb to saddle above the building and follow the ridge N to top.

The road was built in the 1870's for wagons bringing ore from the Hortense (or Lucky) Mine, and is jeepable to timberline and beyond. The first recorded ascent of Mount Princeton was by William Libbey, Jr., on July 17, 1877. His diary records that he encountered no difficulty until within 1500 feet of the top, "when his only way lay over a bed of debris . . . the size of the boulders being such that nothing but the hardest sort of crawling would answer." The hot springs in Chalk Creek Gulch have been used since Indian times, and Father Dyer, the Methodist minister known as the "Snowshoe Itinerant" in the 1860's, enjoyed the hot water after climbing the Chalk Cliffs. Various hotels were built near the springs; the largest, a wonder of Victorian gingerbread, decorated the scene until 1950 when it was pulled down and its fine hardwood shipped to Abilene, Texas.

The white "chalk cliffs" of Mount Princeton are a rough, hard but crumbly rock called quartz monzonite. The crumbly decomposition of this low altitude rock illustrates chemical decay possible in warm temperatures only.

Mount Antero, 14,269′, is a crystal hunter's mountain and has yielded aquamarines and other crystals. The mountain was named for a Ute chief. Lieut. Pike ate Christmas dinner near the base of Mount Antero in 1806. From 8 miles S of Buena Vista on US 285 and 10 miles W up Chalk Creek on State 162, take a road left a little beyond New Alpine (sign "Calupella"). This road has been jeeped to the summit of the mountain, but cars have recently been stopped after ½ mile and jeeps 3 miles up, at 10,533′ Baldwin Creek crossing, from which a good route climbs SSE 2½ miles to the N ridge and summit.

Boulder Mountain, 13,524′, and **Mamma Mountain,** 13,543′, form a horseshoe around Deer Creek. The horseshoe ridge lies between Grizzly Creek, which flows from the S into St. Elmo, and Baldwin Creek, S of Alpine. The route to Boulder Mountain and Baldwin Lakes starts as for Antero but you turn right at the first opportunity, perhaps 2 miles. Double back and forth (with care if you're jeeping) through the timber on Boulder Mountain on a very narrow track. After 2 more miles you'll emerge into a high park, perhaps the site of a homestead or mining claim. (The second right also comes out

Mount Antero from across the Arkansas valley. *H. L. Standley photo.*

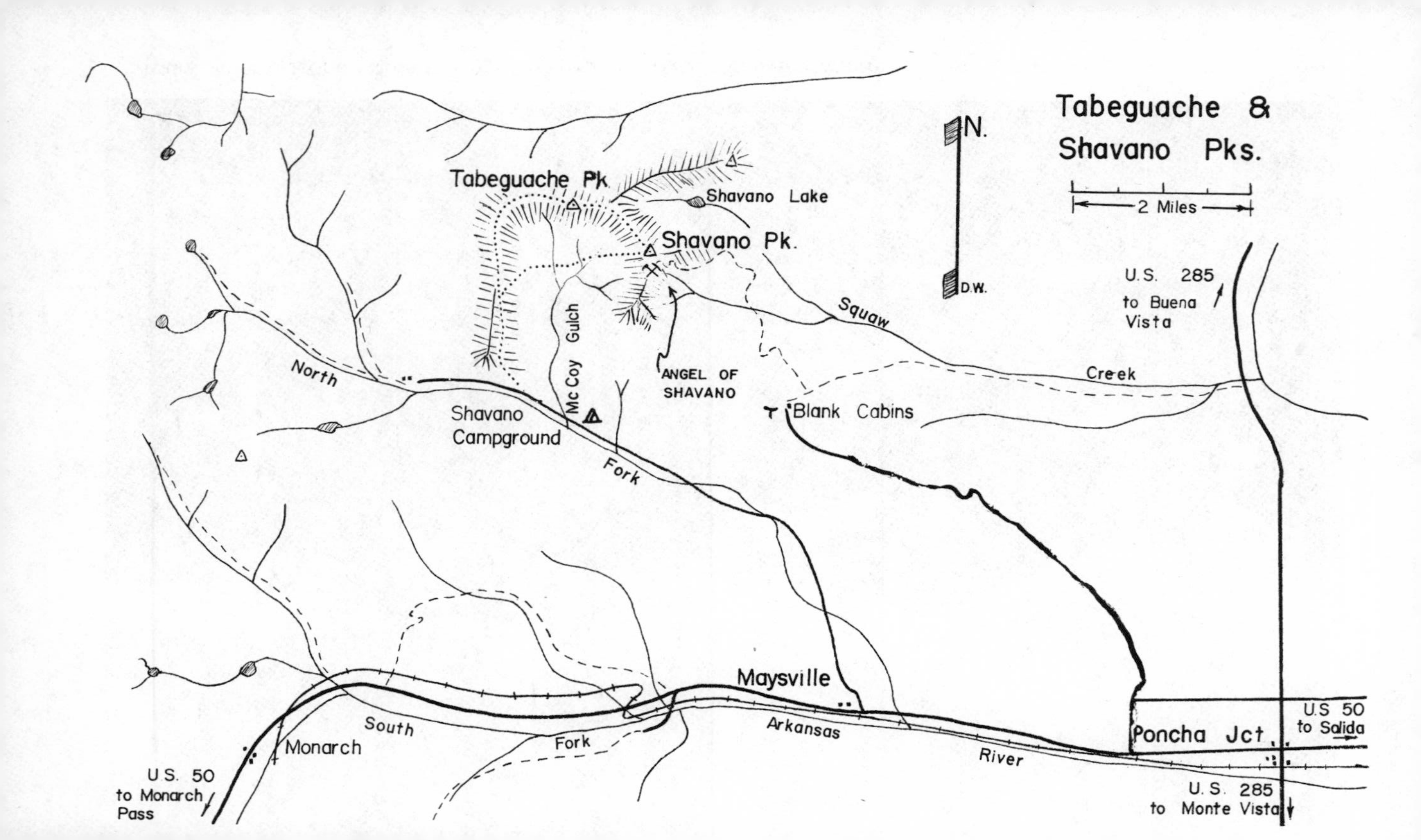
Tabeguache &
Shavano Pks.
N.
D.W.
2 Miles
Tabeguache Pk.
Shavano Lake
Shavano Pk.
U.S. 285
to Buena
Vista
Squaw
Creek
North
ANGEL OF
SHAVANO
Mc Coy Gulch
Shavano
Campground
Blank Cabins
Fork
Maysville
South
Arkansas
Fork
River
Monarch
Poncha Jct.
U.S 50
to Salida
U.S. 50
to Monarch
Pass
U.S. 285
to Monte Vista

at the same place but it's steeper.) At the end of the road, a mile or so on, were located the Merrimac and Tilden mines. The Tilden was the earliest in the vicinity and a big silver producer for a time. The town of Alpine, across Chalk Creek from Boulder Mountain, prospered and declined quickly in response to the fortunes of this mine, although the establishment of St. Elmo farther up-creek hastened its demise.

"A long mile of scree climbing on foot brings you to the top of Boulder Mountain. Here you realize the full extent of the great, precipitous gorge you've been climbing out of—the basin of Baldwin Lakes, backdropped by that unnamed 'thirteen' to the south, and across to the north the white ridges of Princeton."

The above is quoted from Helen Stiles' *Chalk Creek Guide.* We are indebted to this source and to Louisa Arps for information on this area, and to Stiles' *Shavano and South Arkansas Guide* for material below.

Browns Creek Trail gives an approach to the seldom climbed mountains between **Antero** and **Shavano.** From 3½ miles south of Nathrop a road goes straight W 1½ miles. From this junction a jeep road turns S, then W, and after ½ mile splits. Take the left fork 2½ miles to a T road. Turn S and in ¼ mile Browns Creek Trail starts W. It climbs 5 miles to a little lake at 11,300′, where you can camp and try for a fish.

Mount White, 13,600′, is 1½ miles N. Walk ¼ mile beyond the lake and go up the right side of the gully. **Tabeguache** has a good 2-mile climb from the upper end of the marsh, ¾ mile W of the lakelet. Cross the creek there and head SSW up the prominent ridge. **Jones Peak,** which is only an E ridge end off the Shavano-Tabeguache saddle, presents a very broad and rough N face.

US 50 climbs from Salida along the South Arkansas River to its headwaters at **Monarch Pass,** 23 miles, or 18 miles W of US 285. At mile 6 W of 285, the North Fork comes in from a 12-mile valley to the NW, surrounded by high peaks. Cars can reach Lost Lake, 10½ miles from highway.

Shavano Peak, 14,229′, and **Tabeguache Peak,** 14,155′, are separated by a mile of easy walking with a 250′ drop between, and are climbed together. Take the above North Fork road at Maysville (group of cabins at bridge crossing on US 50) and drive to Shavano Campground, at 6.3 miles, and 1.7 miles beyond to Jennings Creek, at 10,500′. Start N up-creek and then angle NE, taking burn route to SSE ridge of Tabeguache, which you follow 1½ miles to summit. Cross to Shavano and for descent return to the saddle and contour into the W fork of McCoy Creek, flowing off Tabeguache. Cross, and regain the ascent ridge above timberline.

A trail leads up the E side of Shavano from the Blank's Cabin site, 9900′, for which you turn off right from Highway 50 on County 15, 1.6 miles W of US 285. As the approach is uncertain and unreliable you should inquire about it at the Salida Ranger Station. The snow angel on this side of the peak is usually in best shape around July 4. Shavano was named for the war chief of the Tabeguache band of Ute Indians of which Ouray was the head chief. The band became known as the Uncompahgre Band when it was moved in 1875 to the Uncompahgre Valley near Montrose, but Mount Tabeguache commemorates the earlier name.

The ghost town of Shavano, at 10,130′, mile 8½ from the highway in the North Fork, was active in 1880–83. An old road now usable as a trail only, turns off right from here and climbs up Cyclone Creek to 12,050′ **Calico Pass,** and then goes N down the 6-mile Grizzly Gulch into St. Elmo, on Chalk Creek.

Calico Mountain, 12,944′, can be climbed from a little short of the pass, where you cut left to its N ridge and summit, 1 mile S.

13,723′ **Grizzly Mountain** is a mile's climb directly NNE up-ridge from **Calico Pass. Cyclone Mountain,** 13,600′, and **Carbonate Mountain,** 12,944′, on the NE side of Cyclone Creek, can be climbed from a start ½ mile up Cyclone Creek, where you turn right and keep to the ridge, or from Jennings Creek, the starting point for Tabeguache. You keep S to the Tabeguache saddle and then turn left up-ridge. Carbonate comes first, Cyclone second, and the full ridge tour around to Grizzly a more ambitious third.

Mount Aetna and **Taylor Mountain** can be climbed from Shavano by way of Hunky Dory Gulch. An intermittent trail takes you W up the gulch and you continue to the N saddle of Aetna for a finish on the ridge. It is a climb of 3000′ in 2½ miles, and Taylor, 1½ miles E on the ridge, involves another 650′. Descend to Taylor's ENE saddle and bushwhack N. (See preferred route below.)

From near Lost Lake, 11,400′, an old road climbed 2 miles NNW past Billings Lake and the Pride of the West Mine to a 12,800′ pass, and dropped 4½ miles down Pomeroy Gulch, area of the Murphy Mine, to Romley. To Billings Lake, the first mile, it can be jeeped. **Sewanee Peak** to the SW, **Pomeroy Mountain,** WNW above the Pride of the West Mine, and **Calico Mountain** to the E are short climbs within a mile or so of the lake. Some of the little herd of mountain goats transplanted from Montana have been seen in this area, others on the S side of Taylor Mountain, and still others far to the north on the Harvard massif. The rangers, who are their foster parents, earnestly request that you report location of any you see.

From 2 miles W of Maysville, 8 miles W of 285, a road starts N up Lost Creek 1 mile and turns off NNW to follow Cree Creek 4 miles to a mine under 12,707′ **Missouri Hill.** The road can be jeeped most of the way, to about 11,000′.

A car road zigzags 3½ miles N up Lily Gulch from the E end of Garfield, 12 miles W of US 285.

Taylor Mountain, 13,657′, and **Mount Aetna,** 13,771′, can be climbed from the Lily Mine, 11,250′. Climb E to the ridge and along it N, NW and N to the top of Taylor, 2 miles, and W via a 750′ ridge-dip to Aetna. Aetna, which presents its long rock slide and squared-off top to the viewer on **Monarch Pass,** can be climbed directly from the valley, on either side of the slide. As on Mount Princeton, the whiteness here is due to quartz monzonite.

From the W end of Garfield the Middle Fork road climbs off NW on the old stage route to **Chalk Creek Pass** and St. Elmo. From Garfield, 9500′, to the pass, 12,070′, it is 6 miles, the first 4 or more drivable by sturdy car or jeep. Starting here at 11,100′ you can walk 1½ miles up-stream, turn right and climb in a mile to the 12,850′ N saddle of **Aetna,** and finish going S on the ridge, another mile.

Monumental Peak, 13,375′, is a steep mile W from about the same 5-mile point in the valley, a little past two lakelets. It can be combined with **Vulcan** and **Clover Mountains,** 12,987′ and 12,935′ ridge points to the S on a 3-mile Continental Divide walk before you return to the valley. If you want to fish more and climb less, take the **Boss Lake Trail** S from 1½ miles out of Garfield on the Middle Fork road, and turn W to Hunt Lake, altogether a 2½-mile climb to 11,500′. You are ½ mile N of **Banana Mountain,** the E ridge of 12,851′ **Bald Mountain,** and you are 1 mile SSE of Clover. The bananas raised here are becoming a major Colorado crop.

Monarch Campground is 2½ miles up-pass from Garfield on 50. Opposite the entrance is the trail to Grass Lake, 1½ miles WNW, where the trail splits W and NE for Waterdog Lake and Pup Lake. Here you are S of the Banana-Bald ridge and can climb the two as an appetizer.

From the **Monarch Pass** crest a section of the **Main Range Trail** not now maintained runs along the W side of the Divide past **Peck, Pahlone, Ouray** and **Antora** to meet the **Indian Creek Trail** N of Saguache. It provides access to the southern Sawatch peaks.

WEST SIDE

A road from the W terminus of **Monarch Pass,** 1 mile N of Sargents, will take you 9 miles N to White Pine, terminus of the original Monarch Pass road, good up till 1921, and 2 more miles beyond to 10,300′. An old road on your right winds up the gulch to a mine at 11,950′ under **Clover Mountain.** You can climb the last 700′ by angling right to the ridge, then up left. Total distance 4 miles; it is another mile and a shorter descent if you go N to **Vulcan Mountain** on the ridge.

Walking up the valley from 10,300′ about 1½ miles, you will be in the basin between **Monumental Peak** a mile E on the Divide and lesser summits to the W. **Granite Mountain,** 12,598′, is 1½ miles W by way of a steep mountainside ridge and a level crest ridge.

The Quartz Creek road from Parlin, 20 miles W of Sargents on US 50, opens access to a farther N part of the western side of the Sawatch and to some westward extensions of them. See Pitkin and Garfield 15′ Quads. Ohio City is 9 miles ENE up this road; Pitkin is 15 miles.

SOUTHWEST AREA

Where the Quartz Creek road divides 2 miles W of Pitkin, you can drive the Middle Quartz Creek road E to the campground at 10,200′, and if you wish, continue around N on the Denver South Park and Pacific grade to Alpine Tunnel, 11,650′, another 5 miles by car. From the bend, 2¼ miles up this road from the campground, you can walk E up an old road to Brittle Silver Basin, 1 mile. Here **Tomichi Pass** and the mountains around it are to the S, **Van Wirt Mountain** on the Divide is SE, and **Hancock Pass** and **Chapman Mountain** are N, all within the radius of a mile or two.

SAWATCH RANGE—FOSSIL GROUP

QUAD: 15′ Pitkin; Gunnison N F.

A long, irregular spur projects W about 12 miles from the Divide N of Quartz Creek to end in Fossil Ridge. Long Trails come in from the W and the N, but the easiest routes of access are from the S. From Parlin, 8 miles E of Gunnison on US 50, the Quartz Creek road runs NE 9 miles to Ohio City, 6 more to Pitkin, and 12 more N to **Cumberland Pass,** where it descends to the Taylor River. At Cumberland Pass, 12,000′, you are 2 miles W of Fitzpatrick Peak and the head of Chalk Creek's North Fork, crossing the Fossil Group Spur.

Fairview Mountain, 13,213′, is 3½ miles W along the ridge from the Cumberland road. A 10-mile jeep road, starting at the upper end of Pitkin, runs all the way N to the summit. On the way, about 11,250′, you pass the Fairview Mine.

A road runs N 7 miles from Ohio City to a strategic campground on Gold Creek at 10,200′. A 3-mile trail takes you N past Lamphier Lake to a 12,250′ saddle en route to South Lottis Creek and the Taylor River Road. **Bronco Mountain,** 12,845′, is ½ mile from the saddle going ENE, and **Squaretop,** 13,012′, is a mile in the opposite direction.

Henry Mountain, 13,286′, is a short mile NW of Squaretop, with a 250′ drop. **Fossil Mountain,** 12,760′, is a mile S from Squaretop, and you can drop E off it to Mill Lake and the Mill Creek trail back to the campground on Gold Creek.

Fossil Ridge, which gets its name from the Pennsylvanian, Mississippian and Devonian rock to be seen there, extends 7 miles WSW from **Fossil Mountain.** The western portion is most accessible from the **Willow Creek Jeep Trail,** which runs N from the Ohio Creek road a mile W of Ohio City. It can be jeeped for about the first 7 of the 8 miles N to the **Fossil Ridge Trail.** From 11,250′ you have a steep one-mile climb up the end of Alder Creek to timberline and the trail, which is on the edge of the ridge itself. The E end can be reached by the descent route given for Fossil Mountain above. For the W end drive N from Gunnison 1½ miles on 135. Leave the highway where starts a 2-mile tangent (straight road section) north. Drive NW and generally W, keeping always to the best road available. If you make the 16 miles to the Fossil Ridge Trail head at 10,500′, you can follow the trail E 2 miles and then cut NE for a rather steep climb of 2000′ altitude and 2 miles to the 12,140′ E end of the ridge. Inquire also about the Dry Gulch jeep road, which, if it goes, will take you in a little farther.

SOUTH END

There are some short roads toward the range crest from the S side of US 50 between US 285 and Garfield. These trails suggest longer ascents of the range crest peaks.

Little Cochetopa Creek, at mile 2 W of 285 will go 4 miles by car and then about 8 more by a trail that climbs all the way to the range crest between Chipeta and Ouray, or from 8700′ to 12,400′.

Greens Creek at mile 4 from 285 goes a mile by car and 2 more by jeep. There are some mine roads on both sides, but the mainliner is a pack trail to the range crest between **Pahlone Peak** and **Chipeta,** about 7 miles walk and 3500′ of climb.

Fooses Creek, at mile 9, 1½ miles W of a hydro plant, goes 3½ miles by jeep to the creek and trail junction at 9600′. The **South Fooses Creek Trail,** left branch, climbs 6 miles to the **Main Range Trail** about 2000′ higher, just off the NW side of **Pahlone Peak.** This was built as a pack trail and though not presently maintained it should be satisfactory for pedestrians.

If you follow the **North Fooses Creek** road it runs into a trail after another mile and continues 4 miles to the range crest and **Main Range Trail** which it meets just N of **Mount Peck.**

Pahlone Peak, 12,667′, is the midpoint between **Monarch Pass** and **Marshall Pass,** 5 miles from either one on the **Main Range Trail,** which runs SW from Monarch Pass along the W side of the range crest. A two-car two-way expedition could meet there for lunch. The peak can be climbed from the **South Fooses Creek Trail.** You would cut sharp left from it at mile 5, a mile short of the range crest, and sidehill 2 miles NE to the summit. You could also climb to it from the **Greens Creek Trail** on the E side, leaving the trail at mile 5 from the jeep road end, about 10,400′. (See trails above.)

Mount Ouray, 13,971′, on Pahlone Peak and 15′ Bonanza Quads, is a pleasant short climb from **Marshall Pass.** Drive S on US 285 5 miles from its junction with US 50. Keep SW (right) up Poncha Creek 3 miles for junction to O'Haver Lake and follow D & RG grade 15 miles or steep shortcut up Poncha Creek to the pass, 10,846′. The mountain looms up 3 miles NE. **Chipeta Mountain,** 12,853′, is an easy 2-mile walk N along the Divide from the end of Ouray's crest ridge, 1½ miles W of Ouray summit. You climb 500′ extra, which is all in a short day's work.

Antora Peak, 13,266′, is the end point of the Sawatch Range and a good lookout point for the Sangre de Cristo peaks and the Cochetopa-La Garita high country. The crest trail S from **Monarch Pass,** once considered part of the **Main Range Trail,** can sometimes be jeeped for 2 miles or so S from **Marshall Pass.** Otherwise it is a 6-mile walk to where you leave it, at timberline on Antora's N ridge. The route is almost level up to this last 1½ miles, where you climb 850′. If this name Antora is a misspelling of Antero we prefer to preserve the difference. Marshall Sprague suggests a Spanish origin.

RED TABLE MOUNTAIN

QUADS: Toner Reservoir, Red Creek, Mount Thomas; and for approach, Glenwood Springs, Carbondale, Cattle Creek, Cottonwood Pass, Leon; White River NF.

This section is entered in our book mainly for the long jeep road and fine view of the northern Sawatch and the Elk Range. Drive to **Cottonwood Pass.** From Glenwood Springs you go to Cattle Creek on State 82, then E and N. From Gypsum on I-70 you go SW. The road to and along **Red Table Mountain** is some 30 miles by jeep. It leaves the Cottonwood Pass road 1 mile E of the pass crest, turning S through a road labeled Cow Camp on the White River N F map. The view of the back of the Sawatch improves as you drive E; the road degenerates.

ELK RANGE

The Elk Range name is here broadly defined as the mountains west of the Sawatch Range and between the Roaring Fork and the Gunnison River tributaries. More precise boundaries are given with the sections.

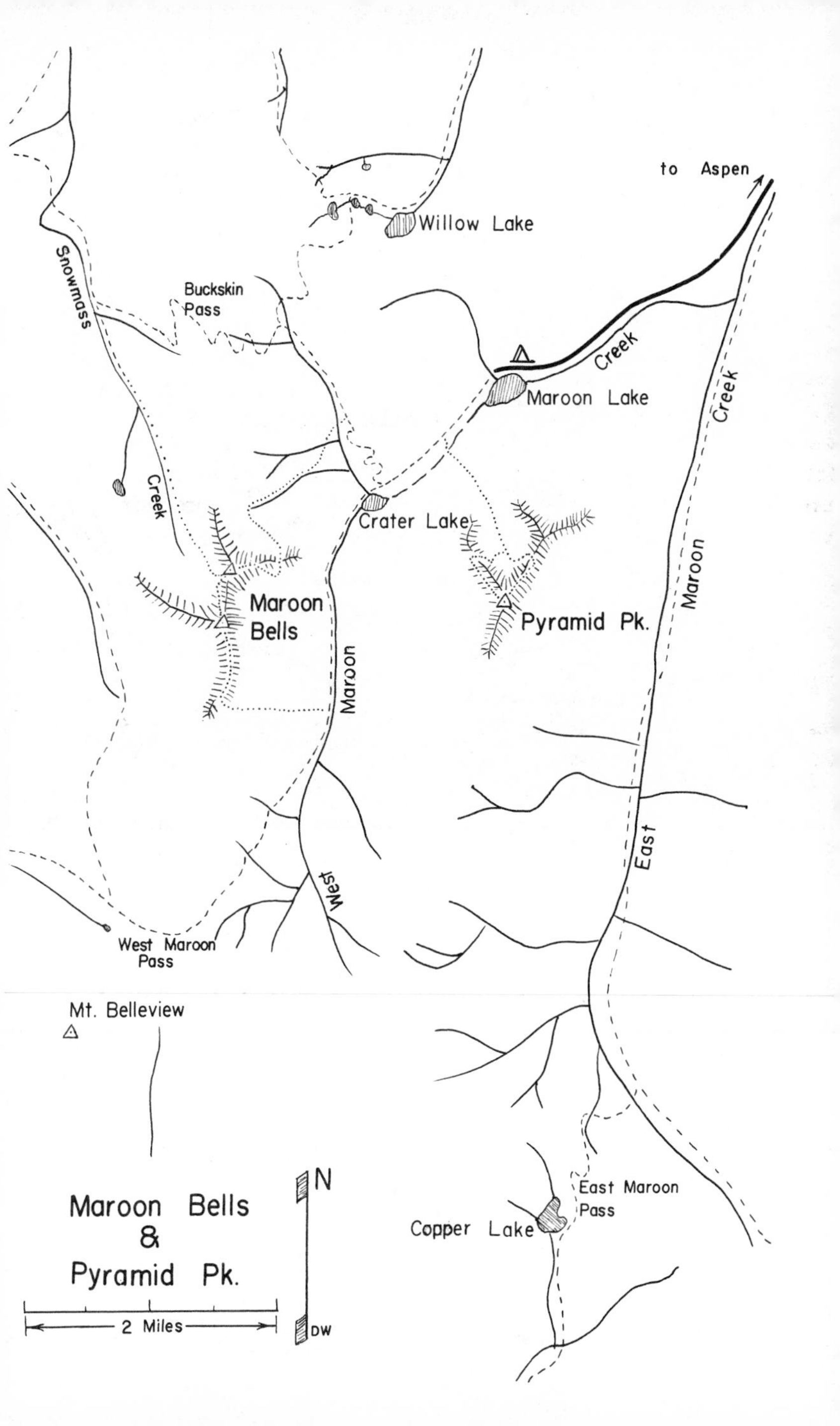
to Aspen
Willow Lake
Buckskin
Pass
Snowmass
Creek
Creek
Maroon Lake
Creek
Crater Lake
Maroon
Bells
Pyramid Pk.
Maroon
Maroon
West
East
West Maroon
Pass
Mt. Belleview
N
DW
East Maroon
Pass
Copper Lake
Maroon Bells
&
Pyramid Pk.
2 Miles

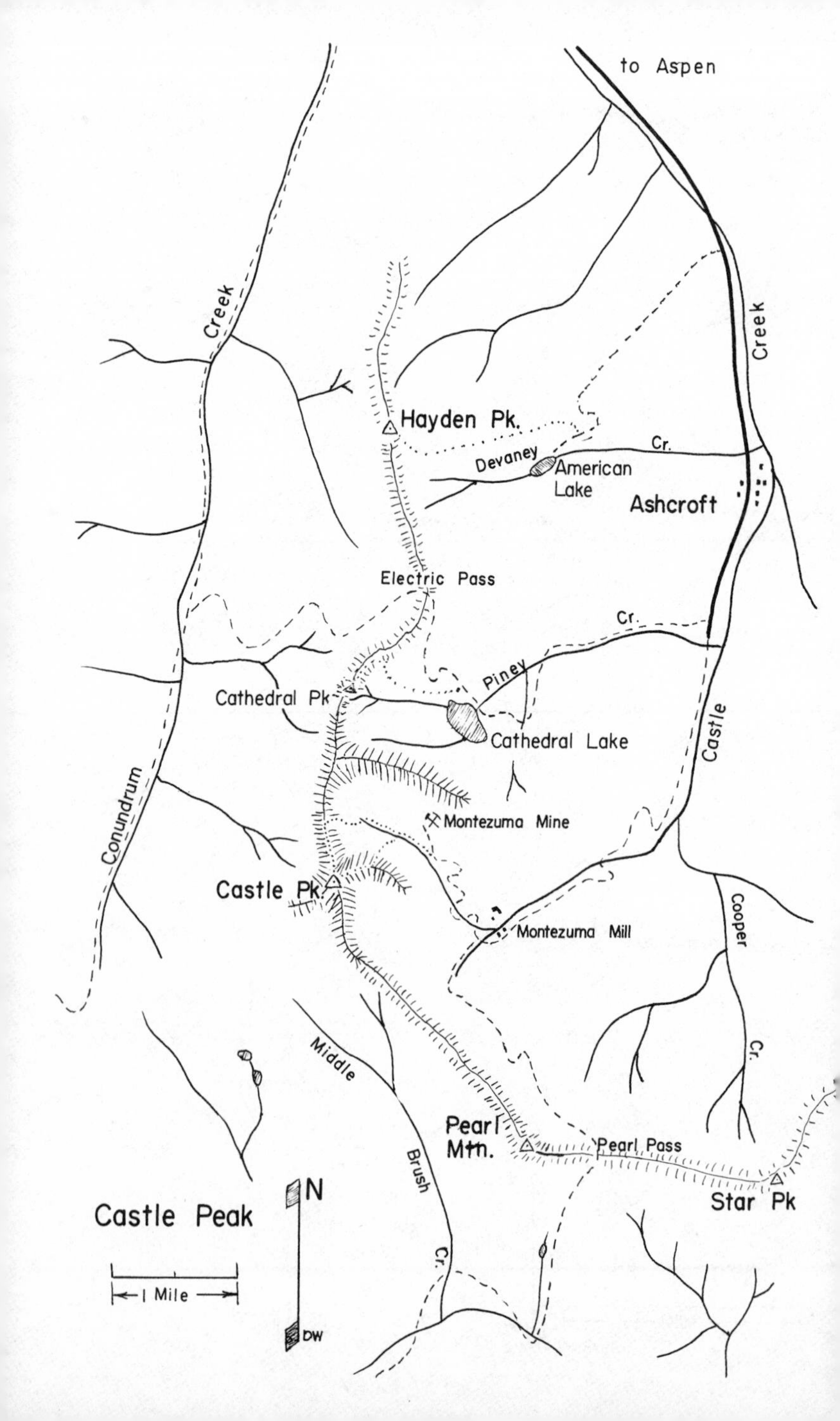

to Aspen
Creek
Creek
Hayden Pk.
Cr.
Devaney
American
Lake
Ashcroft
Electric Pass
Cr.
Piney
Cathedral Pk
Cathedral Lake
Castle
Conundrum
Montezuma Mine
Castle Pk.
Montezuma Mill
Cooper
Cr.
Middle
Brush
Cr.
Pearl
Mtn.
Pearl Pass
Star Pk
Castle Peak
N
DW
1 Mile

ELK RANGE—CENTRAL SECTION

QUADS: Hayden Peak, Pearl Pass, Maroon Bells, Highland Peak, Capitol Peak, Snowmass Mountain; White River and Gunnison N F's; Maroon Bells—Snowmass Wilderness folder.

The fourteener summits are of two geological types: the igneous rock—tertiary intrusives of Snowmass and Capitol, which are eaten away into thin, shattered ridges that swoop and rise gracefully from point to point; and the layered Canadian-style stratified rock of Castle, Pyramid, and the Maroons. The latter are sedimentary rocks of Permian age which have been hoisted up with little folding.

The central Elks run from Lincoln Gulch and the tributary New York Creek west to the Capitol-Snowmass ridge. They include the range crest between Roaring Fork drainage and Gunnison drainage. The Hayden Survey men left some of the first ascents to Percy Hagerman, whose delightful booklet, *Notes on Mountaineering in the Elk Mountains, 1908–1910*, is a rarity in Colorado's mountain literature. These peaks are among the finest in the Rockies for a number of reasons. They have big streams and fine large lakes; they are rugged, steep and forbidding in appearance; some of them are richly colored; and finally, the upper stretches have not been scarred with mining claims which can be converted to private property, and so have achieved Wilderness status.

While the Elk summits generally can be scaled without rope, they are rough enough to offer route problems and give a lively mountaineering experience. For most parties the routes are slower than the distance indicates; early starts are wise. The main peaks are clustered S of Aspen, at the heads of Castle, Maroon, and Snowmass Creeks. The road up Maroon Creek to Maroon Lake gives some of the state's most intimate close-ups of mountain grandeur.

New York Peak, 12,811′, our arbitrary eastern boundary mountain, is on the quad named for it. It offers some routes cleared of timber by snowslides. Drive 2-3 miles up the Lincoln Gulch Road from State 82 and look for a way to cross to the right side of the creek and climb the fall line. You will make 2500′ in the first mile, and 500′ more after you have passed the false summit.

Aspen mining was largely silver mining. The area never died entirely but was a very quiet place when skiing and Walter Paepke brought it to life as a ski resort and culture center.

Two access roads run S into the mountains from ½ mile W of the bridge immediately W of Aspen on 82. The left one goes 12 miles up Castle Creek to the Ashcroft flats beyond Elk Mountain Lodge, where it splits. The left fork, which is a good jeep road, crosses the creek and climbs in 6½ miles from 9400′ to 11,928′ **Taylor Pass.** There is a very steep and washed descent to little Taylor Lake, 11,544′, and what used to be the most dreadful jeep trail you would ever hope to be caught on creeping down to Dorchester on the Taylor Park road. (It has been dozed out and a friend tells me the challenge is all gone.) The top of the pass gives fine views all around, especially of the serrated **Castle Peak** ridge. There is a lot of smooth ridge country from the pass E and N, with jeep trails running off on the tundra. You can drive E a mile to a 12,430′ lookout summit and N from that road to points farther E. You can also follow a long jeep road over **McArthur Mountain** which continues down the ridge to **Bell Mountain** and the town of Aspen.

About 3 miles up the pass from Castle Creek flats a little right hand turn-off takes you off the road for a 50-yard walk to Express Creek Hut, available to cross-country skiers. There is room for summertime camping in the valley here or at the start of the jeep road below.

The road which goes right from mile 12 S of State 82 on the Ashcroft flats (see above) continues on the right hand side of Castle Creek for 3 miles in the flats and 1 mile going uphill SW before crossing to the left. It goes another 1½ miles and re-crosses. The left fork crosses back again and takes a wiggly

3-mile route to **Pearl Pass,** 12,705′, the other early wagon route from the S—this one from Crested Butte and Brush Creek. Like Taylor Pass it can now be jeeped. The junction of these trails is at 11,200′ and hard by is the Taggart Hut, likewise used as headquarters for winter ski touring in the broad valley under **Pearl Peak.** The right hand trail, which turns off NW and zigzags up into Montezuma Basin is the old road to Tam O'Shanter Mine on the right side at 12,700′. Jeeps have gone up 200′ higher than this.

Castle Peak, 14,265′, on Hayden Peak Quad, uses the Montezuma approach. From a camp at 9900′ before the road starts to climb it is 5 miles and 2200′ climb to the flats in the Basin. Camping is also good up the creek a little way and again near timberline at the fork for **Pearl Pass.** Two routes are followed to the summit. The older one takes advantage of the jeep road to 12,900′. From its end, angle SW 1 mile to the N ridge, keeping right of the snow bowl (or up it if you find towing facilities) and go S far enough under the ridge to miss the false summit of **Conundrum,** then up over its true summit and along the dipping ridge ½ mile to **Castle Peak.** A more pedestrian and perhaps better route leaves the road at the flats, 12,100′, and spirals counterclockwise a mile into the upper bowl directly under the summit, then goes SE ¼ mile up a rubbly ridge and finishes on the last ¼ mile of the peak's NE ridge.

Cathedral Peak, 13,943′, is reached from the trail to Cathedral Lake. The trail angles off right from the Castle Creek road ½ mile S of the Ashcroft buildings and climbs in 3 miles to 11,600′, N of the lake (near enough—it ain't purty). Leave the trail to head a little left of the peak and its E ridge. You will work your way W up through willows a mile to the head of the broad gulch and can find a steep but passable scramble of 800′ up the SE face.

Hayden Peak, 13,561′, has a route from Elk Mountain at the lower end of Ashcroft Park. A bridle trail starts across from the buildings at 9400′ and climbs in 3 miles to American

Lake. Leave the trail at mile 2¾, ¼ mile after it crosses a ridge near timberline, and re-cross to the N side. Go WSW 1 mile, most of the way up a cirque, then climb out to right to finish on the E ridge, altogether another mile.

The **Conundrum Creek Trail** leaves Castle Creek 5 miles from 82. It runs the length of the valley to climb out at **Conundrum Pass,** 12 miles S. The first 6-mile stretch is open to jeeps, the second in Wilderness. From Conundrum Pass it traverses the cirque west ½ mile to cross Triangle Pass at 13,225′ and descend in East Maroon Creek 6 miles to a jeep road up East Maroon Creek. This is a good 2-car circle trip with the rather astonishing Conundrum Hot Springs and a piece of high ridge on the way. A car will normally do for the 5-mile lap up East Maroon Creek from the Maroon Lakes road, whereas a jeep is needed for Conundrum Creek. The trail connects on the range top with a trail W from **Triangle Pass** and down Copper Creek 7 miles to the road at Gothic. The lower end of this, too, is jeepable.

At 10,200′, 1½ miles in from the Wilderness boundary, the **Electric Pass Trail** climbs off E from Conundrum Creek in zigzags to a crossing of Cataract Creek at 12,000′ and on up the hill to 13,500′ on the Hayden ridge. It descends to the **Cathedral Lake Trail** on the Castle Creek side. The Trail is labeled 1984. Though the trail is a long climb and on the dull side, it offers the surest route to **Hayden Peak.** From the last long trail lap N to 13,100′ you can work your way N past the first ridge summit to Hayden Peak, ¾ mile from the trail elbow. The Electric Pass peak is still higher and much closer. You almost climb on the main trail to its 13,635′ summit. **Cathedral Peak** is a mile S of Electric Pass and can be climbed along the W side of its pinnacled N ridge. From Conundrum valley to the pass the trail logs out at 3.3 miles.

Hunter Peak and **Keefe Peak** are on the ridge between Conundrum and East Maroon Creeks and can be climbed from the Conundrum side, which is a little higher and closer.

South Maroon Peak from Upper Maroon Lake. *H. L. Standley photo.*

Castle Peak from the east. *H. L. Standley photo.*

Hunter Peak, 13,497′, is climbed from the Wilderness boundary at the jeep trail end in Conundrum Creek, 10,000′. Climb a steep 1½ miles W and WNW toward the NNE ridge, to which you should find access at 12,600′. The top is an easier half mile from there to the left. **Keefe Peak,** 13,516′, starts with a two-mile walk up the trail inside the boundary. Leave the trail at 10,500′ and climb W along the N edge of the trees. This graduates into a good ridge route leading directly to the ENE face and summit, 1½ miles.

The Maroon Creek road, right branch at the start just west of Aspen on 82, runs S and SW 11 miles to Maroon Lake. The East Maroon Creek road turns off left at mile 8½ and keeps S 5 miles to the Wilderness boundary, where it continues as trail (see above, Conundrum Creek).

A trail from the Maroon Lake parking area at 9600′ runs 8 miles SW and SSW 8 miles up the creek to **West Maroon Pass** at 12,500′, where it drops 3½ miles to the road at Schofield Park, N of Gothic. Two miles W from Maroon Lake a trail runs off right, NW, above the little Crater Lake and climbs 2½ miles to **Buckskin Pass,** 12,462′, where it enters Snowmass Creek drainage and descends 4½ miles to the large Snowmass Lake, 11,000′, and the trails there. The **Buckskin Trail** is more open than some of the valley trails and looks out on fine mountain scenery.

Pyramid Peak, 14,018′, is very rough and steep. You see it framed between the canyon walls from a mile below Aspen on 82. The climb starts 1 mile up the West **Maroon Trail** from Maroon Lake, where a cairn tells you to turn off left and pick your way over the moraine toward the basin SSE to S. It is a steep mile into the basin floor. From a square rock cairn you climb a steeper ½ mile to the ridge saddle on the left of the face. Cross the ridge at 13,000′ just before it steepens and angle upward and S across the slopes of loose rock to approach the summit from the S. A party of any size should keep a diagonal route so that no one is under fire from the precariously poised rocks. The climb is about the same from the W side of the face.

There you cross the ridge on a slightly lower saddle and keep near the ridge on its W side.

A Wheeler Survey man climbed to within 200′ of the summit and turned back; Percy Hagerman is believed to have made the first ascent.

North Maroon Peak, 14,014′, and **South Maroon Peak,** 14,156′, loom above Maroon Lake like peaks of the Canadian Rockies. These two and the peaks from **Pyramid** to **Castle** are the only high summits in Colorado of this conspicuously layered late paleozoic sedimentary rock. They are named and photographed for the rich color and its contrast with the blue sky and with the aspens, whether green or gold. Though it goes very well on the right route and under good conditions, the peak has claimed the lives of experienced climbers. We use a helpful representation by Hugh Hetherington with the route description. Take the **Buckskin Pass Trail** from Maroon Lake, and climb on it to about a mile up from the trail junction near Crater Lake. Here at 11,100′ the creek you are on levels off a little and gives a good place to start toward the peak. Cross the stream and climb SW ¾ mile to a timberline bench at 11,750′, between upper and lower cliffs. This takes you under "a small triangular northeast face" to a broad grassy couloir. Climb in this couloir toward the whitish cliff above, and just under the cliff, about 12,400′, traverse left across a minor gully to a wider second couloir, where you can climb to the edge of the N face, 13,200′. Cross on the N face far enough to find the easy white chimney that lets you through to the top. It is important to keep your route in mind for the return trip, especially if there is a chance of fog. Some of us have cut left too soon and visualized ourselves stepping out into nothing.

Other routes on and near the E ridge are used, some of them offering rope pitches. The dyke route, which cuts through the NW ridge from the face and finishes on the NW face, can be used. It is easier except for the short final stretch of the cut itself, which is steep and powdery and requires careful work with a rope. From **North Maroon,** head W and S ½ mile to

South Maroon. The drop is less than 500′ but slow. Continue S $\frac{1}{4}$ to $\frac{1}{2}$ mile or more on ridge and choose a descent route 1 mile E to the trail down West Maroon Creek. When **North Maroon** is climbed alone, descent can be made by the NW ridge and dyke, providing there is rope for the short descent from the dyke out.

It is a slow but not too difficult job to pick your way off W and S on the traverse to **South Maroon Peak.** You lose 300-400′. A couloir descent from the first saddle S of the S peak on snow should be carefully tested and the upper part done with ropes and belays. Shadows create hard places. Open slopes are available from farther S on the ridge, a slow half mile or so.

South Maroon offers approaches from West Maroon Creek, both on the 1-mile E ridge and on the slopes farther south. For a gentler but longer route to the Maroons, see Snowmass Lake area.

The road up Snowmass Creek leaves State 82 4 miles SSE of Basalt and runs 10 miles up the canyon to Snowmass Campground and Snowmass Falls Ranch. There is a shortcut from Aspen via Snowmass Ski Area. It goes up Brush Creek from 4 miles NNW of Aspen on 82 and drops over the ridge to Snowmass Creek. The **Snowmass Lake Trial** climbs from 8400′ to 11,000′ and ends 8 miles from the road end above the campground. At the lake one branch turns back E to Snowmass Creek (the lake is on a sidestream) and up to **Buckskin Pass** as noted above. The other climbs SW 2$\frac{1}{4}$ miles to **Trailrider Pass,** at 12,400′, and drops by Geneva Lake to Lead King Basin. Consult the Forest Service for information about the high country pack trips on these Wilderness area trails.

Snowmass Mountain, 14,092′, is named for the great sheet of snow that hangs between its two summits and is visible from numerous northern summits of the Sawatch Range. From the lake it is an inconspicuous hump to the right of **Hagerman Peak,** which rises handsomely above the water. From the outlet take a fisherman's trail $\frac{1}{2}$ mile along the S (left) side of the lake, climb WNW to the steep summit, which has a pitch of careful though non-roped climbing.

Hagerman Peak, 13,600′, ridge end 1 mile SE of **Snowmass Mountain** and ½ mile NNW of **Trailrider Pass,** is a photographer's dream as seen from the lake beneath. It has been climbed by routes of varying directness from Snowmass Lake, including everything from rope work on the face to full flank attacks on both N and S sides. It combines as a ridge traverse with **Snowmass Peak,** which is a painstaking affair and requires mountain knowhow. The easiest route is probably on the south. You climb to **Trailrider Pass,** contour right (WNW) for a full quarter mile, and go to the right up a couloir to a saddle between the highest point and front point. Go through the saddle and choose your summit—high point or lake overlook point.

Capitol Peak, 14,130′, is the hardest of the Elks to reach and one of the most rewarding to climb. The first ascent was that of Hayden Survey men, who carried 40-pound packs of instruments. Like Whitehouse and Treasury, it was named for a government building. Along with Snowmass it is in a system of thin ridges that sweep from point to point in long, graceful parabolas. Under the north-south connecting ridge between the peaks, and draining E, is Pierre Lakes Basin, a bowlful of broken rock 2½ miles wide. It is named for an Aspen youth who back-packed fingerling trout over the rock benches into Pierre Lakes. Some New York schoolboys built a sketchy trail up Bear Creek and the narrow shelves of the fall section to Pierre Lakes along his route. It is a good way in if you can get across Snowmass Creek near Bear Creek.

Assuming you are camped at Snowmass Lake, climb from the outlet ¼ mile N around the lake end, and NW ½ mile into and up the main ravine to a col N of the lake. This col is a 12,550′ pass 1½ miles ENE from **Snowmass Mountain.** Descend N ½ mile to 11,600′ and head 2½ miles NW across Pierre Lakes Basin. Climb a steep couloir to low point of the E ridge and climb SW ¼ mile on ridge to summit. To climb **Capitol Peak**

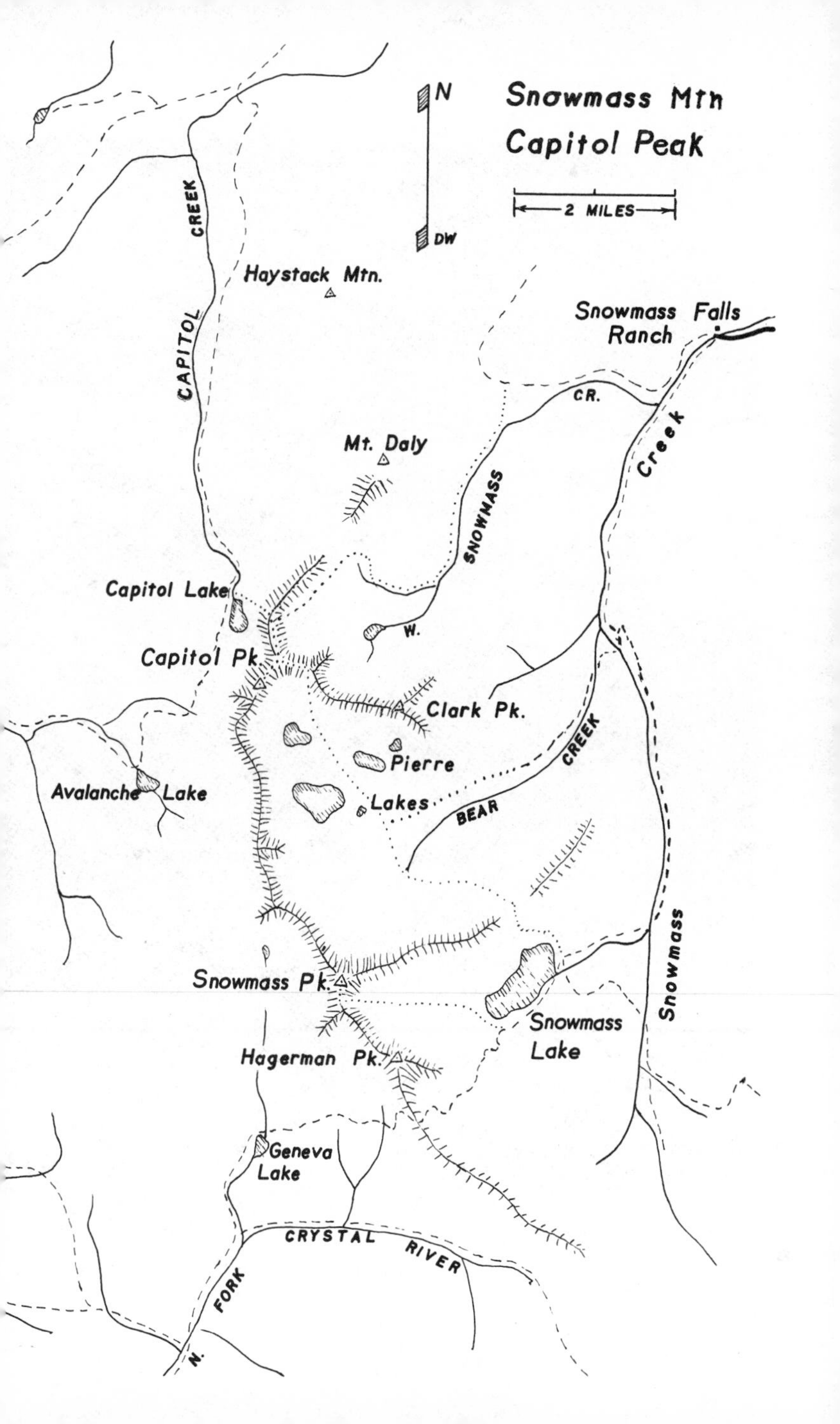
Snowmass Mtn
Capitol Peak
N
DW
2 MILES
Haystack Mtn.
CAPITOL
CREEK
Snowmass Falls
Ranch
CR.
Creek
Mt. Daly
SNOWMASS
Capitol Lake
W.
Capitol Pk.
Clark Pk.
CREEK
Pierre
Avalanche
Lake
Lakes
BEAR
Snowmass Pk.
Snowmass
Snowmass
Lake
Hagerman Pk.
Geneva
Lake
CRYSTAL
RIVER
FORK
N.

Snowmass Mountain with its sheet of white, and Capitol Peak.

from Snowmass Falls Ranch parking area, cross to NW (right) side of Snowmass Creek and with permission walk upstream parallel to the stream 1 mile in pasture. Look along the upper edge of the clearing in order to find the unmarked trail leading W (right) into aspen. This trail keeps to the right (NE) side of West Snowmass Creek for 2 miles and then angles sharply away to NE. You stay on the right side of the valley on sketchy trail above the creek for ½ mile, then along the E side but closer to the creek for a mile. When you come to a creeklet coming E from the banded **Mount Daly,** climb up this creeklet toward Daly for 1000′ altitude, then angle left. If you want to camp in the valley you can stay down and turn W to make altitude later. Continue NW parallel to the Daly-Capitol ridge, keeping to left of the steep rough section. It is about 2 miles from where the creeklet enters West Snowmass Creek to the convergence of the Clark and Daly ridges, at 13,600′. Scramble around a pinnacle or two and then stroll along the knife edge. This all takes time, and for a party of any size, allow for a long day.

The same Daly-Capitol Ridge can be reached from a timberline camp just below Capitol Lake, on the W side of the peak. To reach the lake from Aspen, drive 14 miles NW on State 82 to Snowmass P. O. and 2 miles S up Snowmass Creek. Take the right hand fork SW 2 miles, left road SW 1½ miles, and keep right 6 miles to 1½ miles past Capitol Creek Guard Station, where cars may be left. Continue S on trail 6½ miles to Capitol Lake, 11,700′. Climb E ½ mile to Capitol-Daly saddle and continue as from West Snowmass Creek above. The NW face of Capitol has yielded good rock climbs to roped parties, and final sections of the Cleaver Ridge, coming in from Snowmass Mountain, have also been traversed.

ELK RANGE—CRYSTAL RIVER AREA

QUADS: Carbondale, Mount Sporis, Redstone, Marble, Chair Mountain, Snowmass Mountain, White River N F.

This group takes in the Crystal River drainage.

Crystal River comes into the Roaring Fork at Carbondale. The road, State 133, runs 17 miles S up the valley to Redstone, where a posh hotel reminds one of the world of wealth from steel and coal. The road continues 3 miles to Placita and the McClure Pass road W out of the Elks to Paonia country, and then goes on S and E 8 miles to Marble, where both a steam and an electric railroad brought out gleaming white stone from the quarries up Yule Creek, some of it for the Lincoln Memorial, some of it still about in every size from chips to great drum-shaped hunks that would fill a living room. It was on this river, originally called Rock Creek, that "an evil mule called Gimlet" dumped a load of W. H. Jackson's precious glass plates, so that he had to go back over his weeks-long trail and do the work again. The Crystal River—and it would be nice to know who had the felicitous idea to name it the Crystal and when—is full of interest, starting with Carbondale at its foot. There are fabulous cattle ranches around here, and this was where Eugene Grubb created the finest of potatoes. At Redstone, Osgood of the Colorado Fuel and Iron Company established a model village for the miners and coke workers about 1900, long before day laborers were recognized as human beings.

There is plenty for exploration—two railroads up the valley and a coal road W from Redstone, mines in the high country, and the town of Crystal, 5 miles E of Marble. Crystal is the terminus of car travel, but connects with Gothic and the Crested Butte country by a sometimes-blocked jeep road up steep hillside and a stretch of all-rock canyon. It is 4 miles to good road at Emerald Lake in Schofield Park, 3 more to Gothic.

Mount Sopris, 12,823′, you see coming up the Roaring Fork from Glenwood Springs. From Carbondale drive 1½ miles SW and take the road to the left. After 6 miles on Prince Creek it climbs 2 more to an exit for Dinkle Lake. Keep right instead; 4 miles farther you cross West Sopris Creek. A trail starts off this road shortly after the crossing and climbs S 2 miles to near timberline. Angle slowly right and climb to and along the ridge to one or both summits. An alternative route is not to cross West Sopris Creek but to climb the embankment on the near side and find a horse trail which takes you 2 miles into the upper basin. Sopris' name honors a Denver mayor who took men "over the range" in pre-transportation days.

At mile 12 from Carbondale, 5 N of Redstone, Avalanche Gulch comes into the river, flowing NW off the slopes of **Capitol Peak.** A 2½-mile road runs left to the campground in the gulch at 7300′. **Avalanche Trail** follows the Gulch. At mile 2½, 8200′, a branch climbs out left 6 miles to a 12,050′ pass and drops into Capitol Creek 2 miles above the guard station there. At mile 10 the main trail goes over left to Capitol Lake by way of a zigzag through the timber and a 12,050′ pass.

From the head of Avalanche Gulch there is a quite feasible short cut pass to Siberia Lake in Lead King Basin. Take the left basin above Avalanche Lake, 10,700′, and climb to a lakelet at 12,100′, then head to a 12,650′ saddle ¼ mile S. This report came to us from the Outward Bound lads whose camp is 2 miles E of Marble.

Chair Mountain, 12,721′, is a showpiece from here and there along the valley—a high-backed chair with high arms, facing you. If you use a campground at Bogan Flats, 7 miles upstream from Redstone, drive 1 mile farther (SE) to Prospect Ranch to leave the car and inquire for Genter Mine, ¼ mile W. A trail from the 7800′ mine climbs through timber to 10,500′ before fading out in the main N glacial valley. Keep track of where the trail ends for the return, since bushwhacking here is rough. Work up the valley close to Cleaver Ridge, which is on your left. After you pass the cleaver—east arm of the chair—cross the saddle between that and the summit, and head straight S for ½ mile to a narrow E ridge. The final climb of 1000′ is on this ridge, on unstable rock. Chair Mountain lets you see the Elk Range from the end and looks off SW at the peaks toward Crawford.

Ragged Peak, 12,641′, high point of the 6-mile curved ridge that forms an ending bulwark for the Elk Range, is at the end of the Rapid Creek valley. For any but a very fast team, this should be a two-day excursion, with a camp at timberline on the route to **Chair Mountain.** It appears that the 2-mile ridge between the two would be very slow going, and that even if they are climbed in one day the better plan would be to retreat from Chair Mountain to the saddle between it and the cleaver and continue nearly all the way to Ragged before regaining the ridge. Whatever you try, let us hear.

Treasure and **Treasury Mountains** can be reached from the long trail up Yule Creek. You cross the river at Marble and if the road is open you can drive the first 4 miles to the trail head, in a side drainage ½ mile short of the quarry at 9000′. It is 6 miles to **Yule Pass** at 11,700′, with camping possibilities on the way. **Treasury Mountain** is a steepish but easy climb N a mile and NNW a little farther on ridge. See shorter routes from Crystal below. **Treasure Mountain** is 2 miles WNW along the ridge from Treasury with a loss of 400′ or so between. It makes a good combination with Treasury because of two possible lines of descent: (1) on down the ridge to the Skyline Mine Trail at 12,000′, from which you can zigzag down through the timber to the valley floor; (2) straight off from Treasure Mountain for a visit to the Yule Lakes, benched halfway down to the valley.

Purple Mountain, 12,958′, is perhaps more in the province of the Ruby Range to the S. It is climbed from the pass, however, by a 1½ mile S-curved ridge S. See Snowmass Mountain Marble, Oh Be Joyful and Marcellina Mountain Quads.

John Beyer has written directions for several trail trips and climbs of the upper Crystal River. His article, "Hikes and Climbs from Crystal," which appeared with a map by Bob Hubbard in the October 1968 *Trail and Timberlines*, is the source of the statements below, which are approximate quotations.

A trail leads S 2 miles from Crystal, 8950′, to 10,350′ Bear Basin. Cross to it on the Outward Bound suspension bridge or on logs behind the southernmost house. Climb directly up the hill 75 yards to find the trail. It follows a road upstream ¼ mile then veers off to the right (S) paralleling but staying well to the W of the stream draining the basin. The trail climbs steeply through conifers and meadows, then disappears in a "skunk cabbage" patch just beyond a large outcrop of table rock. The stream is visible about 200 yards to the left (E) where it separates into two branches. The righthand stream branch leads toward a saddle between **Treasure** and **Treasury Mountains,** whereas the left branch leads to a saddle between **Crystal Peak** and **Treasury Mountain.**

Crystal Peak, 12,632′, is climbed from Bear Basin. Cross the stream and follow the left branch stream S near the right side but leave the stream and keep well to the W as a waterfall is approached about ½ mile upstream. Climb steeply and bushwhack through conifers and a few willow patches, until an old cabin is reached on the bench W of the waterfall. Follow the very gradual drainage system S heading directly for the saddle between Crystal and Treasury. Leave the stream well before reaching the saddle but after passing a series of steep ledges and climb E up to the ridge. Follow the ridge N to the summit, avoiding a rock outcrop by passing under and around it to the left (W).

Treasure Mountain, 13,528′, is climbed from the saddle heading the righthand stream branch, by way of a flat ridge to the right. Take an ice-axe for a glissade return but avoid the north side cornices.

Treasury Mountain, 13,462′, has a route from 1 mile upstream on the right fork. Head W toward the prominent nose of the large sloping slab that forms Treasury's N spur. Contour left around the nose then turn S and climb a steep pitch to a false summit above the Treasury-Treasure saddle. Follow the ridge SE to the main summit. Take your ice-axe.

A jeep road runs E ½ mile from Crystal and splits—right for **Schofield Pass** and **Gothic,** left for Lead King Basin. The latter road climbs high above the N fork of the Crystal River and reaches Lead King Basin about 1½ miles from Crystal. The road then crosses the river on a bridge at mile 1¾ and reaches the Geneva Lake, **Trail Rider Pass,** and North Fork common trailhead at mile 2. The road then switchbacks several times while heading W across Silver Creek and down Lost Trail Creek to Marble.

The trail to 11,000′ Geneva Lake continues NNE up-valley, through the aspen and meadows of the basin, and then in the open, keeping to the left fork. For **Trail Rider Pass** (over to Snowmass Lake) go through marshes around the N end of the lake and generally E to the pass, about 3½ miles from the lake.

Meadow Mountain, 11,853′ (labeled **Arkansas** on Snowmass Quad), is climbed from the above Silver Creek crossing, 10,700′. Head W ¼ mile and up the SSE ridge 1 mile.

Mineral Point, 11,025′, rising abruptly E of Crystal, gives fine views of the area. The trail to it starts from a little short of the bridge on the Lead King Basin road 1½ miles from Crystal and climbs by trail SW up a steep draw. Angle right to ridge and down to point.

To climb **Snowmass Mountain** from the lake, head toward the summit and climb high in the basin. Then cut left to the SSW ridge for a finish. It is also feasible to climb N from Geneva Lake 1½–2 miles to Little Gem or to Siberia Lake and climb E from there. Do not get on the ridge immediately, rather pick a route up any of several flutes that lead toward the ridge rather gradually. Expect unstable rock and some exposure, but not ice.

ELK RANGE—CRESTED BUTTE SECTION

QUADS: Gothic, Oh Be Joyful, Marble, Mount Axtell, Pearl Pass, Crested Butte and Cement Mountain; Taylor Park 15′; Gunnison and White River N F's; for the north trails see also Maroon Bells, Marble, Snowmass Mountain and Hayden Peak.

This group covers the East River drainage to Ohio Creek on the W and the Taylor River on the E, and so runs up to the S side of the main Elk Range. Interest centers are the Ruby Range and Teocalli and Italian Mountains.

State 135 from Gunnison N to Crested Butte is 29 miles long. At Almont, mile 11, the Taylor River road turns off NE 23 miles to the Taylor Reservoir, where it meets Cottonwood Pass road over the Divide from Buena Vista.

Park Cone, 12,102′, is the symmetrical mountain S of the reservoir, well timbered below a bare top. We know of no tried route, but inquiry at the Forest headquarters in Gunnison, or at Almont or Taylor River store would probably turn up a helpful lumbering road. The Taylor drains a lot of country and is a most attractive fishing stream with numerous campgrounds.

Matchless Mountain, 12,235′, is 4 miles NW of Park Cone on the opposite side of the valley. From ⅓ of the way up the W side of the 9000′ reservoir from the outlet, the **Matchless Trail** climbs 4½ miles W to a timberline saddle, and then descends 4 miles more gently in Dustin Gulch to the Spring Creek road (see below) at 10,400′. From the saddle, which is less of a pull on the W approach, you climb ⅓ mile SW to the E ridge of Matchless and then a mile up it to the top.

The Taylor road swings NNW from the **Cottonwood Pass** road junction by the lake, and at mile 8 meets a good forest service road where you can turn SW and go up Trail Creek through timbered country and a low pass to the Spring Creek road. The latter comes into the Taylor River about halfway from Gunnison to Taylor Reservoir. The **Matchless Trail** (above) starts SE up Dustin Gulch 1½ miles SW of the pass or, if you are driving north, 3 miles ENE of the Spring Creek Reservoir exit.

From ½ mile short of the above Trail Creek exit, or at mile 7½ from the Cottonwood Pass road, a road runs off to the N side for a mile and then becomes the **Red Mountain Creek Trail.** From the start at 9700′, to Pieplant Mine, 10,243′, it is 3½ miles N and E. The trail continues N up the creek and its right fork 6 miles to the high (12,230′) **Lake Pass.** It descends to the South Fork of Lake Creek proper and also by a branch just N of Lake Pass to Sayres Gulch, a S fork of the South Fork.

The pass has two flanking peaks very close to it: on the left (SW), is one of 12,900′; on the right (E), an abrupt summit of 13,318′. (This is on Taylor Park Quad, but see also Independence Pass Quad on the newer scale.) Though steep, these peaks appear to be of the plodding Sawatch type.

At mile 11, $3\frac{1}{2}$ miles past these junctions, the road turns off for Italian Creek. **Italian Mountain** is about 8 miles W, **American Flag** close and to its left. You can drive a car 2 or 3 miles, possibly more, but it becomes a jeep road a good way before you get in close to high country. As no one guarantees these jeep roads will go, you would do well to inquire about them of the rangers in Gunnison. At about mile 9 from the Taylor road you come to the Star Mine, 11,600′, in a basin with lakelets on the NE side of Italian Mountain. The mountain is a ridge well over 2 miles long, with 4 summit points, altitudes reading N to S as 13,051′, 13,209′, 13,378′ on Pearl Pass Quad and 12,821′ on the Taylor Park Quad. As the maps are not exactly joined, it may help to know that these summits correspond with the following inch distances from the top of the Taylor quad: $2\frac{3}{4}$, $2\frac{5}{16}$, $3\frac{7}{8}$, and $4\frac{5}{8}$. A climb to the N summit should go from the basin N $\frac{1}{2}$ mile into a canyon just N of the basin proper, then SW a mile to the ridge crest at 12,800′, and N $\frac{1}{4}$ mile to the summit.

The 13,209′ summit can go from the same high saddle with the first. For the high peak you should take the jeep out E around the ridge and back into the next valley head, about 4 miles from the first. The road links with one up Cement Creek (below).

The Taylor road continues $2\frac{1}{2}$ miles NW from the Italian Creek entrance to Dorchester Campground and 4 more to Bowman, which is nothing much but the entrance to the Taylor Pass jeep trail. You can drive another 2 miles or so in the valley to about 10,500′, and continue by trail 3 more miles nearly to the head of the Taylor River. The trail climbs out E from the valley to a 12,000′ pass at the head of Cement Creek. Here you are 1 mile W of 12,560′ **Mount Tilton.** Tilton has a name because of its mine; it is only a NW ridge-end of the **Italian Mountain** ridge. From a little off the **Taylor-Cement Pass** a half-mile trail takes you up close to the top of Tilton.

The Cement Creek road provides a more direct route to the Italian Mountain country if a less interesting one. It turns off the Crested Butte road at mile 12 N of Almont, and is drivable when dry through a campground at mile 4 to a fork at mile 9, 9800′. Jeeps can go 8 more miles up Cement Creek to 11,700′, to meet the trail within a mile of the Taylor-Cement pass.

Taking a right at mile 9 up the hillside from the creek, jeeps can go NNE 4 miles to a pass at 11,146′ between Cement and Spring Creeks. The road continues about 6 miles in and out along the SE flank of Italian Mountain to the Stewart Mine cirque, a basin between Italian and American Flag Mountains, where you are at 11,800′. (See above.)

Italian Mountain, 13,378′, on Pearl Pass and 15′ Taylor Park Quads, is a mile WNW from the Stewart Mine. To climb it, look for a route straight W to the cirque head. From the saddle, 12,500′, it is less than a mile N to the top on a steepish ridge. This and American Flag are literally very colorful peaks to climb. They present their best faces to the Taylor River.

American Flag Mountain, 12,720′, is an easy climb from the jeep road saddle a mile ENE of the Stewart Mine on the way to the Star Mine. Starting at 12,000′, you go SE and up the steep N ridge and gentle summit plateau.

At mile 27, 2 miles short of Crested Butte on 135, a road goes off right on the S flank of **Crested Butte** (mountain). It is passable the first 5 miles for cars. At the junction here the left jeep road goes up NNW along the East River on an inferior route to **Gothic.** The right one goes up Brush Creek a mile to another forking: left—West Bush Creek; right—Middle and East Brush Creeks.

Teocalli Mountain, 13,208′, was so called by survey men for its resemblance to temple-like pyramids in Mexico. To climb it, take the left of the last mentioned forks. It climbs on the hillside and goes perhaps as far as 5 miles up West Brush Creek, where you are at 10,000′ on the bare S side of Teocalli Mountain. A trail takes off right (eastward) from near the end of the jeep route, and gives you a half-mile of uphill contouring before you turn off and climb more directly toward the ridge E of the summit on the broad S slope.

From back at the junction at East River plus 1 mile, the right hand road goes E to main Brush Creek, and up that by way of a climb-out on the left side. At about mile 4 you come to the junction of Middle and East Brush Creeks. The left jeep trail stays in Middle Fork 5 or 6 miles and then climbs out to work its way E and N some 3½ miles to **Pearl Pass.** This was once a wagon road, and the hardiest of jeepers go over it in either direction. But not fast.

A similar route goes up East Brush Creek from the last mentioned junction. It may be jeepable for as much as 2 miles E and a mile N. Then a long, long trail takes over and runs up NE under **Pearl Peak** and **Taylor Peak** to **Taylor Pass.** Except for some local fish, anything reached from Middle and East Brush Creeks is better reached from somewhere else.

Crested Butte, 12,162′, is a good show from the S side. The rough cliffs are cut out of early tertiary intrusive rock. To climb it go up the ski area. The gondola top, 1000′ below the summit, gives a good view west, north and east. If you want to see deeper into the Elks you can climb on up to where the ridge ends, at 11,800′. For the summit you have to work round east to a southeast ridge.

Gothic is on up past the ski area at about mile 8 from Crested Butte town. It is a ghost town, revived as a place for alpine biological studies.

Gothic Mountain, 12,625′, is the handsome and appropriately named peak directly W of the town. The ascent should start from a mile down the road at 9400′. Climb directly up W 1000′ to timber and then another 1000′ along the right edge of the timber patch to the top end of the trees. A ridge, first broadish and then narrower, takes you up to easier grades near the top. Come back the same way.

An old road goes E and NE up Copper Creek 5 miles and then off W another 1½ miles to some lakelets and an old mine on the back side of **Avery Peak.** This is jeepable up to Judd Falls, mile 1, and perhaps farther. In any case you are soon in the primitive area. The trail continues up Copper Creek to Copper Lake, 11,300′ at mile 6, where there is camping for trail riders and others. The trail splits, a left fork for **East Maroon Pass,** 1 mile; the right for **Conundrum Pass,** 3 miles.

Whiterock Mountain, 13,500′, is a grandly rambling mass to the E of this trail, and can best be climbed from about mile 4 out of Gothic, a little short of where the trail goes on to a little rib and steepens. Cut ESE from it on a very minor drainage line to the upper end of a strip of trees, then turn NNE to climb 600′ higher in a direction a little left of the summit point. From there angle almost S to the W ridge for the last 1000′ of climbing.

Avery Peak, 12,760′, is named for a mine and mill operator in the heyday of Gothic. To climb it you go to the Virginia Mine in the basin S of the peak. The old road goes N from the E end of Gothic at 9600′ and branches right from the packtrail .1 mile after the start. The mine is at 10,600′, 1½ miles up the basin, and you can climb in the basin the next two miles to 12,200′. As we don't know anybody who has been there you will have to work your way out of the basin on your own. The problem is to decide what to call the summit. Tradition attaches the name to a 12,659′ point visible from the East River above Gothic. It is on the W side of the little cirque. We vote for a point straight N of the cirque, but that only begins the problem. On to the N there is a string of other tops, some over 13,200′, and it gets still higher without any name as part of the Gunnison–Roaring Fork Divide. The cirques W and NW of Copper Lake would be the best place to look into the summits problem for this upper outer NE Avery, or whatever it is.

Three miles up the East River from Gothic at 9700′, an old road goes E, N and E up Rustler Gulch to a couple of old mines, one on each side of the gulch at 11,600′. This gets around behind the same points on the ridge N of Avery, and is close to them—a tempting area for exploration.

A branch road off this trail at mile 1 climbs left to the Silver Spruce Mine at 11,800′, 4 miles N. It is just under and E of 12,519′ **Mount Bellview.**

From a mile N of **Schofield Pass** you find the trail that turns E up the East Fork of the South Fork of Crystal River and over **West Maroon Pass,** 12,500′—a favorite trail route between the drainages. There is differently spelled **Belleview Mountain,** its summit at 13,233′, a mile N along a sharpish ridge from the pass.

There are trails on the other side of the Schofield road. **Galena Mountain,** 12,580′, is approached from 1½ miles N of **Schofield Pass,** where a road runs off through woods 1½ miles NW and W into the North Pole Basin valley. Leave road at meadows to follow stream 1 mile, then cut left across basin to climb to the level S ridge of Galena. If you don't care for the last steep part of the climb to the ridge on rotten rock, you make the mine under the saddle your objective.

From **Schofield Pass** itself an old road climbs off W and S to the Paradise Mine and Paradise Basin, 11,200′ and after a miniscule pass winds down to the Slate River to the great steel mills of Pittsburg. From the Gothic Campground, mile 3 N of Gothic, you can find a trail west to Elkton, a once lively mining area NW of Gothic Mountain. The main approach to the camp was from the S on a road up Washington Gulch; it can be driven a little way in a car, perhaps the whole 8 miles by jeep. You start left from 2 miles N of **Crested Butte.**

RUBY RANGE

QUADS: Marcellina Mountain and Oh Be Joyful.

This long southward extension of the Elk Range is worthy of its separate name but belongs within the Crested Butte sphere of interest. It has had a good share of mining activity high up as well as low. Access is generally from the roads to Pittsburg and to Kebler Pass.

The Slate River road NNW to Pittsburg turns off left 1 mile N of **Crested Butte.** Just short of Pittsburg, which is at mile 7, a road crosses the Slate and goes 2 miles NW up Poverty Gulch on mild grade to 9600′, where an interesting pack trail climbs off SW up 3½ miles to **Daisy Pass,** 11,600′, and then drops S to 11,000′ in Democrat Basin, where there is a trail junction with trails from over the range to the W and down the valleys to the S.

Richmond Mountain, 12,501′, is a mile NW along a sharp ridge from **Daisy Pass,** with a false summit to climb en route. It is on the range crest.

Schuylkill Mountain, 12,146′, is 1½ miles the other way, with a similar wayside obstruction of 100′ or so.

The road in Poverty Gulch zigzags up and across the creek and climbs up the left side to the Augusta Mine at 11,000′. This has generally been rated jeepable. The steep ridge to the S is **Cascade Mountain.** Climb toward it for a pleasant little lake on a bench.

Augusta Mountain, 12,559′, and **Mineral Point,** 12,506′, are a mile NW and ¾ mile N from here. Climb up the creek to another bench lake and choose your route.

At mile 5 from **Crested Butte** an old road doubles back from the Pittsburg road and runs W up Oh Be Joyful Gulch. It is jeepable 2 miles and sometimes the whole 5 to the head of the valley. At mile 4 you are directly S of **Schuylkill Mountain** and 2000′ under it on quite steep but passable slope. **Garfield** and **Peeler Peaks** are to the S.

At mile 5 the trail makes a short steep climb to the main trail along the range, here at 10,500′. A mile N up the drainage is the trail junction in Democrat Basin.

The climb from the basin W to **Oh Be Joyful Pass** makes 800′ in 1½ miles. Over the pass you drop to timber on the W side of the range and go S 9 or 10 miles to the Kebler Pass road, meeting it 12½ miles W of Crested Butte.

On Oh Be Joyful Pass you are at the N end of a string of 4 named 12,000′ summits, all on a 2-mile stretch of ridge.

Hancock, 12,410′, **Oh Be Joyful,** 12,400′, and **Afley Peaks,** 12,646′ involve small altitude losses; south of Afley you drop 600′ before climbing to 12,800′ **Purple Peak.**

The trail S from the Oh Be Joyful trail junction turns E after a mile and crosses a pass at 11,900′ into Peeler Basin, south tributary of Oh Be Joyful Creek. From the pass it is an easy stroll N to **Garfield Peak,** which looked quite high on the valley side, and you can go on a mile E to 12,227′ **Peeler Peak** without loss of altitude. Peeler Basin has several little lakes including two fair-sized ones in the timber. On the S side of the basin is Scarp Ridge, rough toward the basin, smooth along the top. It is a pleasant 4-mile ridge walk at altitudes of 12,000-12,200′, running SE from the Joyful–Peeler Basin to **Gunsight Pass,** backside of **Mount Emmons.**

At mile 4¾ on the Pittsburg road, a mile short of the turnoff for Oh Be Joyful Gulch (8950′), a road cuts back along the old railroad grade to start climbing the steep ridges SE of Oh Be Joyful Creek. This is on easy grades and usually jeepable. It comes to a ragged 11,000′ timberline in Redwell Basin in 5 miles, and in 2 more miles to **Gunsight Pass.** At mile 5 a trail cuts off right and down to Peeler Basin. It is the one which connects with the upper end of Oh Be Joyful Gulch.

Mount Emmons, 12,392′, the summit overlooking Crested Butte from the NW, is a half-mile walk E from **Gunsight Pass.**

As described from the E end the road to **Gunsight Pass** starts off right from the Kebler Pass road 2 miles W of the town and goes a mile W up the hill to the Keystone Mine. Then with one switchback it continues W parallel to the Kebler road 2½ miles to turn N up Elk Creek and to the pass, 4½ miles more. These are rated as jeep roads but little enough used to be good walking routes to **Mount Emmons** and **Scarp Ridge.**

Kebler Pass, 9980′, is 7½ miles W up Coal Creek from **Crested Butte.**

Just short of the pass a secondary road turns off N for the mining camps of Ruby and Irwin, and beyond them Lake

Irwin, prettily reflecting the images of **Ruby Peak** and its apparent twin **Mount Owen** (higher but more distant).

Ruby Peak, 12,644′, and **Mount Owen,** 13,058′ high point of the range, are best climbed from the lake, which you can reach in a car. An old road, probably jeepable for a mile or more but no dish for a car, goes 2 miles NW directly to mines at the base of Ruby Peak and then turns N 2½ more miles to a mine at 11,600′ under the Owen-Purple Peak saddle. You can take Ruby Peak by its SE ridge and lose 800′ of altitude in going over it to Owen, or bypass it. In the latter case take the first mile of the trail from where it turns N, then climb up left to 11,653′ Green Lake on a bench between the two peaks. Then to the saddle W of it and N on the narrow ridge crest to Owen. **Purple Peak** can be combined well with Owen, being only ½ mile around the ridge and rising only 200′ from it.

Whetstone Mountain, 12,516′, is the conspicuous one S of Crested Butte. To climb it start from 1½ miles SW of the town on 135, where from 8800′ a road runs S ½ mile to connect with a trail running SW along the N side of the mountain. Two miles of trail take you to a couple of little ponds and, just beyond them, the end of the flattened end of the N ridge. It is a climb of 2500 relentless feet, all within 1½ miles.

WEST ELKS—OHIO CREEK GROUP

QUADS: Mount Axtell, Anthracite Range, Squirrel Creek, West Elk Peak; Gunnison N F.

The group includes Carbon Peak, the Anthracite and West Elk Ranges. State 341, the access road, leaves State 135 3½ miles N of Gunnison and climbs on Ohio Creek 27 miles NNW to **Ohio Pass,** 10,074′. It then rejoins 135 a mile N at **Kebler Pass. Carbon Peak,** then the **Anthracite Range,** and then **West Beckwith Peak** come into view from the valley. There are glimpses too of the ridge country of the West Elks, bristling for a fight with rock climbers, and as you climb the pass look at the water cascading off the Anthracite.

Carbon Mountain, 12,709′, has a 6-mile trail, not maintained or signed, from 4½ miles NW of Baldwin, at 9000′, through the forest to the mountain's curiously round summit. Baldwin is the ghost coal camp on the right, 19 miles from Gunnison.

Ohio Peak, 12,271′, is the most tempting excursion on the Anthracite Range because of the cascades. Instead of going up to the pass, where you have an altitude advantage, leave your car at mile 24½, 9400′, where the road crosses a stream to go right on the hillside. Climb up the little ridge left of the stream for the first half mile for a close look at the falls, then work farther left for the main E ridge. Where it steepens climb NW to the crest ridge for the major part of the work. The total distance is 3 or 4 miles. The Anthracite "Range" is one 4-mile long E–W curved mountain, with **Ohio Peak** an E summit. The higher W summit, 12,385′, is 2 more miles along the ridge, with a 300′ obstacle summit and a dip to 11,800′ after that on the way. Too much.

The West Elk Range itself has a N–S backbone of some 5 miles of 12,000′ crest points, with long arms extending eastward towards upper Ohio Creek from distances of 8 to 14 miles. It is largely in the West Elk Primitive Area with the deep-in parts accessible only from trails. The best approach by road is from 1½ miles NW of Baldwin (See Carbon Mountain above), where a normally but not always drivable road of sorts takes off W for 6 miles to Castle Creek Cow Camp.

From mile 5 on this road a trail runs S 2 miles to South Castle Creek. It then skirts the range for several miles as the **Lowline Trail,** joining finally with a road up Mill Creek.

At mile 6, the end of the Castle Cow Camp road, there is a 1-mile jeep trail W to a long trunk trail. Going NNW it takes you 16 miles past **East Beckwith Mountain** to State 135, about 10 miles W of **Kebler Pass.** Going S, it takes you first 2 miles S to a pair of shelf lakes above and N of South Castle Creek, at 9900′. It then sidehills SW 4 miles up to and along the creek itself, and at 11,300′ zigzags out S 2 miles to 12,450′ **Storm**

Pass. It then drops down a little basin to the **Mill Creek Trail.** It is labeled the **Mill-Castle Trail.**

The Castles are a rough section of ridgetop between Castle and South Castle Creek, at about 12,000′. To visit the area, turn up the hill, right, from the above trail about where it finishes contouring in close to South Castle Creek. You can climb 700′ on a ridge and then work to the right to get in close to the toothsome rocks. The summits themselves are a matter for the technical climber.

West Elk Peak, 13,035′ high point of the range, goes from the same trail. Keep on it until you have climbed 2 or 3 double elbows toward **Storm Pass** and then head off 2 miles straight W to the SE ridge.

The Mill Creek Road goes W 11 miles from Gunnison, 8½ from 135. It goes in 5 miles up the creek on easy grades but possibly too rough for a car. At mile 4 the **Lowline Trail** comes in; at 9000′, ¼ mile short of the end, the **Mill-Castle Trail** climbs off it on the hillside to the right and then parallels the creek. It finally tops off at mile 9, about 12,700′, 150′ lower than the top of **North Baldy Mountain.** About mile 4 you are under a stupendous cliff, rising some 800′ vertically and 3-400′ more in toto. As there is a junction beyond which this trail is not maintained, you should inquire at the Gunnison Ranger office as to whether you can get through on it at all easily.

The extraordinary cliffs and pinnacles in the West Elks are in a formation called the West Elk Breccia, composed of volcanic agglomerate and breccia, probably Miocene in age.

Other much longer road and trail combinations come into the area from the south—up the Beaver Creeks, Steuben Creek and Sun Creek and a ridge leading to **Middle** and **South Baldy Peaks,** and connecting with these from the west side up Coal Creek and over 11,629′ **Bonfisk Peak,** and up through Big Soap Park and the Soap Creeks, but these do not take you so close to the part with mountaineering interest.

GUNNISON NORTH FORK GROUP

QUADS: West Beckwith Mountain, Marcellina Mountain, Paonia Reservoir, Minnesota Pass, Paonia, Mount Guero, Crawford, Cathedral Peak; Gunnison N F.

Several more or less separated peaks string westward from the Elks and West Elk Range as far as Crawford, between the Gunnison and its North Fork.

Marcellina Mountain, 11,348′, presents to the Kebler Pass road south of it a piece of geography 2000′ high by 2 miles long that is a showpiece of eocene roughness. It appears the rock was pushed up by a tertiary intrusion and is still angry. You could certainly get up there walking from the rear with enough bushwhacking but we recommend you either take rope and gear and try it head-on or leave it alone. The Forest Service is planning a trail from the east end to the summit.

West Beckwith Mountain, 13,432′, is a ridge with 5 almost identical cirques cut into it from the N. The route to it starts 12 miles W of **Kebler Pass** on 135, where you go S on a secondary but probably drivable road 2½ miles to Lost Lake Slough, 9623′. Cross to the E side of the outlet and follow the side of the lake and the creek S all the way up the big cirque; climb out on the cirque's far right corner and finish a little way along the S ridge. To do the whole ridge along to West Beckwith Mountain is perfectly possible but very long, and we understand the traverse back to the lake would take you through very rough country. West Beckwith is one of several mountains in the area which seem to have started out as circular domes. Others are **Carbon Mountain** to the E, and **Sand, Saddle** and **Landsend** Mountains and **Tater Heap.** See Crawford, Paonia and Mount Guero Quads.

Minnesota Pass Trail starts from 14 miles E and S of Paonia at the end of Forest Road #710 at Beaver Dam Reservoir. It crosses **Minnesota Pass** at 9993′ and **Curecanti Pass** at 10,400′ elevation, and runs down Curecanti Creek to the end of Forest Road #720 for a total of 20 miles.

Mount Gunnison, 12,719′, on Minnesota Pass and West Beckwith Quads, is a miniature version of Mount McKinley, given enough ice to fill the scooped-out valleys. They fall off from the massif in all directions from the summit region. It is a mountain not to get lost on. The approach is a long one. From downtown Paonia a road goes up Minnesota Creek 7 miles E and 2 S to a junction. Take a right and continue on a secondary or jeep road 2 miles E and 2 S to Beaver Reservoir, 8100′. You may be able to jeep farther; in any case follow the right side of the reservoir and East Fork to a trail junction at 8500′. Find Hoodoo Creek, probably a little south of the junction, and climb along it E, SE and E for 3 miles. The trail-less climb up Hoodoo Creek may be the hardest part. Where the creek becomes quite steep, at 10,300′, leave it and climb the slope to its right, a 1600′ rise in one mile. Work left near the top and you will come out on the easy SSW ridge a mile from the summit..

The mountain is named for Captain John Gunnison, who was assigned in 1853 to explore the central of four possible railroad routes across the country. For the twenty wagons in his train he built a road—over Sangre de Cristo Pass, over Cochetopa Pass, down the Gunnison, and out to Utah, where he was killed by Indians. Beckwith, who succeeded him in command, is honored in the peak names to the east.

Mount Lamborn, 11,395′, and **Landsend Peak,** 10,806′, are the conspicuous end pieces of the mountains tapering off from the Elks as you drive toward Hotchkiss and Paonia. From the SW part of Paonia take a road parallel to the D & RG tracks and S of the river. It crosses the tracks 1½ miles from town, and a little later, after you have passed a gravel pit, turns off left and S. After ½ mile of S, go E 1 mile and S 1¼ miles to a right turn for Bell Creek Springs, which are 3 more miles SE. You cross to the right side of Bell Creek and can probably drive another mile up SE to the trail head, at 7400′. Trail continues up Bell Creek 3 miles ESE to a saddle at 9600′ on the Landsend–Lamborn ridge. Landsend is 2 miles SW along a flat ridge.

Lamborn is 1½ miles N up-ridge, but if it looks too obstructed keep on the trail. If you take left turns it spirals NE to NW in 3 miles and puts you within ¼ mile and 700′ of Lamborn on its SE side.

North and **South Saddle Peaks,** 9728′ and 10,055′, are climbed from the S side. From Crawford drive ½ mile SE on State 92; go left (E) 1½ miles, S 11½ miles, E and S ½ mile and E 5 miles to the junction at a pond, 8214′. Climb 1½ miles NNW to S peak on the ridge. For N peak you drop to a 9728′ saddle.

To visit **Castle Rock,** the striking 11,205′ S point of Mendicant Ridge, visible from the Black Mesa Road SE of Crawford, continue on above the road about 2¼ miles E of the starting place for Saddle Peaks. From a sharp hairpin, a jeep road leads S 2½ miles to end at about 9250′, a mile NW of Castle Rock.

For climbs farther W, take the Smith Fork Road E from upper level street in Crawford. Go right (E) ¼ mile after the road turns N. You pass close S of the local showpiece, **Needle Rock,** about 5 miles E of town, and go by Smith Fork Campground at mile 7. About mile 10, when the road turns S, at about 7600′, you can trail E 2 miles and NE 1 mile to the 10,984′ mountain called **Tater Heap.** For **Mount Guero,** 12,052′, continue 2 miles farther on the trail and climb a mile NNE.

GRAND MESA

QUADS: Skyway, Hells Kitchen, Grand Mesa, Leon Peak, and peripherally Collbran, Lands End, Cedaredge, Chalk Mountain, Indian Point, Point Creek; Grand Mesa N F.

The Grand Mesa lies between the Colorado and the North Fork Gunnison. Its W end juts prominently above Grand Junction and Delta; the E tapers to lower mesa country W of the Elk Range. The chief charm is the lake-strewn W part, which is reached by State 65, which crosses from the Colorado River S to Cedaredge. It was traversed by Escalante in the year of American Independence, at the time he crossed the Colorado north of Debeque.

Rhythms in the sand, San Luis Valley Dunes. *H. L. Standley photo.*

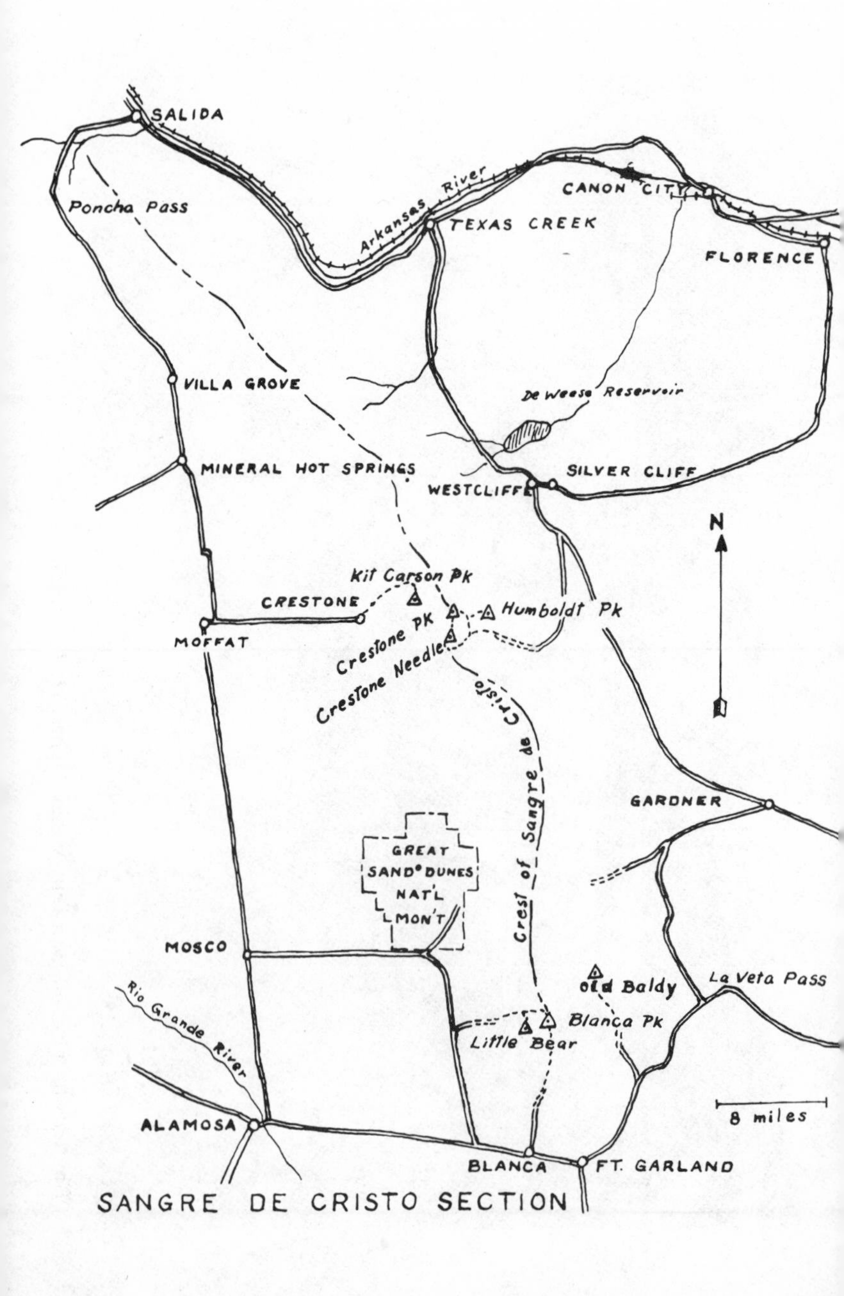
SALIDA
Poncha Pass
Arkansas River
CANON CITY
TEXAS CREEK
FLORENCE
VILLA GROVE
De Weese Reservoir
MINERAL HOT SPRINGS
WESTCLIFFE
SILVER CLIFF
N
Kit Carson Pk
CRESTONE
Humboldt Pk
MOFFAT
Crestone Pk
Crestone Needle
Crest of Sangre de Cristo
GARDNER
GREAT SAND DUNES NAT'L MON'T
MOSCO
Old Baldy
La Veta Pass
Rio Grande River
Blanca Pk
Little Bear
8 miles
ALAMOSA
BLANCA
FT. GARLAND
SANGRE DE CRISTO SECTION

Leon Peak, 11,236′, is a little oval mesa that rises its 200′ gradually from a larger triangular mesa which is 200′ above the surroundings. The approach road is the main one running E from the settlement of Grand Mesa 8 miles to a pair of Twin Lakes a mile S of the peak.

The **Crag Crest Trail** starts on the N side of Island Lake from State 65 ½ mile E of Grand Mesa Lodge. It climbs to, and follows, the Grand Mesa Crest. It drops and terminates at Crag Crest Campground on the Collbran Road. This is a distance of 7 miles. Travel is by foot or horse only. The trail overlooks the Mesa's nearby lakes and much of western Colorado.

The **Land O'Lakes Trail** starts from the parking lot adjacent to State 65 1 mile W of Grand Mesa Lodge. It is a loop trail to basalt rock overlooks which provide a panoramic view of the mesa's lakes. Four interpretive signs assist the traveler. The trail is asphalt paved and limited to foot traffic only. Round trip is roughly ¾ mile.

SANGRE DE CRISTO RANGE

Sangre de Cristo is the Spanish name for the mountain crescent between Salida and Santa Fe. Translated Blood of Christ, it refers to the alpine glow of sunrise and sunset. In Colorado the name is applied only to the chain which runs 75 miles SSE from Salida to Sierra Blanca. On the map it is an exclamation point—a long straight line of peaks with the Blanca group forming a detached dot below. To the west lies the flat-floored San Luis Valley with its artesian water and its national monument of thousand-foot sand dunes. The lower central portion, most interesting to mountaineers, is accessible from the Wet Mountain Valley which parallels it on the east. Except for Blanca, which is of igneous rock, the higher Sangre de Cristo summits are composed of folded and layered metamorphosed sedimentary rocks of Pennsylvanian to Permian age, notably the greenish, durable conglomerate of the Crestones.

Much of the Blanca massif and the area south of the dunes are on the Sangre de Cristo Grant and the Luis Maria Baca Land Grant No. 4. The history of the Baca grant starts in 1821 when the Spanish rulers granted the Vegas Grandes land grant (present Las Vegas, New Mexico) to Don Luis Maria Cabeza de Baca, descendant of the Cabeza de Vaca who walked across the southwest in the 1530's. By the 1860's, when the U.S. Government set out to settle claims for Spanish and Mexican land grants, many families had settled on the Vegas Grandes (Big Meadows) without permission of Don Luis and his heirs. Instead of putting these settlers off the land, the government offered the Baca heirs their choice of equal acreage elsewhere. They chose two parcels in New Mexico, two in Arizona, and one in Colorado in the San Luis Valley—the fourth of the five grants. The Baca heirs (21 of them) ceded the San Luis grant to their lawyer, who sold it to land speculators. The speculators were as unsuccessful as the gold mines that were found near the town of Crestone. Finally, in the 1930's, the Baca Grant No. 4 attained success. A middle-aged Philadelphia tenderfoot with money, named Alfred Collins, turned it into a spectacularly successful cattle ranch. He sold it 20 years later, but today the 99,128.39 acres of the original Luis Maria Baca Grant No.4 are still intact as part of a larger cattle outfit.

Time and again surveyors of this Baca grant tried to get to the top of the Sangre de Cristo range to establish the boundary line, but they always failed. They wrote words like "inaccessible" and "unsurveyable" on their maps across the face of Kit Carson, Humboldt, and the Crestone Peaks.

In the summer of 1961, Bill Arnold, Lester Michel and Jim Michel, aged 14, trekked the range crest from Poncha Pass to Music Pass in a period of 9 days, with the help of food caches.

The names of mountains in the Sangre de Cristo Range which do not appear on Forest Service or Geological Survey maps are from a list submitted for approval to the US Board of Geographic Names by the Names Committee of the Colorado Mountain Club. CMC directors have approved the list.

The range divides itself naturally into three groups: North, Main, and Sierra Blanca.

SANGRE DE CRISTO RANGE—NORTH SECTION

QUAD: 15′ Howard; San Isabel and Rio Grande N F's. The 17-mile string of crests from **Poncha Pass** to **Hayden Pass** is seen from Poncha Pass and south, and from the Arkansas Valley open areas 12-20 miles down US 50 from Salida. The summits are not far under 13,000′.

ARKANSAS SIDE

The north entry point of the **Rainbow Trail** is 4½ miles south of US 50 on the Bear Creek road. Bear Creek enters the Arkansas River 2½ miles below Salida. The trail continues on jeep road up Bear Creek for 3 miles before starting the ins and outs SE along the range. Permission is required to go higher on the Bear Creek jeep road, which climbs to about 10,300′, 1½ miles below range crest.

From Howard, 12½ miles down the river from Salida, a road goes 3½ miles W up Howard Creek to the Calcite quarries at 7600′. It continues as a jeep road (take left fork at ¼ mile) 5 miles and as a trail 1 more mile to Hunts Lake, at 11,300′, where timberline camping is available.

Hunts Peak, 13,067′, N and most conspicuous point of the range as seen from US 285 N of Salida, is a steep mile-long climb by the E ridge, for which you start by going a little N from the lake. It is a good-sized 2 miles SE along the ridge to **Red Mountain,** 12,974′, with a lot of side-hilling or 600′ of lost altitude on the way.

From Stout Creek School, on Cherry Creek, 2½ miles down US 50 from Howard, 9½ up from Cotopaxi, a 2½-mile road climbs first in Cherry Creek and then to Stout Creek (left at mile 1½), at 7200′. A trail, jeepable the first 1½ miles, climbs 3 more miles to the **Rainbow Trail** at 8400′, and across that to a junction 2 miles SW at 10,000′. The right fork climbs 1½ miles to 11,700′ Stout Lakes. This trail, and the branch from it to

Bushnell Lakes, is reached a little more easily from Hayden Creek Road (below).

Twin Sisters Peak, 13,087′, is $\frac{3}{4}$ mile due W of the lakes. You can climb straight to the summit—this is toward and up the right side or head of the cirque. The Twin Sisters were named from the valley, with reference to the two very symmetrical ridge faces they have on the valley side. The left one as seen from the Arkansas Valley is a mile NE down-ridge from the above summit. The one seen to the right is on a parallel ridge NW of Cherry Creek. Its ridge end, the symmetrical part as seen from the valley, is $1\frac{1}{2}$ miles NE of the range crest. **Bushnell Peak** is a mile SE along the ridge from Twin Sisters and can be done with their summit.

The left fork of the **Stout Creek Trail** goes S half a mile to the Bushnell Mines and then $1\frac{1}{2}$ miles along the three little Bushnell Lakes to the valley head. **Bushnell Peak,** 13,105′, high point of this range section, is less than $\frac{1}{2}$ mile S of the uppermost lake. The best route is to use the easiest gradient: work NW to the Stout Creek ridge, and a little right of its high point to the range crest, and SE along that to the summit.

Hayden Creek road leaves US 50 about 4 miles NW of Cotopaxi, 21 SE of Salida, and climbs $4\frac{1}{2}$ miles to Hayden Creek Campground, at 7600′. The Hayden Pass road continues from it SE up the ridge $4\frac{1}{2}$ miles to cross the range at 10,709′, and drop by a very steep route to the San Luis Valley and Villa Grove, $6\frac{1}{2}$ miles. The E side is less steep and short-wheel-base cars can make it for a shortcut of some 45 miles. The **Rainbow Trail,** which comes in from the NW to Hayden Creek Campground, meets a side trail after 2 miles which climbs and crosses another $1\frac{1}{2}$ miles to the Bushnell Mines and a trail from Stout Creek to Bushnell Lakes. It thus provides the best approach from a car to Bushnell Lakes and Peak.

SAN LUIS VALLEY SIDE

Several trails go in to the northern Sangres from US 285 on its 16-mile stretch between Poncha Pass and Villa Grove. The first, from 2 miles S of **Poncha Pass,** goes as a jeep road up Dorsey Creek (keeping right) for 2 miles to the NE, and continues as a trail for 2½ miles from 9200′ through the timber to 10,700′, where it is a mile S and 1000′ below **Methodist Mountain,** a little timber-free N end point of the range. Under the name of **Simmons Peak Trail** it turns SE and contours under the range crest for 3½ miles to a point about ½ mile past little Salamander Lake, 10,800′, where it is ¾ mile SW of Simmons Peak, named for an Arkansas Valley pioneer.

Simmons Peak, 12,051′, is best climbed from ¼ mile E of Salamander Lake via the timber-free slope left of the trail and E along the ridge.

At this point the trail turns S and downhill to cross North Decker Creek after 1½ miles and another mile to a road on Rock Creek. It is possible to come down (or reversing, to go up) North Decker Creek, using cow trails for the first mile and then by pick-up road 3 miles out to Alder on the highway. The Rock Creek road comes out 3 miles SSE of Alder on the highway and requires permission from S. A. Bagwell, owner.

The most useful trail is perhaps the midway one from Alder E and N (keeping left, N at ½-mile point). It takes you 4 miles N by jeep road to Lone Tree Creek at 9600′, and continues as trail from there 2 miles NE to the **Simmons Peak Trail,** reaching it midway between Simmons and Methodist.

A 5-mile road runs N from a mile NNW of Villa Grove on 285, taking you to a T, where you can drive E on jeep road to the forest boundary and 2 miles up the right fork to 9200′. From just short of the road end at the mine a steep but generally open ridge climb of nearly 4000′ in 2½ miles will take you to the summit of **Twin Sisters.** If you want more, go SE a mile passing right of the midway ridge point, and climb **Bushnell Peak,** 13,105′. The WSW Bushnell ridge takes you back to the starting place.

The Hayden Pass road runs E from ½ mile N of Villa Grove, and though not badly surfaced is too steep for most cars, climbing 2000′ in the last 2 of the total 8 miles. From the crest the **Black Mountain Trail** runs SE parallel to the range crest on the W side 6½ miles to a 12,503′ summit point on the long NW ridge of **Cottonwood Peak,** then turns off down Black Canyon to Orient. See Valley View Hot Springs Quad.

Nipple Mountain, 12,199′, is on the above **Black Mountain Trail,** 4½ miles from the **Hayden Pass** end. It is climbed from the point where a branch trail—the **Quarry Trail**—runs off SW. From the trail it is a 600′ summit climb.

SANGRE DE CRISTO RANGE—MAIN SECTION

QUADS: 15′ Electric Peak, Cotopaxi and Howard; Beck Mountain, Crestone Peak, Liberty, Crestone, Sand Camp, Medano Pass, Valley View Hot Springs and Horn Peak (duplicates part of Electric Peak); San Isabel and Rio Grande N F's.

This section runs from **Hayden Pass** to **Mosca Pass.** The crest peaks run generally from well over 13,000′ through 14,000′, with no saddles under 12,000′ except at Hayden Pass and from **Medano Pass** south. Except for a section in the Crestone area the summit climbs do not present problems so long as visibility is good and the cliffs can be seen and avoided.

WET MOUNTAIN VALLEY SIDE

The flanking road for the E side of the range is State 69, which runs from Texas Creek on US 50 through the Wet Mountain Valley and SE to Walsenburg and I-25. The Wet Mountain Valley was settled by several colony groups, including one peopled by Germans from which Colony Creek and Colony Lakes take their names. The valley is one of the lesser of Colorado's large mountain parks, and wide enough so that the summits can be seen all along the road. Some very rich silver mines were developed in the neighborhood of Westcliffe, and two railroads came in, the first a narrow gauge which washed out, the second some time later up Texas Creek. Silver Cliff, a mile west of Westcliffe, came into being when the citizens felt they were being cheated by a water company and so moved their dwellings up the road.

The **Rainbow Trail,** 55 miles long, skirts the E flank of Sangre de Cristo Range from Bear Creek S to Cottonwood Creek Road and **Music Pass,** 22 miles S of Westcliffe. The average elevation of this trunk trail is 9000′. It crosses 40 streams, many of them with side tails running up them to the lakes and range crest of the Sangre de Cristo.

Named for its arc shape, the trail was constructed over the period 1912–1930 at a cost under $15,000. Like the flanking trails it was built largely for fire protection but serves also for horseback and pack trips and is useful as a cross line for backpackers. It is included here because the part in the Main Section of the range is the best maintained and has the most interesting side trips—those to Lake of the Clouds, to Hermit Pass, to Macey Lakes, to South Colony Lakes and the Venable-Comanche loop. For the full trail see Cameron Mountain, Howard, Electric Peak Quads, all 15′, and Horn Peak, Beck Mountain and Hooper 1 NE.

A northern line of access called the **North Lake Trail** goes W from Hillside, 11 miles S of Texas Creek on US 50, 14 miles N of Westcliffe. This road is good for cars up to Balman Reservoir, 9500′, mile 5 from 69 (see Cotopaxi Quad). It continues 7 miles more as jeep road up past Rainbow Lake to the Cloverdale, a mine franchised to operate within the national forest and thus on land open to the public. Take no static. Car can be left near the house at the mining operation. A trail continues up the main drainage to a 12,700′ pass and continues as **Garner Trail** into the San Luis Valley. It is about 6 miles down Garner Creek to the road on that side.

Cottonwood Peak is a little over a mile NW of the **Garner Creek Pass.** To reach it from this side turn off the pass trail about a mile up Cloverdale Basin from the mine dwelling and climb 400 feet on the right side (NW) to Silver Lake. Strike directly up to the saddle N of the lake, then climb SW to summit along the ridge. The ridge climb is 800′ in a mile.

Thirsty Peak is a short climb E from the pass trail crest.

Wulsten Baldy, 12,820′, is a NNE offshoot of Cottonwood, 2½ miles removed.

Though it's ridgedly linked with its mother
And is only a runt
It's so far out in front
That you can't see the one for the other.

To climb it, turn off as for Silver Lake but angle back as you climb so as to come to the ridge N of the big hump between Wulsten and Cottonwood. **Eagle Peak,** 13,221′, rises directly behind the Cloverdale Mine. The best approach however is to stay on the trail till past the last timber, and then angle SE for the ridge leading back N to the top. From the low spot left of the ridge bump you have an easy mile N along the crest.

A trail-bike trail runs in to the Brush Creek Lakes.

Go in as for **North Lake Trail** from Hillside. At mile 4, 8800′, leave the car and go 3 miles S on foot or wheeler to **North Brush Creek Trail.** It is 7 miles to the lakes, which are close under the range crest. The trail turns S and continues as the **Crossover Trail,** a sort of elevated **Rainbow Trail.** From the upper lake, 11,500′, it climbs to 12,300′, then drops S to a cirque heading the S fork of North Brush Creek, at 11,600′, next ascends around the next ridge crossing it at 12,500′, and then zigzags down to timber at 11,500′ in Middle Brush. It climbs Middle Brush to Banjo Lake, 12,400′, and up to the next ridge S, 500 feet higher. It then descends to and along the South Brush Creek. **Electric Peak** is directly above Banjo Lake. It is best climbed however by going up the ridge N of Middle Brush Creek from where the trail crosses it—an easy 1½ miles WSW. The stretch from Brush Creek Lakes across the ridges to timberline in South Brush is about 9 miles in beautiful high country, which makes it very inviting as a backpack loop. Trail vehicles can go along the **Rainbow Trail** but not up South Brush Creek, which is a climb of 7 miles and close to 3000 feet from Rainbow to the climb-out at timberline. The direct road approaches from the E to the Brush Creeks are reported closed to the public, which makes the access routes rather long, particularly to South Brush Creek.

Gibbs Peak, 13,575′, is the most prominent summit from a considerable stretch of the valley. It is climbed from a camp on South Brush Creek, preferably near where Horseshoe Bend Creek comes in from the left (S) at 10,800′. Bushwhack along the E side of this creek through timberline till you are pretty high in the basin, then cut off left (ESE) to the saddle connecting Gibbs to the range crest for an easy finish on the ridge.

Two trails go into the range from a resort place called The Pines. From ½ mile NW of Westcliffe on 69 you drive W 7 miles, jogging N twice and angling WNW at mile 5.

A jeep road goes NW a mile to the **Rainbow Trail,** which you follow a little way NW to Texas Creek. A no-vehicles trail goes in 4 miles from 8800′ to a timberline lakelet at 11,500′. You can get to **Gibbs Peak** by continuing for an 1800′ climb straight W up the narrow gulch to the range crest and then doubling back NE along the easy ridge.

The **Lake of the Clouds Trail** leaves the **Rainbow Trail** S of The Pines. Inquire there for the best route to it (1½ miles or so). The Clouds Trail is open to trail vehicles the full 5 miles to the lakes from The Pines, a climb of 3000′ to 11,600′.

Mount Marcy, 13,305′, 1½ miles NW of the lakes, is climbed most easily from them by a route N to its gentle ENE ridge and up that.

Spread Eagle Peak, 13,481′ and 13,431′, has its saddle 1 mile S (half left as you face up canyon) from the lakes. The climb to either or both summits (the western summit is the higher) goes by way of the saddle and along the connecting ridge. Spread Eagle is descriptive of the formation, the summits being the wings which sweep away from the lower hump or head between.

A road that is roughish in spots runs W from the S side of Westcliffe up Middle Taylor Creek 15 miles to **Hermit Pass,** 13,000′, on the range crest. After the snowbanks are gone most cars can make it to about 12,600′, ½ mile short of the top. The road goes down the W side only a short distance. There are several good camping places in the valley, notably a meadow at about mile 12.

Rito Alto Peak, 13,794′, is a climb of only ¾ mile and 800′ NW from the pass, or from the ridge by Horseshoe Lake 1800′.

Hermit Peak, 13,322′, is an even shorter climb if you go S from the pass. **Eureka Mountain,** 13,489′, is 1½ miles SE along the ridge from Hermit Peak. A trip that looks attractive is to climb from Hermit Lake to the pass on foot, walk down range over Eureka and drop SE on a good slope back of the cliffs to Goodwin Lake, then climb N over the saddle E of Eureka to Eureka Lake, and either contour NW to Horseshoe Lake or cut down the hill E before that.

North Taylor Creek has a trail too. From about mile 8 W of Westcliffe on the Hermit road you can take the **Rainbow Trail** N a mile at 8600′. It is about 4 miles up North Taylor to a little lake under **Rito Alto Peak.** The N ridge of this valley, **Spread Eagle Peak,** is not difficult from here.

The Schoolfield road, which leaves 69 3½ miles S of Westcliffe, takes you W 6 miles to Abbots Lodge and Alavarado Campground, 9100′. This approach is used for each of four valleys.

Goodwin Lakes Trail starts with a mile of **Rainbow Trail** leading WNW to Goodwin Creek from Abbots Lodge. From the Rainbow it climbs 4 miles to the lower lake at 11,500′, where you are under the upper Goodwin Lake and an easy route to **Eureka Mountain** by its SSE face.

The **Venable** and the **Comanche Trails,** the former starting N and the latter S of the lodge, go up to complete a loop at 12,800′ behind the range crest. On the Venable Trail one side-tracks into Venable Falls, looks across S from Venable Lakes at the Phantom Terrace, and cuts left from a little E of **Venable Pass** across the E face of **Venable Peak** on a high shelf route to the range crest saddle, where one meets the other trail from the S. It is about 6 miles to the range crest either way, and ½ mile on the western slope of it.

Venable Peak, 13,352′, **Spring Mountain,** 13,244′, and **Comanche Peak,** 13,277′, are all within half a mile of the trail and present no difficulties beyond a little steepness. The ground trip is a big day without these additions, and since there is camping (preferably on the Comanche side) we recommend it as a deluxe overnight tour.

The fourth valley is Cottonwood Creek, for which you walk S 1½ miles on the **Rainbow Trail** from Alvarado Campground. This trail climbs 4 miles to 11,600′. Vehicles outlawed. **Horn Peak** can be climbed by the long NE ridge from near the start of the trail, or from a route which uses the trail for altitude and takes off SE to climb first a little way toward the bowl behind the peak, then N around to the W ridge and up that. The preferred route is from the S.

The Horn Creek Ranch road turns S off 69 5 miles SSE of Westcliffe and after the first mile goes W 4 miles to Horn Creek parking. It is the starting point for trails up Dry Creek, Horn Creek, and Macey Creek.

Dry Creek Trail is reached from a ½-mile stretch of **Rainbow Trail** running NW from the Horn Creek road. It climbs in 5 miles from 9300′ to 11,800′. Camping is good between the falls and the lakes.

Horn Peak, 13,450′, like **Gibbs Peak** farther N, is far enough E of the crest to dominate its section of the valley. The route climbs NW from the lower lake to the peak's W ridge saddle, thence NE to the top. For little Horn Peak climb S off the trail when it comes back to the creek above the falls. From the ridge, which is low here, it is a good-sized trek—1½ miles and steep—to the top. Trail vehicles are prohibited in this valley.

A more direct route to **Horn Peak** is by Hennequin Creek. From 5 miles W of 69 on the Schoolfield Road, toward Alvarado Campground, go by jeep S and SSW 2½ miles to the **Rainbow Trail;** continue on the trail and up the creek or right hand ridge for 3 miles to summit. If the jeep road to Hennequin is impracticable you get the same sort of a trip by going S 1½ miles from Alvarado Campground on the Rainbow Trail and

1½ miles up the **Cottonwood Creek Trail.** From there you take to the ridge on your left.

The Horn Creek jeep road climbs from the 9000′ terminus of the car road 2½ miles to 10,300′ and as a trail 3½ miles more to the upper lake at 11,800′. Little Horn you pass on the right; Little Baldy is the long ridge running to the valley head on the left.

Mount Adams, 13,931′, is at the upper lake valley head on the right. The ridges cut it off from all but a point or two of State 69. When you do see it it is a wedge shape and looks high, hard and handsome. Climb NNW from the upper lake to the ridge, a mile or less, and then left up that to the finish. A rope is recommended.

Little Horn Peak, 13,143′, and **Fluted Peak,** 13,554′, are connected by a mile of narrow but quite passable ridge. From trail mile 5 take the side trail right to the right basin and lower Horn Lake. Climb N to the low point left of Little Horn and E to summit; reverse on the ridge and go up to the range crest and NW along cirque crest .1 mile to Fluted.

The **Macey Creek Trail** likewise starts in effect from the Horn Creek road head parking place. It is 2 miles S on the **Rainbow Trail,** then 6.5 miles SW to the upper Macey Lake, 11,650′, all open to trail vehicles.

Colony Baldy, 13,745′, ½ mile E of the lake, is climbable on its WSW face. You keep to the left fork of the valley and trail and go up and around the upper lake there. Then you turn right and ascend.

North Colony Creek has a trail which runs 5½ miles in from the Rainbow. It is closed to vehicles and can only be approached on rather long stretches of the **Rainbow Trail** from either Horn Creek or South Colony.

South Colony Creek is a favorite haunt of mountain climbers who go there to enjoy the **Crestones,** the roughest and some of the pleasantest part of the Sangre de Cristo. From Westcliffe, drive 4.6 miles SSE on 69, then S 5.6 miles on Colfax Lane, where you turn W and climb on an increasingly rocky and

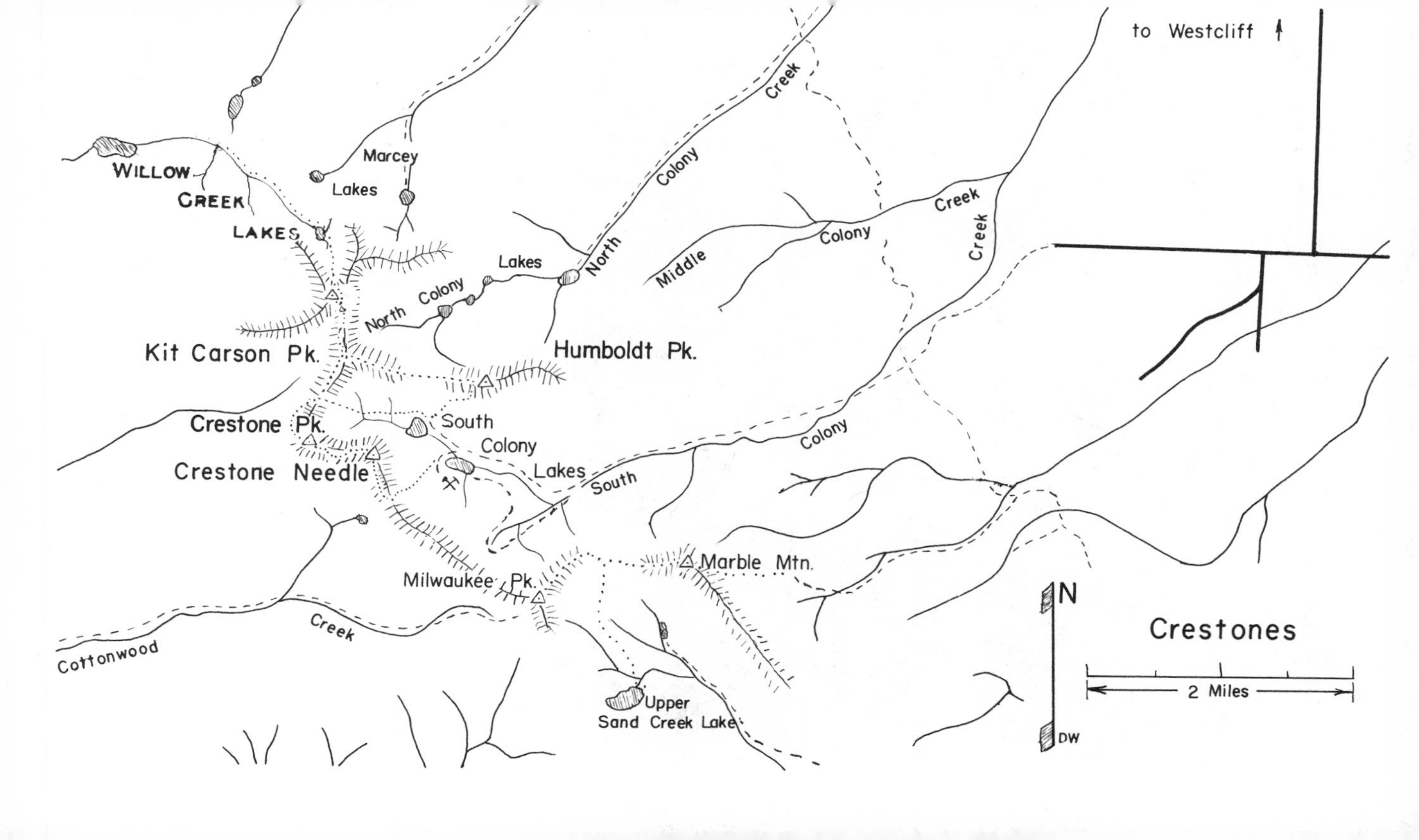
Crestones
2 Miles
N
DW
to Westcliff
Willow Creek Lakes
Marcey Lakes
Kit Carson Pk.
North Colony Lakes
North Colony Creek
Humboldt Pk.
Middle Colony Creek
Colony Creek
Crestone Pk.
Crestone Needle
South Colony Lakes
South Colony
Marble Mtn.
Milwaukee Pk.
Upper Sand Creek Lake
Cottonwood Creek

steep road. The old road to Queen Anne Copper Mine has been replaced by a recent one to a uranium digging under **Broken Hand Peak.** This is a jeep road, and goes about 8 miles in from Colfax Lane. A little before it makes the second crossing of South Colony Creek back to the S side at 11,000′, take the old mine road to the right, which is marked and provides a walking route off WNW to the lower lake. (There is also a trail to the lakes from the end of the uranium mine road.) There are good camping knolls near the lake; a large party is better housed downstairs. For this you make the second crossing of the creek (see just above) and stop there. There is also a good meadow farther down stream.

Humboldt Peak, 14,064′, is an ant hill type mountain (small rocks for sand grains) a mile NE of the first lake, which is 11,667′. The short but tedious climb—best from farther up the valley—offers as reward a fine view of **Crestone Needle** and **Peak** across the valley. Most years it sends a snowslide down its S face to South Colony Creek.

Except for parties thoroughly familiar with the routes, rope should be taken for the other climbs from this camping area.

Kit Carson Peak, 14,100′, is 3 miles NW from lower South Colony Lake, and most frequently climbed from there. Go up the right hand trail from midway along the lower lake to the upper lake and rock-whack W to the head of a cirque and 13,150′ plateau. Pass to the left of the unspectacular rock-pile hump. From the saddle beyond it, 13,450′, you should go over the ridge summit immediately W and climb down to the notch beyond, losing about 350′. The 600′ climb up-ridge to summit is steep but not difficult.

Crestone Needle, 14,191′, and **Crestone Peak,** 14,294′, are often climbed together. From the NW end of lower south Colony Lake, approached as for **Kit Carson** above, climb generally toward the low point of the Needle's left (ESE) ridge, and after .2 mile find a zigzag cairn-marked route more directly up until you cross a ridge at the third pinnacle NW of the low point. Contour left around the first rib to get into an easy steepish hard-rock gully for the summit climb. (The first gully is airier and parties require rope for one short steep section, though the rock is not difficult.) On the descent be looking for the way back left to the ridge or you will get too low. The gully from the lowest point of the ridge is very rotten.

The Needle-to-Peak traverse looks precipitous but though slow it is not difficult. Drop from the Needle to the saddle WNW (fixed hand rope will move your party faster) and keep contouring left. You can begin climbing after you pass the red saddle. (A technically easier route contours 200′ below the red saddle to a huge red gully not previously visible, and up the gully to the high saddle.) From the high saddle between the summits, climb left. Return to same and go down the NW couloir. Sand on smoothed rock or ice problems may make this very slow. Traverse right as soon as you can, and go down to the plateau and a steep couloir for descent. Below the upper lake, keep well to the left to find the trail to the lower lake and so avoid deep willows. Strong parties make three and sometimes all four 14'ers in a day. **Crestone Peak** can of course be climbed by this descent route, but the best traverse from it to the Needle is harder to find going ESE.

13,573′ **Broken Hand** has a flattish face climb most of the way up if you go directly S from the lower end of the lower lake. **Milwaukee,** about 13,522′, is due S up steep rock and ledges from the head of the S (jeep road) fork of (South) Colony Creek. There is on the same massif a higher summit (13,631′) ½ mile to the WSW, as yet unnamed. This may be given the name **Pico Isolado** since it is way out of sight. **Milwaukee** is connected with **Marble Mountain,** the smoother more conspicuous one you see from the valley, by a 1½ mile arc of ridge circling the head of Sand Creek. It is steep and rough on the Colony side, smooth on the S. It is a mile S by crusty ridge from Milwaukee to **Music Mountain,** and another ¾ mile more to **Tijeras Peak.** The first three of these, **Broken Hand, Milwaukee,** and **Pico Isolado** can be reached from Music Pass and the trail to Upper Sand Creek Lake. For **Tijeras Peak** or **Music**

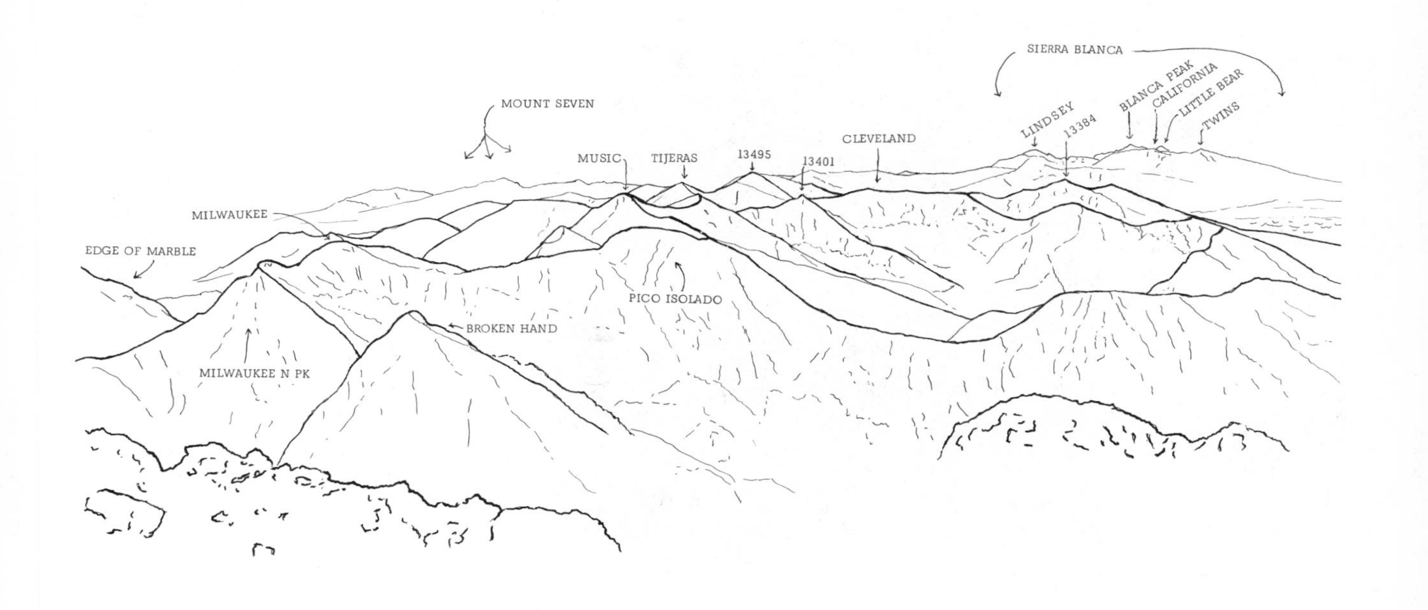
SIERRA BLANCA
LINDSEY
13384
BLANCA PEAK
CALIFORNIA
LITTLE BEAR
TWINS
MOUNT SEVEN
MUSIC
TIJERAS
13495
13401
CLEVELAND
MILWAUKEE
EDGE OF MARBLE
PICO ISOLADO
BROKEN HAND
MILWAUKEE N PK

Looking south from Humboldt Peak, the Sierra Blanca group. *H. L. Standley photo.*

Peak, or both, you would best go from **Music Pass** W past Lower Sand Creek Lake to their connecting ridge.

Broken Hand Peak, 13,573′, is directly south of the lower South Colony Lake. There are interesting routes on this side, and an easier approach from beyond the notch separating this peak from **Crestone Needle.** The notch itself is rather too steep and dirty for comfort, but you can get behind it from higher on the right as for Crestone Needle, and then drop to it on the easy side.

Milwaukee Peak can also be reached from the back, or SW side of **Broken Hand.** It goes best if you drop to about 12,500′ to traverse across the slope of Broken Hand to get into the W basin of Milwaukee for the ascent. Climbers have also gone directly up from the S or uranium mine fork of South Colony directly up-cirque to the saddle between Broken Hand and Milwaukee, then up the sharp W ridge of Milwuakee's false N summit, and S to top.

The **Marble Mountain Trail** runs up most of the way to the **Rainbow Trail** as jeep road. Turn W from the end of Colfax Lane as for South Colony Creek, but after $\frac{1}{4}$ mile go S a mile and then SW 2 miles along the SE side of Hudson Creek. If this fails, go back the 3 miles to the E-W road and another mile W on it. Turn S again and inquire at the Henrich Ranch for the best way to the **Main Range Trail** S of there. You should be able to drive close to 9000′ in a 4-wheeler. The trail continues for pedestrians only for 3 miles above the Rainbow, and is used as the approach for the Marble cave and other caves.

Marble Mountain, 13,262′, is a smooth frontal ridge running parallel to the valley and range. It climbs on this steep side, more or less directly from the trail end at 11,500′. Marble can of course be approached from the South Colony road. The **Rainbow Trail** crosses the latter 4 miles W of Colfax Lane and $\frac{1}{2}$ mile E of the road's lower stream crossing. From this point it contours S 3 miles to Hudson Creek and the **Marble Mountain Trail.** It is also possible to climb Marble Mountain sans trail, by climbing straight up the first ridge crest S of South Colony Creek. This way you use the Rainbow Trail for only $\frac{1}{4}$ mile.

The trail to **Music Pass** is open to 4-wheel drive vehicles. For this you take the same road as for South Colony Creek, but at the end of Colfax Lane go one half mile E and then turn S. Keep right at $\frac{1}{4}$ mile and left at mile 2 after the jog W. About 3 miles S, where you come to Grape Creek, you enter the forest boundaries at about 9300′. Rangers rate the road jeepable the next $5\frac{1}{2}$ miles up west to the pass, 11,400′. Sand Creek, on the other side of the ridge, gives access to several fine rough peaks.

Music Peak, 13,369′, is a little over 2 miles W and a little N from Music Pass. Walk on a trail from the pass 1 mile into Sand Creek and up to about 50 yards past the first timber. Here you should pick up a trail cutting left for lower Sand Creek Lake, 11,471′, 1 mile SW. Go counterclockwise around the lake to the N side, where from a clearing a game trail leads to timberline and good slopes.

Tijeras Peak, 13,604′, has not been honored with a route description. It is 1 mile SSE along the ridge from **Music Peak,** and presents a formidable ridge-crowned wall to Lower Sand Creek Lake. The likeliest way for a trail seems to start up as for Music Peak, from the N side of the lake, then to turn S from about half way up the Music basin. Look for a break through the steep midsection of the canyon side. The upper slopes lead SW less steeply to a short stretch of NW ridge for a finish. Tijeras can easily be combined with Music Peak since their connecting ridge is the likeliest route for the latter.

Milwaukee Peak, 13,522′, heads the Sand Creek Valley. It should be approached from 11,745′ Upper Sand Creek Lake. From the lower lake you head NE far enough to pass under the cliffs, then up the slopes NW for a mile. Cross the upper lake outlet and climb 200′ or more on the ridge that ends at the outlet far enough to let you cross, NE, losing some altitude, into the long NW basin heading Sand Creek. Continue NW all the way to the South Colony ridge, 12,750′, and follow it left around to Milwaukee. Taken this way the peak has a false summit, 13,436′, .2 miles short of the top. When you are camping high and have time, Marble Mountain can be combined with Milwaukee. It is about 2½ miles N and E along the ridge, with some 500′ drop to regain. As for **Pico Isolado,** the higher summit ½ mile WSW of Milwaukee, we will leave that to adventurers up Cottonwood Creek on the W side.

Cleveland Peak, 13,414′, 2 miles SSW from Lower Sand Creek Lake, suggests a long airy approach from a camp there. Go SE ½ mile from the lake's outlet across flats until you can climb S up the broad north-facing ridge there. In ¾ mile you should rise 1800′ to the ridge crest (as far right as practicable). Continue W ½ mile toward Tijeras' S ridge point, and then turn to contour S along the E side of the ridge all the way to Cleveland, passing the 13,405′ midway point about 200′ below its summit.

The Medano Pass road is a jeep trail, viable part way by car. It leaves 69 8 miles WNW of Garner and continues in that direction 2 miles to South Bradford School and thence N ¾ mile where you take the right hand choice of two roads at the junction. From here it is NW 2 miles to the forest boundary and the 1.7 mile jeep trail via Muddy Campground to **Medano Pass,** 9950′.

Mount Seven's top summit, 13,350′, is just over 3 straight miles W of **Medano Pass.** From Muddy Campground, 9125′, you take the jeep trail over the pass and ½ mile down the other side to the trail junction at 9600′ on Medano creek. The right fork goes W, NW and SW 5 miles to little Medano Lake, 11,515′. You can climb the left (S) side of the cirque to a bench 400′ higher, then if the S face looks too steep cross to the N side, ½ mile NNW, and take the more reasonable ascent route there. When you reach the bench after 200′ of climb, head W to the ridge saddle and S ½ mile to the summit. See Medano Pass Quad.

SAN LUIS VALLEY SIDE

From near the junction of 285 with State 17, 4 miles S of Villa Grove, a road runs E 7 miles and N a mile to Orient, once an iron source for Pueblo's Colorado Fuel and Iron Company, and hence a rather interesting place to prowl about in the red ore.

From mile 3 on the Orient road a road runs N, and at mile 2 on the N road a jeep road turns off NE 2½ miles to become the **Quarry Trail** at 8475′. It climbs 5 miles to the **Black Mountain Trail** at 11,600′ on **Nipple Mountain** (see above with N Sangre de Cristo section).

The left fork of the Orient road goes N a mile beyond Valley View Hot Springs, where you can pick up the **Black Canyon Trail** at 9000′ and climb NE 3 miles in the valley to a trail junction at 11,000′. The left fork zigzags N 3½ miles to the 12,503′ end of **Cottonwood Peak's** NW ridge. The right fork continues ½ mile toward the canyon headwall under the NW face of Cottonwood Peak. One can continue to the basin head and then climb out SW to the ridge to make a round trip with the better route below.

Cottonwood Peak, 13,588′, has a trail to within easy distance from the summit. From Valley View Hot Springs you can drive a jeep 2½ miles up Hot Springs Canyon road (starting SE from the settlement) to 10,200′, and continue by trail 3 miles to near 13,000′ on the peak's W ridge.

The **Garner Trail** starts from the right fork at mile 7 of the Orient Road and climbs over the range crest to Cloverdale Basin and Rainbow Lake down the other side. Turn left on a jeep road after 1 mile and go right (E) along Garner Creek one mile, end of permission for cars or jeeps, at 8900′. Trail bikes are permitted for the next 4½ miles to the 12,650′ crest.

Thirsty Peak, 13,217′, is a short clamber ESE from the Garner Trail pass. It takes its name from the Michel-Arnold traverse of the Sangre de Cristo. The trio arrived at this peak in a dried up condition and had to satisfy their thirst by gazing down at the Brush Creek Lakes. They survived and two days later began to get daily drenchings.

The **Major Creek Road** leaves the road S from Orient 1½ miles farther S than the **Garner Creek Trail,** and runs 4 miles ENE up the canyon to a fork at 10,000′. The left fork, which is restricted to horse and foot travel, climbs 2½ miles to the crest at 12,450′ and continues ½ mile on the other side to a junction with the **Crossover Trail** in the head of the S fork of North Brush Creek.

Electric Peak, 13,621′, the highest point N of **Rito Alto Peak,** is most easily approached from this range crossing. It is 1½ miles SE along the crest ridge—a pull of 800′, a level-off, and a pull of 400′ more.

Mount Niedhardt, 12,863′, whose name honors an early settler, is a mile-long ridge walk due S off the crest from the above halfway level stretch NW of **Electric Peak.** You lose 400′ altitude that way, but can use it for descent down the trough due W to the S fork of the Major Creek road.

Cotton Creek road, the next S, is best approached from 1½ miles S of Mineral Hot Springs on State 17. You drive E 5 miles, N 2 and E 5, the last on a jeep road to and up Cotton Creek to 10,000′. Travel above this point is restricted to horse and foot. The trail continues a mile up-canyon to a junction, and on the right 5 miles SSE to Cotton Lake at the 11,500′ timberline. It continues S a long mile to the 12,500′ pass separating the long **Mount Owen** massif from the main range, and then heads around W down Rito Alto Creek.

Mount Marcy, 13,510′, is about 2 miles NE of the lake on good slopes. From the pass top you can skirt E and S around the bowl to climb **Spread Eagle Peak,** or head NE to the higher 13,521′ peak 1½ miles WNW of Spread Eagle.

The left fork of the **Cotton Creek Trail,** mile 1 beyond the end of jeep travel, climbs 1½ miles of steep slope to cross the range crest at 12,800′, and drops a little way on the other side to the **Crossover Trail,** meeting it at its S end, head of South

Brush Creek. This suggests a loop trip with the **Major Creek Trail** via the cirquier side of the range.

The road to Cherry Creek goes straight W from 5 miles S of Mineral Hot Springs on State 17. It is 8 miles, the last 1 or 2 perhaps requiring jeep. **Cherry Creek Trail** climbs 5½ miles from 8600′ to Cherry Lake, 11,800′. No vehicles are permitted.

Mount Owen, 13,387′, is a steep but climbable mile due N from the lake.

Rito Alto Creek route starts as for Cherry Creek but turns S at mile 5 E of State 17. At mile 3 S go E again 2 miles, where jeep road runs off NE 2 miles to forest boundary and all-vehicle restriction. The trail climbs 4½ miles ENE up to Rito Alto Creek to 10,900′, junction point for the pass trail N to Cotton Lake (above), and a 1½-mile continuation S to Rito Alto Lake, 11,350′, and E 3 more miles up to meet the Hermit Pass road at 13,000′. **Rito Alto Peak** is an 800′ 1-mile climb NNW up-ridge from the pass.

South of Rito Alto Lake, about ¾ mile up the Hermit Pass road, there is a junction with a trail (the **Rito Alto**) S over the ridge at 12,200′ and around the head of San Isabel Creek, then over a 12,400′ pass and down the N fork of North Crestone Creek. The high pass offers a short brisk climb of 1000′ NW up the ridge to **Eureka Mountain.**

A mile S off this pass at 11,700′ another trail comes in from the E over Venable Pass—the one from Alvarado Campground. **Venable Pass** is 1½ miles E and a climb of 1100′ to 12,800′ from the trail junction.

More trails are reached from State 17 on the latitude of Moffat, which sends a 12-mile road E along the N side of Baca Grant No. 4 to the village of Crestone.

For Dimick Driveway drive a jeep road 1½ miles NNW to San Isabel Creek, where from about 8400′ an 8-mile horse-and-foot-only trail climbs NE to San Isabel Lake, at timberline (11,600′) in the right fork. The trail also cuts up S to the **Rito Alto Trail** under **Hermit Peak,** and so suggests loop trail trips of various kinds.

For the **North Crestone Trail** go straight N from the E side of **Crestone** 1.2 miles and 1.5 miles NE up-creek to road end, where all vehicular traffic stops at 9000′. At mile 2 up the creek the N fork trail turns off left, climbs 2½ miles in the North Fork and then up the ridge ½ mile to a junction. On the left is the **Rito Alto Trail** to the NW, well under the range crest and parallel to it. On the right is the trail to **Venable Pass,** 12,800′. Turning that way you can follow the **Venable Trail** S on the far side of the range crest to Phantom Terrace and then along the near side to **Comanche Pass** and then descend on the Crestone Creek Middle Fork to the junction with the North Fork. From the road end this makes a 13-mile loop, more or less comparable with the Venable-Comanche one from the Alvarado side in the Wet Mountain Valley.

By keeping right at mile 2 above the road end in North Crestone Creek you pass the **North Fork** and **Middle Fork Trails** above and take the Lake Fork, which takes you 3½ miles ESE to North Crestone Lake at 11,800′ on the Lake Fork, under **Mount Adams.**

Fluted Peak, 13,554′, is a short stiff climb of 1800′ from the lake. Go N up the cirque and NE to the ridge saddle, then S to the top. **Mount Adams** goes by its steep and airy NE ridge. First climb SW from the upper lake end to the saddle, 900′, then the ridge, for which maybe you should have a rope along.

There is a road, open for 2½ miles to jeeps, E from Crestone to two trail heads. The left one follows South Crestone Creek 3½ miles to South Crestone Lake, still in timber at 11,800′. **Mount Adams** is a climb of 2 miles and 2100′, ending upside the basin or on either side ridge, whichever looks better.

The **Willow Lake Trail** takes off E from just E of the start of the Crestone trail and climbs from 8400′ to 11,560′ Willow Lake (the lower one) on a 4-mile route restricted to horse and foot travel. A camp in this valley gives short routes to **Mount Adams, Crestone Peak** and **Kit Carson.** For the last it is the easiest approach.

To climb **Kit Carson Peak,** take an angling route up the slope facing Willow Creek to where a high contour ESE lets you into the notch E of the bulkier end of the peak (14,084′) for the steep climb to the true summit, 14,165′. If you want to go on to **Crestone Peak,** descend 550′ to the gash ESE, climb over next point (320′) and head along and on the right side of the ridge on easier terrain toward Crestone Peak, 2½ miles E and S from Kit Carson. Climb Crestone Peak in the reddish or snow-filled trough, a rather slow and dirty passage and a bit loose for a crowd. Rope and an ice axe may be needed. For Crestone Peak alone the best route takes you in Willow Creek to the upper lake, 1½ miles upstream, at 12,325′. You can then climb E to the headwall saddle a little over 13,000′ there, and S up the ridge a way, where you will look for a high traverse right to bypass left of **Obstruction Mountain** as we might call it, and so make your way to the golf course section.

The Baca Grant #4, a little square of some 12½ miles on each side, has its NE corner close in to the Willow Creek Lakes and contains about half the trail up Cottonwood Creek 7 miles to **Milwaukee Peak**'s E cirque. If you want to investigate the trail, turn in at the Baca gate, some 10 miles E of Moffat on the Crestone road, and inquire for permission, conditions and location. The creek is 7 miles SE from the ranch. You should make sure where you are to go and not squirrel around; this is in sand country and even your jeep can go down wallowing. With luck however you may back pack in to a camp at the mile 5 meadows, about 11,400′. **Milwaukee Peak** is 2 miles straight up the valley, all trail except the last little steep pitch.

Pico Isolado, 13,631′, is just right of Milwaukee Peak and best climbed from the saddle between the two whether alone or with the latter. The saddle is at 13,200′, the last 400′ very steep. From it you turn back to the right along the ridge. This peak, though it is the highest point between Crestones and the Sierra Blanca massif, is all but invisible from both the valleys flanking the range. Hence this tentative and unofficial name.

The Crestones are also within reach of the camp on Cottonwood Creek. For **Crestone Peak** go back from the camping area ½ mile or less, to where you can contour right into a north fork of the creek. Follow the line of this fork, climbing 800′ in a half mile to another drainage fork. A little way up the right fork is a lakelet under the usual approach to **Crestone Needle.** The lake has an old Indian name: Lake-you-come-down-to-when-you-come-down-wrong-way. You can follow the left fork all the way to the red saddle between the Needle and Peak. You can also get to the Needle and to **Broken Hand** by taking another north route from Cottonwood Creek—to the side cirque near the upper end of the valley.

Another Baca jeep road of interest if passable goes to and up Pole Creek to a mile beyond the land grant boundary, where you are at 9600′, about 3½ miles WSW of **Cleveland Peak.** If there is any sort of fisherman's trail up the rest of Pole Creek it would be a good way in to Cleveland Peak. Pole Creek Lake, at 12,000′, is directly W of and 1000′ below the very flat W ridge of Cleveland, which rises at the far end to a 13,414′ summit.

Two Baca roads converge at Liberty, name of the quad and start of the **Sand Creek Trail.** If you do not gain permission from the ranch, or are camped at the Dunes Monument, you can get to Sand Creek another way, suggested by the Dunes' superintendent:

> "By 4-wheel-drive vehicle, go north of the Monument Visitor Center on the Medano Pass Road. Park near Little Medano Creek and hike across the top of the dunes to Cold Creek and go down Cold Creek until Sand Creek is reached. This is about a 6-mile hike, all unmarked with only game trails to follow and most of it through sand. You get a great appreciation of the size of the Sand Dunes and there is little problem in finding your way if you have any directional sense."

From Liberty the **Sand Creek Trail** goes a mile SE, a mile E and 6 miles NE, and 5 miles N and NW to the head of the valley. Little Sand Creek comes in from the E side of the Tijeras-Cleveland N-S ridge at mile 8. The top of that creek to some lakelets there was pronounced "real rough" by a pioneer. It pretends to no trail. At mile 12 of Sand Creek, the trail over **Music Pass** comes in from the E across the low S ridge of **Marble Mountain.** This is about even with Lower Sand Creek Lake, which is up on a bench on the E side of the valley. Upper Sand Creek Lake is benched above the valley head in like manner. Since Sand Creek is more easily approached from the E side the climbs in it are treated with those on that side of the range.

The Dunes are an extraordinary playground and camping spot reached by driving 22 miles E from $\frac{1}{2}$ mile N of Mosca on State 120. (Mosca is on State 117), or by driving N 16 miles from 160, 6 miles W of Blanca, to State 120. The white sand, rising 1000′, is that of an inland sea.

The Medano Pass road goes N for jeeps 6 miles N from Dunes headquarters and turns up Medano Creek going 7 or 8 miles more to **Medano Pass,** 9950′. The grade is very gentle up to the last half mile, and possible there, but it may be closed to vehicles, and in any case is not of great interest. From 3 miles off the top it connects with a better road up from Bradford on State 69.

The Mosca Pass jeep road goes directly east from Dunes headquarters, but is washed out and closed to traffic. One breezes up the E side in a car.

SANGRE DE CRISTO RANGE—SIERRA BLANCA

QUADS: Blanca Peak, Twin Peaks, Mosca Pass, Zapata Ranch; Rio Grande and San Isabel N F's.

The name sierra is often used for a whole range. We apply it here to the massif of which Blanca Peak is the highest individual mountain or peak. It includes besides Blanca the cluster around it: Little Bear, California, Lindsey and their ridges. As usual we add to it anything in the neighborhood that seems convenient.

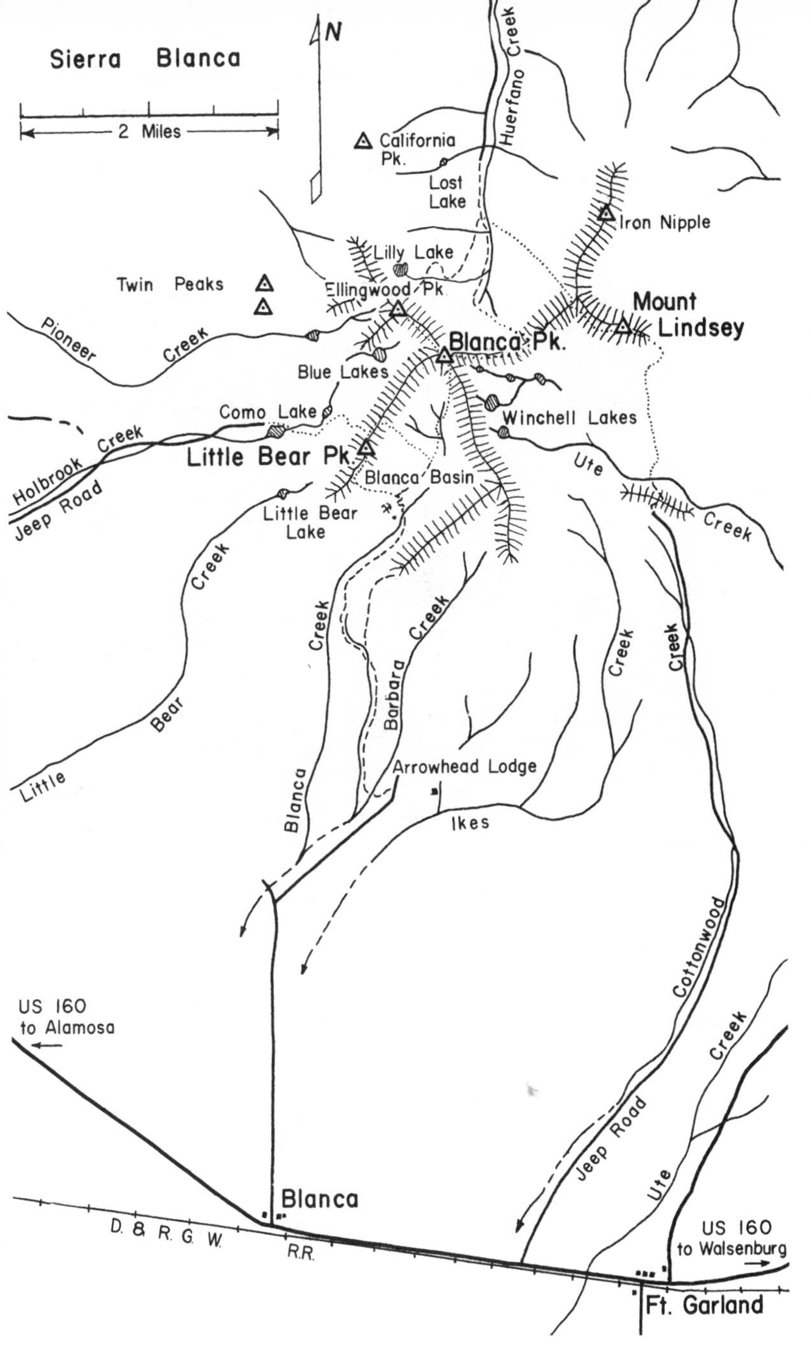

Looking south from Crestone Needle.

Blanca Peak from Mount Lindsey with Little Bear to the left and Ellingwood to the right. *H. L. Standley photo.*

The Mosca Pass road turns off State 69 WSW from Gardner and is the main road west all the 18 miles to **Mosca Pass,** 9750′. It goes a little higher to a relay installation with no special advantages for viewing. You can drive ½ mile down the W side for a campable area or for a walk down to the Dunes and back. It is a touch over 3 miles to the highway, where you are at 8200′. The return over the same route is approximately 4½ miles.

At mile 12½ from Gardner, where the Mosca road changes from SW to WNW, you can leave it to go SW up the **Huerfano.** The road is good enough to mile 4, where there is a ranch. Beyond that you will need a rough-country vehicle for the stony road and can go only another 4 miles or so to the main E-W forest boundary line and probable end of driving. You can camp here at 9950′ or farther up. A mile farther S in the valley brings you to the **Huerfano Trail,** a route across the valley connecting on the W side with **Zapata Drive Trail.**

California Peak, 13,849′, is climbed from this trail, which zigzags to the right up to the ridge, 2 miles. From this point, at 11,845′, it is 2½ miles S on good enough footing to the summit.

Mount Lindsey, 14,042′, was known as **Old Baldy** until renamed in 1954 for a devoted leader of Denver's Junior group in the Mountain Club. To climb it continue on the **Huerfano Trail** from the forest boundary 4½ miles to just beyond Lily Lake turnoff trail. A trail of sorts can be found in the first draw coming into Huerfano Creek from the left. You follow this and climb 2 miles to the ridge saddle at its end, at 12,500′. From here you climb NW ¼ mile to the higher ridge, 13,150′, and then right a mile to the summit.

Iron Nipple, 13,828′, is a respectable summit 1½ miles N of Lindsey and can be climbed from the same 13,150′ ridge saddle. You head N and NE on the ridge for a curved mile.

Blanca Peak, 14,338′, shows a fine steep N face to this valley. The best route for a party of any size is probably the one that starts up the **Lily Lake Trail** and from the farthest S bend of the trail cuts directly W up the slope to the ridge. The mile and a half of ridge from there up is not difficult despite the loss incurred by going over **Ellingwood Peak,** 14,042′, ½ mile short of the summit. Smaller groups can have good and not too slow rope play at the right edge of the N face, where there is a couloir and rib combination. The gash ridge on the left goes, too. The gash itself is no problem, but just above it the rock is smooth, sandy and disconcerting for a short piece. To get to the NE ridge (Gash Ridge) leave the Huerfano at or N of the exit for Lily Lake, and head SSE up the drainage basin to the left of the ridge point .3 mile ENE of the Blanca summit. To get to the ENE ridge you best go to and over the ridge point that is .3 miles off the Blanca summit. Go up the drainage to the left of it on grassy slopes till you reach the ledge 1000′ above the valley. Go right and get on the prominent N ridge, which takes you up to the main Blanca ridge. The summit block goes best from 100′ to the left of the ridge crest.

The traditional S route up **Blanca Peak** is reported closed by the present owner, but is described here with the hope that it may again be approachable. From US 160 at Blanca, turn N at the intersection with a stone shelter. Jog W, then N; 4 miles from 160 keep right; after 2 miles park at the former Arrowhead Lodge, 8300′. The trail goes N past cottages, skirts a dump, crosses a stream and follows a jeep road N to a grove of cottonwoods; it continues N on the W side of a dry gulch toward the ridge, and 3½ miles from the lodge reaches Blanca Creek at 9400′. A climb of 2 miles along the creek trail brings you to abandoned mine cabins in a good camping area at 11,000′. A trail continues N up the valley another 2 miles to Blanca Basin, from which a route to the summit may be selected.

Little Bear Peak, 14,037′, is also climbed from this camp. Go only a short way up-trail toward the basin from the cabins and strike left (S) up S slopes and a rotten S ridge to the summit. Continue N along the ridge for ¼ mile or less to find a descent route. Able climbers have sometimes done the full ridge to

Blanca, but the ridge gives most of us too much the impression of having to be held together.

Lake Como, on the W side of the massif, gives a jeep road access to both **Blanca** and **Little Bear** which involves less altitude and mileage for climbs. From US 160, 6 miles W of Blanca (15 E of Alamosa) drive N on a dirt road toward Dunes Monument 5 miles. Turn NE and follow the car road 2-3 miles, then proceed on rough jeep road 4½-5½ miles more up Holbrook Canyon to Lake Como, 11,750′. A trail climbs another 2000′ to the valley head, 3 miles. **Blanca Peak** is on the right, and 14,042′ **Ellingwood Peak** on the left, of the 13,750′ saddle. To climb **Little Bear,** which is only 1 mile E of Lake Como, keep up valley 1 mile and then head a little left of the summit to finish on its NE ridge. Crest rocks there are precariously poised. Ellingwood Peak is named, tentatively as yet, for the first Colorado climber to try peaks the hard way. A Rhodes scholar, he had learned balance climbing in England's Lake District.

As Lake Como is privately owned, climbers would do well to seek permission at the restaurant in Fort Garland, or at least to refrain from fishing the lake. In starting up the road, keep generally right, which is the most used track.

The Zapata Ranch entrance is at mile 12 N from 160 on the same road, and 1 mile S of State 150, the road to the Dunes from Mosca. Three trails, one up North, one up Middle and one up South Zapata Creek, start E from the ranch as a single jeep road. Ben King, an old timer there, reports that the **North Zapata Trail** was built by Coley King up the N side of the canyon many years ago and that it is still in good condition. It crossed the range crest to connect with routes to Gardner. It would give access to the long smooth far-north ridge of **California Peak** for an attractive high country walking trip. **Middle Zapata Trail** is rated very rough.

The **South Zapata Trail** climbs to South Zapata Lake, the first 5 miles of it by jeep to Zapata Falls. The remaining 3½ miles, open to 2-wheelers, climbs from 9400′ to 11,900′.

Twin Peaks, 13,580′ and 13,534′, are a mile up the South Zapata Lake basin on the right (W) side on quite climbable grades. **Blanca Peak,** which is 2 crow miles SE from the lake, has a feasible route from here that includes also **Ellingwood Peak.** Go SE and ENE a mile to the ridge crest, 13,000′, and then climb as from the preferred large party route from the N (see above).

Mount Mestas, 11,569′, and **Rough Mountain,** 11,138′, flank US 160 on the route from I-25 W to **La Veta Pass.** Mount Mestas, named for a La Veta (town) soldier lost in combat, is so near and so conspicuous that it must have been climbed or at least tried a number of times on impulse from the road. The best route would take off less spectacularly from a mile short (SE) of the pass at 9200′, and bushwhack 1½ miles ESE to the saddle between **Mestas** and **Rough,** 10,600′. Rough is close at your left and 300′ higher; Mestas, steep at first, becomes a 1½-mile ridgecrest walk.

WET MOUNTAINS or CUERNA VERDE RANGE

QUADS: Beulah, Wetmore, St. Charles Peak, Hardscrabble Mountain, Deer Park, and Rosita (N half of range only); 30′ Pueblo, Canon City, Huerfano Park and Walsenburg; San Isabel N F.

These mountains are a short NNW trending range; they represent a southward structural continuation of the S end of the Front Range. The range is bordered on the E by a thrust fault along which the core rocks—precambrian granites and metamorphics—were shoved up and eastward over the younger flanking sedimentary rocks. The western edge of the Wet Mountains seems to consist of a series of steeply upturned sedimentary rocks which have been faulted. Tertiary volcanic rocks and quaternary alluvial deposits obscure the western border structure at the northern half of the range. Greenhorn Mountain, at the S end, is a large anticlinal structure.

The range is the broad 45-mile-wide NNW-SSE frontal ridge seen from the Pueblo-Walsenburg highway. Except for a short crest at the S end it is all under timberline—an area of woods, meadows, campgrounds, brooks and a few lakes. There are two blacktop roads: State 165 from Rye NW along the range, and State 96 from Wetmore across it into Westcliffe. The latter gives a fine look across at the Sangre de Cristo.

There are two dirt roads. One leaves State 165 at Ophir Creek Picnic Ground, 7 miles NW of Lake San Isabel, and runs down off the SW side to State 69 near Gardner. The other branches off the first 7 miles SW of its exit from 165 and runs 16 miles SSE parallel to the range crest all the way to the W side of Greenhorn Peak, giving a farther S view of the Sangre de Cristo peaks.

There are several trails in the Greenhorn whose moderate ups and downs are well-suited to horsebacking. In general these are open to 2-wheel and snow vehicles.

The **South Creek Trail** starts at the S boundary of Pueblo Mountain Parks area, 2 miles W of Beulah, and bears W on old road back of Walters Ranch. It runs for 10 miles over Greenhill Divide and circles N to Davenport Campground near Greenhorn Highway. Branches of this good trail run into Squirrel Creek and Middle Creek.

From mile 2½ of the Gardner road (above) there is a close approach to the well-timbered **St. Charles Peak.** You go by way of the **St. Charles Trail** and have a 2-mile walk and short climb. The other terminus of the trail is on 165, 2½ miles SSE of Ophir Creek and ¾ mile N of Greenhill Divide. St. Charles Peak is 3 miles from that (E) side.

Greenhorn Peak, 12,349′, is a very short climb from the plateau where the road ends. To treat it as a mountain, climb up to it from the W end of Rye on the **Greenhorn Trail,** which starts at about 7200′ and takes you 7 miles up Greenhorn Creek to the same road. You are at the N end of the 4-bump summit ridge, and can either flank it on the road for a mile or so and then climb up, or go up directly and follow the ridge to Greenhorn, 1½ miles SSE.

The **Maes Creek Trail** starts a little higher—7500′—and brings you to the road next to the summit in 4½ businesslike miles. Drive to Farista, about 6 miles ESE of Gardner on State 69, then 8 miles N on dirt road. The second right turn after that should take you another 1½ miles on jeep road back to Maes Creek and the trail head.

CULEBRA RANGE

QUADS: Trinchera Peak, El Valle Creek, Culebra Peak, Cuchara, McCarty Park, Stonewall, Torres, Taylor Ranch; Spanish Peaks 30′; San Isabel N F.

Culebra is Spanish for snake, a name first given to a creek. The range runs S 30 miles from **La Veta Pass** to the New Mexico line, with the high section centering S of the middle. The Spanish Peaks, E of the range, are taken with it.

The W slope of the Culebras is on the Sangre de Cristo Grant, the vast tract which includes the lower Trinchera Ranch. It was deeded in the 1840's by Governor Armijo of Santa Fe to Narcisco Beaubien and Stephen Lee of Taos. Narcisco was a 12-year-old boy, Lee a sheriff and distiller of Taos lightning; they received the grant for no other reason than that they asked for it. When both were killed by Indians, Beaubien's father inherited his son's share and bought out Lee's heirs for $100. In 1867 ex-Governor Gilpin of Colorado and associates bought the Grant, and divided it into the Costilla and Trinchera Estates, the better to peddle it to colonists in Europe. Their London-published promotion books are lavishly illustrated and one contains the statement that the San Luis Valley never gets cold.

The Culebra peaks are not difficult climbs but access routes are limited. On the W side there is a jeep road in to McCarty Park, but this is N of the high section. There are some long trail approaches but all through private land and closed. Official names of summits in the high part of the range include only Trinchera, Culebra, Vermejo, Purgatory and Red Peaks. The rest that are used here are proposed names under

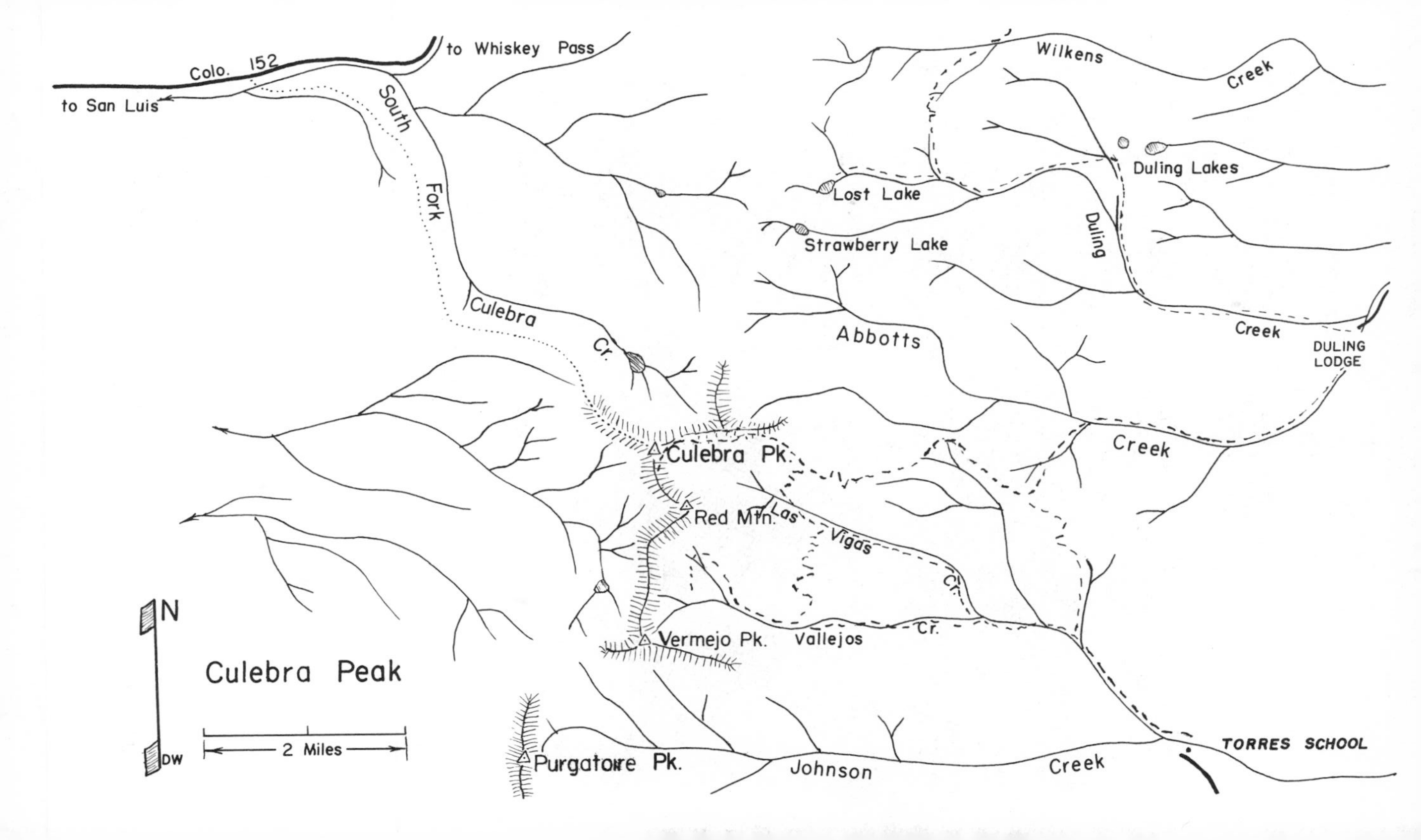
to Whiskey Pass
Colo. 152
to San Luis
South
Fork
Culebra
Cr.
Wilkens
Creek
Duling Lakes
Lost Lake
Strawberry Lake
Duling
Abbotts
Creek
DULING
LODGE
Creek
Culebra Pk.
Red Mtn.
Las
Vigas
Cr.
Vermejo Pk.
Vallejos
Cr.
Purgatoire Pk.
Johnson
Creek
TORRES SCHOOL
N
DW
2 Miles
Culebra Peak

Looking toward Crestone Needle from the Bears Playground. *H. L. Standley photo.*

consideration by the U.S. Board of Geographic Names. Among the proposals is a change from Red Peak to Espinazo Rojo, a Spanish equivalent (red spine or ridge).

SAN LUIS VALLEY SIDE

Culebra Peak, only 14'er of the range, has been traditionally climbed from the W side, where changing-owner situations keep putting the print out of date. See Culebra Peak, El Valle and Taylor Ranch Quads. Currently one can drive from San Luis 13 miles through Chama and E on State 152 to a junction. Take the right fork down across the stream, where you can camp comfortably but should not trust the water for drinking. This is at 9500′. Follow the jeep road 100 yards beyond creek crossing and take a right course S to the S fork, which you ford. Continue on the road and turn left through a small cow pasture, where you can turn right (W) and mount the ridge. Follow the ridge SE, E and S 5½ miles to summit, using trail as far as timberline. The first and second false summits may be skirted on the SW side of the ridge crest to cut loss of altitude in the deep saddle.

Lomo Liso, 13,128′, and the more interesting **Peak N,** 13,468′, can be reached from the same camp. Instead of crossing the S fork of Culebra Creek as for **Culebra Peak** you keep left up the valley on a jeep trail that climbs 3 miles to 10,600′, almost directly west of Lomo Liso. Climb E on a ridgelet N of the creek for a way and then veer left to get on the main E ridge of the peak. It is 2½ miles in all from the trail's end. Go E and S along the ridge crest overlooking cirques. In the first mile you drop to a 12,600′ saddle. It is another mile S around the crest and up to Peak N. You can descend directly W into the bowl and past lakelets and bushwhack down-creek to jeep road, altogether 3 miles WNW.

The Whiskey Pass road, 152, continues E from the above point of departure, mile 13 from San Luis, to a junction at mile 16½. It is currently closed before you reach this point, but we optimistically present some possibilities. From the junction, the main road continues 1½ miles, first on the left hillside and then back to the creek, to a second junction at mile 18, 11,000′. The right or main branch doubles back and into a S branch where it dies, close to but 1000′ under the pass. Cars have gone to this point. See El Valle Quad.

Beaubien Peak, 13,188′, is ½ mile S of the 12,550′ **Whiskey Pass** saddle. **Francisco Peak,** 13,135′, is 1¼ miles S of Beaubien over an easy ridge with a drop to 12,700′. On return you can work W from the latter saddle and avoid a second-time climb before the descent.

From the mile 18 junction a left fork continues straight up the left creek on jeep grades 1½ miles ENE to an 11,600′ saddle one mile W of the range crest.

Cono De Anza, 13,333′, and **Mount Maxwell,** 13,405′, are within a 2-mile radius of this trail ending. Climb E .3 mile to the ridge and S on it ½ mile to a flat on the range crest. Turn NNE ½ mile up ridge to Cono De Anza. Drop N along the ridge to 12,850′, and climb NE up-ridge 1 mile to Maxwell. 13,335′ **Mariquita Peak** is a mile farther N along the ridge. As the W side is quite rough you will have to return over Maxwell, a climb of 350′ from the saddle to the N of it, to get back to base.

Purgatory Peak, 13,676′, and its 13,466′ north twin are a handsome ending to the main range string. They lie only a mile apart at the head of San Francisco Creek, but are separated by a 12,827′ saddle. The approach, which we have not checked for private closure, is from San Francisco, where you drive a jeep-rated road 2½ miles ESE and 3 more E from the town up the creek to 10,300′ and then bushwhack or wade or whatever's right to the end of the valley, some 4 miles up the drainage to the saddle. See La Valle and Culebra Peak Quads.

EAST SIDE

At the N end of the range the approaches are from the east. County road 410 leaves State 111 a mile S of La Veta and goes about 9 miles by way of Indian Creek into the wooded country near **Veta Pass** (the railroad one). The **Indian Trail** takes off at mile 8 and runs down, generally on the E side of the crest, to Blue Lakes. There it continues as the **North Fork Trail** SSE down the North Fork of the Purgatoire. See McCarty Park, Trinchera Peak and Cucharas Pass Quads.

12,265′ **Park Mountain** and 12,565′ **Teddys Peak** are within reach of the trail. From the S side of Cuchara—½ mile S of the main part—drive W on a jeep trail 3½ miles to the Dodgeton Creek fork, 9500′, and perhaps a little way south. Climb S 2½ miles on the trail past a first saddle and up to a second saddle at 10,600′. From here make a short steep climb up 600′ W to the E ridge of Park Mountain, and continue W and then S 2 miles to the top. Teddys Peak is 1½ miles S along a not very steep ridge with 200′ altitude loss. You can come down a mile E off Teddys to the top of **Steep Mountain** and a mile down Steep's NE ridge to the trail on Baker Creek. The **Baker Creek Trail** climbs from 8800′ to 10,200′ on the NE ridge of Steep Mountain in 5 miles. USFS Steep is USGS Sheep.

The road in to Blue Lakes gives the best approaches to the northern Culebras. It turns off from 111 4 miles S of Cuchara and climbs 4 miles to 10,400′. If you follow the road another two miles to the N lake you are again within striking distance of **Teddys Peak** by way of a stiff bushwhack WNW to a range crest saddle and then north. Total: 4½ miles, generally steep and with deadfall on the mountain side.

Trinchera Peak, 13,530′, is the main northern one—prominent as a symmetrically rounded summit from as far off as I-25. There is a trail most of the way to it from the S bend of the road between the S and N Blue Lakes. It takes you in 5 zigzag miles to 12,600′ (jeeping prohibited). You are just as well off, however, to leave it at 12,000′ and stay on the NE ridge.

English Saddle, 12,955′, is a mile N of Trinchera with a 350′ dip between.

Leaning North Peak, 13,100′, and **Leaning South Peak,** 13,320′, are within reach from the saddle S of Blue Lakes on the **Purgatory North Fork Trail.** The **North Fork Road** and **Trail** meet 6 miles W up the fork from North Lake, at 9700′.

Mariquita Peak, 13,335′, is directly up a ridge from about half a mile short of the road end, at 9400′. A 4½-mile trail zigzags up the ridge to timberline and gives you a 2-mile, steep, open ridge route to the top. **Quatro,** one of the livelier looking peaks, is a mile N along the ridge, with a drop to 13,000′ and some bumps and steep stuff en route. On your right is Hell Canyon, one of those places where a Hollander looks around and says, "Where are the people?"

The E road toward **Whiskey Pass** goes in W 6 miles from ½ mile S of Monument Lake and dead ends on the side of Whiskey Creek at 10,218′, where it is helpful with 2 trails. The right-hand one goes N and W 4 miles to the head of Whiskey Creek's N branch and way up the cirque to 12,300′ on the S face of **Mount Maxwell.** The mountain is a pull of ½ mile to the N and **Cono De Anza** about the same distance SW. See El Valle and Stonewall Quads. The left hand trail from the road end doubles back S and splits after ½ mile. Its right branch goes up to 10,500′ in a middle branch of Whiskey, but too far below the range crest to help much. The leftmost trail goes 3½ miles up a S fork to 11,900′. It is an easy climb on to **Beaubien Peak,** ¾ mile SSE up a rather steep slope.

At a point 1½ miles down the Whiskey road from its upper end there is another trail head. A trail winds off S 2 miles, W 4 miles and S again, where at altitudes around 10,500′ and 11,000′ it flanks the range crest about 2 miles E of the cirque heads in the **San Francisco** to **Peak N** sector. (A side trail climbs W from it to a lake at 11,525′, one valley N of Peak N.) When it turns E this trail connects with the jeep trail system W from Duling Lodge, below.

Duling Lodge is a mile S of Stonewall Gap and behind the wall. A jeep road runs W from the lodge up Duling Creek 3½ miles to a junction. The right fork turns N 2 miles for Duling Lakes, near the linkage point with the trail above. The left fork goes W in the main creek bed and then winds several miles up a ridge and back into a N fork of Abbotts Creek, where at 11,200′ it is about 3 miles E and a little S from Peak N. See Stonewall, Torres, El Valle and Culebra Peak Quads.

A jeep road runs from Duling Lodge up Abbotts Creek and after about 12 miles divides on the back side of a 12,000′ cone. The left fork zigzags down to Vigas Creek, where it meets another 4-wheel drive road up from Torres. The Torres road may be the better of the two approaches; inquire at the Stonewall store. (For the Torres road go right from 5½ miles S of Stonewall on Tercio road.) In any case, the right hand trail goes up-ridge from the 11,800′ saddle behind the cone and climbs in 3 brisk miles to 13,600′, about 2 blocks off the top of **Culebra Peak.** The terminus is a little lower on Culebra's S ridge, ½ mile farther W and S.

Espinazo Rojo, 13,800′, the peak with the long E ridge, is a mile-plus S of Culebra, with a double dip to 13,500′ between. If you left a car on the cone saddle, cut down the smooth Rojo ridge 2 miles to the trail and go N and up the hill to retrieve. This summit may remain on maps as Red Peak.

Vermejo Peak, 13,723′, is a tent-top at the head of Johnson Creek. Take the Torres Road for 7 miles, keeping right at mile 1 and mile 3 and left (in the valley) at mile 6. A car might go to here but a jeep is recommended, and will be needed for further progress. At mile 7, where the road splits, take the left side. You can probably do another mile or two to perhaps 9600′. Continue on foot up the canyon trail 4 miles, where at 11,300′ you can cut left 2 miles up the slope of the peak.

SPANISH PEAKS

QUADS: Cucharas Pass and old 30′ Spanish Peaks; San Isabel N F.

These visually paired mountains are a little farther E than Pikes Peak and so share with it the honor of being first seen by people who come to southern Colorado from the East. Indians called the pair the Wajatoya, breasts of the world. As you approach them you begin to see the radiating dikes, pieces of vertical rock wall, which run along for miles and usually more or less lined up with the summits. These came when the mountains, or the uplift of which they are a surviving part, were cracked in many places by a second intrusive mass that forced its way toward the surface from beneath. The summit rocks are intrusives, generally tertiary. The dikes at Stonewall are a part of this system.

A road goes S, E and S from La Veta 6 miles to the Wajatoya School, and perhaps 2½ more miles S to the **Wajatoya Trail,** which climbs 5½ miles to the saddle between the peaks at 10,400′. It then descends 2½ miles to a secondary road up the S fork of Trujillo Creek. To reach the trail and saddle from the S side, drive 10 miles W from Aguilar (2 past Gulnare) and take the right fork for **Apishapa** and **Cucharas Passes.** Six miles W of the forks take a road N 3 miles to the S fork of Trujillo Creek. From here on NW up the creek to the trail head it is 4 miles by jeep road. You then climb on the trail about 1700′ in 3 miles to reach the saddle.

East Spanish Peak, figured as 12,708′ in 1897, is a 2½-mile ridge climb to the E, once you have reached this saddle. It may seem more attractive to shortcut toward the peak from the trailhead, using a ridge route. My preference is for a route farther E on the S side. Leave the main road at mile 4 SW of Aguilar. Right 2 miles, then left 2 miles. You are headed W; keep straight W (right) 4 more miles and continue W 4–5 miles up Middle Trujillo Creek. You are close in on the S side at 8500′ or so. You will be tempted to do some dike scrambling on the way up, especially if it gets you out of the snow.

The road to **Apishapa Pass** is very pleasant when it gets high. The pass is 18 miles from Gulnare, 29 from Aguilar, and 7½ from **Cucharas Pass** on the W end. It does not seem like a pass, but you are on the ridge connecting the Spanish Peaks with the Culebra Range.

West Spanish Peak, 13,623′, is a climb of very modest proportion from Apishapa Pass. Starting at 11,243′, you move off N and NE along the ridge a couple of miles before you do any climbing. I recollect this as a sort of stone stumbling cross-country walk, but the maps indicate a trail now takes you to 11,900′. The West peak can also be climbed from the saddle between the two, but it is a long hard ridge for a hot summer day.

The **Spanish Peaks Trail** starts on the Echo Creek road 7 miles S of La Veta. It climbs S on the W side of West Spanish Peak, and using occasional pieces of road, makes a 29-mile circle of the two peaks, ending 7 miles S of La Veta on Wajatoya Creek. With the **Wajatoya Trail** it makes an almost closed figure 8. The trail was recently reported in pretty good condition, but as the E part is not under maintenance we would not recommend it for horse travel. The West peak can be circled alone on good trail.

Fishers Peak, 9586′, is the highest of the late tertiary or quaternary lava flow mesas E of I-70. Its block top is detached from Barilla Mesa to form an abrupt though flat summit. It is visible from far N, and conspicuous S of Walsenburg. You can inquire in Trinidad for the start of an 8-mile trail to it, but the more natural and shorter approach is from about 2 miles south of Starkville, 4½ miles N of Morley, on I-25, where a jeep road goes ½ mile ESE up a draw. There are two trails from the road end. Take the left one up onto a ridge, and keep to this ridge, which ends up running ESE to the summit. At the top where you are confronted by vertical rock, you can find a chimney to break through. It's a good fall climb, with Persian carpet colors to compensate you for having to push the oak brush around. See Starkville and the 30′ El Moro Quads.

In the cool months, Walsenburg mountaineers take out their climbing shoes and go NE to visit Indian shelters, teepee rings, petroglyphs, and the like along a 12 mile stretch of the Cucharas River. For a sampling of the sites drive from Walsenburg 7 miles NE on State 10; 10 miles N on Turkey Ridge Mail Route; 3 miles E, 4 miles N, and 1 mile E on section line roads; and 4 miles winding E to the canyon rim.

From this point a trail can be found into the canyon. The area is covered on Walsenburg Quad.

SAN JUAN MOUNTAINS

We tend to speak of the whole aggregation of peaks and ridges in SW Colorado as "the San Juan," thinking rather of a large and varied mountain area than of a range. While the outlying La Plata Mountains form a Range and the San Miguels are likewise set off from the rest, the other groupings used below are merely conveniences, suggested more on the basis of approach than anything else. Besides the Bend and the Northeast San Juan, they include the Lake City Group, its northern offshoot the Courthouse Group, the Sneffels Range, an East and a West Silverton Group, the Telluride Group, the San Miguel Range, the Needle Mountains, the Rico Mountains, the La Plata Range, and the southeast San Juan.

Parts of the San Juan, particularly around the present day towns of Creede, Lake City, Ouray, Telluride and Silverton, were prospected and mined from the sixties on. Old homes, stores, churches and courthouses preserve the flavor of earlier times, and the abandoned mines with their dumps of colored rock, the mills, the tramways are all a part of the scene for the visitor, while the old mine roads, built to carry lettuce up hill and bring ore down, have introduced a whole new way of going into the mountains which fits with our motor-married generation. More old valley roads and old passes are being opened up and improved each year. Jeep tours and rentals are an established business, and maps like that of the Telluride Jeep Club and books like that of Robert Brown are on the go.

Fortunately not all the San Juan produced pay metal enough to be built up with towns and roads. The Needle Mountains are roadless, almost trailless, hard to reach, hard to get around in and very wild and rough when you *are* there. All of us who have been there hope that man's propensity to develop things will never succeed in overcoming the better

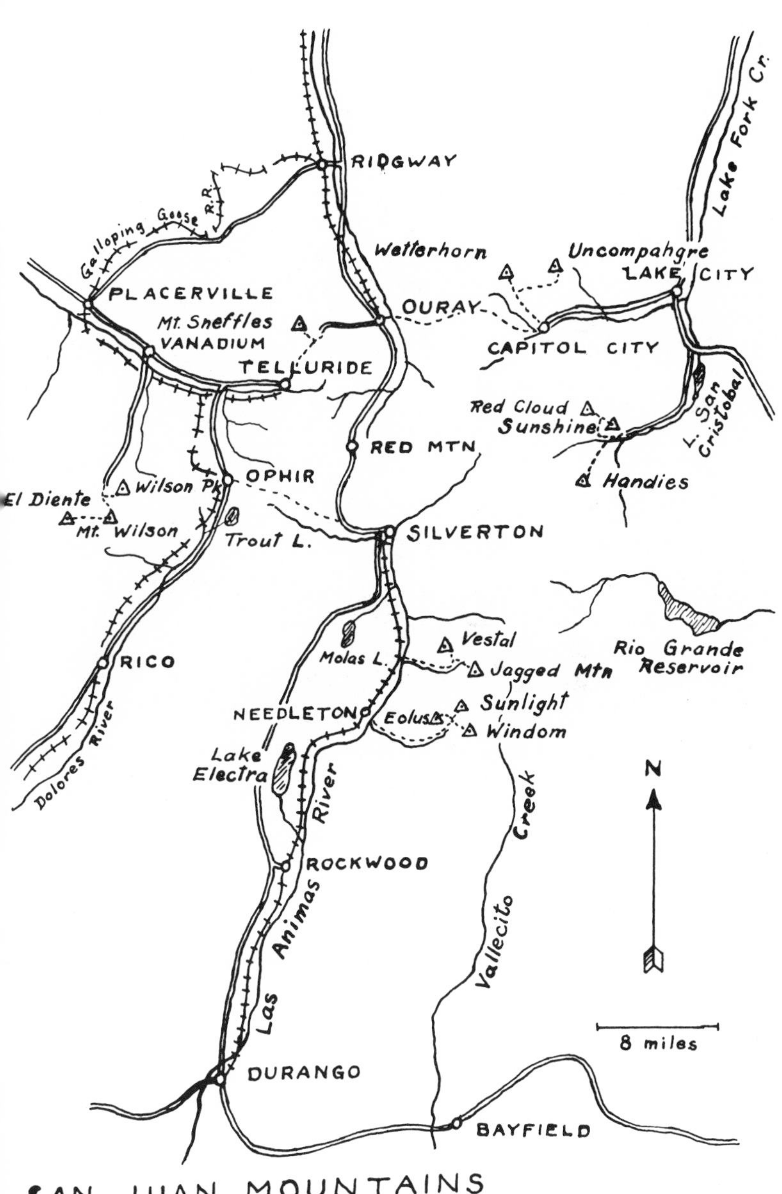

SAN JUAN MOUNTAINS

Uncompahgre Peak from the southeast approach. *H. L. Standley photo*

development of recent wise men—the permanent setting aside of wildernesses.

Geologically the San Juan region is a mass of varied rocks too complex for easy generalization. There are thick sedimentaries like those along the San Miguel, and many sorts of volcanic and metamorphic rocks, some of which we mention where they are conspicuous.

There is trail on or close to the Divide for almost the entire length of the crest where the Cochetopa Hills start and the Sawatch Range leaves off. Segments have different names. A good deal of the N half is the **La Garita Stock Driveway.** S and E of Beartown most of it is called the **Continental Divide Trail.** There is some talk now of making continuous and marking a Continental Divide Trail through the entire length of the Divide in the state, estimated when Carl Melzer and his son walked it as some 800 miles.

COCHETOPA HILLS

QUADS: Chester, Sargents, Sargents Mesa, West Baldy, Razor Creek Dome, Sawtooth Mountain, Cochetopa Park, North Pass, Elk Park, Chimney Rock; 15′ Creede; Gunnison and Rio Grande N F's.

The Cochetopa Hills carry the Divide SW 50 miles from the three-county corner 5 miles S of **Marshall Pass** to the junction with the La Garita Mountains 7 miles NNW of Creede.

The **Cochetopa Passes,** "Old" and North, cross the range midway at 10,000′. Cochetopa is Indian for buffalo. The summits, most of them along the Divide, tend to be smooth and broad. If you walk there, leave your rope and carry two canteens.

From 5 miles W of Sargents on the **Marshall Pass** railroad grade, which is good for cars, a jeep road goes S 8 miles to the Divide and several miles W along it to very near Long Branch Baldy. A trail up Tank Seven Creek, from 4 miles farther E on the railroad road, links with this jeep road, and continues W beyond it on the Divide to **Middle Baldy,** where it runs off the NW side down Razor Creek.

A 9-mile road runs N from US 50 at Doyleville up Needle Creek to the Needle Creek Reservoir. From its end there is a trail circling 11,449′ **West Baldy.** Its length, including the above Razor Creek segment, is 18 miles.

Long Branch Baldy, 11,974′, is the high point of a long section of the Divide. Besides the jeep road along the Divide, from which it is a climb of 400′ in 1½ miles, there is a good pedestrian route. From Sargents on US 50, drive SW a mile and SSE 2½ miles to Long Branch Guard Station. Jeeps go 1½ miles farther on poorer road to forks at 8800′. Take the right fork and go 3 miles W on pack trail to a trail junction on the ridge. Take the left trail 1-2 miles S and climb S to summit. For a bath, drop off the steep side ¼ mile to a lake and trail. See Sargents and Sargents Mesa Quads.

Cochetopa Dome, 11,132′, on Cochetopa Park Quad, is a large massif with rather abrupt drop-offs from 1 to 3 miles away from the summit. To climb it drive 5½ miles SW from **North Pass** on State 114 (26½ miles SE from US 50) and take the Cochetopa Pass road, State 114, 18 miles to a right hand exit. Follow this road 5½ miles S to the latitude of Cochetopa Dome, at 9000′. It is a 2100′ climb E, moderate, steep and gentle by turns.

Razor Creek Dome, 11,530′, is climbed from State 114, at mile 20 SE of US 50, ½ mile SE of the exit for Flying M Ranch, 9000′. Climb 3 miles NNE.

Stone Cellar Campground is a curiously remote place between the Cochetopa Hills and the La Garita Mountains on the middle fork of Saguache Creek. The road to it turns S from 7 miles W of **Old Cochetopa Pass** and runs 14 miles, crossing the Divide at 10,658′.

Chimney Rock, 10,242′, or about 100′ high, is approached from 1¼ miles N of the campground on the road in. You have a 200′ ascent W from the road. Try it with lariat.

LA GARITA MOUNTAINS

QUADS: Lookout Mountain, Bowers Peak, Mesa Mountain, Pool Table Mountain; 15′ Creede; Rio Grande N F; La Garita Wilderness Trail Map (U.S.F.S.).

The La Garitas run W 25 miles from W of La Garita in the San Luis Valley to join with the W end of the Cochetopa Hills, farther N. The E part is largely in timber; the W end rises higher and is more distinctly a ridge or range.

The town of La Garita, 6 miles W of US 285 (17 miles S of Saguache), has a road running 10½ miles NW up Carnero Creek to a junction. The left road, in South Carnero Creek, runs from this junction 12 miles WNW to **Moon Pass** (for which you keep right) at 10,600′. Beyond the pass a lumber road continues for 6 miles to the N side of **Bowers Peak.** Short of the pass, at about ¼ mile N of where the road leaves the creek (mile 19 from La Garita) a road runs off left and W along the creek for 3 miles to 10,850′.

The **La Garita Stock Driveway** starts with this road and runs 170 miles to Beartown on the Bend, first along the **La Garita** crest and afterwards on and near the Divide. It is well-marked, though sometimes steep and rough.

Bowers Peak, 12,449′, is at the head of South Carnero Creek and a mile N of the stock driveway. From the road end on the creek (the mile 19 road above) continue W on the trail up the creek for 2½ miles and cut off right at the end for a half-mile climb NW. See Bowers Peak and Lookout Mountain Quads.

Pool Table Mountain, 12,218′, is approached from South Fork on US 160. Drive W on State 149 toward Creede ½ mile. After crossing the Rio Grande go right to Alder Creek Guard Station, 4 miles, and continue N 12 more miles to the N end of Pool Table Park, 11,000′. The mountain top is 1½ miles N.

La Garita Peak, 13,718′, is on Creede 15′ Quad, the SE corner piece of a 4-mile NW-SE ridge of middling high 13'ers 7 miles NE of Creede. A trail from Creede's lower E side at 8800′ climbs 6 miles to the 11,300′ flats E of **Mammoth Mountain,** then loafs 3 miles more to the La Garita Stock Driveway.

From there the route proceeds directly NE to the peak, 1700′ higher and 1½ miles distant.

A forest service road runs E 8 miles from 1 mile NW of Wagon Wheel Gap on State 149 to Hanson Sawmill on East Bellows Creek, at 10,800′. A jeep trail continues 8 miles NNW to Wheeler Geological Area, the former national monument, with its Bryce Canyon-like erosion pinnacles. This replaces a permission route through the Phipps Ranch, 2 miles nearer to Creede on 149 than this turn-off. From 2 miles beyond Hanson's Sawmill on the jeep road one can drive E and NE 2 miles by jeep to the N side of **Pool Table Mountain** for a short climb of 1000′ altitude to the mountain's summit.

NORTHEAST SAN JUAN

QUADS: Mineral Mountain, Cold Spring Park, Stewart Peak; 15′ Bristol Head and Creede; La Garita Wilderness Trail Map (preferable to Rio Grande and Gunnison N F's).

This section of Continental Divide is the stem of a Y whose arms are the La Garita Mountains and the Cochetopa Hills. It runs W from their junction 7 miles NNW of Creede to **Spring Creek Pass.**

La Garita Stock Driveway connects **Spring Creek Pass** with **Half Moon Pass** in the La Garita on a 27-mile route close to the ridges at the ends but halfway down to Creede in the middle. There are numerous roads N from Creede, some of which are jeeped for several miles. They go up both East and West Willow Creeks and Rat Creek to the W. One can drive a car up West Willow Creek 3 miles and a jeep might go on for as much as 5 more to the Equity Mine at 11,150′. This line continues 3 miles as trail to **San Luis Pass** at 12,000′. Just N of the pass it connects with the **Skyline Trail,** which runs E 5 miles on high ground to Cochetopa Creek and W a few miles with the branches of Mineral Creek. Going on N it drops into Bondholder Meadows, above Powderhorn and Cathedral.

San Luis Peak, the high point and only 14'er in this sytem E of Lake City, is on a smooth massive ridge with 3 peaks to

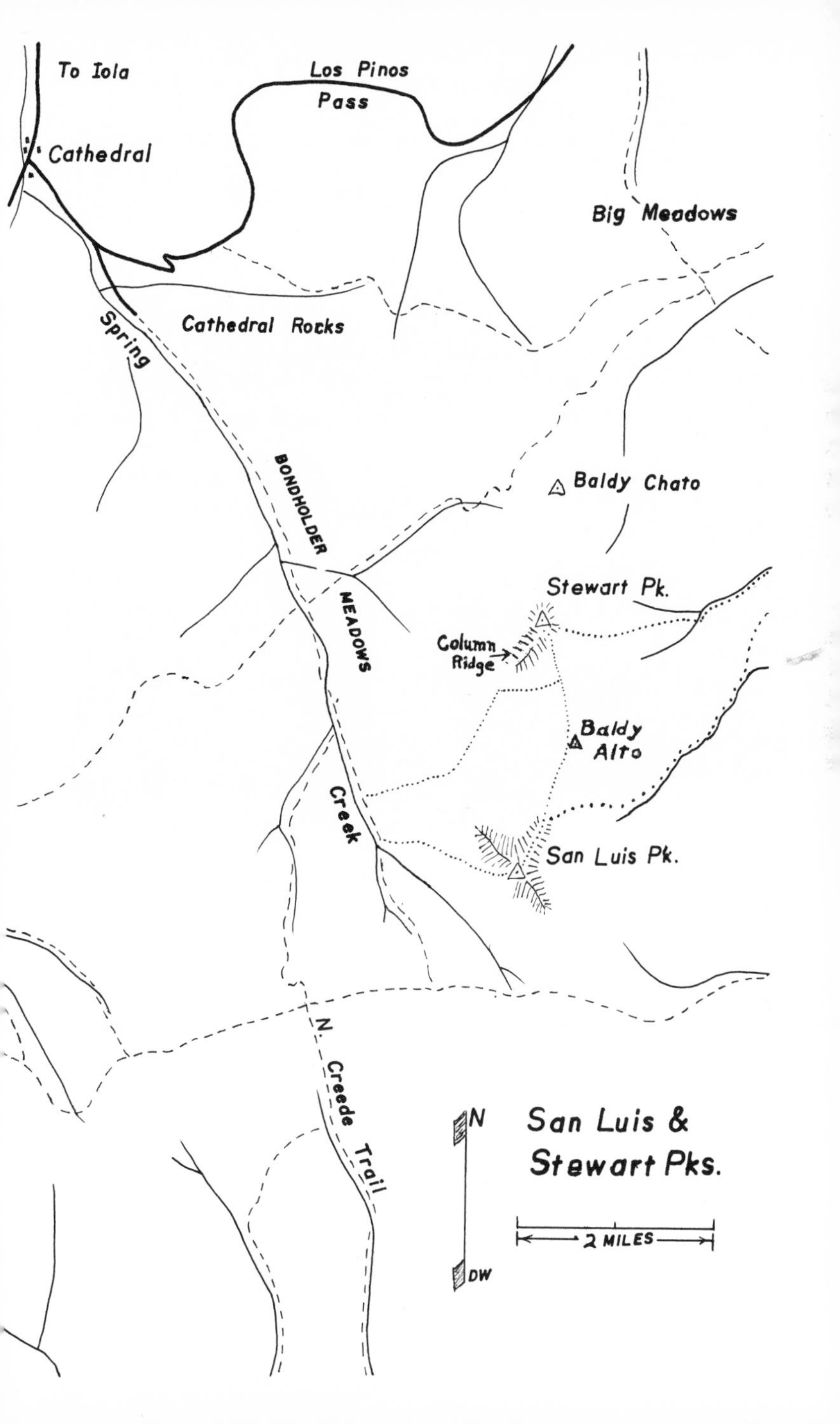
To Iola
Los Pinos
Pass
Cathedral
Big Meadows
Cathedral Rocks
Spring
BONDHOLDER
MEADOWS
Baldy Chato
Stewart Pk.
Column
Ridge
Baldy
Alto
Creek
San Luis Pk.
N. Creede Trail
N
DW
2 MILES
San Luis &
Stewart Pks.

Mount Stewart looks at San Luis Peak. *H. L. Standley photo.*

the N: **Baldy Alto,** 13,698′, **Stewart Peak,** 13,983′, and **Baldy Chato,** 13,401′. The traditional route for Stewart, formerly rated a 14'er, and San Luis, has been to drive from 7 miles W of Gunnison on US 50 via State 149 to Powderhorn, 18 miles SSW, and from there 15 miles S up Cebolla Creek to Spring Creek, where a road comes in from the left. Take this, and check in with the owner of the ranch, about 2 miles up toward Cathedral Rock, and obtain permission to drive up Spring Creek 1½ miles farther to where road crosses creek, at 9300′. Walk about 5 miles to and up the side valley; keep left around the box canyon.

San Luis Peak, 14,014′, and the others on the ridge with it are now more easily approached from the NE on Forest Road 791, which brings you to Stewart Creek. At 19 miles S of US 50 on State 114, keep right (S) on the Old Cochetopa road for 6 miles (not Old Agency road, mile 3 on the latter). Jog right to cross Archuleta Creek and go S again for 3 miles. Turn right and cross Cochetopa Creek by an old ranch. Well-graded timber road 791 takes you from Cochetopa Creek ½ mile NW, 3 miles SW, 8 miles S veering to SW and 3 miles SE over Nutras-Stewart Creek divide. **Stewart Creek Trail** climbs from 10,500′ to timberline, 4½ miles SW. Continue up-creek to the saddle and to the summit of San Luis, another 1½ miles. For terrain, see Cochetopa Dome, Elk Park, Cold Spring Park and Stewart Peak Quads.

Mineral Mountain, 12,097′, 4 miles W of Stewart Peak, is an easy climb by the **Cebolla Pack Trail** crossing the lower end of Bondholder Meadows. The trail climbs SSW 2½ miles and NW 1½ miles to a ridge at 11,600′, where you are ½ mile S of the summit.

Baldy Cinco, 13,383′, high point of the Divide between Creede and Lake City, is a climb of 4 miles E and NE along the Divide from 10,898′ **Spring Creek Pass.** See Bristol Head Quad.

One sees parts of these peaks from the interesting 11-mile road from Cathedral to **Slumgullion Pass.** Trail 459 runs in and out midway between the Divide and the road, and trails from the road climb to the Divide on Tumble Creek, Rough Creek and Mineral Creek as well as Spring Creek.

LAKE CITY GROUP

QUADS: Uncompahgre Peak, Wetterhorn Peak, Redcloud Peak, Handies Peak, Lake City, Lake San Cristobal; Uncompahgre N F.

The mountains covered here are those around the two streams flowing from the west into Lake City—the Lake Fork, named for Lake San Cristobal to the S, and Henson Creek. Roads now drivable for long distances by cars go up both valleys and continue over the Bend as jeep passes into the Silverton–Ouray country. The one straight W up Henson Creek is the more scenic, climbing in 19 miles from Lake City to 12,950′ **Engineer Mountain Pass,** with a little vertical side road to the 13,218′ peak and its 360° view of the San Juan. Although some small cars make it this is not a guard-rail excursion. The other road, climbing for 26 miles to near the end of the Lake Fork, crosses at **Cinnamon Pass,** way down at 12,600′ where you can't see out much. Both go down the Animas to Silverton or by a rougher more northerly course down Mineral Creek and the Uncompahgre to US 550 and Ouray.

Uncompahgre Peak, 14,309′, is climbed by trail from Nellie Creek. Drive 5½ miles W up Henson Creek from Lake City. Starting at 9310′ climb or jeep S up-creek 5-6 miles, taking a left at the junction. The trail continues W 3 miles to the summit, whose N slope is too hilly for the sense of security which this tilted plateau has induced. This mountain is often climbed with Wetterhorn.

Wetterhorn Peak, 14,017′, is 3 miles W of **Uncompahgre** over rolling plateau, with a drop to 12,000′ and a not very imposing **Matterhorn,** 13,590′, for the ambitious to climb en route. If there is fog when you leave Uncompahgre, head WNW magnetic for a mile or so to pass Matterhorn, then W. The ascent of Wetterhorn is by the ridge which steepens as it curves from

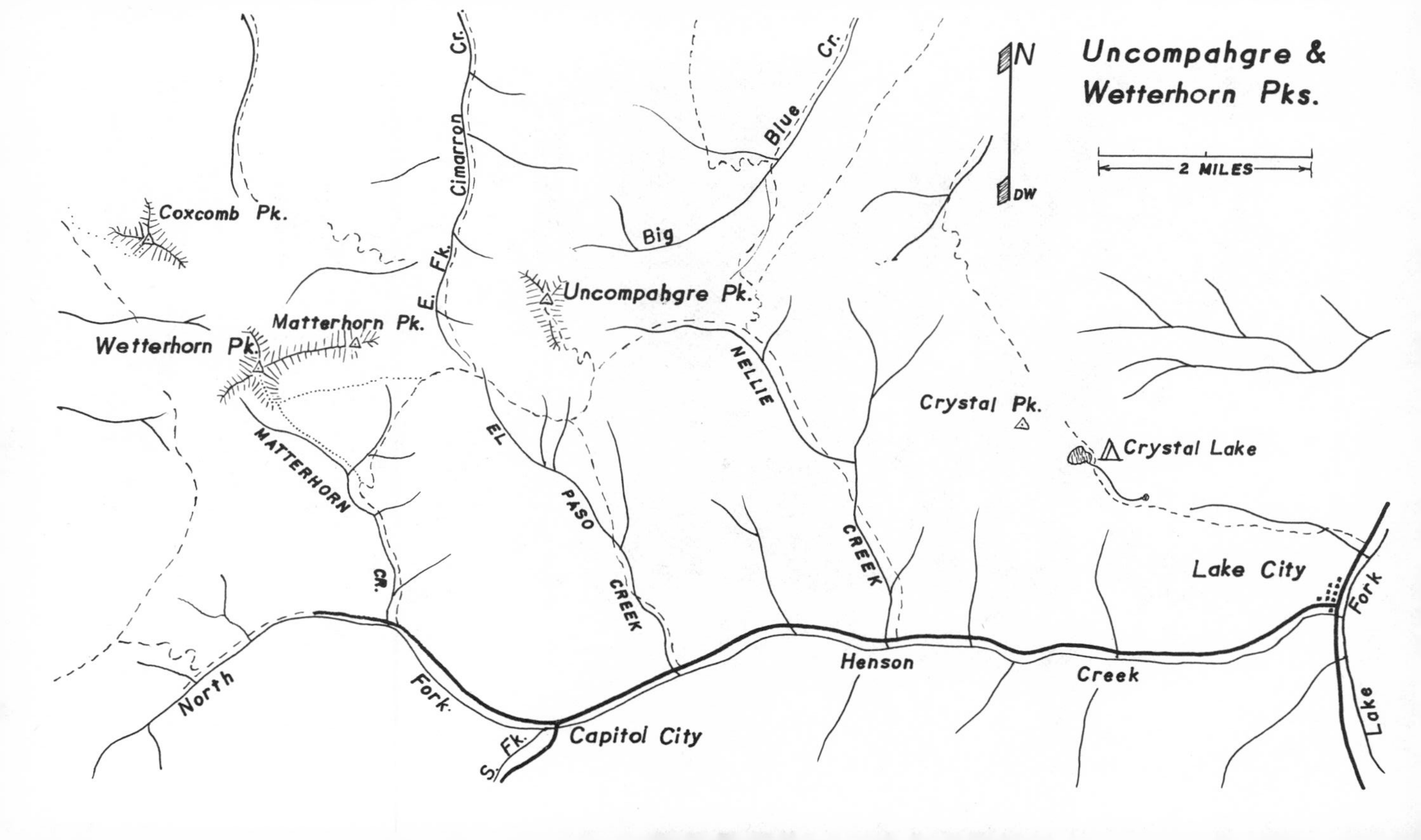
Uncompahgre &
Wetterhorn Pks.
2 MILES
N
DW
Coxcomb Pk.
Cimarron
Cr.
E. Fk.
Blue
Cr.
Big
Uncompahgre Pk.
Matterhorn Pk.
Wetterhorn Pk.
NELLIE
CREEK
Crystal Pk.
Crystal Lake
MATTERHORN
CR.
EL
PASO
CREEK
Lake City
Fork
Lake
Henson
Creek
North
Fork
Capitol City
S. Fk.

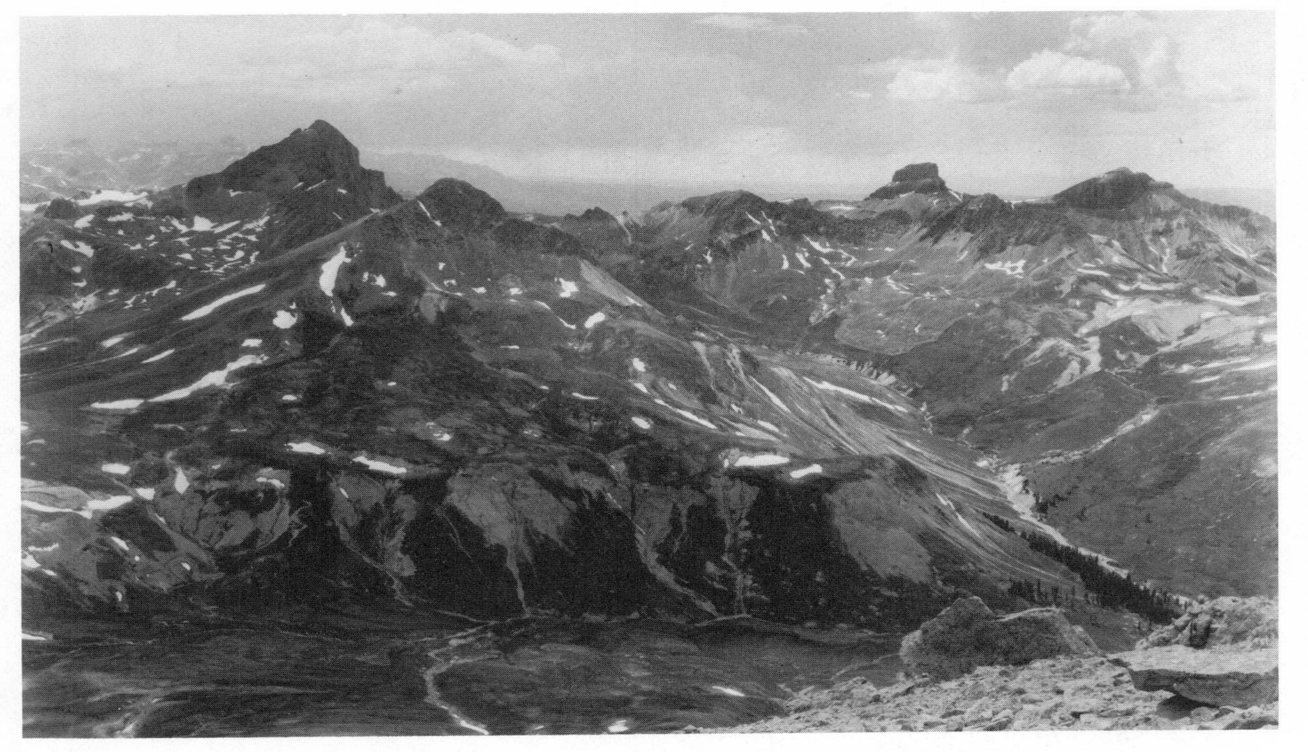

Wetterhorn, Matterhorn and Coxcomb as seen from Uncompahgre Peak approach. *H. L. Standley photo.*

NE around to N. Near the top it is too sandy for easy scrambling; parties should have a rope along. On the route for Wetterhorn alone, or a second route for both peaks, you drive 9½ miles W from Lake City to Capitol City (not much there) and take the right fork (on which there is good camping 1.4 miles from the junction) for 2 miles to Matterhorn Creek, 10,350′. The old road which climbs 3 miles up the creek was being jeeped to the E side of Matterhorn and all the way down the East Cimarron, but is now within the closed Uncompahgre Primitive Area. You can walk the 3 miles and then cut across WNW a mile to the climbing ridge. Climbers have also made it to Wetterhorn Peak from a camp on West Cimarron Creek at 10,400′. A trail leads 4½ miles S up-valley to the 12,500′ pass at its head; then you lose 400′ or more on the 2½ mile trek to the peak.

Coxcomb Peak, 13,656′, is 2 miles NW along a ridge from Wetterhorn and can be easily approached that way. See Cimarron group below.

Wildhorse, 13,266′, is an abrupt and conspicuous peak when seen from Montrose and from the Cow Creek road to **Owl Creek Pass.** From a little off **Engineer Mountain Pass** on the Lake City side it is a 3-mile walk mostly by trail N over American Flats. The climb is from 12,300′.

The ridge between Henson Creek and the Lake Fork has several high points that are easy enough to climb if you have the ambition. **Red Mountain,** 12,826′, is directly up W from Lake San Cristobal. 12,821′ **Grassy** is 2 miles SSW from Red. From Grassy the ridge goes W to higher summits. I like to call the one whose altitude is 13,688′ **Three Faces Mountain.** It has a sort of trail—an old road—from 2½ miles W of Lake City on the Henson Creek road, where Alpine Gulch comes in from the S. The road climbs 2 miles S and 3 or 4 more SW, to 11,900′, 1½ miles NE of the summit.

Bent Peak, 13,393′, and **Carson Peak,** 13,657′, can be reached from the Wager Gulch Road. Drive 8½ miles up the Lake Fork road from its junction with State 149 2 miles S of Lake City.

The Wager Gulch jeep road takes you S 6 miles past the settlement of Carson to a saddle at 13,000′ on the Divide. Bent Peak is a mile WNW, Carson another mile. The road continues S and E as a rough jeeper to Heart and Pearl Lakes, the latter available from 149. See Lake San Cristobal, Finger Mesa and Pole Creek Quads for the road and topography.

Redcloud Peak, 14,034′, **Sunshine Peak,** 14,001′, and **Handies Peak,** 14,048′, are often climbed from the same camp. Drive 15.2 miles up the Lake Fork from Lake City (13 from junction with state 149) and take the right hand road toward **Cinnamon Pass** for 4.2 miles to Grizzly Creek and Silver Creek at 10,400′. For Redcloud, go 200 yards up-road from the Silver Creek crossing to a cabin site. Trail starts with a cairn between the cabins and a mine dump and goes 2 miles NE up the NW side of a creek. There is a cairn-marked route up a steep side creek on the right side to Redcloud, but we prefer to continue in Silver Creek on the trail which climbs NE and S to the 13,000′ saddle. The saddle is 5 miles from the Lake Fork; the NE ridge on which you finish is a long ½ mile more.

Sunshine and Redcloud are in the area of flows and intrusive rock of which the most prevalent is called Sunshine Peak Rhyolite.

For **Handies Peak** follow an old trail 4 miles up Grizzly Gulch to summit.

There is also a shorter and opener climb of Handies Peak. From 4 miles farther up the Cinnamon Pass road, where it hairpins right to climb, keep S up the Lake Fork a mile by foot or car to 11,600′ and another 1½ miles by trail S to Sloan Lake, then E to the saddle and N to summit, another mile. In Model T days we came up the Animas to Burns Gulch and finished climbing Handies this way with the help of a dip in Sloan Lake. The world is going to the dogs.

COURTHOUSE GROUP

QUADS: Courthouse Mountain, Sheep Mountain, Wetterhorn Peak; Uncompahgre N F.

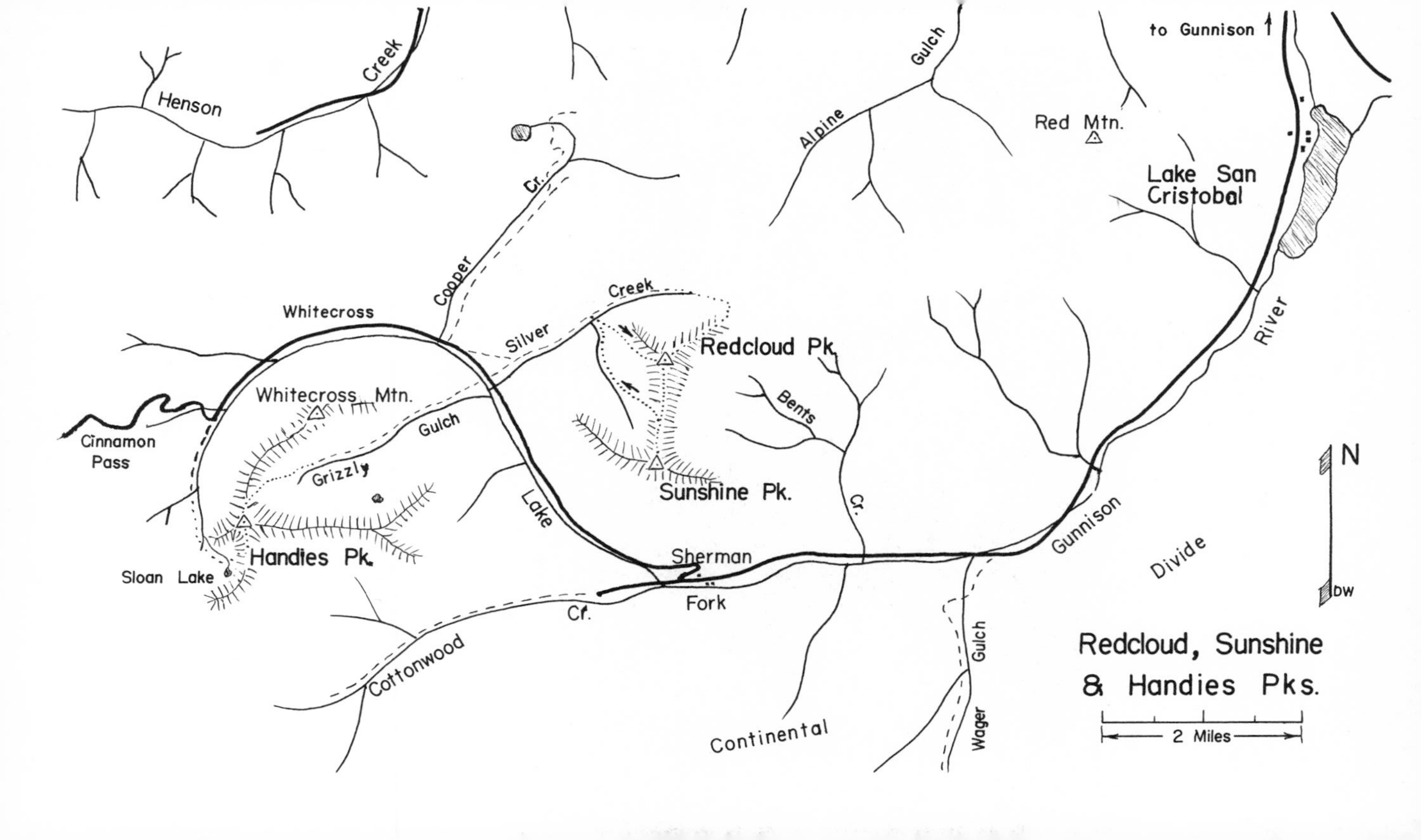
to Gunnison
Henson
Creek
Alpine
Gulch
Red Mtn.
Lake San Cristobal
River
Cooper
Cr.
Whitecross
Silver
Creek
Redcloud Pk.
Bents
Cr.
Whitecross Mtn.
Gulch
Grizzly
Cinnamon Pass
Sunshine Pk.
Lake
Handies Pk.
Sloan Lake
Sherman
Fork
Cr.
Cottonwood
Continental
Divide
Gunnison
Gulch
Wager
N
DW
Redcloud, Sunshine
& Handies Pks.
2 Miles

Strange figures appear to huddle around the summit of Precipice Peak. *Waddington photo.*

This group centers around the Cimarron Creeks, mainly the West Cimarron. The higher peaks are capped with tawny and gray rock, and the ridges along the canyons below them are so lined with little salmon-colored buttresses and pinnacles as to suggest a whole lifetime of rock climbing possibilities. Both the pinnacles and the thicker layerings above are typical of the San Juan Tuff, a tertiary fragmental volcanic, or pyroclastic, rock.

From near Ridgway on US 550 you have glimpses of the Courthouse–Chimney Peak ridge. This with the connecting Cimarron Ridge to the N is one of 4 parallel ridges lined with enough little towers and pinnacles to keep you out of the office for an entire lifetime. Camping and approach are best on the West Cimarron Creek. Leave US 50 2½ miles SE of Cimarron and drive S 18 miles to 1 mile past Jackson Guard Station. Keep right twice, circling W to the W fork of Cimarron Creek and S up the creek.

Camping is good about 9 miles from the Guard Station, 1-2 miles N of the junction with Owl Creek Road. (The latter comes from US 550, starting 12 miles N of Colona, 2 miles S of Ridgway. It climbs 16 miles through **Owl Creek Pass** and a little way S to meet the Cimarron road.) The peaks nearly all have a pitch or two where rope is required.

Courthouse Mountain, 12,152′, and **Chimney Peak,** 11,781′, are at the ends of a mile-long ridge of curious cliffs and pinnacles that one sees from time to time on the parallel section of US 550 in the Ridgway vicinity. Courthouse has some wicked overhangs on three sides, but it is no problem to climb from the Cimarron side. From 1½ miles S of the road junction near **Owl Creek Pass,** climb a mile W to the ridge N of the mountain and go S and SE ¼ mile to the top. Chimney is climbed by an obvious south-side chimney with a large chock rock high up. Though vertical it is an easy ascent for a small roped party with experience. The first ascent climbers record a curious booboo. When they found the second man had climbed up the opposite side of the chock rock from the leader they concurred in his retreating and doing it over instead of sitting on top to untie and retie. Must have been excited.

Coxcomb, 13,656′, is at the head of the valley on the left, a strangely imposing peak and well-fortified against walking routes. To reach it climb to the 12,500′ pass and drop 100′ into Wetterhorn Basin. Traverse ¼ mile SE to a ridge from which Coxcomb summit is visible ½ mile to the E. Continue to its southernmost buttress. Dave Waddington describes in December 1965 *T & T* three routes from here, including the usual, the couloir left of the buttress. It starts with a difficult 10′ climb into the couloir. Then after some scrambling comes a 50′ chimney where pitons have been used. Scramble to the ridge crest and climb E along it to a notch, where parties sometimes leave rappel rope to facilitate the return; finish not difficult.

Red Cliff, 13,642′, is ½ mile N of Coxcomb on the West-Middle Cimarron ridge. To climb it go up the **West Cimarron** to timberline and head ESE 1 mile to the saddle N of Coxcomb, which you identify by its flat top and big notch. The S ridge of Red Cliff is an easy half mile with 400′ rise.

Precipice Peak, 13,144′, is 2 miles ESE of the junction of **Courthouse Trail** and the West Cimarron road. Bushwhack toward the ridge which comes W south of the peak, bearing a little S to keep clear of the gray cliffs, then E to and up the ridge. Above timberline look for an outcrop with a big hole in it about 100′ from the cliffs of Precipice. The rock is 25′ high; the hole has room for 2 couples. From this rock work E along the S cliffs to the third big couloir going N. Climb in it to near the end, where it gets too steep and a ledge takes you W to a branch couloir. A grassy slope leads to the easy summit ridge. In case of doubtful weather note your point of ascent to that ridge for return use, says Dave Waddington (who supplied the following Dunsinane route also).

Dunsinane Mountain, 12,742′, is across the valley and a touch S from **Courthouse.** As soon as you can pass the lower gray cliffs, head for the ridge running NNE from the summit. Climb up the ridge or arete until you reach a ledge averaging

10′ width, outsloping and containing loose rock. Follow the ledge 100 yards or so, until you find a steep couloir running N to the summit.

Heisshorn, 13,411′, which is 1.3 miles N of Wetterhorn, is described as looking from the N or S, endwise, like an upthrust tooth. It is climbed from a flat stretch on the N ridge at 13,250′, by a route that works around to the E face and then returns to the N edge. One can reach the platform either by climbing the N arete or using a gully on the W side.

El Punto, 13,280′, is 1.8 miles N of Matterhorn Peak, on Uncompahgre Quadrangle. It has an aiguille summit like a small replica of the Lizard Head. Dwight Lavender and F. Greenfield climbed it in 1929, approaching by a couloir on the SW side. The final pitch was made by a little 15′ ledge on the SW side.

Sheep Mountain, 13,168′, gives a very fine look at the rough and steep N faces of Uncompahgre, Wetterhorn and company. To reach it from a Cimarron approach walk up the E fork road and trail 3½ miles from the Jackson Guard Station to where the left side couloirs offer some hope of a passage. It goes pretty well from 9600′ on the creek to the N end of the summit plateau at 12,600′, 1½ miles distant. The plateau is a tilted stroll.

OURAY GROUP

QUADS: Ouray, Ironton, Handies Peak, Wetterhorn; Uncompahgre N F.

The territory covered in this group lies W of Poughkeepsie Gulch and E of Canyon Creek S of Ouray, and farther N between the Uncompahgre River on the W and Cow Creek on the E as far S as Engineer Mountain.

Hayden Mountain, 13,206′, is the bulky unexciting ridge between Canyon Creek and Ironton Park. From a mile NE of the last U-bend of 550 as it descends **Red Mountain Pass** toward Ouray, at 9900′, two trails climb NW. The right one takes you up 3 miles to 12,657′ **Richmond Pass,** and then down to the Campbird Mine in Canyon Creek. Hayden Mountain is

¾ mile N from the pass, the first part along a very choppy ridge. The SJM-designated **T8,** 13,315′, and **T7,** 13,359′, are a greater distance up-ridge in the opposite direction, and easily climbed. The last has good views into the Needles and everything N of there to Wetterhorn. It also gives a good look at the Sneffels Range.

Red Mountain No. 3, 12,890′, is one of those things people climb because there they are in plain sight. Turn off the highway at the Idarado Mill and cross to Ironton to leave your car. Climb SSE to and up the N ridge from about 10,700′. For **Red Mountain No. 2** get as far as you can NE from Ironton on the mixed-up road system there. You will be able to climb from 10,600′ to the 12,219′ summit on a steep NW ridge. **Red Mountain No. 3** is best reached from the trail up Corkscrew Gulch, 1½ miles NE of the lowest U-bend of 550. If you have to go downstream past the tailings pond to get across the stream, take the trail there SE up Gray Copper Gulch instead. It is 4 miles and 2000′ to the pass into Cement Creek, then a mile W along the ridge to the 12,592′ summit.

Brown Mountain is the long ridge E of Ironton Park, tapering bumpily from 13,339′ at the S end to 12,801′ **Mount Abrams** at the N. Abrams is of interest because of the framing it gets as you look up the valley from Ouray. As you come up from Ouray to Ironton Park there is a trail that climbs E from .2 mile S of the last climbing bend in the road. It climbs from 9600′ to a mine at 9300′, directly W of the summit on a steep but easily climbed slope.

If instead of keeping on US 550 S of Ouray you take the left fork at mile 4, you are on the worst of two W side routes to **Engineer Mountain Pass** and Lake City (the better being from Silverton and the Animas). From the flats close under the W side of **Engineer Mountain** a trail goes N a mile to the 12,500′ saddle W of Engineer and descends to the main Bear Creek and its trail, 2 miles farther N.

The **Bear Creek Trail,** though not maintained and so impassable for horses, is a very exciting trip. You start up it from just short of the highway tunnel at 8500′, 3 miles S of Ouray. Some of it has slid out of existence with chiprock, but when you have gained the level-off at 9400′ it is an obvious shelf route high above the waterfalls of Bear Creek. In time you get up E to the meadows and American Flats, and have trail connections with the **Horsethief Trail** from farther N and the routes to Lake City.

The **Horsethief Trail** climbs S 4 or 5 miles from the hot springs pool at Ouray, 7700′, to a ridge at 10,400′. Here it climbs E and SE 10 miles to American Flats and the **Bear Creek Trail.** A branch trail runs over to the E rim of Ouray's Amphitheater. The trail reaches 12,700′ at the **Wildhorse Creek Pass,** where it is 1½ miles W of **Wildhorse Peak.** One can save some of the starting altitude and mileage by coming into the trail from a road up Dexter Creek. This starts 2½ miles down the river from Ouray, and jeeps a mile or so E from the highway.

From mile 3 E of 550 on the Owl Creek Pass road (it starts 2 miles N of Ridgway) you can keep right on a road that takes you 4 miles E to upper Cow Creek. It goes SSE up Cow Creek as jeep road for 6 miles, to the junction with Oben Creek at 8300′. The next part of Cow Creek for 5 miles is fully lined with the same San Juan Tuff pinnacles that decorate the Cimarron valleys to the E. The **Cow Creek Trail** climbs out of the valley from the road end and crosses E to 12,600′, where you are 1½ miles W of **Coxcomb Peak** and a little under its W ridge.

SNEFFELS RANGE

QUADS: Sams, Mount Sneffels, Ouray, Gray Head, Ironton, Telluride; Uncompahgre N F.

This range is north of the San Miguel River and Imogene Pass, northwest of Canyon Creek and west of Ouray. It is treated in some detail in the *San Juan Mountaineers Climbers Guide to Southwestern Colorado*, by David Lavender, Carleton Long and Thomas M. Griffiths, who did some triangulating in this range and climbed all over the San Juan country between

1929 and 1932. Their book, which has supplied much of the information below, is in typed and xeroxed form but not published.

The main approach road for Mount Sneffels and the eastern portion of the range runs SW from US 550 ½ mile S of Ouray. It follows Canyon Creek to the split at mile 4. The left fork goes S past the Camp Bird Mine and continues by jeep road 4 miles to **Imogene Pass,** 13,114′, and then descends 7 miles to Telluride. The Camp Bird road is generally closed, but the Campbird operation can be by-passed. Take instead the right fork and follow it 2 miles to the one-time village of Sneffels and a jeep road left to the Imogene Pass road. This is very rough and wet for over a mile. The right hand road continues to a junction a mile farther W, where you keep right for Yankee Boy Basin or jeep left to high mines in Governor and Sidney Basins.

St. Sophia Ridge, 13,000′, is a showpiece of rather unstable pinnacles. The higher (left) fork of road takes you via Sidney Basin to upper Governor Basin and the Humboldt Mine at 12,600′ under St. Sophia Ridge for a close look or a visit. Melvin Griffiths found the traversing on the SW side of the ridge full of unstable rock and the needles themselves generally too rotten to be tempting.

Mount Virginia, 13,581′, and **Mendota Peak,** 13,275′, are at the NW and SE ends of the St. Sophia Ridge, 1½ miles apart, and can both be climbed easily from the basin. A trail from a mile short of the road end at 12,050′ climbs over the ridge a mile S at 13,050′ and divides for two routes into Telluride, the shorter one to the right, the handsomer one to the left through Marshall Basin, where it meets the Imogene Pass road.

The Yankee Boy Basin road goes for small cars when it is in normal condition, and can be driven for 2 miles beyond the forking to 11,800′ where you are N of Stony Mountain. On the way you pass through a tilted field of innumerable columbine.

From the road end a trail climbs W 2 miles to **Blue Lakes Pass,** 13,000′, and zigzags down through the Blue Lakes to the

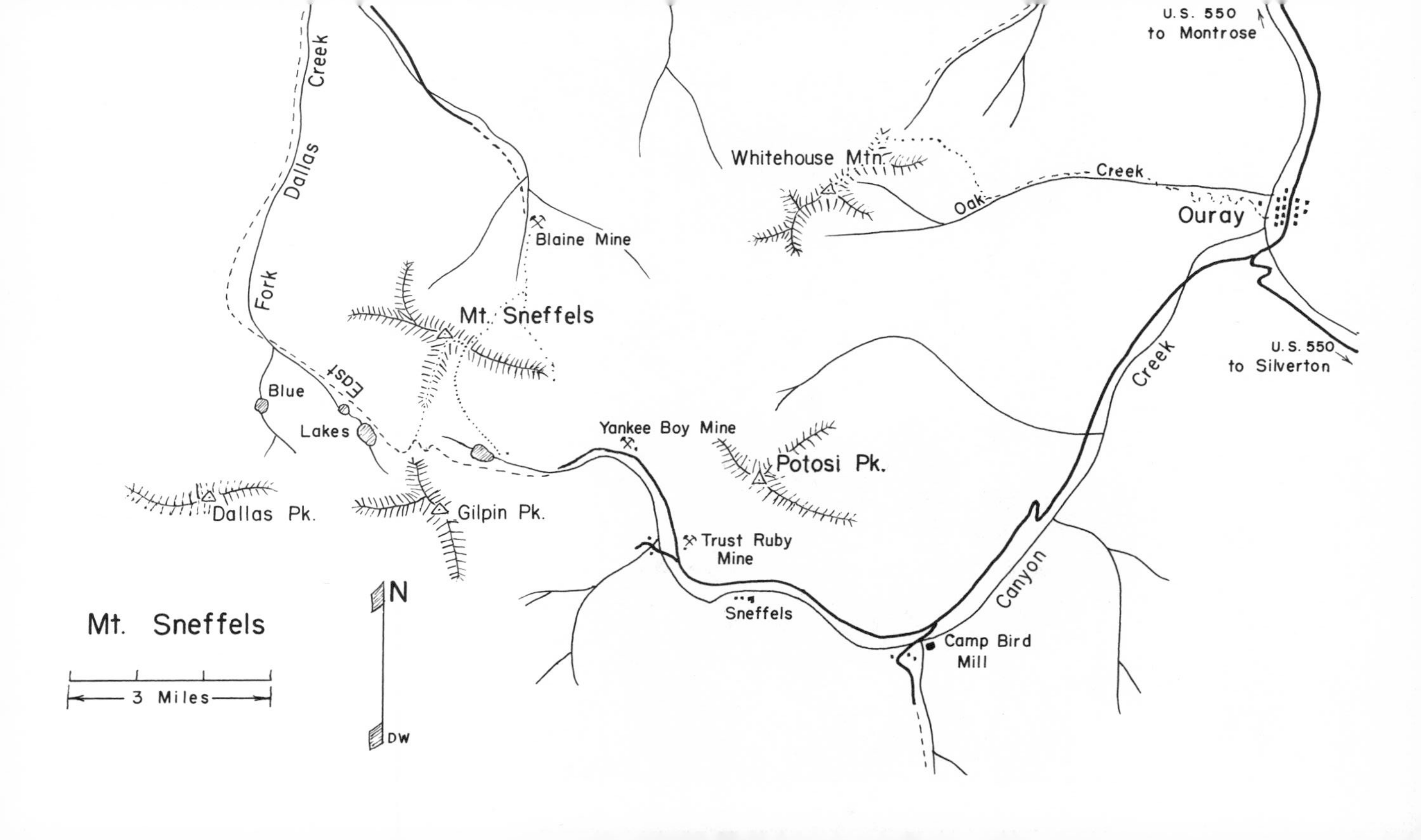
U.S. 550
to Montrose
U.S. 550
to Silverton
Ouray
Oak
Creek
Whitehouse Mtn.
Blaine Mine
Mt. Sneffels
Creek
Dallas
Fork
East
Blue
Lakes
Dallas Pk.
Gilpin Pk.
Yankee Boy Mine
Potosi Pk.
Trust Ruby
Mine
Sneffels
Camp Bird
Mill
Canyon
Creek
N
DW
Mt. Sneffels
3 Miles

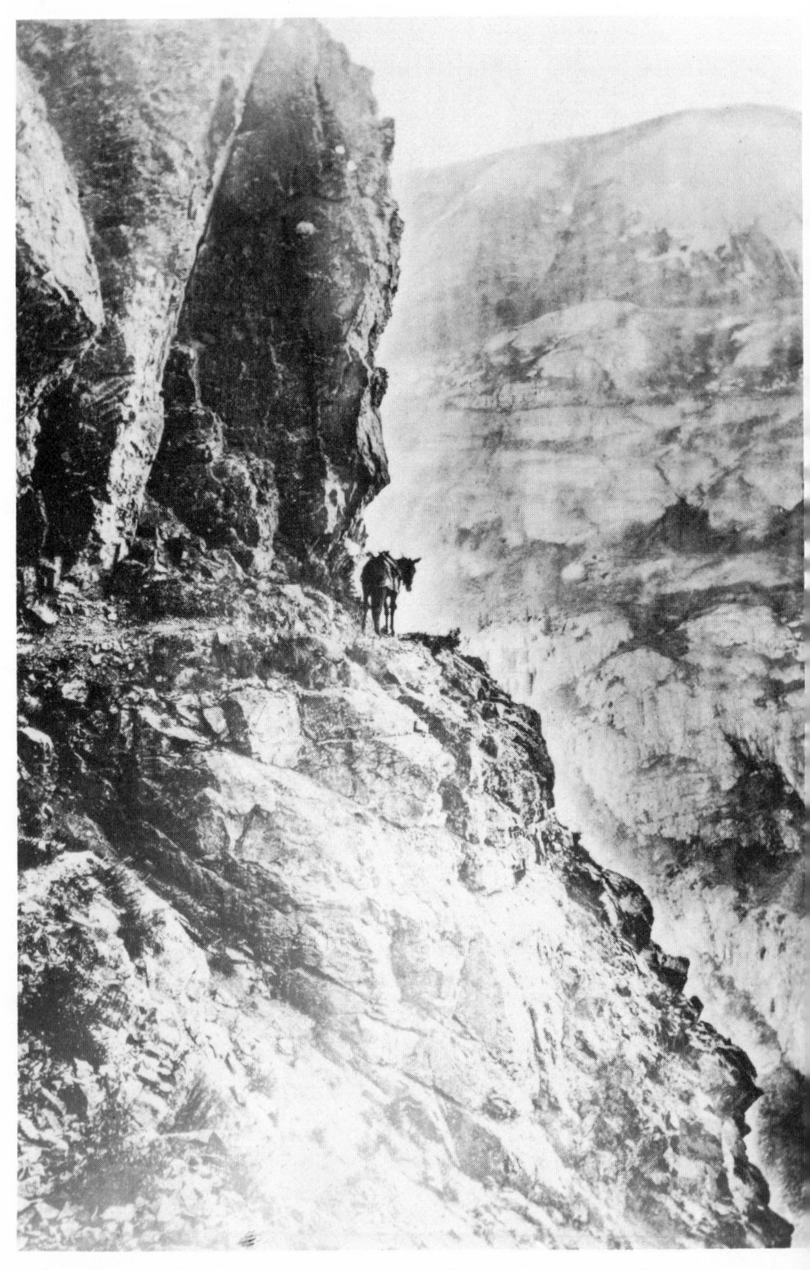

A William H. Jackson photo of the Bear Creek Trail.
Denver Public Library Western Collection.

East Fork of Dallas Creek. It is about 6 miles from the pass to the road, which it meets at 9400′.

Mount Sneffels, 14,150′, has a Nordic name meaning snow-field which Jules Verne used in his *Journey to the Centre of the Earth.* It was given the peak by Endlich and a companion member of the Hayden Survey, about the time of the 1874 first ascent. The usual route goes from Yankee Boy Basin, where you climb ½ mile from the road end most of the way to **Blue Lakes Pass** by trail. Leave the trail and head N in a broad gulch, and work to the right under cliffs until you reach the saddle where it ends. A steep and much narrower couloir climbs out to the left over large rocks. Keep left again in a smaller branch couloir to the top. The couloir is not a rock climb, yet steep enough to create a rolling rock hazard. Mount Sneffels itself is part of a volcanic rock flow; the range crest rocks in general belong to the Potosi volcanic group, which often has the kind of layering seen on Potosi Peak.

Gilpin Peak, 13,694′, can be climbed from Yankee Boy Basin. From the road end at 11,800′, cross the basin to the SW, climbing a mile to a little flat spur ridge off the S main ridge of the peak. Climb the steep 200′ pitch to the main ridge and follow it N.

Dyke Col, a 13,050′ pass, about half way between Kismet and Cirque Mountains, though steep on the N side, is the best route between Blaine and Yankee Boy Basins. It is named for the rhyolite dyke on its W side.

Kismet, 13,694′, is the cluster of points including a very spectacular NW one, that lies 1 mile ESE of **Sneffels** on the range crest. The route leads directly N from Wrights Lake on the **Blue Lakes Pass Trail** to the left of the prominent SE needle and directly to the SE side of the peak itself. This involves the likelihood of rope work at the top, where the route comes around to the S or SSW side.

Cirque Mountain, 13,686′, is 1.2 miles E of Mount Sneffels. It has a gentle W summit and ridge, but is rough on top. The big cliffs on the N and E sides are described as too rotten and soft for climbing, but it is easily approached from the S face or by way of **Dyke Col** and the W ridge.

Teakettle Mountain, 13,819′, is 1 mile NE of the flats N of Stony Mountain. The easiest approach starts at the timber patch at 11,400′ 1 mile up the Yankee Boy road from the exit for Governor Basin. Start N toward the jutting S ridge of the peak, and then as you climb veer right until you reach the ridge across the gully from it. Keep on or just right of this ridge till you reach the flats, 13,400′, under the point SE of the summit, which you bypass as you turn NE to the col and summit.

Potosi Peak, 13,786′, is well-armed with cliffs. Start as above but instead of climbing all the way up the ridge go right above the steep section and head E ½ mile or less to the 13,000′ saddle NW of Potosi. Climb on the ridge toward Potosi for about 250′ of altitude, then contour SE ¼ mile to the S ridge. Use the S ridge and the face to the right of it to gain the summit.

Whitehouse Mountain, 13,492′, is the large NW corner ridge of the Sneffels Range. Two trails run up toward it from Ouray. The more direct of them starts at the W end of the town's southernmost cross street, at 7950′, and climbs, first on the S side and then on the N side of Oak Creek, beyond timberline. From its end take a half right, or northwesterly, route up to the ridge and get on the E ridge for an easy finish. It is about 6 miles. The second trail starts one block farther N and angles NE up the ledges and timber to the Speedwell Mine, then S and W to **Twin Sisters** about 3 miles from town. You can continue bushwhacking and climbing W on the ridge another 3 miles to the Corbet or NE ridge of Whitehouse, which you meet ½ mile below the Whitehouse summit. The San Juan Mountaineers liked Corbet ridge for its more challenging possibilities, which are on the northern side. To get there use the second trail and work around to the right of the ridge a mile or so W of the Twin Peaks.

The *San Juan Guide* discusses several summits which interested its writers as high points or rock climbs, either potentially or as a result of their experience. Those not named they

Cirque Peak, Teakettle Mountain and Potosi Peak, from the south approach to Potosi. *Walker photo.*

North ridges of Mount Sneffels from high in the Blaine Basin. *Ormes photo.*

designated as S1, S2, etc., the S standing for Sneffels. We will identify these on the newer Sams and Mount Sneffels Quads. (S1 is on Telluride Quad.)

S2, 13,468′, is the summit 1 mile WSW of **Whitehouse,** about midway between it and **Teakettle.** To reach it from Whitehouse involves first ¾ mile of level ridge walking, then another ¾ mile with a 600′ dip. It is also available from canyons to the N. **S1,** 13,568′, on the SE ridge of **Teakettle,** is described as a little block aiguille best reached from the basin S of Teakettle, probably difficult.

The others are W of Sneffels: **S3,** 13,410′, is 1½ miles W of the lowest of the Blue Lakes, at 11,000′. It is reachable and easily climbable from that side. **S5,** 13,363′, is ¼ mile N of S3, with some rough bumps and a dip of 250′ between. It would not give trouble climbed separately from the cirque or from its E saddle. **Wolcott Peak,** 13,242′, has striking frontal cliffs facing upper Dallas Creek, but can be approached from the same cirque W of Blue Lakes. Climb to its W saddle, which connects it to S5.

S6, 13,441′, consists of a whole group of summits, several of which seem to offer "good bits of climbing." From Blue Lakes it is best reached over the S5-S3 saddle, 13,050′, where a drop of 100′ should suffice for the traverse NW.

Northern approaches to the Sneffels Range, especially to Mount Sneffels and its immediate ridges, give the most exciting prospects. The peak is both symmetrical and rough. Together with the Uncompahgre region it is visible as a long stretch of rugged summits from 80 miles away, near Grand Junction. The scene reappears in increasing magnificence as one drives south.

Driving W from Ridgway on State 62, you come to Dallas Creek 4½ miles W of US 550. The East Fork road turns off at this point and goes 2 miles S to a junction. Keep right, around the hill, and continue on the best road 5 miles to the meadow on East Dallas Creek, 9150′, the end of car road. (You can jeep in farther if you turn off left 1 mile earlier and stay parallel to the canyon but above it.) From the meadow climb left 300′ on steep hillside to old mine road and follow it S 4½ miles to a camping space a little beyond 11,083′ Blaine Mine, in Blaine Basin, where you are a mile NNE of the cliffs of Sneffels.

Blaine Peak, 12,910′, is ¾ mile N of Sneffels. The E summit first ascent (SJM) went easily by the short SW ridge, which the climbers reached by climbing 1¼ miles SW up the basin under Sneffels.

Some of the agiuilles are located as follows: **Purgatory Point,** 13,650′, ¼ mile NNE of the Sneffels summit, looked impossible to the SJM, but has a perhaps climbable summit. **The Hand,** 13,022′, the **Penguin** and the **Thumb** form a 3-part summit ½ mile NW of Sneffels. All are approachable from Blaine Basin. The first two were climbed by the San Juan Mountaineers.

Blue Lakes, mentioned above as over the pass from Yankee Boy Basin, are near the head of the East Fork Dallas Creek, for which you follow the route for Blaine Basin as far as the 9150′ meadow at mile 7. Instead of climbing left you walk the jeep road and trail up the creek 5½ miles to the lowest lake for camping at 11,000′, or 7 miles to the middle one at 11,600′.

Mount Sneffels is rated a good climb, not without a problem or two, from the top of the **Blue Lakes Pass** via the S ridge. There are some other summits available from the lakes besides S 3, 5, 6 and Wolcott. **Wolf Tooth,** 12,720′, is .6 mile W across the cirque from the Sneffels summit. The **Monolith** and the **Blue Needle** just W of it, are .3 mile down the SW ridge from Sneffels. They are all rated difficult and beautiful, like Cleopatra. The SJM report describes numerous climbs up Sneffels and around its crags from Blaine Basin and the lakes.

Dallas Peak, 13,809′, shows a very steep N face to the Blue Lakes. One is tempted to suggest doing the full 5-mile ridge S of the Blue Lakes Basin for a high time. This could start with a climb of 2½ miles to 13,735′ T-O at the W end of the basin grand cliffs. Next the tour would pass close under the summits of the **Block-tops,** 13,543′, which excited great enthusiasm in the San Juan'ers. From there, go **Gilpin Peak** or a shortcut ridge descent N to **Blue Lakes Pass** and the trail. The total climbing is close to 5000′, with numerous intermissions.

State 62, running from 550 W to Placerville over 9000′ Dallas Divide, has fine views of the Sneffels Range from the N and NW. From 1½ miles W of the divide a road runs off left across Hastings Mesa and around the end of the range on **Last Dollar Pass,** 10,663′. You keep left at mile 6; the pass is at mile 11. The road descends to the San Miguel River 3½ miles W of Telluride. **North Pole Mountain,** 12,208′, and **Hayden Peak,** 12,987′, can be reached from this road. At mile 7½ from State 62 you come to Alder Creek, 9000′. Take the trail off left, keeping to the N fork of the creek. Trail climbs you to timberline, and you continue E to a saddle between the above summits. Both are available by ridge. The U.S.G.S. attaches the name of Hayden to the lower summit, .3 mile NW of one which measures 13,012′.

Mears Peak, 13,496′, is very good looking from the N but hard to reach. Drive up the Last Dollar Road from the Telluride end (3½ miles E of Telluride) to Deep Creek, 8750′, and go 4½ miles NE (not N) up the left side of Deep Creek's middle fork on the trail to 10,900′. Take a drink. Mears Peak is 1½ miles NE and 2600′ higher.

Ruffner Mountain, 12,304′, is directly N a mile and climbable from about mile 3 of the same trail.

The **Hayden Peak** summits, 13,125′ S9, and 13,242′ S8, can be reached from the main or W fork of Deep Creek. The route starts as a road from .2 miles W of the crossing of Deep Creek on the Last Dollar road, and runs N 2 miles to a pack-trail continuation. Follow the latter ½ mile to 10,000′, where it turns off right, and work your way up the drainage to the mountain tops. SJM writers have much to say of **S9**, whose northern cliffs are among the most imposing of the range. The S approaches are all easy. Deep Creek is recommended as the best climbing center camp for the W end of the Sneffels Range, even though it is a toilsome pack-in.

NEEDLE MOUNTAINS

QUADS: Storm King and Snowdon Peaks; 15′ Needle Mountains; San Juan N F.

In its general sense the term Needle Mountains subsumes the Grenadier Range, the Needles proper and perhaps the West Needles. Unlike the mining town San Juans, the Needles have few roads and trails. This fact and their steepness have tended to make them a preserve for mountaineering. Much of the Needles area is in the San Juan Wilderness. Except for the West Needles the mountains are between the roadless Animas River and the Vallecito, also roadless from 4 miles N of Vallecito Reservoir. The main peaks are approached by railroad. Here as always, steepness and weathering make rotten rock problems. The general rule in the Needles is to take with you rope, ice axe and experienced companions.

The southern and West Needles are of Eolus granite; the Grenadier end is of slate, quartzite and conglomerate.

The Grenadier Range is a single ridge running ESE from **Mount Garfield,** prominently seen 5 miles SE from **Molas Pass,** to the **Guardian,** with a 2-pronged northern spur at the head of Elk Creek. Two or three of the sharpest summits are visible 10 miles S from the W end of Silverton. They are 13'ers with steep faces and ridges of a hard quartzite which makes for sporty climbing.

Elk Creek, the northernmost approach, has an old road which serves as a trail. This runs E from Elk Park 7 miles down the railroad from Silverton. From Molas Lake, 6 miles SSW of Silverton on US 550, there is a 4-mile trail dropping from 10,500′ to an Animas River bridge in Elk Park at 8900′. We do not have reports on the approaches to peaks from this side, though we know it has been used; we can only speculate from the map. The **Elk Creek Trail** climbs 9 miles to the Divide,

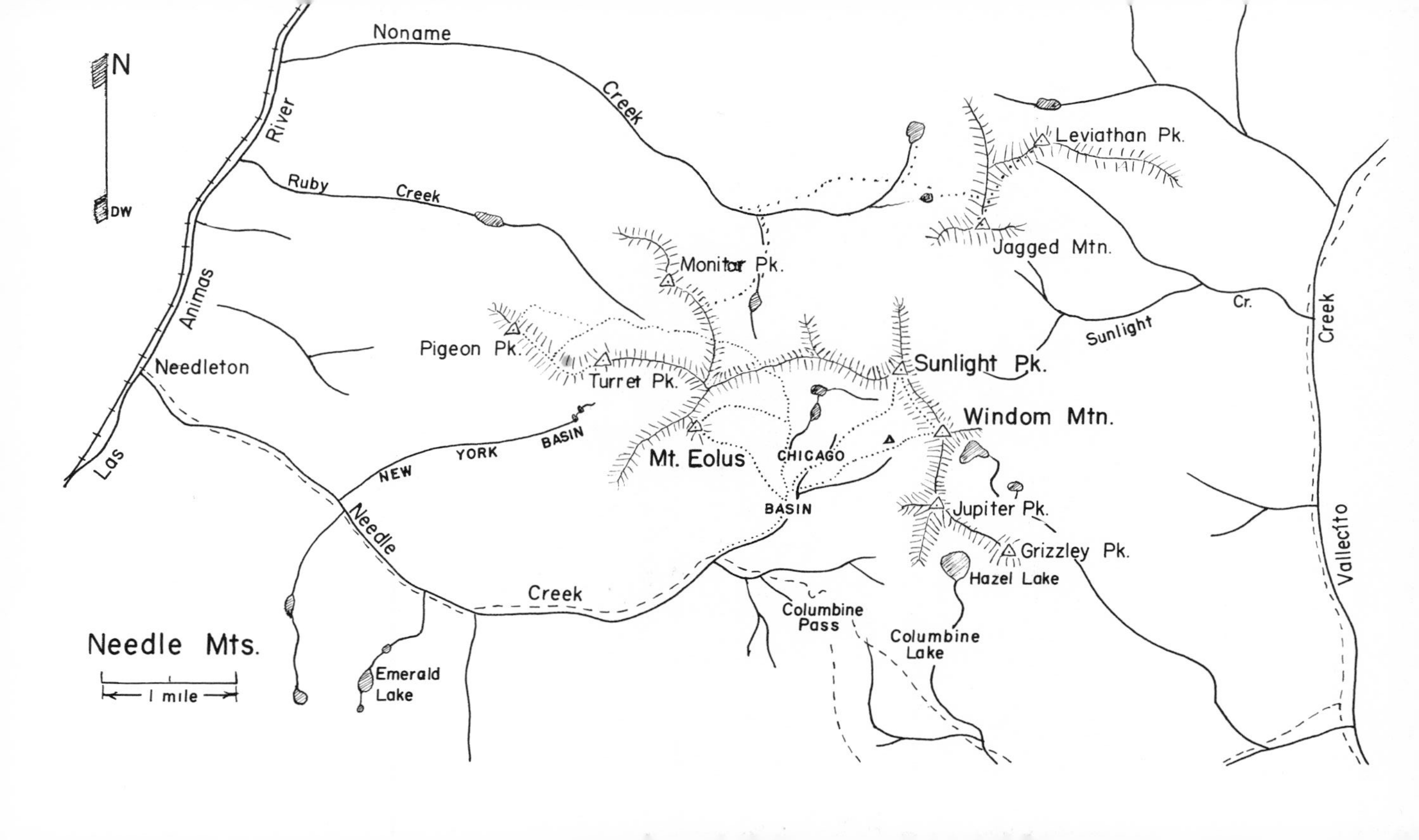

N
DW
Noname Creek
Animas River
Las
Ruby Creek
Needleton
Monitor Pk.
Pigeon Pk.
Turret Pk.
Mt. Eolus
NEW YORK BASIN
CHICAGO BASIN
Needle Creek
Leviathan Pk.
Jagged Mtn.
Sunlight Cr.
Sunlight Pk.
Windom Mtn.
Jupiter Pk.
Grizzley Pk.
Hazel Lake
Columbine Pass
Columbine Lake
Emerald Lake
Vallecito Creek
Needle Mts.
1 mile

Close to the clouds on Needle Ridge. *Griffiths photo.*

where it meets a crest trail, the jeep road to Beartown, and the **Kite Lake** and **Hunchback Pass Trails.**

Mount Garfield, 13,074′, presents its likeliest route from the lower end of Elk Park, where the N and NW ridge comes off the peak to end. The chief unknowns are the steep section of 400′ near the top, and a possible problem or two along the summit ridge to point 3, the summit.

Electric Peak, 13,292′, could be started from ½ mile W of the Animas. It looks like a dry 3-mile ridge climb, sometimes steep but without important problems.

Peaks Two and **Three,** and **Arrow, Vestal** and the **Trinity Peaks** are all approachable from the Vestal Lake creek. The route should leave Elk Creek 2½ miles E of the Animas, where the trail comes to a lakelet in a flat. One should work S and a little E, at first on the E side of the creek and then on the W, to a level-off at 11,400′ for camping.

We have unfavorable reports from Carleton Long on the dip of the quartzite layers on the N side of the peaks, but **Vestal Peak** has been climbed more than once by the Wham Ridge, and we would like to see a route on Arrow parallel to the Wham on the E side of the broad NNE face. The face starts about ½ mile S of this putative camp.

West Trinity Peak has a sharp 1000′ NNW ridge, but the two first **Trinity Peaks** would be best taken from the rear by a route up-canyon past Vestal Lake, SE over the saddle at 12,050′, and thence NE by optical conjecture. If the **East Trinity** proved too much we would recommend coming around to it from the E end. You would walk up canyon to the 13,000′ pass and turn right. The middle **Trinity Peak,** 13,805′, is the highest of the Grenadiers.

Tenmile Creek, 10 miles down the river from Silverton, climbs 2800′ in less than 5 miles to Balsam Lake. The route starts with the drowning of all but the fittest—a crossing of the Animas that is impossible early in the year—and continues with a line of march which has only occasional resemblance to a trail. As blazed in 1941 by the CMC, it went up the right side 1½ miles, then crossed creek. "A possible game trail route leads from Elk Creek to Tenmile over the saddle between **Vestal Peak** and the first **Trinity Peak.** The 1500′ drop in altitude from the 12,850′ saddle into Tenmile Creek valley is awesome. However, a faint trail immediately below the saddle appears to travel east for several miles beneath the Trinity Peaks and pass Balsam Lake to the **Storm King-Silex Trail.** Karl Zeller believes that one could travel with difficulty from Elk Creek to the saddle over trail-free terrain."

The camp at Balsam Lake is so satisfactory for climbers that several parties have gone there. From the lake they climb SW on a tiresome talus slope and cross cirque country to **Peak Four** and the **Heisspitz,** taking them from the ridge or south side. The same start and an angling S to the saddle goes for Peaks Five and Six.

Arrow Peak, 13,803′, has no walking route. The first climb, accomplished in 1932, is described in the *San Juan Guide* by Carleton Long, one of its authors. Starting from Balsam Lake he and John Nelson contoured a mile WNW and climbed N to Arrow Lake. "From the west end of the lake go north and a little west to the water gully . . . in the western portion of the south face of the peak. Follow up the eastern of the pair of gullies thus offered. Just below the band of red rocks is Long's overhang, which may be avoided by swinging left up and over a vertical sheet into a jam chimney."

Vestal Peak, 13,664′, has been climbed in a number of ways from the S. A good route takes you to the Arrow-Vestal saddle (as for the first ascent of Arrow), then angles up the SW face. The sharply jutting E end of the S face, called the Kurtzhorn, forms part of a route which then goes into the chute to the S. Rit Burrows reported the first and a quite merry ascent of the Wham Ridge on the N side in *Trail and Timberline*, October, 1941.

Storm King Peak, 13,752′, and the **E Trinity Peak,** 13,745′, can be climbed from the upper cirque, a mile E of Balsam Lake. You climb N from the lake ½ mile, turn E ½ mile and look

Mount Silex and The Guardian behind. From Tenmile-Trinity Creek Pass. *Rosenbaum photo.*

Windom Peak as seen from Sunlight Peak. *H. L. Standley photo.*

things over. East Trinity is on your left, Storm King on your right. From the same place you can go on across the Storm King–Peak Eight saddle, 12,800′, and losing 600′ or so, climb to the next saddle at the same altitude for an ascent of **Mount Silex,** 13,628′ on its SW ridge. **The Guardian,** 13,617′, is another ⅓ mile SE along the ridge. The return from it to 12,050′ on the second dip in the ridge between the two gives you a good traverse to the Silex SW ridge without extra climbing. For upper Noname Creek peaks, use the approach for Peak 5 and cross the saddle W of it into the lake basin of Noname's N fork.

Noname Creek Trail, the third line of approach from the Animas, has been popular enough to rate two climbing guides printed in *Trail and Timberline*: the first by Henry Buchtel in September, 1947; the second by William E. Davis in October, 1960. Davis begins by stressing the rotten rock problems which increase with the great steepness of these peaks, and then expands and adds to the route information given in the non-available *San Juan Guide*. Although Davis' material is for Noname Creek it covers a wide circle of routes, some reached by fly camps. He omits technical climbs—Gray Needle, the Index, Monitor's E face, Eolus' N face, the Needle Ridge and others—but remarks that rope, pitons and ice axes may be called into play for short parts of many of the climbs.

Noname Creek is 13 miles S of Silverton and the Animas has to be forded. (The stream widens ¼ mile below the creek and can usually be done in August.) Recently the railroad has refused to stop at Noname except on the downhill run from Silverton. Try a tip. The climb to camp starts at 8430′ and for the 3½ miles to the meadows is no formal trail but a fair, cairn-marked route that zigzags left of the creek. Camp can be made anywhere from 4 miles E of the river at 10,200′ to the forks at 10,750′, 6 miles up. The latter is as central a place as can be found for combining the southern 14'er climbs with those in the Grenadiers. It is used as the point of reference in the Davis Noname Guide. The following paragraphs are largely written from his statements. We have also made use of the trails material in the *T & T* article of August 1969, "Trails of the Western Weminuche", by William Weihofen, Ralph Tosenbaum, and Henri Navelet. The ridge between Noname and Tenmile Creeks, an easy climb of 2,000′, gives a good look at the Grenadier. **Peak 4** goes best by the ridge to the right of the main gully above camp on the NNW side. For the **Heiss-pitz** one can drop S off Peak 4 and traverse along the ridge, or start ¼ mile down canyon to climb it alone. **Peak 5** goes from either of the lakes which flank it on the E and W. For **Peak 10, Jagged Mountain, Leviathan,** and **Peaks 5, 6, 7,** and points N you start by angling ENE up the left branch of Noname to a flat and a higher little lake at 12,200′. (From camp you can climb N to timberline and follow game trails E.)

Jagged Mountain, 13,824′, is "one of the more difficult and certainly one of the most rewarding climbs in the Needles." From the lakelet climb E ¼ mile to the 13,000′ saddle N and slightly E of the peak. Summit is the first aguille to the right of a prominent snow couloir on the N face. Traverse from the col just short of the couloir, where a series of ledges leads up to an impasse under which you traverse W into the next gully. This leads to a ridge just W of the summit. Here you swing to the SE face and contour to cracks which lead to the summit. Avoid starting in a good-looking gully to the left of that specified. It leads to a lower summit separated from the true summit by a gap. Avoid also the snow couloir; it leads to summit ridge but not to summit. "Finding the route on Jagged is a delight." **Leviathan,** 13,528′, is climbed by the SW ridge. The approach is to the same col as for **Jagged Mountain.** From here you traverse NE ¼ mile to the col which starts the ridge. It is not hard to descend the SE ridge to 11,250′ and go up 13,428′ **Vallecito Mountain,** half a mile E.

Knife Point, *c.* 13,200′, and **Peak Ten,** *c.* 13,400′, "are climbed from the col between them. Approach them by the E branch of Noname Creek, but instead of climbing northward to the high basin, swing southeast along the main watercourse. A prominent gully will be seen leading to the col. To ascend the lowest cliffs, get into the bottom of the main gully. When you are really in it (rock on both sides), work up to the second couloir on the south (right) and follow this out onto the upper grassy slopes. From the col it is an easy walk up the Knife Point ridge to the top."

Sunlight Peak, the **Needle Ridge,** 13,400′ plus, and **Peak Eleven,** *c.* 13,500′, can all be reached from Noname camp. Climb to the first bench ½ mile E of camp and turn S as for Knife Point (above), but keep to the valley.

"At the valley's head, either contour on the right (western) side or attack the lowest cliffs directly. Either way brings one to upper boulder- and snowfields. It is a straightforward march across them to the pass between Sunlight and Needle Ridge.

"A choice must be made at this pass. One alternative is to climb Sunlight directly; the other is drop into Chicago Basin and ascend the peak by the regular route. Choose the former if your objective is Sunlight only; take the latter if you are trying to climb both Sunlight and Windom.

"To climb Sunlight directly from the pass, start eastward along the ridge. After about ten feet it is possible to pass behind a large north-facing flake. Doing this brings one to a ledge about three feet wide which traverses for some distance along the northwest face of the peak. Follow this ledge upward to the main couloir at the intersection of the west shoulder and the north ridge; then ascend the couloir to the ridge to meet the regular route.

"To climb Windom and Sunlight, it is necessary to drop into Chicago Basin. From the pass, descend as closely to the cliffs as possible. Do this by keeping as high on the southwest flank of Sunlight as is comfortable; or, in other words, keep to the left. This brings one into the basin between Sunlight and Windom. The regular routes are then available. Windom should be climbed by the west ridge; the easiest route to the ridge is up to the saddle between Windom and Peak 18. The ridge is then worked eastwardly to the top.

"Sunlight is approached by the southeast ridge. To gain this, climb to the yellow-dirt saddle obvious from the basin. The route then generally follows the ridge to the summit. Incidentally, local ground rules still require that each member of a party stand up on the true summit!"

Chicago Basin can be reached with about the same effort by way of **Twin Thumbs Pass,** 13,050′, for which you climb directly up the S fork 2 miles from camp, keeping E of the creek and lake. To ascend **Mount Eolus,** traverse W from Twin Thumbs Pass and climb by easy ledges up the E slopes. Not much altitude needs to be lost recrossing the S ridge of **Glacier Point.**

Other peaks reached from the left or E side of the watercourse in this S valley are **Peak Eleven, Twin Thumbs** and **Glacier Point.** For the first two, climb SE from E of the lake through the lower cliffs into the cirque between Peak Eleven and Twin Thumbs. A direct ascent of the snow N of the Thumbs will lead to chimneys and slabs NE of the Thumbs summit. A col on the ridge provides access to both peaks. Pitons and rope must be carried. For Glacier Point take the next W indentation of the cirque head (straight N from the lake) and climb it easily from the S side of **Twin Thumbs Pass.** Taken more directly from the N side it makes a good ice climb.

To climb 13,120′ **Peak Twelve,** start as for the above but after $\frac{1}{2}$ mile up the S fork angle right and climb to the 12,750′ col S of the great wall of **Monitor Peak.** Carry with you your July, 1969 *T & T* to trace out the routes on this face (a Davis idea updated). Peak Twelve goes easily up the ridge left from the col.

Pigeon Peak, 13,972′, is approached from Noname Creek over the same col W of Peak Twelve. Drop into Ruby Creek drainage a mile for a fly camp in the broad meadow N of Turret Needles or keep higher for a direct ascent. The usual route from Ruby Basin lies W of the first large gray rock ridge that runs from the N face of Pigeon almost to Ruby Creek. It climbs grassy ledges and continues up the NW ridge. Another route in this neighborhood has been described which climbs by way of a N couloir to 200′ below the summit on the NW ridge. There are too many technical overtones for reproduction here but with some more experimentation it might well work out as the best approach from Noname Creek. See Robert M. Smith in the October, 1960 *Trail and Timberline.* Pigeon offers a roped-up chimney climb from the Turret saddle—a route which is used for descent by long rappels. Hard hats help. To find it from the top, use a couloir which descends S from W of the summit and splits about 400′ down into the chimney. Two double-rope rappels take you down, the first from a chockstone 30′ below the start, the second, 120′ long, from hardware, 80′ lower. **Turret Peak,** 13,835′, is climbed from this saddle, 13,100′ where the Pigeon Chimney starts up.

The longest rock climb we have record of in the Needles is that of the **East Face of Monitor Peak,** which presents a spectacular 1200′ wall. The first ascent, by Joe Stettner (of the Stettner Ledges on Longs Peak), was made in 1947 and reported in the December *Trail and Timberline* that year. The July 1969 *T & T* has Jack Fralick's report of a second and more direct climb by Paul Stettner and Larry Dalke.

The Index, though no such feat as this, belongs in the technical list. It is the point at about 13,150′ 1 mile NW of **Monitor Peak** and .4 WNW of **Animas Peak.** It has been visited by parties who attained the ridge just W of it. They traversed the W face of the third summit, went through the center to the E face of same, traversed upward to the shelf between the third and second summits, rappelled E to the base of the second, and traversed S and up along the E face of the high summit to its S face for the finish.

Ruby Creek has been used for short-time camps, but the climb of 2½ miles to Ruby Lake is trailless and very steep and the repertory more limited than farther E. The creek out of New York Basin, tributary to Needle Creek, is likewise hard going and limited.

Needle Creek Trail, 16 miles down the Animas from Silverton, is the main route to the southern Needles. The conductor on the train will let you off at the Forest Service bridge (not Needleton Bridge), close to where an old mine road starts at 8150′ and climbs 6 miles E up the creek to Chicago Basin and camping places at 11,000′ there. This gives the easiest access to the 14'ers and can be used for longer trips N, preferably with fly camps. The 14'ers are not difficult, but rope should be carried and probably ice axes. The cirque is bounded clockwise by **Eolus, Glacier Point, Twin Thumbs, Peak Eleven, Needle Ridge, Sunlight** (with **Peak Eighteen** in front), **Windom, Jupiter,** and S of the high **Columbine Pass Trail, Aztec Mountain.**

Mount Eolus, 14,084′, is about 1 mile NW and can be climbed directly by its SE ridge or by gentler gradients from farther up the basin. For the latter, a trail leads you N to the E side of peak. Climb W to a snowfield, N to the low point on the ridge, NW 100 yards to low point of the N-S Eolus ridge, S to the E face and up a middle route to the summit, or directly up the ridge.

Windom Peak, 14,087′, and **Sunlight Peak,** 14,059′, are usually climbed together, with Windom recommended as first. From the camping part of the basin start N on trail, following it to an E bend from which you hike ENE a little right of **Peak Eighteen** and climb to its E ridge. This leads E to **Windom Summit,** $\frac{1}{2}$ mile. In continuing N to Sunlight keep to right or E of the notch on the latter. Climbers usually return down ridge from Sunlight to descend, but direct S face routes have been used for both ascent and descent of Sunlight when not coupled with Windom. The route up in this case keeps left of Peak Eighteen. Mel Griffiths and I finished our Windom-Sunlight day with **Needle Ridge,** E-W. I remember it as airy, with firm rock and no problems but the rappels.

The **Columbine Pass Trail** is recommended as a warm-up and scenic trip.

WEST NEEDLE MOUNTAINS

QUADS: Snowdon Peak, Engineer Mountain.

This name applies to a 20-mile chain of fairly rough mountains S of **Molas Pass** and paralleling the Needles section of the Animas River on its W side. We do not have records of routes and can only suggest lines of approach.

Snowdon Peak, 13,077′, is at the N end, 2½ miles S of **Molas Pass.** The route would seem to start at 10,400′ with a trail 1 mile W of the pass. It goes SE and S halfway to the mountain on its NW side. Cut E for ½ mile around the S side of a hill and another mile to a saddle NNE of the peak and try the narrow half-mile ridge from there.

The Twilight group (13,079′ **North Twilight,** 13,158′ **Twilight,** 13,100′ **South Twilight,** and 13,045′ **West Needle Mountain**) are E to SE from Lime Creek Campground and 1½ to 2½ miles away up ridged faces that climb steeply from a little over 9000′. Approached from the W sides their summits should not prove any more difficult than the bushwhack to them.

NEEDLE MOUNTAINS—VALLECITO BASIN

QUADS: Needle Mountains 15′, Storm King Peak, Rio Grande Pyramid.

The Vallecito Reservoir is 14 miles N of Bayfield on good road. The road on the W side of the reservoir continues 8 miles N to Vallecito Campground. The **Vallecito Trail** runs 19 miles more N up the river to **Hunchback Pass,** 12,487′, to meet the trail from the Rio Grande and Beartown. The Vallecito is a very full creek, especially up through midsummer. The trail, once it gets into the mountains, is on the E side except for a mile or so above mile 5, and there are no bridges for trail departures on the W side.

Emerson Mountain, 13,147′, and **Amherst** and **Organ Mountains,** about the same height, are on a ridge to the W at mile 5 to mile 7, and visible in part from the Reservoir. They can be climbed on the 4-mile ridge to the right of Sheep Draw. Bushwhack W up the slope from mile 6 to this ridge, which climbs from 8700′ to the top of Organ Mountain. If you go S to Emerson you can drop off E to the creek between the peaks and then contour out to your approach route.

At mile 8 from the Vallecito Campground, a trail climbs from 9200′ up Johnson Creek WSW and WNW 5 miles to Vallecito Basin, 11,300′. The trail continues 2 miles more to the top of **Columbine Pass,** about 12,650′, and down to Chicago Basin. It was made horse-worthy in 1966 but is reported very muddy when wet.

In the Vallecito Basin you are surrounded by the southernmost summits of the Needle Mountains. **Florida Mountain,** 13,076′, is at the left or S, and can be climbed most of the way (to **Trimble Pass,** ½ mile SW of it at 12,800′) by an old road. **Aztec Mountain,** 13,250′, is a mile S and ¾ mile W from **Columbine Pass** on quite passable ridge with little altitude loss. **McCauley Peak,** 13,551′, is up a 2-mile steep slope NE. **Hope Mountain,** 13,000′ plus, which splits the upper basin, is a mile E of Columbine Pass, and can be approached from the pass on an old road that crosses N of it going E to Hazel Lake. The trail across to Hazel Lake is about 1½ miles long. Here you are looking at the rough cliffs of the S face of **Jupiter Peak** and the SW face of 13,695′ **Grizzly Peak,** both within a mile. Jupiter can be climbed from the long SSW ridge, the same route normally used from Chicago Basin.

Grizzly Peak's western face is split by a broad gully. If the couloirs above the gully seem too steep for comfort, work N before climbing. The ridge from Grizzly to McCauley is bumpy but offers no real difficulties.

Sunlight Creek Trail leaves the Vallecito 3 miles N of the Columbine exit, 2 south of the Rock Creek exit, and climbs 4½ miles from 7900′ to 12,033′ Sunlight Lake, close under **Sunlight Peak.** There is good camping en route and a passage into the Needles by **Knife Point Pass,** 12,350′. To cross this way leave the trail on your left above timberline and climb W. Our informants say it is steep, long and grassy on the Vallecito side, and somewhat frightening when you look down into Noname

Creek. You can slide loose scree down to a CMC trail which skirts above the dangerous cliffs.

The most convenient northern pass into the Needles leaves the Vallecito to climb up into Stormy Gulch where the Vallecito grows suddenly steep, at mile 17. The route climbs into the left branch to Lake Silex, 12,100′, where you are between the cliffs of Silex and the steep ridge of **Storm King,** and beyond the lake is **Peak Nine.** The pass is on the right, between the two last, at 12,800′. The descent to Balsam Lake is about 2½ miles long. Keep well right of the creek where it steepens.

For the Hunchback approach to this pass, see the **Bend.** You come down the **Vallecito Trail** to where Nebo Creek comes in on the left and contour right off the trail to Stormy Gulch and its trail.

There are some summits worthy of attention on the E side of the Vallecito.

Irving Peak, 13,210′, is at mile 8 N of the campground. From a little N of the Columbine exit, at 9100′, you climb 2 miles NNE up a S ridge.

Mount Oso, 13,706′, on the San Cristobal 30′ Quad, appears to be a very hard 1½ miles ENE from Irving Peak. The more natural approach to it however seems to be from Rock Creek. The good **Rock Creek Trail** climbs ESE from the Vallecito 13 miles N of Vallecito Campground, 5 south of **Hunchback Pass.** From a start at 10,100′ it goes SE to very near Rock Lake, 12,000′, 2 miles ENE of the peak. Climb SE from the Rock Lake Basin, then head toward the peak WSW, looking for a gap in the defenses. The map shows it a steep climb; we have no report as to how it can be done.

Emerald Lakes might seem an interesting goal in themselves, and quite as practicable a way to approach **Mount Oso** and some of its rough, steep neighbor summits. From the lower end of the lakes, 10,020′, there is a 6-mile trail N past Moon Lakes to a lakelet under the saddle 1¼ miles east of **Mount Oso,** which was on the route not described just above. To reach Emerald Lakes, take the Pine River road E from the E side of the Vallecito Reservoir. You can drive 4 miles to the Pine River Campground at 7900′, and perhaps a mile farther to the ranch. It is 5 miles to the trail junction, where you take left and climb in the steeper Lake Fork 5 more miles N to the big and little Emeralds.

Mount Nebo, 13,205′, affords a marvelous view into the Needles. It can be reached on a 3-mile walk S along the Divide from **Hunchback Pass,** with one 400′ summit to climb or bypass. From the Vallecito the best route starts up a steep watercourse 1 mile N of the **Rock Creek Trail** exit. After you reach timberline head a mile NE for a drink in the 12,500′ lake, and take your peak by the SE ridge.

TELLURIDE GROUP

QUADS: Telluride, Ophir, Silverton, Ironton; San Juan and Uncompahgre N F's.

This arbitrary section consists of two ridges: the N-S ridge W to Telluride between Marshall Basin and Bridal Veil Basin, and the E-W ridge connecting with it S of Bridal Veil Basin and running W of Ophir Needles. In this group we made use of the San Juan Mountaineers' explorations. Nomenclature for the unnamed summits is theirs.

T5, 13,436′, is a flat-summited ridge point reached from the **Governor Basin-Marshall Basin Trail,** which crosses the ridge at 13,050′, $\frac{3}{4}$ mile W of the summit. **Chicago Peak,** 13,385′, is $1\frac{1}{2}$ miles NE of 13,114′ **Imogene Pass,** easily reached along the ridge with a loss of 300′ of so. **Telluride Peak,** 13,509′, is an easy $\frac{3}{4}$ mile in the opposite direction from Imogene Pass.

The Imogene Pass road on the Telluride side is much easier for a small car than on the Canyon Creek side. From the N side of town drive E up the hillside, and keeping generally to the best road, you will come to the Tomboy Mine area at mile 7, and 13,114′ **Imogene Pass** $2\frac{1}{2}$ miles beyond. From the pass and the lookout $\frac{1}{2}$ mile to the E you see a good deal of the Sneffels Range and of the ridges way off E.

About mile $5\frac{1}{2}$ from Telluride, at 10,900′, a road climbs off for Marshall Basin and the Smuggler Mine 2 miles NNW. It is another mile N to the 13,050′ pass into Governor Basin of Ouray's Canyon Creek noted above.

T5, 13,436′, is a $\frac{3}{4}$-mile ridge climb E from this pass, quite gentle except for the first bit. After that the ridge narrows but continues without violent ups and downs via 13,385′ **Chicago Peak** SSE for a total highland tour of 5 miles to **Imogene Pass.** For this leave the car at the Tomboy and take the higher road directly from there into Marshall Basin when you start.

The road to **Black Bear Pass,** which climbs W from 11,100′ **Red Mountain Pass** on US 550, and then drops in Ingram Basin to Telluride, is a little easier on the 4-mile E side than on the 8-mile W side. Consequently round trip jeepers from Ouray go Black Bear, Telluride, Imogene. Its views include the Silverton mountains around to the Needles.

Black Bear Pass and **Imogene Pass** are about 4 miles apart by ridge. The summits between are **Telluride Peak,** 13,509′, an easy trip of $\frac{3}{4}$ mile S from Imogene Pass, a 13,510′ extra summit of same around another $\frac{3}{4}$-mile bend southward, and **Trico (Three-county) Peak,** 13,321′, an easy $\frac{1}{2}$ mile NNE up ridge from Black Bear Pass. The Black Bear Mine is not near the pass but farther N in the cirque W of the Telluride Peak summits.

The two 13,477′ summits of **T 10** are $\frac{1}{2}$ mile SW of **Black Bear Pass** and easily reached from it.

Three Needles, 13,481′, receives high SJM praise for its beauty and climbing possibilities. It is $1\frac{1}{2}$ miles SW of **Black Bear Pass,** and separated from **T 10** by a 500′ gap. One can get there from the pass but the summits themselves are another matter.

Blue Lake, 1200′ down the cliffs from Three Needles, is the largest in the Telluride sphere of interest. One can drive a small automobile from Telluride up to the vicinity of the magnificent Bridal Veil Falls on the Black Bear road, and climb by foot (or go much farther by jeep) up the right fork of the road just short of the falls. The first right trail, ½ mile above the road junction, takes you up to Jackass Basin under 13,472′ **La Junta Peak.** The latter can be climbed by a long, steepish NE ridge from near the end of the trail at 11,800′. The jeep trail goes S up Bridal Veil Creek 5 miles to the Lewis Mine at 12,450′, and continues as trail another mile to a 13,058′ pass over the ridge and down to Mineral Creek on 550, about a mile N of the start for **Ophir Pass.**

T 11, 13,510′, is 1¼ miles S and ½ mile W of Three Needles, and can be reached from the Lewis Mine, ½ mile W of it. The N ridge of this one rather than the summit appealed to the SJM visitors, who eye-climbed several pinnacles there.

T 12, 13,614′, is ½ mile N of **Lookout Peak** on a ridge with bumps but no great dip. It is most approachable from about timberline about 1½ miles W of the small-car **Ophir Pass.** Climb up left of the roughest part of the Lookout slope. T 12 is also approachable from Bridal Veil Basin.

Wasatch Mountain, 13,555′, is best reached from Bear Creek, where there is an old road which climbs S 3 miles to 9800′ from 8800′ on the S side of Telluride. Near the end of the road there is a water wash down the left side of the gulch which you ascend several hundred feet to a little below some mine buildings. A trail can be found here which leads right to the "rocky, cliff-guarded entrance to La Junta Basin. Go to head of the basin and climb the north shoulder of the peak and follow on up to the top." The SJM report points out that Little Wasatch, the ridge point a mile NNW of Wasatch, is generally confused with the mountain itself from Telluride. This lower part of the massif has fine north-side cliffs.

Palmyra Peak, 13,319′, is a N ridge end off **Silver Mountain,** likewise decorated with excellent cliffs on the N face. Mine trails way up the W fork of Bear Creek will take one to Lena Basin and out N to the peak's NE ridge for a finish.

San Joaquin Ridge, 13,446′, at its junction with **Silver Mountain,** is an offshoot of Silver on the E side of Lena Basin and can be reached by a steep climb up to and out of the basin's

E fork. The narrow ridge drops off in steep cliffs on both sides and the N end.

The Boomerang Road, which runs S, W and S from 1½ miles W of Telluride, climbs 7 miles through the forests to the ghost town of Alta, 11,000′, and descends to State 145 2 miles NW of Ophir. Alta has some curious buildings and a fine look across at the Wilsons and Lizard Head.

From the descent road and from the approach to Ophir on the highway you look up at the Ophir Needles as they climb toward the sky. There are surely some excellent climbs on these pinnacles, whose outer sides have very long stretches of hard-looking rock.

RICO MOUNTAINS

QUADS: Rico, Hermosa Peak; San Juan N F.

Although Rico itself is a mining town of long standing, the activity has generally been in lower altitudes than the two groups of 12,000′ mountain summits east and west of town. You have some glimpses of the Wilsons from the highway, State 145, but the Rico mountains keep out of sight. Scotch Creek, 2 miles S of town has a jeep road, pretty rough, leading E over the ridge to Hotel Creek and the Hermosa Creek road. For cars there is a road across the same ridge (Hermosa Divide) from State 145 7 miles up the Dolores River from Rico. It is 9 miles to **Bolam Pass,** 11,200′. From mile 1 to mile 6 it is on the flank of a 12,098′ **Flat Top Mountain;** from mile 7 it is only a mile S to 12,579′ **Hermosa Peak,** and at mile 9 you have a good look across NW at Grizzly and associated peaks S of Ophir.

12,681′ **Dolores Mountain** (U.S.G.S. labels it **Blackhawk** and calls the point 12,112′ 1 mile WSW, Dolores) is 2½ miles E of Rico. There is a network of roads up the lower slope to mines at 10,000′, but the better approach is on the road up Silver Creek if it can be driven for the first two miles to 10,200′. Climb or jeep 2 miles E to Section Point, 11,700′, where a 2-mile trail leads SE close under the summit. 12,579′ **Hermosa**

Peak is 3 miles E along a mild up-and-down ridge from Section Point, but it is much closer—almost on—the Bolam Pass road.

For the mountains W of Rico there are two good approaches. You can cross the river and climb the zigzag road to the mine at 10,600′ on Sulphur Creek, and continue W over 12,071′ **Expectation Mountain,** named for the mine, to **Anchor,** 12,327′. By going a mile NW along the ridge you meet with the second route to the topland.

From town you can cross the river and drive 2 miles N to Horse Creek, which has a mile of road to the Puzzle Mine, 9500′, and then continue on a pack trail 3 miles to **Calico Peak,** 12,026′. 12,113′ **Eagle** is a mile W, 12,012′ **Johnny Bull** is a mile N, and from there you can go W along the stock driveway over 12,308′ **Sockrider** to 12,340′ **Elliot.** You can come down-ridge toward Rico from here and work over to the Puzzle mine or lower on the road.

LA PLATA RANGE

QUADS: La Plata, Hesperus, Rampart Hills; San Juan N F.

The ridges of this highly colored 12-13,000′ range lie E and W of the La Plata River. The road up the river starts N from US 160 just W of Hesperus and is good by car for 9½ miles to the Gold King Mill, 9400′. From half a mile farther, a 3½ mile jeep road climbs to the right up Lewis Creek and the hillside to **Eagle Pass,** 11,800′, and goes down to mines on the E side.

Lewis Mountain, 12,720′, is the highest of the group E of the La Plata canyon. It is a climb of 1000′ in less than a mile, going N up the ridge from Eagle Pass.

Pickups can go up the river beyond the Gold King Mill the full 5½ miles to **Kennebec Pass,** 11,850′, where the road connects with various trails from north of Durango on the Animas.

Cumberland Mountain, 12,388′, and **Snowstorm Peak,** 12,511′, are ¼ mile and 1 mile respectively SSW of **Kennebec Pass.** To do both, you go up 500′, down 400′, and up 500′, and

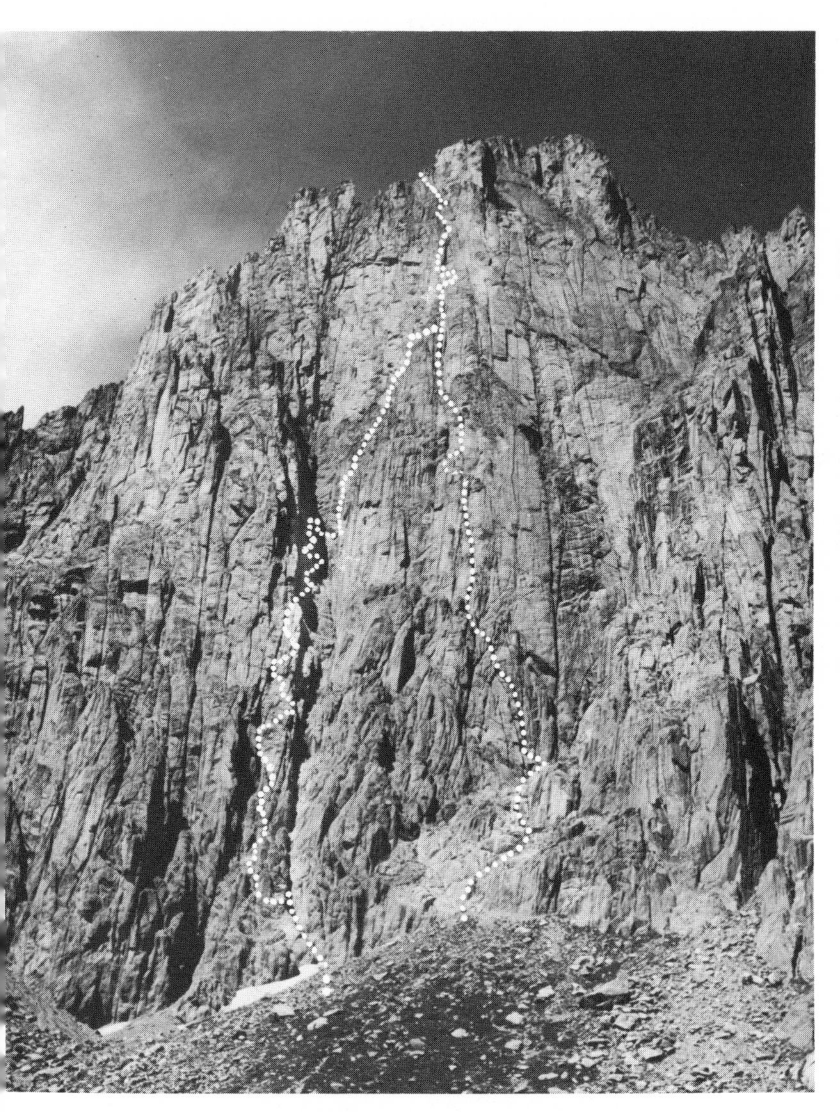

Two routes on the east face of Monitor Peak. *Lumby photo.*

From Courthouse Mountain to Chimney Peak as seen from across the West Cimarron.

return N from the saddle between them on Bessie G Mine road.

If you go up-canyon 3½ miles from the Gold King Mill to Columbus Creek, 10,450′, you can climb, keeping right at mile 1, on a combination of road and trail to the crest at 12,200′. You can go down the other side 400′ to the **Bessie G,** or S to **Lewis Mountain,** or N to **Snowstorm Peak** and down N to the Kennebec Pass road in Cumberland Basin.

Parrott Peak, 11,857′, and **Madden Peak,** 11,972′, are the conspicuous S end points W of the river. The former commemorates Tibercio Parrott, an absentee prospector from California, whose Colorado representative was Captain Moss. (Moss' pyramid is 4 miles W on the same ridge.) The climb starts 6½ miles from US 160, where Root Creek comes into the La Plata at 8900′. Go up to the Comstock Mine by a roadway and then cross the creek to the N side, about ¼ mile from main road. It is about 1¼ miles W up the hillside and back S across the creek to the Lucky Discovery Mine at 10,200′, and a climb of 1600′ W up the steep drainage line to Parrott Peak. You drop 300′ to cross to Madden.

Gibbs Peak, 12,286′, and **Burwell Peak,** 12,664′, are in reach from the 2.7 mile 4-wheel La Plata Ranger Road, which turns off left at Bedrock Creek, mile 8 N of US 160, and climbs to a ridge point at 10,900′. You climb 400′ more on a mine trail and continue W up the short ridge to Gibbs Peak, which is a mile from the jeep road end. Burwell Peak, 2 miles NE of Gibbs, involves a 200′ obstacle hump and a drop to 11,900′ en route.

To reach the thirteeners, for which you had better have a rope along, drive or walk 1½ miles up-river from the Gold King, and then up the jeep road which cuts S and W into Basin Creek and climbs 1½ miles to the Tomahawk Mine, 10,700′. Continue up the valley on a trail until it cuts right at 11,000′. Go on up the basin, 1½ miles in all from the Tomahawk, to 12,200′.

Babcock Peak, 13,149′, is on your left, ½ mile away, and **Spiller Peak,** 13,123′, is ½ mile behind it (W) and out of sight.

To climb them we would recommend climbing SE around the ridge of Babcock to its easier E ridge, and then on a high S side traverse to the gentler Spiller ridge. The SJM Guide describes lively north-side climbs of the four summits of Babcock. The ridge in local parlance is **The Knife.** In traversing it one keeps N of the crest and is careful not to cut his hands on the sharp-edged rectangular blocks and pinnacles with which it abounds. The ridge can be reached from old **La Plata,** ½ mile short of the Gold King Mill. You climb left on an old road and keep left at the junction of Boren Creek with Shaw Creek.

Mount Moss, 13,192′, is on the right side of the Tomahawk Basin at the NW corner. **Banded Mountain,** 13,062′, is a mile N of it, and **Hesperus,** 13,232′, is a mile W. Head up the talus slope for the left side of Mount Moss and an ascent from the S. If you have camped high in the valley, you may have time enough to make all three. The route to Banded Mountain and back is likely to be slow, with either a low off-ridge traverse or a climb along the pinnacled crest. Hesperus, both mountain and town, take the name from Longfellow's poem "The Wreck of the Hesperus." Mount Moss is not named for the soft vegetation on top.

NW of **Mount Moss** ¼ mile is a steep-sided summit of the same altitude, fantastically spired with monzonite pinnacles, particularly as seen from Hesperus Peak. It can be by-passed on the way to **Hesperus** as well as to **Banded Peak.** The SJM called it **Peak L.** There is a movement to name it Lavender Peak for David Lavender, SJM who died young.

The La Platas are sharp and rough, and they look very handsome from the Mesa Verde road and from Transfer Campground, 10 miles NNE of Mancos. As climbs, they are in beautiful country but involve long pulls up the flatrock pieces which cover the slopes.

From 2 miles E of Mancos on 160, a road runs NE 8 miles, where it meets itself coming back from a circle trip of 8½ more miles around Burnt Ridge. Taking the left route around the circle you come to a jeep road after 3½ miles—½ mile after you have turned S—at 10,150′. Keep right on the jeep trail; it will take you 1½ miles to a prospect hole at 11,200′, 2 miles W of **Spiller Peak** and directly under its long W ridge. The ridge loses 200′ but divides the steep climb in half with a long level section.

By leaving the same jeep trail at mile 1.2, .3 mile below the prospect hole, you can cut off left over Jackson Ridge and contour from the far side of it to the West Mancos, about where there is a timber patch at 11,700′. Early the next morning, dash SE up the 2300′ mountainside and ridge to **Spiller Peak.** Go E ½ mile to **Babcock's** W summit, with loss of only 100′ or so, and then head for **Mount Moss** a mile N and 500′ above the saddle. It is another mile NW along the N side of the ridge and a climb of 400′ to **Hesperus Mountain.** Then 2500′ down the slope to camp.

A 10½ mile 4-wheel road climbs to the Doyle Mine, 11,400′, S of the Spiller W ridge. The mine is only a mile WSW from the top of Spiller, but you are out of reach of the other peaks here. The road leaves the Burnt Ridge circle road 1 mile N of 160 and goes off right. You should have the Thompson Park, Rampart Hills and La Plata Quads to keep track of where you are going.

From Transfer Campground, for which you drive from Mancos N 1 mile and keep right to go 9 more miles, a road good for cars for 6½ miles, and jeeps 2½ more, goes E to about 10,500′ on the N fork of the West Mancos River, where you are 2 miles from **Hesperus Mountain,** 2700′ above you to the SE. On the road from the campground you keep right at mile 2½, left at mile 4, and right at mile 6. Hesperus goes well on a direct route from the road end. You can also climb from the road end ½ mile NE in a clearing and go a mile ESE on a hillside trail to the Windy Williams Mine at 11,400′.

Sharkstooth Peak, 12,462′, is a mile ENE up-slope from this mine, and easy to ascend if you don't mind long talus slopes. The summit is climbed on the SW side.

Banded Mountain, 13,062′, is 1½ miles SSE of the mine. Go E to the saddle and S up the ridge.

SAN MIGUEL RANGE

QUADS: Mount Wilson, Dolores Peak, Beaver Park, Lone Cone, Gray Head, Little Cone; Uncompahgre and San Juan N F's.

The range is a westward extension of the San Juan uplift in the latitude of Telluride and Ophir. The group has three rugged steeply sloping 14'ers and two others of the state's most striking peaks. State 145, which crosses from the San Miguel to the Dolores River at **Lizard Head Pass,** is the E boundary and main access route.

Jeepers can make a W country circuit around the Dolores group. They go S up Fall Creek from 3 miles SE of Placerville, go W 6 miles from just short of Woods Lake, and S and E about 12 miles to a car road just E of Dunton. They also get up close to **Sunshine Peak** from both Bilk Creek and Howards Fork drainage, 6 and 7 miles E of Telluride on 145.

Lone Cone, 12,613′, sweeps upward to a sharp summit from the contrasting flatness of mesa country surroundings. It has a reputation for brewing murderous electrical storms. From 1½ miles E of Norwood drive 11 miles S on State 147. Turn E. Follow Beaver Park road signs 5½ miles to ½ mile inside Uncompahgre National Forest Boundary. Take right turns at miles 2.8, 4.5 and 6.1 inside the boundary. Leave your car at the 10,250′ road fork at mile 6.9. Continue W in the left creek fork 1 mile, then right to the NE ridge and up it to timberline. Continue on the loose rock of that ridge to finish on summit slabs or cross the cirque N a little above timberline to an easier NW ridge to finish.

Dolores Peak, 13,261′, and **Dunn Peak,** 13,290′ are on a single massif sometimes called the Dolores Peaks. Take directions as for Lone Cone but continue to follow Beaver Park signs until 100 yards from main Beaver Creek where the road forks. Follow the jeepable forest service trail S up the W side of the

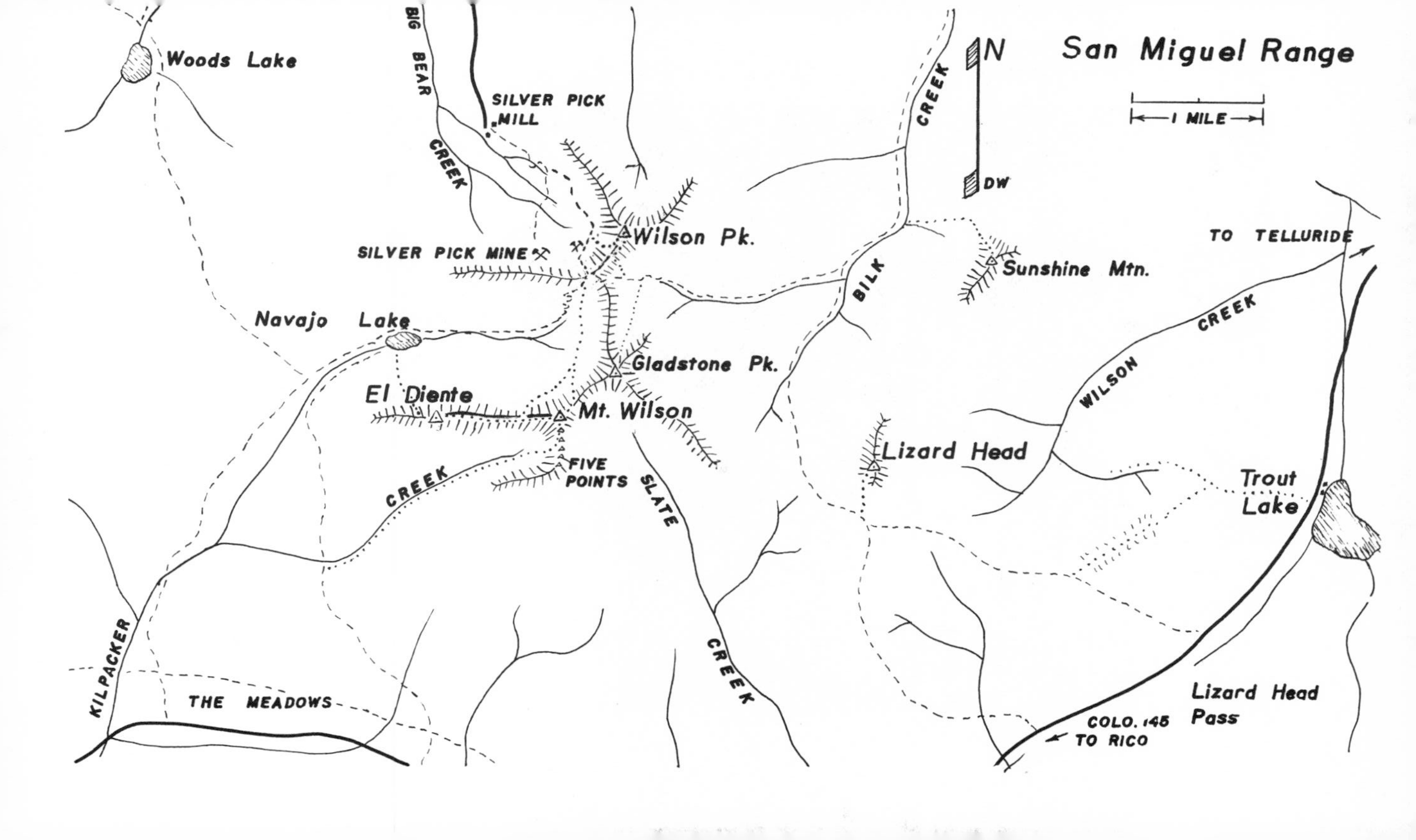
San Miguel Range
N
DW
1 MILE
Woods Lake
BIG BEAR CREEK
SILVER PICK MILL
SILVER PICK MINE
Wilson Pk.
Navajo Lake
El Diente
Gladstone Pk.
Mt. Wilson
FIVE POINTS
SLATE CREEK
CREEK
KILPACKER
THE MEADOWS
BILK CREEK
Sunshine Mtn.
TO TELLURIDE
WILSON CREEK
Lizard Head
Trout Lake
Lizard Head Pass
COLO. 145 TO RICO

El Diente in the center with Mount Wilson immediately to the right and behind.

creek 3 miles from this road junction, marked "Dunton 15 miles." After crossing the creek on the trail, at 9800′, climb W 3 miles up the ridge and W face of peak. Dunn Peak is another 1½ miles SE with a drop to 12,600′.

Wilson Peak, 14,017′, **Mount Wilson,** 14,246′, and **El Diente,** 14,159′, are climbed from both N and S. For the N route drive to Vanadium, 7 miles SE of Placerville on State 145. Turn off right and continue 9 miles S up Big Bear Creek and Wilson Mesa to Silver Pick Mine to camp at 11,000′. At 2½ miles S of Vanadium keep right (W, then S); at 4 miles (firetool box) take the center choice of 3 roads; at 6 miles keep left (S). For the last 5 miles jeeps from Telluride are preferable. For Wilson Peak, climb SE 1½ miles. Where the trail turns S at 12,800′, climb ESE ¼ mile to the summit ridge. This short climb is a conditioner for the much longer trip to Mount Wilson and El Diente from the same camp.

For **Mount Wilson** climb 1½ miles SE as for **Wilson Peak,** and from the 13,000′ saddle head across Navajo Basin toward Mount Wilson, 1½ miles S. It pays to lose 600′ altitude instead of hugging the Gladstone cliffs on your left. **El Diente** is 1 mile W from Mount Wilson along a slow, rough ridge. People complain to me bitterly about this ridge, but I do not consider it my responsibility. There is perhaps only a 300′ loss of altitude, but it takes time. El Diente alone can be climbed more easily by the N face, for which you cross the valley lower down on the way from the 13,000′ pass; the N face also provides a descent route, but steep enough to call for ice axes if it is snowed under. The Wilsons were named for A. D. Wilson who climbed there in the 70's with the Hayden Survey party. The rock is intrusive, probably late Miocene.

To climb by the southern route, which is easier than the N for Mount Wilson and El Diente, drive 7 miles N from Rico or 6 SW from **Lizard Head Pass,** and on the Dunton road 5½ miles NW to where it starts to lose altitude at 10,100′. The trail contours W 1 mile and N 1½ miles to Kilpacker Creek, which you follow 5 miles ENE to the **Mount Wilson** summit. One moves over a great deal of talus. For a camp in Dunton Meadows take water to avoid the taste of wool, etc., in the local supply.

For the ascent of all three peaks from the S it is best to camp at Navajo Lake. Use the same trail to Kilpacker Creek but cross and continue N and W 3½ miles to the lake, at 11,154′. **El Diente** has a fair W ridge and an easier N face than the S. The trail continues up the valley to the vicinity of the two Wilsons (it crosses the 13,000′ pass W of **Wilson Peak** at mile 3 from the lake). It has usually been possible to obtain the services of a packer from Dunton.

The approach to the Wilsons from the east leaves State 145 10 miles up-river from Placerville or 2½ miles W of the Telluride exit. At mile 5 on this road (mile 4 from the other end at Ophir) a road zigzags W up the ridge 1½ miles to a forking at 9000′. If you are fortunate you can jeep 4 more miles on the left fork—up-ridge toward Sunshine and around NW of it to Bilk Creek, where you meet the **Bilk Creek Trail** at 10,100′. The right fork meets Bilk Creek 2½ miles farther N (lower) and goes back down the E edge of Wilson Mesa to meet 145. If you learn that it is better to come up to Bilk Creek this way, leave 145 at the same place as for the road system above but turn W (sharp right) after .1 mile. After you cross Bilk Creek take the right hand branch up the hillside to Wilson Mesa rather than the one which stays with the creek. There is camping at whichever level of Bilk Creek you come into.

Sunshine Mountain, 12,930′, has superb views into the Wilsons and across at the crusty ridge back of **Ophir.** It is best climbed with a start from .1 mile N of the 10,100′ road end in upper Bilk Creek. You climb along the N side of the side creek 600′ to the falls, and then angle left to the ridge N of you, which you use for a 2000′ rise to the top. The total is about 2 miles.

From the road end the **Bilk Creek Trail** climbs 2 miles S to timberline and divides. The left fork becomes the **Lizard Head Trail;** the right, which gets rather sketchy, climbs 2½ miles over the S saddle of **Wilson Peak,** 13,300′, and drops W along to the 13,000′ W saddle. The route to Wilson Peak departs from this trail a little short of the high pass and angles right to the S ridge.

Gladstone Peak, 13,913′, makes a steep snow climb from the N, and is reached from high up on the trail to the Wilson Peak ridge. It is very slow to go off Gladstone and work your way W and S to **Mount Wilson** from the saddle between the two. Mount Wilson is more easily reached from the low point of the **Wilson Peak** to Gladstone saddle, where you drop 300′ or so on the chiprock on the W side and go W far enough to get a good purchase.

The **Lizard Head Trail** properly starts from 145 at Trout Lake, but the shorter and higher entry point is 2½ miles WSW of **Lizard Head Pass,** 4 NE of the Dunton road exit, at 10,000′. This way it is 4 miles to the 11,979′ pass into Bilk Creek.

The **Lizard Head,** 13,113′, on Mount Wilson Quad, is a volcanic neck. It is the most difficult of Colorado's summits to reach. In fact the rottenness of its 400′ rock tower makes safety too much a matter of luck for comfort. Where the trail comes to the S ridge of Lizard Head at mile 3, head N to the base of the peak. The only route to date has been that pioneered by Albert R. Ellingwood and J. Barton Hoag in 1920 when they left their rope on the peak in order to get down. P. D. West and H. G. Wilm recovered the rope 10 years later, and in the years before 1940 several other ascents have been made. Returning visitors have formed the opinion that the peak has become noticeably rottener and more dangerous. The climb route starts on the W side just N of the SW corner. The first 150′ is in a near vertical chute whose crumbling walls will not give sure lodgement to a piton. Good rock with an overhanging chimney make the upper half better going.

There is a route on the S that will go. It is quite nasty at the start—up an unstable flake—but it gets to the reliable rock above sooner than does the ordinary route.

UNCOMPAHGRE PLATEAU

QUADS: Sams (S end), Norwood, Windy Point, Pine Mountain (for SW edge), Battleship Rock, Colorado National Monument (N end); Uncompahgre N F.

The plateau is a 90-mile ridge running NW from Dallas Divide to W of Grand Junction. The southern portion has some ranches and farms and is mainly in the national forest; the lower north end is rather dry and largely within the Bureau of Land Management sphere of control. The smooth highlands run up to 10,000′, often in fine pine and aspen forest.

The Colorado National Monument Road, signed, can be found by taking US 50 S across the river from Grand Junction. It connects at the other end with a short road S across the river from the middle of Fruita, off I-70 W of Grand Junction.

SOUTHWEST CORNER

Mesa country, particularly the Mesa Verde of cliffdweller fame, takes up much of the land S of the main cross highway in southwestern Colorado—US 160. There are a few summits near the Four Corners which rise respectable distances from their surroundings: **Ute Peak,** 9977′, on Moqui SE Quad and **Hermano Peak,** 8959′, on Sentinel Peak NE Quad. Inquire in Cortez as to whether permission should be obtained from tribal headquarters for the Ute Indian Reservation.

THE BEND

QUADS: Lake San Cristobal, Finger Mesa, Pole Creek Mountain, Howardsville, Storm King Peak, Rio Grande Pyramid and Weminche Pass; San Cristobal 30′ and the 15′ Needle Mountains and Silverton cover the same ground; Gunnison, Rio Grande and San Juan N F's.

Mountains along the Bend of the Divide lie in a 50-mile horseshoe curve between **Spring Creek Pass** at the NE end and **Weminuche Pass,** S of the Rio Grande Reservoir at the SE end.

Bent and **Carson Peaks** have been mentioned with those associated with Lake City. There are some more in the same class that have no names, yet are high and rough—some summits S of Cottonwood Creek, the tributary of the Lake Fork which comes in at Sherman, mile 16 from Lake City. (Sherman is where the road to **Cinnamon Pass** climbs N on a sidehill.)

The jeep road W from Sherman can be followed for 4½ miles up Cottonwood Creek to the mouth of Cuba Gulch, 10,800′. As trail it continues 5 miles SW to the crest trail on the Divide at 12,900′.

At mile 1 W of Sherman, the **Cataract Gulch Trail** runs steeply up S to 11,600′ in 3 miles and gentles along northward 2 more miles on flatter ground to Cataract Lake, 12,802′. On the way it gives access to some fine 13,000′ summits 2 miles to the W. Notable among these is a 13,841′ one we could call **Three-corner Table,** on Pole Creek Mountain Quad 2 miles NW of Cataract Lake. At the Divide, a little beyond the lake the trail comes into the **La Garita Stock Driveway.** From the driveway to the E there are trail connections down both East and West Lost Trail Creeks to Lost Trail Campground. From the driveway to the S and W there are trails up the W and N forks of Pole Creek to Divide passes. These go down Minnie and Maggie Gulches to the Animas Forks road out of Silverton.

Some of the Bend summits are best reached from these Silverton approaches, and some more from the **Vallecito Trail** to the S.

The main E route to the Bend leaves State 149 20 miles W of Creede and runs west 10 miles to the Rio Grande Reservoir site. From Thirty Mile Campground at the E end of the reservoir it is 7 more miles W and NW to Lost Trail Campground and Ranch, at 9800′.

From this campground the road continues as jeep W 15 miles up Rio Grande to 12,588′ **Stony Pass** and 4 more down to car road in Cunningham Gulch en route to Silverton. Keep right at mile 8½ from Lost Trail Campground, where trail for Beartown exits left.

The Beartown jeep road branches S from the Stony Pass road, and goes W and SW 12 miles to Beartown at 11,200′. The **Hunchback Trail** can be reached (a) by continuing on the jeep road to Kite Lake, 2 miles W, where it leads off S on a cairn route, or (b) by climbing a steep slope to the S of the highest part of Beartown and intercepting the constructed trail there. The jeep road is next to impossible in wet weather.

Beartown and Kite Lake are connected by trail with a trail from the Animas River up Elk Creek. The latter comes up past Eldorado Lake, 12,500′, which is a mile down the W side, using 26 switchbacks.

White Dome, 13,627′, at the E end of the Grenadiers, is 1 mile S of Eldorado Lake, and can be climbed on a clockwise route, or more directly and steeply.

Peak One of the Needles is a 2½ mile climb. The route goes E ¼ mile from the lake and then S to the saddle and SW past the ridge point to the summit.

Ute Ridge is a curious eastward off shoot from the Divide. Its 6½ miles have a profile of ten summits, the first five above 13,000′ and the second five above 12,000′. Just E of the decaying buildings at Beartown there is a good trail which leads SE 2 miles to the first saddle—12,702′ **Ute Pass.**

Rio Grande Pyramid, 13,821, has its shortest approach from Thirty Mile Camp Ground, 9300′. From State 149 about 20 miles W of Creede, you drive W 10 miles to the campground, and take the trail W 1½ miles along the S side of the reservoir site and SW up Weminuche Creek 4 miles to **Weminuche Pass,** 10,550′. Go W (right) along the ridge 5 miles to the summit, passing **Fools Pyramid** and the **Spanish Window** on the left at about the altitude of the saddle W of the first knoll, mile 3. See Rio Grande and Weminuche Pass Quads.

SILVERTON EAST GROUP

QUADS: Silverton, Howardsville, Handies Peak, Ironton; San Juan N F.

All the Silverton East group and the range crest above Ice Lakes Basin as well are taken together as Silverton volcanic group from the geological point of view. This grouping takes the mountains off the Continental Divide Bend from Animas Forks and the Red Mountain ridge S to the Needles and E of Mineral Creek. The mountains are steep but seldom rugged. Old roads and trails lead up the gulches and attract more jeep explorers than mountain climbers. The maps show an infinity of mines and names on all the summits; Houghton, Tuttle, California, Hurricane, Treasure, Eureka, Hanson, Bonita, Emery, Storm, Macomber, Dome, Tower. All can be climbed in different ways, but for a sampling we would recommend driving out 4 miles E on 110 from Silverton to ½ mile short of Howardsville. A trail of many steps takes you from 9,600′ to Hematite Lake, 11,850′. **Tower Mountain,** highest of the whole ridge at 13,552′, is a mile further in the same direction.

Another large collection of 13,000′ peaks clusters about Silver Lake, 4 miles ESE of Silverton. The W half is called **Kendall Mountain.** A road leading to active mining is visible across the Animas from Silverton. Jeeps have a route almost to the summit. Silver Lake, is reached by driving on 110 2¼ miles W to the Mayflower Mill, where you turn SSE and perhaps try for the mine, 3 miles of not-too-steep road up the gulch. It is at 11,200′, and another 1½ miles takes you to the lake. 1,000′ higher.

A few of the Bend peaks are best reached from the Animas Forks road, where short steep gulches climb to the Gunnison-Animas Divide south of **Cinnamon Pass.** Grouse Gulch, 11 miles up the river from Silverton, has a trail on its N side climbing 2½ miles SE from 10,800′ to 13,000′, and dropping to the Lake Fork west of **Handies Peak.** From just south of Grouse Gulch a road sidlehills SSE 2 miles into and up Burns Creek. There is a mine at 11,900′, under **Niagara Peak's** rough N face, at which you can turn to the right or left. For a tour, we suggest going right and keeping right of Niagara to go S a mile to **Crown Mountain,** 13,569′, then N a mile to 13,807′

Niagara, and on up the ridge another mile to 13,860′ **Jones Mountain.** Then come down or go on N to the Grouse Gulch road. Maximum route, 12 miles, 4000′.

A spur ridge S from the **Red Mountains** divides Mineral Creek from Cement Creek drainage and provides for some 12,000′ of jeeping from Gladstone to the ridge and down its gentler W side slope past **McMillan Peak** toward **Ohio Peak.**

The jeepers have routes to the ridge from the N up Poughkeepsie Gulch, from Animas Forks W and back past **Hanson Peak** to the mouth of Picayune Gulch, and up Eureka Creek and past **Bonita Peak** to **Gladstone,** on Cement Creek, with branches over the uplands. On the other (E) side of the upper Animas River road they climb up into Minnie Gulch and Animas Gulch and climb clear over **Stony Pass** to the upper Rio Grande.

About 50 years ago a friend and I started confidently up **Stony Pass** in a model T. It was on the map. A few rods above the Animas it began to be rough, and we found a man to talk to. "Well," he said, "the first car into Silverton came over this road. But it was in some wagons."

Canby Mountain, 13,478′, is a steep mile NNE from the 12,588′ pass crest. From **Stony Pass** to **Hunchback Pass** there is a 10-mile trail on and close to the Divide, not all of it under maintenance. The Divide trail links with a trail W down Elk Creek to the Animas, with the Beartown jeep road to the E, and with the **Hunchback Pass Trail** down to the Vallecito.

SILVERTON WEST GROUP

QUADS: Silverton, Ophir, Engineer Mountain, Snowdon Mountain; San Juan N F.

This grouping centers about the S and middle forks of Mineral Creek and extends S to the **Engineer Mountain** W of US 550. Except for some obviously smooth climbs, these peaks call for ropes. **Ophir Pass,** normally one of the easiest of the jeep roads to drive, starts 5½ miles NW of Silverton on US 550

A William H. Jackson photo of Ice Lake Basin in the 1870's. *Denver Public Library Western Collection.*

A glissade for easy descent.

and climbs Middle Mineral Creek 5 miles W to 11,789′, then descends 6 miles to Ophir on State 145.

Lookout Peak, 13,661′, a mile N of **Ophir Pass,** is the rough, brightly tinted profile you see from a little below the top on the W side. From .2 mile E of the pass climb N and a little W up a wide trough to S ridge. You may have to look around or by-pass the summit on the left to get to it, but as it is only a mile and under 1000′ it should not take long.

South Lookout Peak, 13,357′, is 1½ miles SSW along the ridge. Leave car 1.5 miles E of pass top near sharp bend and contour S across N fork to S fork of drainage; climb to Paradise Basin and look for a way to get S to the E ridge of the peak for final climb. It is a 2-mile climb of 1200′. The Lookout Peaks are well-named: you see high mountains in all directions and at various distances. Rotten rock is the price.

South Mineral Creek Campground is 5 miles W of US 550 on a good road starting 2 miles WNW of Silverton. A whole circle of sharp interesting peaks are available from this 9800′ start. For **South Lookout,** you start W on the **Ice Lake Basin Trail** and then walk the jeep road or scramble up Clear Creek and pick your route NW from the lake—total 2½ miles or so. Ice Lake Basin, center for several more summits, provides a higher and more isolated camping area. The lower basin, about timberline (11,500′) is reached by a 2-mile trail W from road's end. The peaks you climb are some of those which look so handsome from down toward Ophir and at Trout Lake: 13,767′ **U.S. Grant,** well-named 13,738′ **Pilot Knob,** 13,760′ **Golden Horn,** 13,894′ **Vermillion,** and 13,761′ **Fuller.**

Among the reports of a 1932 outing, we find **Pilot Knob** was climbed by going up the talus at the N end, around the high corner to the W and up a chimney there. Later an easier route was found up the E face to the middle summit, and N along the ridge. The climb to **US Grant** was on a long steep trail and talus slopes to the SW ridge. The way to the summit went up a difficult little cliff and along a ledge to the S face, where the last part became an easy matter.

Besides their route to Clear Lake the jeepers go a long way up the S fork of Mineral Creek on to the range crest at the saddle a mile N of Rolling Mountain. The road is a left hand continuation of the car road into South Mineral Campground. From a little beyond the Bandora Mine, 2½ miles from the campground, you can climb a mile to the steep-sided saddle separating **Fuller Peak** from 13,342′ **Beattie.** Both can be ascended in short order.

Rolling Mountain, 13,693′, is a larger and more separate massif than the others, and has a good deal of cliff scenery here and there. The easiest route is to keep left at Bandora Mine and follow the **Rico-Silverton Trail** 2 miles S to a stream which flows E off the back or S side of the mountain. The watercourse takes you to a south ridge which in turn lets you get on the W ridge for the final pitch. A climb on the other side of the canyon leads to **Twin Sisters.**

The long ridge known as **Yellow Mountain** has doubtless been explored, but we have no material on climbs from that side. The steep N face of **Sheep Mountain,** W extremity of **San Miguel Peak** 2 miles S of Trout Lake, is an ice axe climb. If you go there bring a friend and expect steep ice.

For the rest of this group you drive S from Silverton on US 550. **Sultan Mountain,** another multi-summited massif like Kendall across the Animas, lies 3 miles SW of Silverton. It was climbed by a group which started on a dirt road ½ mile N of **Molas Pass** and led to Little Molas Lake, 10,900′, a mile W, where they camped. The route goes N 3 miles, up through 2 saddles and along or over the summits labeled **Grand Turk.** This is gentle terrain.

12,968′ **Engineer Mountain** is attractive for the odd reason it is the only summit that stands alone in the whole area. We never go by without thinking we would like to climb it and look around. Straight W 2 miles from 10,660′ **Coal Bank Pass** is probably the shortest way, but San Juan Mountaineers thought better of the footing on their route from Cascade Creek.

SOUTHEAST SAN JUAN

The long SE arm of the San Juan Mountains runs 50 miles SE from **Weminuche Pass** to **Ellwood Pass** and S through the New Mexico line, which is 30 miles beyond. It is on Rio Grande and San Juan Forests except for the land grant at the S end, which has **Chama Peak** and **Banded Peak** on its E boundary.

PIEDRA MOUNTAINS

QUADS: Granite Peak, Bear Mountain, Oakbrush Ridge, Chris Mountain, Pagosa Peak, Pagosa Springs; 15′ Creede, Spar City and Wolf Creek Pass; 30′ Pagosa Springs and San Cristobal; San Juan and Rio Grande N F's.

The group consists of the peaks on and near the Divide between the Rio Grande on the N and the Pinos, Piedra and San Juan on the S. Most of the routes touched on are reached from US 160 to the S.

The Piedra road turns off US 160 3 miles W of Pagosa Springs, and runs NNW 18 miles to a junction for the Middle Fork (Piedra (right) and Williams and Weminuche Creeks (left). The right hand fork goes NNE 4 miles for cars, and to another junction. The right hand jeep trail, good for 2 miles from the junction to the Wilderness boundary, stays on the Piedra.

Piedra Peak, 12,300′, has an 8-mile trail route to the summit from the end of this jeep road at 8400′. The first part is a steep climb-out from the canyon; the rest winds ENE on the hilly SW ridge of the peak.

The left fork from the junction above goes N also by jeep 2 miles to a short trail that heads for Palisade Lake, 9300′, where you are under some of the sharp ridge ends that you have seen jutting out from down the Piedra road. A trail continues W across a saddle, 9300′, and descends to the **Williams Creek Trail.**

The Williams Creek road, left road fork at mile 18 from 160 goes N 5 miles to another fork, mile 23 from 160. The right one continues N past Williams Creek Reservoir 2 miles to a campground on the Wilderness boundary. Long trails take you up Williams Creek, up its tributary Indian Creek, and up Cimarrona Creek, to the Divide. There they meet the **Little Squaw Creek** and **West Trout Creek Trails** from the Rio Grande on the N side. The most interesting of these is the westmost one, up Cimarrona Creek. It climbs quickly from the 8400′ campground to the 12,400′ N ridge of Cimarrona.

Cimarrona Peak, 12,600′, a handsomely jutting point 1 mile S of the Divide, is approachable from this trail by a short climb upridge from the NNE. A trail of the same length and climb leads to the peak from the end of the ranch road up Weminuche Creek, 5 miles SW. The **Divide Trail** and the **Squaw Creek-Squaw Lake Trail** lie just to the N.

Graham Peak, 12,531′, on Granite Peak and Bear Mountain Quads, is conspicuous for its notch and for its isolation as you drive up the Piedra Road. If you keep left (W) into Weminuche Creek where the Piedra road to Williams Creek forks at mile 23, a drivable branch road off to the left crosses the creek and the high timbered country W of it for 7 miles, until it intersects the Stock Driveway about 10,100′. The **Driveway Trail** leads 2 miles NW and N to the top of the mountain. **Granite Peak,** 12,147′, is 2 miles SW along the easy ridge from Graham.

Pagosa Peak, 12,640′, is high point between the Piedra and the Wolf Creek Pass roads. To reach it get a jeep and drive north from Pagosa Springs (W part of town) 12 miles, or 1 mile N of the Cade Ranch, where there is a spring and camping place at 9600′. A trail runs NNE 4½ miles to the falls on Fourmile Creek, and 4 more miles to Fourmile Lake at 11,200′. From a mile N of the falls, ½ mile beyond the steel bridge, you turn W and climb and contour 2 miles into the bowl, 11,100′, immediately NE of the peak. Climb out SW, NW and S another mile to the summit.

Eagle Mountain, 12,007′, is a rougher proposition. Try this on it: from ½ mile short of the falls on Fourmile cross the creek and head straight E up a shallow drainage depression and after a mile turn S with its right fork. Work your way out of it on the left side near the end and head S until you get on the SSW ridge of the mountain not far from the top. Go counterclockwise around the tower and look for a route up the steep E face.

South River Peak, 13,145′, is a mate to **Piedra Peak,** which is about 2½ miles W of it. You get a little start toward it from the campground at the foot of **Wolf Creek Pass** on 160. You can drive W and N 2½ miles or so to near Borns Lake, 8400′, where a 10-mile trail will take you up the West Fork of the San Juan to a meeting point on the Divide with both a range crest trail from the E and another trail which, with jeep, provides a closer way in from Spar City to the N. From 7 miles SW of Creede on 149 take the Spar City road. Instead of going to Spar City keep right at mile 5 and left at mile 7½ to follow the old road up Red Mountain Creek or South River. You can drive to the campground at mile 10, and you can jeep to the Weminuche Wilderness boundary at Red Mountain Falls, 2 or 3 miles north of the Divide. Piedra Peak is directly S. It is climbable by the ridge between the forks, followed by a clockwise spiral for the top part. It is easier however to keep on the left fork road to the pass top, 11,500′, where you can climb W 1½ miles to Piedra Peak or E 1½ miles to Piedra Peak, or both.

SUMMITVILLE GROUP

QUADS: Elwood Pass, Summit Peak, Summitville, Platoro, Jasper, Greenie Mountain; Rio Grande N F.

Between the Conejos River and the Rio Grande, and bordering the San Luis Valley on the W, is a delightful plateau of grassland, timber and moderate but varied and well-separated summits. Main roads in are (1) SW from the W end of Del Norte to Summitville, 25 miles (this has a bad stretch beyond Summitville); (2) W up the Alamosa River from 12 miles S of Monte Vista on State 15; (3) W to N up the Conejos River from Antonito, leaving the La Manga-Cumbres Pass road about mile 24 and continuing 25 miles to Platoro; (4) a road 14 miles long climbing SSE from Park Creek, SW of South Fork on US 160, to the W of Summitville. This road and the one up Alamosa River connect with a road joining Summitville and Platoro.

Summit Peak, 13,300′, and **Montezuma Peak,** 13,150′, at the W edge of the plateau, are off the road between Summitville and Platoro. To get to them drive W and S from Summitville or NW and W from Platoro to Lake Denalda (De Nolda?) Drive W 2 miles (Horseshoe Park is 1 mile) to 10,800′, and climb in the same valley 1 more mile to Treasure Creek. Work off to the right. Keep W up the left side of Treasure Creek for about 2 miles; then cut S a mile to get past the E ridge of Summit Peak and come to the summit, another mile, on the SE face. For Montezuma, which is 2 miles N of Summit Peak drop N on steep ridge or E to **Continental Divide Trail** and pick a route for the final 500′ climb. Return E and S to Treasure Creek.

Conejos Peak, 13,172′, is on Platoro Quad. Drive W up the Saddle Creek road from 7 miles SE of Platoro or ½ mile S of Lake Fork Campground on Conejos River Road. About mile 6, 4th right-turn hairpin, at 11,300′, take the trail 3 miles W and S past Tobacco Lake to summit.

Lookout Mountain, 12,488′, is tempting for the flat rhombus which is its summit, and for its high coloring. From 1 mile E of Lake Denalda, where the road from Platoro crosses Iron Creek at 10,500′, follow a jeep trail about ¾ mile and climb to the right 1 mile to the summit on one of the ridges. 12,578′ **Cropsy Mountain** is 1½ miles N over a ridge that drops off sharply at both ends to a low point of 11,800′. See Platoro and Summitville Quads.

Bennett Peak, 13,203′, on Jasper Quad (see also Greenie Mountain Quad) is the easternmost high point of the region. From Monte Vista drive on State 15 2 miles S, then 3 W, 1 S, 1 W, 1 SW, ¼ S and follow the main road to Rock Creek Campground, 10 more miles, and up-creek 3 miles to Comstock

Campground, 9700′. Take the trail W 1 mile and NW 4 miles up to the head of S Fork Rock Creek and the saddle S of the peak, whence a 1½-mile trail leads N over the summit. Bennett can also be climbed from Jasper, 9114′, for which you drive S from Monte Vista 15 miles on State 15 and 21 miles W and find a trail just W of the settlement. Drive .6 miles N on the stage road. Climb N 3½ miles to a divide; follow **Dry Creek Sheep Drive** 1 mile E and go N 1½ miles to summit.

NAVAJO-CHAMA GROUP

QUADS: Chama Peak, Chromo and Chama, all 15′; San Juan and Rio Grande N F's.

This group consists of some striking 12,000′ summits E and W of the Navajo River and close to the New Mexico line.

US 84 crosses the Navajo River between Chama, New Mexico, and Pagosa Springs, at Chromo. The Navajo River road runs E from Chromo and turns N to the Hughes Ranch and the Tierra Amarilla Land Grant it is on. About mile 7 there is a 14-mile shortcut road SE over an 8500′ pass to the N side of Chama. From near the junction of the Navajo River road and the shortcut, a lumber road runs N 5 miles to Price Lakes, at 8800′. A trail from the lakes takes you NW 4 miles to the Little Navajo River and 6 more miles across NW to Buckles Lake, under the W side of **V Mountain.**

Navajo Peak, 11,323′, dominates this part of the valley with its belligerent rock face. To climb from the lakes under it, continue NNW 2½ miles on trail toward Little Navajo River to where you are 1 mile WNW of peak. Cut E ½ mile to where the likeliest ridge for the climb starts. The ridge runs ESE, rising 1200′ to a saddle a short way N of the peak. Let us know what happened.

At mile 6 NNE from Chama on the Cumbres Pass road, the 6½-mile Chama River road runs N into the Rio Grande Forest.

Chama Peak, 12,019′, is 4 miles WNW from the road end on Chama River at 8800′. To climb it cross the river and from a little S of the road go NW 2½ miles on a trail up Archuleta

Creek. When the trail turns N up a side creek, leave it and take the stream fork which goes WSW. After about 2 miles of climbing work off to the right of the peak to finish on the NE ridge.

Banded Peak, 12,778′, is very handsome from the W side, which you see from the shortcut road and along the Navajo River. A trail runs 2½ miles up the W side of the Chama River from the road end, and taking the left of two forks there continues N, W and N 10 miles more to Chama Lake, at timberline (11,530′). From the lake it is a 3-mile walk SW to the peak, easily climbed on this side. If you don't care about the lake you can shortcut up a steep creek 1½ miles S of the lake and camp where it levels off. Distance to peak 2 miles. Banded Peak and a lot of the top country NE of it belong to the Potosi volcanic series, which have layering and a tendency to flat-topping.

ROCK CLIMBING

Presence of a rope is the main dividing line between rock scrambling and rock climbing. Most people who climb long with the CMC learn some simple belaying techniques, how to rappel over a short cliff face, and how to tie into a two- or three-man rope for the mutual belaying system that is used. A fair number make some simple climbs with hardware and work up a taste for descents by rappel. Climbing is graduated from there on up to the Yosemite School type of climbing which stops at nothing. The ascents of the Diamond on **Longs Peak's** E face are examples. Strong parties make ascents in winter which were considered impossible two or three decades ago. Specialized rock climbing must be learned from those who know, and there is no better way than to enroll in a school such as the CMC conducts every year for the various levels. Most of the climbs of any difficulty are given classifications according to a system used throughout the world.

A few general precautions are in order.

People, especially children, can often climb up a steep slab surface and then find they can't come down again.

Loose rock is often more of a hazard than mere height.

Darkness or bad weather can change an easy climb to a dangerous one in short order.

Half-understood techniques are more dangerous than none at all.

Many of the favorite areas for rock climbing are relatively obscure canyon walls, where the rock is reasonably dependable but the routes lead to nothing in particular. Most rock climbers are mountaineers as well and like their climbing best when it is in the country of cold streams, high camps and the flowered meadows of timberline country.

With cliffs as with caves, the only way to know exactly what has been done and what the newest areas of challenge are is to join the young active group who are too busy to write up what they are doing and who carry on most of their intelligence work colloquially and who can give helpful information on the classifications as to difficulty. Your initial query can go to the Colorado Mountain Club Secretary.

We have given in the main text a number of the peaks whose routes have short to middling inclusions of technical climbing. A brief recapitulation may be useful here.

Rocky Mountain National Park sees much climbing: **Longs Peak** has everything from the easiest digressions from the trail routes to the boiler-plate Diamond topping the E face. Nesbit's book keeps track of the variations with periodical revisions. **Spearhead, Notchtop,** the E face of **McHenrys, Arrowhead,** the Sky Pond face of **Taylor,** the **Little Matterhorn,** the **Cathedral Spires,** notable **Sharkstooth,** and the cliffs of **Hallett,** and lower granites such as the **Needle** and **Thumb** and **Teddys Teeth,** all offer good climbing.

Lone Eagle has seen some good climbs besides the ordinary, and there are less-visited peaks of the Indian section of the Front Range with horrendous walls. **Blanca's** N face has seen some climbing, the **Crestones** more, and the Sangre de Cristo Range has some other cliffs that will be heard from—between **Milwaukee** and **Cleveland,** and here and there N of the Crestones.

The best rock in the Elk Range is that of **Capitol Peak,** but the stratified **North Maroon** has seen more technical climbs.

Many places in the San Juan area have fine climbs, some of the best and longest in the Grenadier Range and other Needle Mountains. Blaine Basin, N of **Mount Sneffels,** was a favorite hangout of the San Juan Mountaineers. The **Lizard Head,** in the San Miguel Range, has been climbed a fair number of times because it is the only pinnacle high enough and separate enough to be considered a peak. The first 180′ of the 375′ total is made just inside the S edge of the W face, starting in a steep shallow trough too rotten to take pitons. Above the trough the rock becomes more reliable, with a final difficulty in the form of a climb-out from a little overhang or cave. The summit holds one climber.

Several San Juan climbs made in the years 1965–69 were reported in brief form in the October 1969 *T & T* by Martin Etter. These include a **Coxcomb** N face, the NE cliff face of **Wildhorse,** the NW face of **Arrow** via the **Arrowhead** pinnacle on the W shoulder, and the E face of **Vestal.** Etter winds up his report with a query about a dozen other climbs in the **Needle Mountains,** indictating one might still find some very hilly country there.

SKI TOURING

The Colorado Mountain Club schedules ski tours which are well-led and graded for different levels of endurance and difficulty, and conducts training sessions to acquaint beginners with techniques and safety requirements. Anyone starting this activity should take advantage of these or other qualified groups to learn the ropes. The equipment differs from that for ski area skiing mainly in that touring requires skins for the climbing and bindings which permit the heel to lift well off the ski without swivelling loose. The best bindings for the purpose keep the toe and foot rigidly in line with the ski and yet permit the arrangement to come open with strain.

Touring takes you away from the crowds, but also from the patrol and the warm hut. Instead of packed slopes and tailored trails you run the gamut of snow conditions from flour-soft powder to rock-hard wind crust to slush. It is important that you ski more conservatively and be ready for dangerous surprises. Parties of four or five people are safer than couples, given some evenness of abilities. Leaders must know avalanche possibilities. Good touring places are innumerable; CMC schedules give an indication of some that are convenient to reach and usually have reliable snow conditions. From I-70 Dry Gulch and Herman Gulch are easily reached. They are E of Loveland Basin. From the bottom hairpin on the S side of **Berthoud Pass,** on US 40, trips go up the **Jones Pass** road. The region S of **Vail Pass** and W over **Shrine Pass** has snow of moderate gradient. The **Trail Ridge** above Hidden Valley Ski Area usually has good snow.

A frequent pattern is to put on skins, climb at a steady, leisurely pace to some high lunch spot on a sunny rock outcrop, and then glide off again. Many of the high bowls and peaks have been climbed this way. Summits and summit ridges are usually blown too clear for skiing and skis are left somewhere under the top. **Mount Elbert** has been ski climbed many times—**Mount Sherman, Quandary Peak, Mount Audubon, Castle Peak** and others, too.

CAVES AND SPELUNKING

by John A. Streich

Caves have long been the subject of wild tales and superstitions. These stories are based on a fear of the unknown and yet it is this same fear which entices and challenges the adventurous to exploration. While there are few places above ground which have not been trod by foot of man, many such places exist below ground only waiting for someone to discover them. The relatively new science of speleology and the sport of spelunking have provided the explorer with a last frontier.

Organized speleology started in this country in 1939 with the incorporation of the National Speleological Society in Washington, D.C., and spread to this area with the formation in Denver in 1951 of a Colorado Grotto which has served as collecting point for cave information about the Rocky Mountain states in general. In 1968 a Colorado School of Mines Grotto was organized and in 1969 a grotto was formed at Colorado State University. Many of the more frequented Colorado caves have been mapped and the search for new caves is ever continuing. Any information concerning caves not herein mentioned would be deeply appreciated.

The same rules of caution apply as for climbers: cavers should check in and check out with someone who knows their plan. Parties of three are safest, and soloing in caves is even more dangerous than climbing alone, because of the difficulty of attracting attention in case of trouble.

Most Colorado caves can be negotiated without ropes. Rope techniques when used are like those of the rock climber except that the spelunker's first interest is exploring the cave, and he makes extensive use of cable ladders and ascenders. He is always belayed while on a ladder. Where there is rope he must be particularly careful of the open flame of a carbide lamp.

In spelunking, lights are obviously of primary importance. So important, in fact, that the well-equipped spelunker carries three light sources, a lamp or lantern, a flashlight, and candles. The primary light is usually a headlamp, either carbide or electric. These headlamps give a large amount of sidelight, enabling one to walk without turning the lamp toward his feet; indeed they are so effective that one loses all sense of being in the dark because wherever he looks is light.

Carbide lamps have many advantages. They are economical, using only calcium carbide and water. The fuel supply for many hours of light may be carried in a pocket. Although malfunctions are not uncommon, the lamps are simple enough that repairs can almost always be made on the spot.

Flashlights are very useful as a second light but should not be used as the primary one. Besides their lack of sidelight they are uneconomical in their use of batteries. A set of batteries seldom lasts over three hours in continual use. They also require the use of a hand often needed elsewhere. Flashlights should be provided with a cord tied to the caver so that they may be dropped when necessary.

Candles are usually reserved for an emergency, although they give a suitable light if nothing else is available. Whatever the choice of light, plenty of fuel and spare parts should be carried as even the most simple caves are hopelessly complex in the dark.

Hardhats are a very desirable piece of wearing apparel especially in deep caves where climbers above may dislodge pebbles or drop equipment. Hardhats should be equipped with a chinstrap to keep them on when the caver is crawling head-first down a hole.

Any old clothing will suffice for cave exploring but expect it to suffer considerable abrasion and soiling. Cave temperatures average about 50° F. in Colorado both winter and summer. Caves at higher elevations are somewhat colder than lower ones. Gloves are useful to protect the hands from sharp rocks and cactus spines.

Low topped hiking boots are preferred for footwear although tennis shoes and oxfords are suitable. There are many opinions about what constitutes suitable footwear but leather soles lack the necessary traction on rocks.

Caves may have several origins but the vast majority of them are formed by solution of the rock by underground water. The most common rocks subject to water solution are limestone and dolomite. With only one exception, all of the known caves in Colorado are in either limestone or dolomite. Since the cavernous portions of the state are limited to areas containing these rocks, a geologic map such as "The Nonmetallic Resources of Colorado" published by the U.S.G.S. may be used as a guide.

Cave entrances are sometimes very inconspicuous and it is often possible to walk near them without noticing. For this reason it is strongly recommended that local inquiry be made and a guide secured if possible when searching for a cave.

The only commercial cave, operating in Colorado at this time, is **Cave of the Winds.** It is located on the west side of Williams Canyon just N of Manitou Springs. It undoubtedly contains more stalactites, stalagmites, flowstone and various other speleothems than any of the "wild" Colorado caves. If you have never visited a cave, this is the logical place to start.

Lower in Williams Canyon, on Cave of the Winds property, are two smaller wild caves. The larger of these, **Huccacove,** is located on the E side of the canyon directly above the "Narrows." The entrance is in the bottom of a small gully about 200 yards above the Williams Canyon road. The smaller cave, **Pedro's** or **Broken Rock Cave,** is located about $\frac{1}{4}$ mile below the Narrows on the W side of the canyon across from but on the same level as the road. These two caves are well-known and because they are so near Colorado Springs and are so easily accessible, they have more visitors than any of the other wild caves in the state. Both caves can be negotiated without the use of ropes although a 50′ rope may be used for belaying on a short section in Huccacove Cave. Since these caves are on private property, permission should be obtained at Cave of the Winds before entering them.

Clear Creek Fault Caves are located just W of Golden in Clear Creek Canyon. Drive W from Golden on US 6. After passing through the first tunnel, the road curves to the right. Where the road first starts to curve back left, park the car and follow a poor trail up a gully on the N side of the canyon. There are numerous cave entrances located on the hillside E of the gully starting about 300 yards above the highway. The main entrance to the largest of these caves lies just below and on the W side of a rocky ledge which runs N-S along the eastern side of the hill. These caves were caused by a movement of the mountainside and are the only notable ones in the state which are not located in limestone. A network of cracks underlies this whole hillside connecting the numerous cave entrances although many of them are too small to be passable. Heavy clothing is advised in exploring these caves to ward off the cactus spines which are mixed into the dirt on the floor.

In the rocks around the Red Rocks Theater, W of Denver, there are many small shelters and crevices. Across the road to the E of the theater a high narrow crack is found in the rocks which is narrow at the top and wider at its base. This is called **Cave of the Seven Ladders** and is a true cave, containing areas of total darkness only on a dark night.

Marble Cave, Fly Cave and **Wilson Cave** are located N of Canon City on State 143 (Garden Park Road). Marble Cave is on the Freek Ranch in the SW¼ of the SE¼ of Sec. 33, R70W, T168 (Cooper Mountain Quadrangle 1954). Permission to enter Marble and Fly Caves should be obtained at the Freek Ranch. After passing the Ranch, cross three dry washes and park the car 200 yards beyond the last one. The 15′ deep pit entrance of Marble Cave is 150 yards E of the road across a meadow.

Fly Cave is ¼ mile NE of Marble Cave on the edge of the canyon of Fourmile Creek. Follow the W edge of the canyon to its highest point. The entrance is on a small ledge 15′ down from the top. This cave is named for the cloud of flies which live in its entrance.

Wilson Cave is reached by continuing N on State 143 through Helena Canon. This is a shelf road, one lane wide, and should be attempted only in dry weather. After crossing Fourmile Creek, the road goes up over a rocky point and descends to the level of Wilson Creek. Park here and continue up the road 200 yards. The cave is located 100′ above the road on the W side. This area is covered by the Cripple Creek South Quadrangle and the cave is in the NE¼ of the SW¼ of Sec. 15, T16S, R70W. The lower entrance is equipped with a wooden door. A second entrance is 30′ above and slightly to the S of the lower entrance. The cave is dry and dusty, and contains long passages where crawling is required.

One of Colorado's largest caves, **Fulford Cave,** is located 17 miles S of Eagle near Yeoman Park Ranger Station. Follow road S from Eagle along Brush Creek. Forest Service signs direct you to Yeoman Park. Go to Fulford Campground. From the campground follow a ½-mile marked trail E up Craig Peak to the cave. The cave has two main entrances—the lower one, very tight, is located at the bottom of a funnel shaped sink and the upper entrance, as large as a doorway, is plainly visible above it. If the upper entrance is used, a 30′ piece of rope is needed to descend a pit to the main part of the cave. This cave contains a small stream which emerges as a spring near the campground.

In the same general area is the deep vertical shaft of **Sinking River Cave.** Again follow the Brush Creek road S from Eagle but take the fork to Woods Lake (and the Frying Pan River). A Forest Service trail leads from the S side of Woods Lake to Tellurium Lake. About 2½ miles from Woods Lake this trail passes within 5′ of two sinkholes. They are located in an open valley and cannot be missed if you stay on the trail. A small stream flows into the upper one to land 165′ below as spray. This shaft opens only slightly toward its base and there are no side passages. The stream sinks into the debris on the floor and probably reappears as a spring in Lime Creek canyon a mile to the NW. Both Sinking River Cave and Fulford Cave are covered by the map of the White River National Forest.

Near Glenwood Springs is found Colorado's largest concentration of caves. Fairy Cave, Cave of the Chimes and Cave of the Clouds are all located N and NE of town on Iron Mountain. Hubbards Cave is located high in the south wall of Glenwood Canyon above the Shoshone Power Plant.

Hubbards Cave, one of the state's largest, is reached by going S on State 83 for 3 miles and turning left onto the Lookout Mountain road (Red Canyon). This road leads to a lookout point above Glenwood Springs. About 2 miles before reaching the lookout a jeep road turns off and leads 7 miles NE to the cave. The jeep road, marked by flying red horses cut from oil cans, ends in Deadman Gulch. A $\frac{1}{2}$-mile trail from the end of the road holds the same elevation and traverses the east side of the gulch and the south wall of Glenwood Canyon ending at the large main entrance to the cave.

Fairy Cave may be reached by driving N on the main street of Glenwood Springs, crossing the bridge and US 6 and continuing to the end of the street. Park here and follow a driveway E, climbing to a wooden water tank. The trail starts here and leads to the top of Iron Mountain, about $1\frac{1}{2}$ miles. Fairy Cave is located nearly on top of the mountain on its S side. A useful landmark is a telephone line which runs N-S directly over the cave entrance. Do not overlook any crawlways in this cave as the main areas are connected by small inconspicuous holes. This cave is now gated and locked.

Cave of the Chimes is reached by driving E on US 6 from Glenwood Springs to the city limit sign. Park here and follow a rocky couloir $\frac{1}{2}$ mile upward to a cliff at its head. The cave opens into the middle of the cliff and may be reached along a narrow ledge. This small cave was once very well decorated but has been badly vandalized. Cave of the Chimes may also be reached from the Fairy Cave trail but there is no visible trail.

Cave of the Clouds is reached by driving E on US 6 about $\frac{1}{2}$ mile from Glenwood Springs. Turn N and climb the steeply switchbacking road up Cascade Creek to the water tanks. Park here and follow the flume E $\frac{1}{4}$ mile until a tunnel is reached. A faint trail starts here and climbs NE for 400 yards to the cave. Although the entrance is very large it is not visible from any distance because of the terrain. This cave contained massive draperies and stalagmites but like Cave of the Chimes it has been badly vandalized.

Spring Cave is marked on maps of White River National Forest. To reach it drive E from Meeker to Buford on State 132. At Buford turn S on the road which follows the S. Fk. White River. Leave the car at the campground at the end of the road and follow the marked Forest Service trail $\frac{1}{2}$ mile to the cave. The complete exploration of Spring Cave is prevented by a large underground stream which fills the back passages.

The honor of being the most difficult cave in Colorado belongs to the legendary Caverna Del Oro. **Caverna Del Oro,** the Cavern of Gold, is also known as Spanish Cave or Marble Mountain Cave. This cave, according to legend, was known to the Spanish conquistadores, serving as a cache for their ill-gotten gold. They were supposed to have marked its location with a maltese cross and indeed the remains of such a cross is found on the rock beside the entrance. A folder containing the legends and accounts of Caverna Del Oro is maintained in the Western History Division of the Denver Public Library.

Caverna Del Oro is located 15 miles SW of Westcliff on Marble Mountain. From Westcliff drive 4.6 miles SSE on State 69. Turn off and drive due S 5.6 miles, W $\frac{1}{8}$ mile and S another $\frac{1}{2}$ mile to the Caspar Henrich Ranch. Inquire here for detailed instructions. It is possible to reach a private ranch road from here which follows along the S side of Hudson Creek and ends at a pole corral. From here follow a trail $2\frac{1}{2}$ miles up the S. Fk. Hudson Creek to Marble Mountain. At the head of the trail is a collapsed prospector's cabin. To the NW of the

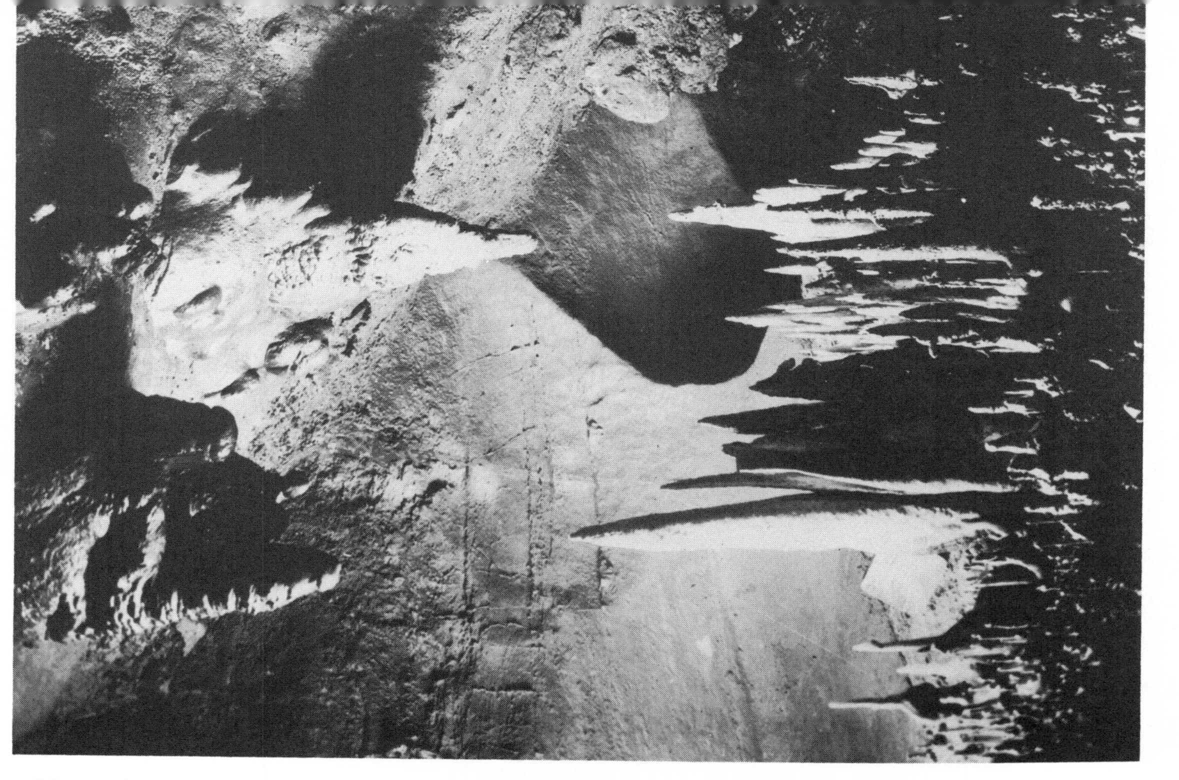

The underworld of spelunkers, in a limestone formation. *Stewarts Commercial photo.*

White water boating on the Arkansas. *Mason photo.*

cabin, on the face of Marble Mountain, is a circular outcropping of limestone cut down the middle by a rocky ravine. The entrance to Caverna Del Oro is located in the middle of the outcrop on the north wall of the ravine at an elevation of 11,550′.

The cavern is steeply inclined reaching a depth of 300′ and having an 80′ vertical pit. A minimum of 500′ of rope is required. The temperature is 34° F. and the humidity is above 95%. This, coupled with the cold wind and snowdrifts which extend 180′ into the cave, make it far from pleasant.

Also on Marble Mountain are found six other caves, the largest of which is called **White Marble Halls** from an inscription near its entrance. It is the lower of two holes plainly visible on the south face of the limestone outcrop.

Bell Cavern is located N of Durango near Rockwood in the Bell Limestone Quarry. It is the only cave in Colorado in which bad air has been reported. Apparently carbon dioxide gas accumulates in one dead end passage. Although carbon dioxide is not poisonous it excludes enough oxygen to make breathing difficult or impossible.

People interested in exploring Colorado's caves should contact the Colorado Grotto by inquiry at Denver Public Library or any mountaineering shop.

WHITE WATER BOATING

The fur trappers—Mountain Men—learned to build bull-boats from the Indians. These were made of buffalo hides stretched over frames of bent wood, with the seams tallowed. The first definite date is one left on a rock by General Ashley, head of the Rocky Mountain Fur Company. He and his wreckless young trapper companions maneuvered two bull boats down the **Green River,** starting in Utah, through **Flaming Gorge** and over what is now **Ashley Falls.** In present Colorado they floated through Browns Park and slipped between the rose-red portals of **Lodore Canyon** and kept on past **Disaster Falls** to east-central Utah.

Powell came on his 1869 voyage down the **Green** and the **Colorado** through the **Grand Canyon,** and seeing "Ashley 1825" (which he read as 1855), named the nearby falls.

In 1901 Torrence and Fellows ran down the **Black Canyon** far enough to locate a mouth for the Gunnison Tunnel which carries water for the Montrose farming area. They used only a rubber raft to carry instruments, sometimes clinging to it and sometimes easing it down ahead with a 500-foot silk line they had. The full length of this gorge was first run in 1917.

People who can manage themselves in mild water can do some self-training. One way is to run several times over a short stretch with a problem or two, and then apply the method to a more complicated piece of water. The basic precaution is a life jacket, and a preliminary inspection is necessary. Have a towel and a change of clothes as you are pretty likely to get wet. Go in pairs or groups, and where you try something a little fancy have a well-stationed man with a rope and grab stick.

Ordinary speeds for active streams run from 4½ to 6½ miles per hour. A good deal can be learned about many of our streams from the river plattes available at the Map Distribution Center of the U.S. Geological Survey, in Denver Federal Center.

Boating as sport has generated the CWWA—Colorado White Water Association. Activities include sponsoring, along with similar groups across America, of Wild River legislation, fighting against no-purpose dams, and the promotion of water safety regulation. The members participate in slalom and down-river racing meets and in spring they conduct training sessions to prepare paddlers for a graduated schedule of cruises up through advanced boating. They have rated most of the Colorado stream segments according to the scale below, taken from the International River Classification.

Class 1—very easy, with waves small and regular; passages clear, with sandbanks; artificial difficulties such as bridge piers; riffles.

Class 2—easy, with rapids of medium difficulty; passages generally clear and wide; low ledges; spraydeck useful.

Class 3—medium, with waves numerous, high and irregular; rock; eddies; rapids with passages that are clear through narrows, requiring expertise in maneuver; inspection usually necessary; spraydeck needed.

Class 4—difficult, even for experienced boatmen, with long rapids and powerful and irregular waves; dangerous rocks, boiling eddies; passages difficult to reconnoiter; inspection mandatory first time; powerful and precise maneuvering required; spraydeck essential.

Class 5 and 6 water is increasingly dangerous and difficult; not for treatment by this editor, who is seized with shuddering at the contemplation of class 4, probably because he went down a waterfall backward in class 3.

While there are some canoes on the streams and quite a number of people play with the relatively safe but not very manageable inflated rafts, the main boat of the sport is the kayak. Kayaks are now mainly fiberglass and usually one-man affairs.

Ron Mason, who heads the CWWA, has furnished nearly all the information below covering the better-known runs.

ARKANSAS RIVER

The Arkansas is rated as tops, with plenty of water of all classes and generally a long season of reliable flow. The stretch from Leadville to Granite, called polite, often has enough water for at least early season running. From **Pine Creek,** which flows under US 24 3½ miles S of Granite, to highway 285 crossing 2 miles below Buena Vista, the river is rated 4 and 5 and considered the classic US stretch for kayaking. It has seen slalom events and will see more. The upper end, from Pine Creek to 10 miles N of Buena Vista, is too dangerous during the high water season for any but exceptional boaters. The road is quite close.

There is a 12-mile stretch between the bridge at Nathrop, 5½ miles S of the US 24 and US 285 bridge at Johnson City, and the State 291 bridge. The upper end is class 2 or 3 water through fairly flat country with a bridge and exit road at a resort about 2 miles along. Then comes 5-mile **Browns Canyon,** with class 3 and 4 water—short lively rapids with pools between, canyoned, with large rocks at the edges. There is a side road about 2 miles from the lower end which meets US 285 ½ mile north of the junction of that highway with State 291. The highway is distant but the railroad runs along one side.

Between Salida and Cotopaxi is the 26-mile stretch of class 2 and 3 water which has been known for years as the best down-river race course in the world. Most of it is quite close to US 50. The **Bear Creek, Tincup** and **Cottonwood Rapids,** which are all class 4, have been sworn at in a dozen languages.

The **Royal Gorge,** between Parkdale and Canyon City, is again roadless but parallel to the railroad. The spectacularly canyoned upper part is class 4 and 5 water. It is a run of about 8 miles.

SOUTH PLATTE RIVER

The closest running to Denver is reached from US 285 W of Schaeffers Crossing, where you take the road to Buffalo and downstream to Foxton and South Platte, or from just S of Sedalia (US 85) where you take the Jarre Canyon road to Deckers. From 3 miles above Twin Cedars Lodge (downstream from Deckers) to South Platte there is excellent class 1 and 2 training water, with the short Slot rated class 3. It is a good 8-mile stretch, paralleled closely by road.

From Foxton, on the North Fork, to South Platte, there is a 5-mile stretch of class 3 and 4 water excellent for the learning of techniques and kept dependable as to supply by the Roberts tunnel. The road closely parallels it.

Waterton Canyon, from South Platte to Waterton, has class 4 and 5 plus water and is very difficult, with big drops and gradients over 100′ per mile. Numerous small dams have to be portaged, and there is an infamous rapids known as the Widow-maker. This stretch of 10 miles has no road.

ROARING FORK RIVER

From Aspen to the Woody Creek bridge, 10 miles, is a scenic run with tree-covered canyon walls. The many rocks in the channel make it technically demanding or class 4. The 30 more miles from **Woody Creek** to near **Glenwood Springs** is generally class 3 with some cross roads which make it easily divisible into segments. State 82 is parallel to both stretches and generally not far away.

BLUE RIVER

Between the Dillon Dam and the Green Mountain Dam reservoir the Blue River runs parallel and usually close to State 9. The first stretch is class 1 and 2 water, good for beginners for about 8 miles north from Silverthorne to Blue River Campground. It is punctuated by occasional barbed wire fences which must be portaged. The next 3 miles to where it lakes out is class 3 and 4 water and not always ample for boating. Dillon is about 70 miles west of Denver on I-70.

Below Green Mountain Dam is a stretch of beautiful tree-lined canyon with class 3 water but no roads or trails for 4 miles. Below the bridge at this point the shallow canyon frames Eagles Nest Mountain to the S while it runs 9 miles more through ranch lands to a bridge short of Kremmling. It is class 1 and 2 water, again good for beginners.

CACHE LA POUDRE RIVER

The **Cache la Poudre,** augmented by water from the Never Summer Range's **Grand Ditch,** one of Colorado's earliest diversion projects, flows by a long tortuous route to the plains. To reach it drive 10 miles NW from central Fort Collins on US 287 and take State 14 W. From the Water Works Plant near Seaman Reservoir turnoff at mile 5½ there is a 4-mile stretch of cold class 3 water with a good many sharp rocks. State 14 is parallel and close. Another stretch of the Poudre, with class 3 and 4 water, begins at the lower end of **Big Narrows Canyon** 13 miles farther W—a mile W of the Stove Prairie road—and runs down to the small water diversion dam above the water works.

COLORADO RIVER

US 6, which is becoming I-70 as it 4-lanes, parallels the Colorado River below Dotsero, 18 miles E of **Glenwood Springs.** There are long stretches of class 1 water with a class 2 stretch of two both above the Shoshone Power Plant lake out and below Glenwood Springs, the latter often some distance from the road. For a generally slow and easy 18-mile run through cottonwood and ranch country, with now and then a heron to watch, start below Glenwood Springs and take out at the side road bridge beyond Silt.

More of a challenge is the class 4 water from a little below **Shoshone Dam** to **Grizzly Creek.** This is followed by 5 miles of class 2 water before you reach **Glenwood Springs.** The upper stretch of the above is in true heavy water with lots of waves and holes and much turbulence. It is recommended to experts only during the high water period, when the river may run a volume of 10,000 cubic feet per second. There are stories of all sorts of hard times with the **Tombstone, Wall** and **Superstition Rapids.**

OTHER WATER

These are a large beginning, but there are plenty more rivers with runs. A 15-mile stretch of scenically pleasant class 1 and 2 water parallels State 149 from Lake City to the bridge where the road turns E. One must be on guard however for numerous fence portages, some in difficult or even dangerous places. The **Rio Grande** is a beautiful stream with one of its good class 2 stretches between Wagon Wheel Gap and Masonic Park alongside State 149, about 10 miles long. The **Taylor River** and the **Yampa** are likewise inviting. There are stretches of the **Eagle** below Minturn which can be estimated from the adjacent I-70.

LIST OF 14,000-FOOT PEAKS

The altitudes below are the most recent figures furnished by the U.S.G.S. (1969)

No.	Peak	Altitude
1	Mount Elbert	14,433
2	Mount Massive	14,421
3	Mount Harvard	14,420
4	Blanca Peak	14,338
5	La Plata Peak	14,336
6	Uncompahgre Peak	14,309
7	Crestone Peak	14,294
8	Mount Lincoln	14,286
9	Grays Peak	14,270
10	Mount Antero	14,269
11	Torreys Peak	14,267
12	Castle Peak	14,265
13	Mount Evans	14,264
14	Quandary Peak	14,264
15	Longs Peak	14,256
16	Mount Wilson	14,246
17	Mount Shavano	14,229
18	Mount Princeton	14,197
19	Mount Belford	14,197
20	Mount Yale	14,196
21	Crestone Needle	14,191
22	Mount Bross	14,172
23	Kit Carson Peak	14,165
24	El Diente Peak	14,159
25	South Maroon Peak	14,156
26	Tabeguache M'tain	14,155
27	Mount Oxford	14,153
28	Mount Sneffels	14,150
29	Mount Democrat	14,148
30	Capitol Peak	14,130
31	Pikes Peak	14,110
32	Snowmass M'tain	14,092
33	Windom Peak	14,087
34	Mount Eolus	14,084
35	Mount Columbia	14,073
36	Missouri M'tain	14,067
37	Humboldt Peak	14,064
38	Mount Bierstadt	14,060
39	Sunlight Peak	14,059
40	Handies Peak	14,048
41	Culebra Peak	14,047
42	Mount Lindsey	14,042
43	Little Bear Peak	14,037
44	Mount Sherman	14,036
45	Redcloud Peak	14,034
46	Pyramid Peak	14,018
47	Wilson Peak	14,017
48	Wetterhorn Peak	14,017
49	North Maroon Peak	14,014
50	San Luis Peak	14,014
51	Huron Peak	14,005
52	Mount of Holy Cross	14,005
53	Sunshine Peak	14,001

Ellingwood Peak, 14,042′, is a tentatively named subsidiary summit of Blanca Peak; 14,022′ Conundrum is a north ridge point of Castle Peak; South Elbert Peak is a SSE summit of Mount Elbert.

ABBREVIATIONS USED

CMC — Colorado Mountain Club
Cpgd — Campground
Crk — Creek
E — East
FS — Forest Service
GS, USGS — United States Geological Survey
Glch — Gulch
GR — Gore Range
L, Lk — Lake
Mt — Mount
Mtn — Mountain
N — North
Quad — USGS Quadrangle, $7\frac{1}{2}'$ latitude $\times$ $7\frac{1}{2}'$ longitude unless otherwise designated
Pk — Peak
Pks — Peaks
Pt — Point
R — River
Rd — Road
Res — Reservoir
RMN — Rocky Mountain National Park
RR, Ry — Railroad
S — South
Socty — Society
Sprs — Springs
Sta — Station
T & T — *Trail and Timberline*, the Colorado Mountain Club periodical
W — West

INDEX